Reflections on British Royalty

THE MASS-OBSERVATION CRITICAL SERIES

The Mass-Observation Critical Series pairs innovative interdisciplinary scholarship with rich archival materials from the original Mass-Observation movement and the current Mass Observation Project. Launched in 1937, the Mass-Observation movement aimed to study the everyday life of ordinary Britons. The Mass Observation Project continues to document and archive the everyday lives, thoughts and attitudes of ordinary Britons to this day. Mass-Observation, as a whole, is an innovative research organization, a social movement and an archival project that spans much of the twentieth and early twenty-first centuries.

The series makes Mass-Observation's rich primary sources accessible to a wide range of academics and students across multiple disciplines as well as to the general reading public. Books in the series include reissues of important original Mass-Observation publications, edited and introduced by leading scholars in the field, and thematically oriented anthologies of Mass-Observation material. The series also facilitates cutting-edge research by established and new scholars using Mass-Observation resources to present fresh perspectives on everyday life, popular culture and politics, visual culture, emotions and other relevant topics.

Series Editors:

Jennifer J. Purcell is Professor of History and Chair of the History Department at Saint Michael's College in Vermont, United States. She is the author of *Domestic Soldiers: Six Women's Lives in the Second World War* (2010); *Mother of the BBC: Mabel Constanduros and the Development of Popular Entertainment on the BBC, 1925-57* (2020); and editor of *Mass-Observation: Text, Context and Analysis of the Pioneering Pamphlet and Movement* (2023).

Benjamin Jones is Lecturer in Modern British History at the University of East Anglia, UK. He is the author of *The Working Class in Mid-Twentieth-Century England* (2012), which was positively reviewed in *Sociology, American Historical Review, Journal of Modern History, Journal of*

British Studies, *The Historical Journal*, *Economic History Review*, *Contemporary British History*, *Twentieth Century British History* and *Planning Perspectives*.

Lucy D. Curzon is Professor of Art History at the University of Alabama in the United States. She is the author of Mass-Observation and Visual Culture (2017), as well as several book chapters and articles on Mass-Observation's use of photography, painting, and other forms of visual culture to examine everyday life. She also publishes on contemporary queer painting and photography.

Editorial Board:

Fiona Courage, Deputy University Librarian and Director of the Mass Observation Archive at the University of Sussex, UK.

Claire Langhamer, Director of the Institute of Historical Research, University of London, UK

Jeremy MacClancy, Professor of Anthropology, Oxford Brookes University, UK

Kimberly Mair, Associate Professor of Sociology, University of Lethbridge, Canada

Rebecca Searle, Principal Lecturer in the School of Humanities and Social Science,, University of Brighton, UK

Matthew Taunton, Associate Professor in the School of Literature, Drama and Creative Writing, University of East Anglia, UK

Published Titles:

The Biopolitics of Care in Second World War Britain, Kimberly Mair (2022)

Mass Observers Making Meaning, James Hinton (2022)

Mass-Observation, edited by Jennifer J. Purcell (2023)

Reflections on British Royalty

Mass-Observation and the Monarchy, 1937–2022

Edited by
Jennifer J. Purcell and
Fiona Courage

BLOOMSBURY ACADEMIC
LONDON · NEW YORK · OXFORD · NEW DELHI · SYDNEY

BLOOMSBURY ACADEMIC
Bloomsbury Publishing Plc
50 Bedford Square, London, WC1B 3DP, UK
1385 Broadway, New York, NY 10018, USA
29 Earlsfort Terrace, Dublin 2, Ireland

BLOOMSBURY, BLOOMSBURY ACADEMIC and the Diana logo are trademarks of
Bloomsbury Publishing Plc

First published in Great Britain 2024

Published in partnership with the Mass Observation Archive

Copyright © Jennifer J. Purcell and Fiona Courage, 2024

Jennifer J. Purcell and Fiona Courage have asserted their right under the Copyright,
Designs and Patents Act, 1988, to be identified as Editors of this work.

Cover image: Coronation Street Parties. June 1953 © Mirrorpix/getty

All rights reserved. No part of this publication may be reproduced or transmitted in
any form or by any means, electronic or mechanical, including photocopying, recording,
or any information storage or retrieval system, without prior permission in writing
from the publishers.

Bloomsbury Publishing Plc does not have any control over, or responsibility for, any
third-party websites referred to or in this book. All internet addresses given in this
book were correct at the time of going to press. The author and publisher regret any
inconvenience caused if addresses have changed or sites have ceased to exist,
but can accept no responsibility for any such changes.

Every effort has been made to trace the copyright holders and obtain permission to
reproduce the copyright material. Please do get in touch with any enquiries or any
information relating to such material or the rights holder. We would be pleased to
rectify any omissions in subsequent editions of this publication should they be
drawn to our attention.

A catalogue record for this book is available from the British Library.

A catalog record for this book is available from the Library of Congress.

ISBN: HB: 978-1-3501-0714-4
PB: 978-1-3501-0713-7
ePDF: 978-1-3501-0715-1
eBook: 978-1-3501-0716-8

Typeset by Deanta Global Publishing Services, Chennai, India
Printed and bound in Great Britain

To find out more about our authors and books visit www.bloomsbury.com and
sign up for our newsletters.

CONTENTS

Acknowledgements viii

Introduction Jennifer Purcell and Fiona Courage 1

PART I Mass-Observation, 1937–55 13

1   Coronation of George VI 1937 15

2   Royalty in wartime 1939–45 38

3   Princess Elizabeth's wedding 1947 64

4   Coronation of Elizabeth II 1953 86

5   Townsend Affair 1955 114

PART II Mass Observation Project, 1981–2022 139

6   Jubilees and weddings – 1977 and the 1980s 141

7   Divorces and funerals – the 1990s 167

8   A tentative recovery? The Royal Family in the 2000s 192

9   A decade of recovery? The 2010s 218

10   The British Royal Family in 2022 248

Epilogue 259
Notes 267
Bibliography 290
Index 292
Index of Mass Observer locations 304

ACKNOWLEDGEMENTS

The editors would like to thank the Mass Observation team, Jessica Scantlebury, Kirsty Pattrick, Suzanne Rose and Charlotte Robinson, for all their help in making Mass Observation available for us to use. Insights from Karen Watson and Jessica Scantlebury into the royal family and royal gossip have been invaluable and delightful.

The librarians at Saint Michael's College, especially Laura Crain, Anthony Bassignani and Kristen Hindes, have been wonderful throughout this project. Their hard work and thoughtfulness are much appreciated, always. Many thanks also to Lily Denslow and Rachel Daby for their work in transcribing portions of the 1953 Coronation responses.

The editors would like to thank the Trustees of the Mass Observation Archive, at the University of Sussex, for permission to reproduce original Mass Observation material. We would especially like to thank Trustees Professor Claire Langhamer and Jane Harvell for supporting our endeavours in writing this book.

Finally, special thanks to the Mass Observers for sharing their lives and opinions with us. Their writing is an important and valuable contribution to how we and future researchers and readers will understand British history, society and culture.

Introduction

Jennifer Purcell and Fiona Courage

On the evening of 8 September 2022, news flashed across Britain, the Commonwealth and the globe of the Queen's death. Queen Elizabeth II, the longest-reigning British monarch, passed away at the end of a summer of Platinum Jubilee celebrations commemorating the seventieth anniversary of her accession to the throne. Born in 1926, Queen Elizabeth's life spanned nearly a century of social, cultural and political change, accompanied by the increasing availability of media and technology that enabled an unprecedented level of visibility of, and public engagement with, the British royal family. Understanding these interactions not only provides insight into the relationship between the monarchy and the people but also narrates the changes and continuities in British society and culture, signalling moments of subtle or overwhelming shifts in ideas, expectations and values and charting the impacts of technological change in everyday life.

As the ten days of national mourning for Queen Elizabeth II began, the media covered every possible angle of the moment, witnessing both intimate and popular scenes of mourning alongside national ceremony and spectacle all played out on a global media stage. Britain and the world watched as the Queen's children, and then her grandchildren, stood vigil at her coffin in Westminster Hall and buzzed over the spectacle of 'the queue' – a line that stretched for several miles and had an online 'queue tracker' to measure the length of wait (as much as sixteen hours) to pass by the Queen's coffin lying in state.

Punctuating this royal spectacle were anti-monarchists, republicans, hecklers and protesters holding signs that read 'not my king' or blank pieces of paper in recognition of the fact that animating anti-monarchical sentiment was liable to have you arrested or at least pushed around or harassed by royal well-wishers and the police. The Queen's death occasioned larger debates and criticisms about the crown and colonialism; the right of British museums, and the British Crown, to continue to harbour other countries' treasures; and the violence and racism endemic to that colonialism.

While the media did indeed report on protests and debates about the monarchy, much of the reporting assumed collective grief of the nation and the world and insatiable interest in the traditional rites of royal passage and the decoding of pageantry and ceremony. Creating a space for public criticism, or even for reflection on the relevance of monarchy in the twenty-first century, amid this sea of royal flag waving, felt challenging for many – even the most hardened republicans. In the week following the Queen's death, *Guardian* reporter, John Harris, travelled to several locations around England to understand public feeling about the Queen's death and found few who would express pure criticism of her. In the online video of his travels, Harris reflects on this reluctance: 'For better or worse . . . this moment requires that people fall into line. And that's not a really good atmosphere to do journalism here, is it?'[1]

As Harris learned in his peripatetic quest for attitudes about the Queen's death, gauging private thoughts, feelings and frustrations in moments such as these can be challenging and probing the complexities of relationships between individuals and institutions near impossible. Sparked by another moment of royal significance, Charles Madge was similarly frustrated by an inability to judge popular mood at such moments. As reporter for the *Daily Mirror*, Madge witnessed what he felt was manipulation of public opinion by the press during the Abdication Crisis of 1936.[2] Spurred on by this revelation, and worried that ordinary Britons might not know how they truly felt, or what they truly thought, about such issues without the media or politicians' spin on them, Madge and amateur ornithologist/social explorer Tom Harrisson gathered in London with several other young intellectuals to discuss how to tune out the politicians and media outlets that claimed to speak for the people and instead work out ways to illuminate popular feeling from within: to discern, in their words, 'an anthropology of ourselves'. The result was the creation of Mass-Observation (M-O).

Mass-Observation

Within weeks of the establishment of the organization, a national panel of volunteers was set up through personal contacts and adverts in *The New Statesman*. Anticipating the Coronation of George VI on 12 May 1937, the organizers of M-O asked participants to keep a diary on the twelfth of every month. This way, it was hoped, the ordinary and extraordinary could be observed and compared. As a result of these efforts, a massive volume placing extracts of newspaper reporting alongside Observers' writing about their behaviours, conversations and observations on Coronation day, *May the Twelfth*, was published in August 1937.

During the Second World War, Mass-Observation evolved from an amateur organization, scraping by on donations, a few government and commercial contracts as well as Tom Harrisson's speaking fees, to an established research organization. As the war ended, so too did Mass-Observation's income from its work for government departments, leaving

INTRODUCTION

it increasingly reliant on commercial research as an income generator. In the late 1940s, Mass-Observation became a limited company and despite continuing to undertake social research, including recording large social events such as royal weddings and Coronations, it moved its day-to-day work towards its commercial arm.[3]

Though the organization would shift to an emphasis on observing the everyday, its fascination with popular attitudes towards the British royalty would never go away, and M-O would continue to capture and catalogue attitudes and behaviour surrounding the royalty through 1960. When the project was revived as the Mass Observation Project in 1981, it was spurred on by yet another royal event: Prince Charles and Lady Diana's wedding. Royal fortunes and attitudes towards the royals have been captured ever since, up to, and including, the Queen's death in September 2022.

Measuring public opinion

The genesis of Mass-Observation took place at a particular moment in which academic and popular interest in the everyday and in the ordinary was increasing. The interwar period saw the rise of popular psychology, the nascent disciplines of sociology and marketing and the popularity of entertainment that dealt in the day-to-day life of 'ordinary' Britons.[4] Interest in popular attitudes and opinion polling was also on the rise, as politicians sought to maximize their visibility with a burgeoning electorate in the wake of the 1918 and 1928 Representation of the People Acts, which enfranchised men and women aged twenty-one and over regardless of class or property. Responding to similar pressures in America, Gallup began its famous opinion polling operations in 1935 and came to Britain in 1937.[5] In contrast to Gallup, Mass-Observation hoped to engage beyond the limits of quantitative data and opted instead for a qualitative solution. Quantitative opinion polls offer a satisfying solution to the problem of discussing popular feeling: percentages lend themselves to neat and confident reporting and easily digested visual aids; even more, reliance on numbers lends scientific credibility to the quantitative method.

The leaders of Mass-Observation, however, were confident that their qualitative method also had scientific value and offered important insights. Indeed, M-O's wartime work predicted Labour's sweep into power during the 1945 General Election, surprising most everyone who assumed Churchill's Conservatives would easily prevail. Still, the qualitative is messy and uncertain: no two responses to Mass-Observation's qualitative surveys (directives) are entirely alike. At a time of heroic scientific certainty, Mass-Observation's methods were skewered and lambasted, the butt of jokes: a load of nosey parkers listening into and reporting on conversations on the buses.

Responding to these criticisms, Mass-Observation branched out into the quantitative realm, sending investigators out into the streets to collect data

– the yes, nos and maybes of the opinion polls – in order to provide their qualitative material with the solid confidence of percentages. In its early inception, from 1937 to 1960, the Mass-Observation archives are filled with words peppered with scatterings of investigators' charts and numbers. Weighing up the words with the numbers in the Mass Observation Archive, it is the words – rather than the numbers – that bring clarity; the numbers lack certainty, and feel less meaningful, perhaps *because* they are weighed against the words, which always unsettle the possibility of confidence in the numbers. The opinion polls and percentages can only offer generalities as data points skip across the surface of popular feeling, while the richness and complexity of the words from the Observers – and the frustration of discovering clear and coherent answers – offers depth and insight.

How, for example, might pollsters accurately capture the following sentiments written by an Observer on the occasion of the Queen's death in 2022:

> I have watched the events since the Queen's death with little emotion other than a sense of passing history mixed with a sense of loss. I'm not a royalist but not quite a full-blown republican. I see the need for a non-political Head of State but I cannot think of any satisfactory solution which would do away with the absurdity of one unelected family having the right to 'rule'. We should never have a politician as Head of State. We need only look to the United States to see where that might take us.[6]

If faced with a handful of choices, would this Observer choose to support the monarchy or republicanism, or would he choose to err on the side of 'not sure' and thus add little to our understanding? Sophisticated polling techniques could get closer to the core of this individual's thinking on the matter, but his full response enables deeper insight into why individuals may support the continuation of the monarchy while also being fairly critical of, or apathetic about the institution, or wish to continue with a reformed monarchy, as the Observer goes on to record in the entirety of his response.

Support for republican attitudes – the desire for an elected head of state – and anti-monarchist feeling in Britain have long been minority opinions and those who would like to do away with the monarchy often feel sidelined, silenced and alone in a sea of royalists. In times of royal crisis and at moments of royal transition, discussions about the vitality and relevance of the British monarchy, and potential alternatives to the institution, become more prominent in public discourse, but rarely do these discussions result in long-lasting calls or popular movements for a republic or the dissolution of the monarchy. Opinion polling on attitudes towards the royalty was rarely done in the mid-twentieth century since pollsters felt frustrated with a lack of change regarding public attitudes towards the monarchy.[7] Based on sources that do offer insight into public attitudes about the monarchy since the 1800s, it seems likely that support for the monarchy was always in the majority;

however, that support has fluctuated across time and differs widely based on age, and reasons for support or criticism are rarely articulated in much detail.[8] Certainly since the 1990s, when regular polling of the issue started in earnest, there have been striking ebbs of public support for the monarchy, but the 1990s were perhaps the worst decade for the royals since the Abdication Crisis in the 1930s, seeing the Queen's *Annus Horribilis* in 1992, numerous royal divorces and, of course, the 'War of the Waleses' and subsequent death of Princess Diana.[9] Support for a republican solution, for instance, was its highest since modern polls began tracking the question in January 1997 (eight months before Diana's death), 2001 and 2003, running between 33 and 38 per cent. However, the height in 2003 at 38 per cent reflects a polling question that might be more reflective of public attitudes towards Prince Charles's right to accede the throne than about the institution itself, as the question posed in that poll was, 'When the Queen dies, do you think that Prince Charles should inherit the throne, or should the next head of state be elected instead?'[10]

As a volunteer organization, Mass-Observation's panel cannot be considered representative of the nation. Still, responses to M-O directives from the 1980s to today can be mapped against poll numbers to allow for more clarity about what the numbers might mean and why they shift in particular ways over time. Chapters in the second half of this volume allow readers to consider Observers' responses alongside polling numbers which have been gathered for the past forty years. Further, the fact that Mass-Observation has been conducting qualitative research since 1937 offers a solution to the paucity of polling data in the mid-twentieth century and opens up the possibilities for more clarity on attitudes towards the royal family over the past eighty-five years.

Thinking about the Windsor Brand

This volume covers 85 of the 113 years of the Windsor dynasty, which begins with the reign of George V (1910–35), who changed the royal name from the very German-sounding Saxe-Coburg-Gotha of his grandmother Victoria (1837–1901) and father Edward VII's (1901–10) reigns to Windsor during the First World War. The change in the royal name reflects George V's interest in protecting and modernizing the Crown from the very beginnings of his reign and underscores how anxious he and his royal advisors were to cultivate popular support of the British monarchy during a time in which European monarchs were becoming increasingly endangered and reminds us of the interest in, and management of, British popular opinion at the highest levels.[11] This concern over the opinion of subjects increased as the franchise expanded and the constitutional power of the British monarchy diminished across the nineteenth and early twentieth centuries.

With the rise of popular newspapers during Queen Victoria's reign, the media played an important role in shaping the relationship between monarchy and the people.[12] Announcements and descriptions of royal events in the newspapers encouraged public participation in royal events, while photographs of Victoria and her family cultivated a sense of intimacy and shared values between sovereign and subject.[13] Victoria and her family sat for portraits in 'sober' nineteenth-century fashion, not in royal regalia, thus radiating a sense of ordinariness and underscoring the centrality of domesticity and the family in British life: as the institution's political power diminished, the monarchy was refashioned as the model of British morals and values.[14]

The monarchy was increasingly presented as the symbol of the nation in the popular press, and criticism of the monarchy and the royal family in the press and political cartooning waned.[15] This represented a profound change from the way in which the monarchy was imagined earlier in the century, especially during the Regency and George IV's reign, which were marked by profligate spending, womanizing and the rejection of quiet and sober family life. Never known for adhering to a quiet, domestic life, Edward VII placed his stamp on the modern monarchy in his emphasis on royal ceremony.[16] The sober domesticity of the Victorian age and ceremonial splendour of the Edwardian merged in the reign of George V.

This volume begins after the death of George V in 1936, but his presence can be felt hovering over its pages. As a second son, George was brought up to be a servant of the Crown, and as King he retained this view, placing 'an emphasis on duty to the Crown and all that it stood for, rather than on the privileges of royalty'.[17] In this model, the roles of the monarch and the royal family became 'jobs' to fulfil in order to protect the Crown, regardless of personality, personal inclination or individual desire.[18] In a media and consumer age, such parameters – or royal job descriptions – ensured that the public knew what to expect and could thereby judge whether they were getting good 'value for money': George V not only created the House of Windsor, he also established the Royal Firm and, with it, the Windsor Brand.[19] Mass-Observers' writing in this volume often engages with and negotiates the boundaries of this Brand.

At its foundation, the Windsor Brand rests on a commitment to service and an expectation that all members of the royal family actively demonstrate a strong sense of duty to serve the public. This duty and service must be virtuous: it must be seen as meaningful and relevant to the public and must not be apparently self-serving. Beyond virtuous, royal service must also be understood as a personal sacrifice or burden to be borne with grace and gratitude.[20] This royal duty and sacrifice is underscored by an expectation to provide moral leadership to the nation, acting as living embodiments of ideal British values, rejecting personal desire for the sake of Crown and People, and for the Church of England, which has, since its establishment under Henry VIII, had at its head the British monarch.

Projecting the burdens of royalty may be the most important aspect of the Windsor Brand, for it enables identification with ordinary Britons who

INTRODUCTION

might otherwise be jealous of the enormous wealth and privilege of the royalty. While the royal family may wield immense wealth, that wealth must be understood to have come at a steep price so that ordinary people might consider the economic constraints of their own lives as preferable to the sacrifices of individual choice, time and happiness that the Windsors must endure in service to the nation and to the people.[21] Some take this further and assert a collective ownership of the royals that gives ordinary Britons the right to dictate how the royal family must act.[22]

In sacrifice of individual choice and predilection, the Windsor Brand also expects silence from members of the royal family, especially the sovereign, on political matters, ensuring that the Crown operates above the fray of factional politics. Amplifying important trends in the Victorian period, this stance eases the symbolic connection between Crown and nation and can act as a unifying force for the nation, especially in uncertain and difficult times. This symbolism provided reason for the continuance of the Crown as its political power diminished. The mass media participates in underscoring this connection through a steady stream of reporting on the royal family, and its activities, serving as 'banal reminders of nationhood'.[23]

Equally important in projecting the unifying and symbolic connection of Crown and nation are royal ceremonies, in which intertwine the religious and traditional aspects of the monarchy and the nation. These ceremonies, while intended to cast an image of continuity and history in the nation through the monarchy, stretching back 1,000 years, are, as historian David Cannadine has famously argued, more often modern inventions that go back no further than the Victorian age. 'In such an age of change, crisis and dislocation,' Cannadine stressed, 'the "preservation of anachronism", the deliberate, ceremonial presentation of an impotent but venerated monarch as a unifying symbol of permanence and national community became both possible and necessary.'[24] At the end of Victoria's reign and during Edward VII's time on the throne, traditions and rituals were invented, reinvigorated and embellished; music was written by Elgar to provide majestic atmosphere and underscore the emotional power of these royal moments.[25] George V leveraged these ceremonies to modernize the monarchy and burnish the Windsor Brand.[26]

Windsor royal ceremonials are meant to remind the nation, and the world, of the long history of monarchy in Britain and to legitimize the Windsors by connecting them into a seemingly unbroken royal lineage that can stretch as far back as Alfred the Great. Royal ceremonials, such as Coronations and funerals of sovereigns, are constructed collective national moments of reflection, communion and identity. The oaths, rituals and traditions (even if modern inventions) remind the nation of connection and collective national identity through the monarch and across time. After witnessing Queen Elizabeth II's Coronation in 1953, sociologists Shils and Young were fascinated by the communal aspect of the ceremony, writing, 'In a great national communion like the Coronation, people became more aware of their dependence upon each other, and they sensed some connection between this and their relationship to the Queen.'[27] While the Coronation encouraged feelings of national connection and identity, it went further, highlighting main tenets of the Windsor Brand, such as moral leadership. Shils and Young explained, 'The Coronation Service itself is a series of ritual affirmations of the moral values necessary to a well-governed and good society.'[28]

Popular participation in royal ceremonial has long been an important way for royal subjects to acknowledge a connection with the monarchy. Local and London-based activities have commemorated Coronations for centuries: cities and communities often observed such events with the firing of guns, music, bonfires, drink and processions, as has been documented for the Coronations of Tudor monarchs and James I in Norwich.[29] Samuel Pepys recounted his experiences of the Coronation procession of Charles II through the streets of London in April 1661, remarking upon the 'ladies out the windows' who joined in watching the festivities.[30] Processions through the streets of London, in which the public could see the monarch and the spectacle of their wealth and connection to the empire, would come to mark royal ceremony in Victoria's and Edward VII's reigns and become key sites of popular participation for the Windsors. Royal funerals have served as moments to reflect on the qualities of the Windsor Brand and the job performance of the monarch during their time on the throne.[31] Local celebrations for major royal events such as Coronations and funerals continued into the twentieth and twenty-first centuries, but technological advances have facilitated public participation in and ownership of national events, increasingly bringing the royalty into closer proximity with people across the country and empire (and later, Commonwealth). This is not, of course, an unmixed blessing as social media has also heightened opportunities for the articulation of criticism and anti-monarchism.

At the end of Victoria's reign, newspapers reported 'the great royal ceremonies ... with unprecedented immediacy and vividness in a sentimental, emotional, admiring way, which appealed to a broader cross section of the public than ever before'.[32] Cameras captured a grandmotherly Victoria in the processions celebrating her Diamond Jubilee in 1897, marking the moment when film and cinema became an important vehicle drawing sovereign and subject together through royal ceremony and spectacle.[33] Film cameras and radio microphones were present at the crowning of George VI in 1937, and television cameras captured most of the Coronation of Elizabeth II (excepting the mystical moment of anointing), thus giving ordinary people unprecedented access to royal rituals traditionally hidden behind the doors of Westminster Abbey: no longer did the people have to witness the spectacle of royalty from the streets; now they were invited inside the Abbey, placed on the same level as aristocrats, clerics, politicians and notables. Whereas once it was argued that the monarchy must maintain mystery and distance from subjects, technologies such as film, wireless, television and social media 'replaced ... the magic of distance with ... the magic of familiarity', fundamentally changing the relationship between royals and the people.[34] As these technologies opened up royalty to the public gaze, royals had increasingly to balance the lofty and extraordinary requirements of the Windsor Brand with expectations that the royal family be relevant, ordinary and approachable. The media have become important in both projecting the majesty and mystery of the royalty and cultivating its ordinariness. Royal weddings and funerals, for instance, resonate with national significance and project the Windsor Brand, but they are also significant moments of identification between the royal family and the people. While the Coronation places the monarch firmly at the head of the nation, divinely elevated above the people and politics, weddings and funerals emphasize the human qualities of the royal family. On the occasion of Princess Elizabeth and Prince Philip's wedding, some Mass-Observers imagined the feelings of George VI and Queen Elizabeth must be like all parents on their daughter's wedding day.[35] In the wake of Elizabeth II's death, many reflected upon her qualities as monarch and assessed her performance on the throne; at the same time, many sympathized with the grief of the royal family and some connected the mourning to recent personal losses of parents and grandparents.[36]

As mass media carry both momentous and mundane royal moments into homes across Britain and the world, ordinary people might imagine and construct relationships between themselves and the royalty. With the advent of wireless in particular, listeners could hear the voices of royals and, they felt, assess the character and personality of the speakers.[37] Film, newspapers and magazines carried stories of royal life and duty alongside portraits and snaps which acted to reinforce these assessments, increasing intimacy and familiarity with the royals; television and social media are now important sites in this process.

This process is reminiscent of the imagined parasocial relationships constructed between the public and celebrities, and the British royalty can be considered within the realm of celebrity given their coverage in the media.[38] However, there are important aspects of the royalty that make them different from a celebrity. Tom Nairn has argued that royalty and celebrity differ in that celebrity does not carry the 'mystique' of royalty, which embodies 'a dialectic of the normal and the (utterly) extra-ordinary far more compelling than anything found in stardom or the realms of hype'.[39] As sociologist Michael Billig has shown, there are limits to regarding the royal family as celebrities: rarely are celebrities guaranteed a lifetime of fame nor are they 'held to embody a national heritage or the future continuity of a nation'.[40] As symbols of the nation, the British public can imagine the royals as something that is collectively owned. This collective ownership is demonstrated in the ubiquitous use of 'our', which may be expressed, for example, by a resident of Sussex feeling a sense at having lost 'our prince' when Prince Harry left for America. On the affair between Group Captain Townsend and Princess Margaret, one Observer wrote, 'one tends to regard members of the Royalty as "public" property, they are in effect our servants.'[41]

Mass-Observation and royalty

Mass-Observers offer unique insights into the ways in which the British public engages with the Windsor Brand. Their responses demonstrate the relevance and resonance of the major pillars of the brand, while pointing to other important aspects of the relationship between the British people and the monarchy. The qualitative nature of Mass-Observation highlights the diversity of ways in which aspects of the British royal family and the monarchy are understood, accepted, negotiated, criticized or rejected.

This volume is a curated collection of Mass-Observers' writing about the royalty over an eighty-five-year period, stretching from the inception of Mass-Observation in 1937 to the Queen's death in 2022. And while the volume most certainly takes stock of popular sentiment and thinking regarding the British royal family, it would be more accurate to see this book as a social and cultural history of Britain in the twentieth and twenty-first centuries. Mass-Observers' responses to royal events are not simply commentary. They provide insight into the temporal changes in values, ethics and beliefs within our society. They chart the impacts of technological change on our everyday lives and how that change impacts our cultural response to events. Observers, for instance, comment on their attitudes towards divorce in the 1937 Coronation responses as well as in numerous other questionnaires involving divorce and the royal family, such as the Townsend Affair in 1955 and Prince Charles and Camilla's wedding. In the Townsend Affair writing, we can also observe attitudes and anxieties about a perceived decline in religion and emerging concerns about the behaviour of the press in pursuing its journalistic (and royal) prey.

Throughout the writing presented in this volume, we are witness to the rise of the Welfare State, increasing affluence and the impacts of austerity in the postwar years and, more recently, in the 2010s and 2020s. Observers' writing on royal events, such as Coronations and weddings, provides windows into the experiences of emerging technological innovations such as radio, television and social media. Observing the royalty knitted into everyday life, as Mass-Observers do in this book, welcomes thinking about the ways ordinary Britons imagine the place of royalty in their lives as well as the relevance of monarchy in British society. Indeed, the main object of this volume is to encourage readers to ask such questions about connections between the royalty and British society and culture and to find connections beyond the ones we, the editors, have suggested. As historian of Mass-Observation James Hinton has said, 'Mass Observers are good to think with.'[42]

* Editorial note: We have selected a range of writing to represent Observers who responded to specific directives on royalty or who wrote about the royalty in diaries. They have been selected to illustrate facets of the overall themes found in the archive. Most of the writings included here are extracts,

INTRODUCTION

though some are full accounts. Where possible, we have not broken up Observers' accounts across the text but rather kept them intact so that readers can understand the context within which the account was written. The varied nature of the original 1937–55 archival material has suggested the formats of the chapters in Part I: the wartime chapter uses diaries and as such is written chronologically, while the 1953 Coronation chapter mixes a chronological approach with Directive reporting seen in the rest of the book. Finally, this volume is not an exhaustive record of Mass-Observation writing on the subject – indeed, this volume only scratches the surface of what is available in the archive – and we encourage readers to research the rich Mass-Observation materials further.

PART I

Mass-Observation, 1937–55

Jennifer Purcell

Mass-Observation was spurred into life in late 1936, following in the wake of the spectacle of the Crystal Palace fire and the Abdication Crisis hitting the news just days later. In the early days of 1937, the group brought together acquaintances and volunteers to participate in recording their lives on the twelfth of every month. This would coincide with the coronation of George VI on 12 May 1937, thus enabling M-O to compare the everyday with the extraordinary. The group would continue gathering volunteers who wrote up day diaries every twelfth of the month and posted them to the group in London into 1938 when M-O began to collect directives or qualitative questionnaires that asked Observers to respond to specific questions or issues. With war clouds on the horizon and uncertainties hanging over the continuation of services such as the post, Observers were asked to keep diaries on a monthly basis. As it turned out, postal services remained stable during the war, and M-O continued to issue directives and collect diaries into the postwar period. Nonetheless, stable funding for the organization and its work was challenging to find, and by the late 1940s, Mass-Observation shifted to become a consumer marketing research group. Leveraging their panel of Observers, market research became the focus of the organization. Still, some Observers continued writing and posting diaries to the group well into the 1950s – indeed, a few posted monthly diaries up until 1967 and 1968. Fewer directives were issued in the 1950s and the last official directive featured a royal scandal in 1955: the Townsend Affair. Mass-Observation Limited continued its work into the late 1950s, and a few staff members of M-O worked sporadically through the 1960s and into the 1970s when Tom Harrisson decided to house the organization's archives at the University of Sussex. During this first phase of Mass-Observation, interest in the royalty featured in the 12 May day diaries and in several post-war directives, including the wedding of Princess Elizabeth and Prince Philip in November 1947. Interestingly, though numerous topics were covered in wartime directives, none addressed the royals. Therefore, the only way to assess public feeling through Mass-Observation is via the diaries. The organization failed to issue a directive for the death of George VI in 1952 but launched a major effort to collect observations and data on the coronation of his daughter in June 1953. After the 1955 Townsend Affair directive, Tom Harrisson published some of the 1950s royalty material in Britain Revisited (1961) and an associate of Mass-Observation, Leonard Harris, wrote a book in the 1960s entitled Long to Reign Over Us? The Status of the British Family in the Sixties featuring Mass-Observation Ltd. material. In this Part, we feature Observers' responses from the May the 12th day survey to the 1955 Townsend Affair directive.

1

Coronation of George VI 1937

On 10 December 1936, the British public learned that their popular King, Edward VIII – the once charming Prince of Wales, the man who aspired to modernize the monarchy and become known as 'Edward the Innovator' – had decided to abdicate.[1] Emotions ran high the following day when Edward took to the microphone to declare allegiance to his brother, speaking to the people of his unenviable position, entreating them to believe him, 'when I tell you that I have found it impossible to carry the heavy burden of responsibility and to discharge my duties as King, as I would wish to do, without the help and support of the woman I love.'[2] Opinion was divided: on one hand, many believed that the King should be able to marry whomever he loved, even if she were divorced and an American; on the other, many felt the King should place his duties to the Crown and the people before his own personal desires and needs. Such opinions underscore the complicated and often contradictory expectations the British public place upon royalty: as a symbol of the nation, it is imperative that the monarch – and the royal family more broadly – discharge their duties virtuously, without regard to their own needs and wishes; yet, the public also have a desire to see the monarch as human and 'like us'.

Outside the government, the white dominions and court, few in Britain were prepared for the storm that broke over them in the first week of December.[3] Whispers of Edward's deepening relationship with American divorcee, Wallis Simpson, had circulated in the foreign press throughout the summer, but British news sources refrained from printing potentially libelous news which might scandalize the Crown until details were certain.[4] In August, American papers carried stories of Edward's cruise along the shores of the Mediterranean with Simpson, while the Times *reported details about the Coronation, official souvenir programmes and the extension of the Coronation procession route. Not until December, when talks between the government and the King pointed inexorably towards abdication, did British media begin to cover the deepening crisis. Journalist and novelist*

Philip Gibbs asserted in his 1937 book about the 'nightmare year of 1936' that in the wake of the abdication:

> *England was shaken by profound emotion which went deeper than a sense of sensation or scandal in high places. Every man and woman felt personally affected, with a sense of calamity as close as their own household and touching all their loyalties, and all their code of moral values, and any tradition that was in them. They waited under an intolerable strain for the outcome.*[5]

The crisis unfolded quickly in the first week of December, such that by the 4th, potteries production was suspended on Edward VIII Coronation mugs, which had already churned out around 8 million mugs.[6] The nation paused in a moment of uncertainty, and it looked as though the Crown itself might be in mortal danger when Parliament debated the Abdication Bill on 10 December, and ILP member from Glasgow, James Maxton, moved that the monarchy be dissolved and a republic declared in its place. Labour leader Clement Attlee supported the Crown and argued against Parliament becoming distracted from the urgent social and economic problems facing the nation by 'abstract debates about monarchism and republicanism'.[7] The Crown survived the crisis – the republican measure was handily dismissed 403 to 5.[8]

King George VI was proclaimed in London on 12 December, and proclamations were heard across the empire over the ensuing week. New designs for Coronation souvenirs were showcased in London on the same day. Two days later, all speculation was ended when the King decided that his Coronation day should take place on the date appointed for his brother's Coronation. Indeed, the King, who had been the chair of the Coronation Committee for Edward, decided to retain much of what was already planned, including the highly popular extension of the Coronation procession route to include Oxford and Regent Streets and a drive along Hyde Park after the ceremony in Westminster Abbey. Planning for the Coronation continued as scheduled and grew apace in February and March 1937.

It was the abdication crisis, along with the destruction of the Crystal Palace on 30 November, which inspired action from intellectuals around Charles Madge to organize Mass-Observation (M-O).[9] Poet David Gascoyne, who was involved with M-O from its beginnings, remembered how the Crystal Palace blaze 'represented in a sort of symbolic way an image of world-conflagration which we were already beginning to think of as about to break out, and we felt that it meant this, unconsciously, to the general public, hence the unusual fascination it seemed to have for everyone at the time'.[10] With details of the abdication crisis breaking in early December upon the British reading public, the embers of the Crystal Palace blaze seemed to settle upon the throne and threaten annihilation of the monarchy. Further, mass unemployment continued to dampen the prospects of a prosperous Britain. In mid-November, Edward had visited unemployed miners in south

Wales, where he promised, 'something must be done . . . and I will do all I can to assist you.'[11] Meanwhile, many anxiously watched developments on the continent which saw the rise of fascism and Nazism, political and civil strife in France and civil war in Spain.

The first M-O panel began in February 1937 with friends of M-O founders and volunteers from advertisements in the New Statesman. *The panel wrote day surveys, where Observers would take note of dreams, conversations and events occurring on the twelfth of each month. The twelfth was chosen to coincide with the Coronation date, set for 12 May, so that Charles Madge and his London team might compare the ordinary to the extraordinary.[12] About thirty Observers posted their observations in February, and month after month the numbers steadily increased. Forty-three of the established Observers sent in reports for Coronation Day. Additionally, the organization had distributed 'several thousand leaflets' beforehand asking, 'Where were you on May 12? Mass-Observation Wants Your Story.'[13] Along with personal details, such as marital status, religious affiliation and political views, respondents were directed to note whether they saw, or wanted to see, the procession; to describe their activities on the day in 'short hour by hour description'; to discuss their attitudes as to whether the Coronation benefited the nation; to note the most 'stirring . . . peculiar . . . and funniest incident that you saw or that you heard of during the day'; and finally to note the views of the respondent's neighbours.[14] Seventy-seven people responded to this call; these and the established Observers were augmented by twelve mobile Observers deployed throughout London to collect data on the day's events in the capital.[15]*

The M-O publication, May the Twelfth, *which came out in September 1937, was presented by documentary film-maker and photographer Humphrey Jennings and Charles Madge as a 'textual montage' of preparations recorded in the press and by Observers for the Coronation, experiences and observations in London and elsewhere by the panel of Observers and by a mobile squad of twelve Observers in the capital; a larger group of volunteers responded to a special questionnaire.[16] In its final section, the editors juxtaposed the extraordinary with the ordinary by including observations from the 'Normal Day Survey'.[17] Placing the gaze of the reader firmly on individuals and those assembled in the streets rather than on the King and royal personages, the publication might be read as subversive: certainly, to a young David Pocock (who would later revive M-O in 1981), the effect of reading the book felt like a 'magnificent subversion of authority'.[18]*

Nonetheless, as Hinton points out, the subversiveness of the text is 'contained' by 'a sense of national occasion, and the story May the Twelfth *tells is of a kind of unofficial national unity running alongside the official celebrations'.[19] This ambiguity, and the sense of confident certainty that eludes readers of Observers' writing, instead invites us 'to become detectives in a case that can never be closed: an unrelenting investigation of everyday life'.[20]*

What follows intentionally shifts the camera from the May the Twelfth *volume, and the majority of responses included here were not included, or only partially covered, in the 1937 publication. It is hoped that this shift will open new lines of investigating the evidence as well as new ways of thinking about how the original volume was constructed.*

Few of the Observers who responded to the May 12th survey wrote enthusiastically about the Coronation and associated festivities, yet many took to heart the charge of M-O to observe and document the day regardless of their personal feelings or political views. A handful intentionally avoided the Coronation by engaging in outdoor activities that took them away from crowds and the wireless.[21] Some of the Observers noted that they, or others close to them, would have been more engaged in activities if the Coronation was for Edward VIII and not his brother.

The observations give the reader a sense of the variety of ways in which the Coronation was experienced. While mobile M-O units wended their way in and out of London crowds, others biked through villages and observed the local activities, still others prepared lunches and organized street parties and fetes or braved the rain to attend these local celebrations, and many others listened in – with varying degrees of interest or attention to the broadcast – on the wireless. Observers noted how others reacted to the festivities of the day, some of whom were critical of patriotism and knee-jerk support of the monarchy which they assumed was particular to the working classes. Others could not block out the reality of the grave domestic and international situations, reflecting on the civil war in Spain or the severe dislocation of long-term unemployment. Finally, concerns for the royal family and fears of impending doom (followed by relief that the day ultimately finished without incident) threaded through some of the accountants.

Observations

A number of Observers wrote about activities in London, and commented on the procession, and whether and how they watched it. Many of these observations were documented in M-O's May the Twelfth *publication. This one, written by a 22-year-old socialist accountant, did not appear in the publication. The Observer documents his anti-imperialist, anti-monarchist feelings and his exasperation in finding few fellow travellers on the procession route:*

Let me first of all state that I did not wish to see the Coronation procession, as I am not at all interested in the jingoistic emotionalism with which it is connected. I had been given a first rate seat gratis by one of my more patriotic clients, and had been prevailed upon to take the opportunity to report the procession and its etceteras by my friends in Mass Observation.

Being one of those more fortunately placed than those poor devils who had to remain all night on the procession route, I enjoyed a perfectly dreamless night and rose at eight-thirty a.m. . . . I had stated that I did not care 'tup-pence' about the Coronation, and was sorry that I had had to rise so early on the morning of a holiday. They [parents] however trotted me out the usual stuff about 'glorious spectacle' 'great show' etc., either sincerely or otherwise, and the conversation turned upon whether the pomp was worth seeing. I hazarded a guess that the spectacle would not be as great as that of the May Day demonstration and certainly would not be as sensible and representative of the life of ordinary men and women . . . There was to be no inconvenience while these middle and upper class people waited until the King passed by. I was rather fortunate in that I knew many of the people present and the next five hours of waiting did not seem to go too slowly. We talked; we ate; we drank; we played on the pin tables; we amused ourselves generally . . . The wireless had been switched on at ten o'clock, and occasionally a few of us did stop to listen to the broadcast from the Abbey. We were conscious vaguely of its dreary music all the morning . . .

Soldiers, soldiers, soldiers. Uniforms, uniforms, uniforms. England's might. The Empire's might. For all the world to see. Then a few carriages containing foreign Royalty. Then the Empire Prime Ministers. I could just see their vague outlines in the sorry black carriages. Poor. Then more sol-diers, more uniforms. Boring. Then Queen Mary and the two Princesses. A tremendous cheer from the crowd. More soldiers. Then a fairy-like, Cinderella coach containing Their Majesties. People all round me cheer-ing like mad. The Dukes of Gloucester and Kent. A few more soldiers; and then the insignificant end of the procession.

A few of the remarks cast around by some of my more delirious compan-ions, both employees and guests:

A was cheering wildly when the Household Guards marched by, their band at their head. 'Now you'll see some marching', he cried. 'Look at the way they hold their rifles. Look at 'em! Now we're showing that not only Hitler can have soldiers. We'll show 'em. We'll show the World. Look at 'em.'

A Scotch employee named Jock banged on the wooden partition in front of him, when the Scots detachments marched by. He was absolutely in-sane with excitement; his passions inflamed. Patriotism gone mad. 'Up Mack! Come on Jock! Listen to the pipes, mon!' . . .

While some of the workers were taking down the temporary stand, I took the opportunity to engage one of them, a young man aged about twenty, in conversation. I said: 'Well what do you think of the show? Did you like it?' His eyes glowed appreciatively. 'Jolly fine. Why, it would have been worth seeing even if there was nothing else but the King's coach. That coach was marvellous, sir. They say it cost thousands.' I tested him. 'Bit of a waste', I ventured.

The youngster, who probably earned thirty shillings a week, looked at me reproachfully. 'It's only now and again', he said. 'Besides, he's a King;

he can't ride in a wooden carriage on a State show like this. Look at the money that Hitler and Mussolini spend on their processions. Millions.' I was squashed. 'Not as big a crowd as I thought there'd be', I muttered timidly. He was at me again. 'I don't know, sir –' (Notice the 'sir'. He was addressing an evident superior.) – 'They say there's three million lining the route. These processions are good now and again. They show the loyalty to the throne.' . . .

I remember my last thoughts well. I know that I said to myself that the May Day demonstration licked the Coronation procession into a cocked hat, both in length, and in meaning and association. I also remember feeling delighted that I had not cheered a single thing or person all day, nor had I bought a red-white-and-blue Coronation emblem. That was my only satisfaction on Coronation Day.[22]

One of the mobile Observers posted in London fixes the lens directly on the crowd and their conversations:

7.45 Primitive lavatory in South Bruton Mews, hard to find, in fact invisible, only holds 3 – one man in when I get there, but enter S. Johns Amb man 'What a gift! This is hard to find! I've been looking for one everywhere, and couldn't discover one.' Other man says 'At the ladies' lav in Hanover Sq there are 250 lined up' A big detachment of S Johns Amb arrives same lav, jokingly call to comrade inside, 'Knock Knock. Who's there?' On wall beside lav is out of date Fascist sign, 'Stand by the King!'[23]

Vigo St . . . 2.15 Crowd sings 'It's a long way to Tipperary.' More remote portion strikes up 'Land of Hope and Glory', then 'Rule Brittania'. Woman says 'It's lovely.' Drops of rain begin.

2.20 Nearer crowd sings 'God save the King'. One verse sung, then a cheer and whistles. Ambulance man leads away youth.'

. . .

3.10 The troops lining the route unfurl the Royal Standard and present bayonets.

Woman: 'No not yet. I think the Duchess first.'
Another: 'That's the Queen.' Then, disappointed: 'No.'
'That's Queen Mary.'
'That's Princess Marina.'
'Princess Royal, that is.'
'The Queen of Norway.'
'I saw Marina.'
'I'm sure Queen Mary's next.'
Man shouts: 'Hullo, George, boy. Well, Marina.'
Woman: 'This is Queen Mary's coach next.'

1937 CORONATION OF GEORGE VI

(It is evident that no one in the crowd actually knows who is who.)
3.13 Hats off. Men yell Hurrah. People are pointing and jumping.
'Queen Mary, that is'.
People hysterical.
'There are the Princesses. Aren't they sweet?'
Woman: 'They're well trained.'
'After the King comes the Duke of Gloucester'.
'That one's piebald!'
A policeman's eyes are shining
Woman: 'I saw Queen Mary'. 'Did you?' 'Yes'.
'See, here's the coach'.
Again a man's particularly raucous hurrah.
Woman laughs at uniform of Horse Guards.
. . .
Hysteria again. (Hysteria renews in waves. When crowd finds itself
mistaken in thinking one lot of coaches royal, it greets next lot.)[24]

*Another Observer, who was not interested in the events of the day, nevertheless
documented how they pressed in upon his activities and experiences:*

I did not see, neither did I wish to see, the coronation procession. Although
I was near London throughout the day, I felt no desire to attempt to see
what was going on. Neither did any of the four people who were with me.
When I did go into the town in the evening it was with some misgiving,
since I had no wish to miss my train back. I was lured into London by an
interesting appointment which had no connection with Kings and Dukes.

I have spoken to ten intelligent people on the subject, and none of them
wanted to go near the City on that day. There was almost an air of apathy
about their remarks.

12.30–1pm I (and a young woman) had a beer in a public house near
Ruislip. We listened to the radio, and when the King was acclaimed, we
toasted him. The pub was very full, and everyone seemed to be talking
about the Abbey. We had some difficulty in getting the car away from the
pub, since many other cars had driven up while we were inside . . .

2.30 pm – 4.30 pm We went for a ride in the car through Uxbridge and
Slough, to Windsor and back. About 3 pm we ran into a small procession
near Uxbridge, and had to wait while it passed. All the motorists seemed
annoyed. Uxbridge was lined with people waiting for another procession.
Windsor seemed very apathetic after this. There were few people about,
and few flags. We had to return for 4.30, since I wanted to catch the 5.10
train into London, in order to keep an appointment.[25]

*Outside London, Observers recounted parties and celebrations that at
once connected the modern with the historic, the national with the local. A*

nursery school teacher from Ashford, Kent, described the festivities in her town:

> I went to the adult's tea and then we patronised the fortune teller's tent where it appeared they (the 2 fortune tellers) were doing quite good business . . . There was quite a crowd . . . watching the various events – various kinds of motor byke races, then a display by the local fire brigade who put out a fire which they started on a car. We walked round to see the various side shows which were doing the normal amount of business. I then reflected that the general atmosphere was absolutely the same as at all other galas I had seen in the park, in fact people seemed even more sedate than usual but this was probably due to the general feeling of dampness, especially under foot . . . [around 8 pm] we walked to the bandstand enclosure from where the King's speech was to be relayed. There were about 200 people there, most of the people were too busy watching the events in the field etc. to listen . . . At the end of the speech an official said 'Now let us all give three cheers'. This was done in a subdued kind of way, the only comment I heard was from the lad standing near me to another, 'Well that wasn't much of a one' (meaning the cheers).
>
> 9.0 pm Returned to the High St, part of which had been roped off for dancing in the street. The town band was on a platform in the centre and this part of the town was brilliantly lit. This innovation seemed to be very popular. There were large numbers of couples dancing watched by a large crowd. About half past nine I began to find it rather monotonous, so I returned home.[26]

Another Observer, in Orford, Suffolk, documented local celebrations with no reference to the radio or to other twentieth-century technologies, reminiscent of traditional, local ways of celebrating royal or national events:

> Just before noon I go up to the Castle (a cement-bound ruin with a caretaker's room, which can be climbed for a small fee) where perhaps twenty people have collected in drizzling rain to drink a glass of free beer to the health of the King and Queen. The local MP is haranguing the small crowd from a platform, leaning earnestly over the iron balustrade at the entrance to the castle. We are too far off to hear what he is saying until he is about to give three cheers for the King. Two men are hurrying round among the people, filling the Coronation mugs (which they have prudently brought with them) with beer from large enamel jugs . . . People stand about dismally in raincoats, fumbling with their mugs; several have rosettes of red, white and blue . . . Guns are heard somewhere in the distance, and we drink the health of the King, then the Queen, then the young Princesses and the rest of the royal family. The wife of the local member comes up to Miss B. with a look of personal enthusiasm and relief, and says ringingly, 'Well, he's crowned, and that's all that matters.'[27]

A young journalist cycled through several villages in Kent to gather information for his newspaper and for M-O. His report for M-O highlighted the holiday atmosphere of his travels, but he also noted conflicts between business interest and politics. Similar to the earlier account, the journalist mused that local identity and experience superseded national:

As I left the house I was struck by the holiday atmosphere of general goodwill. A middle class woman and her little girl were cheerfully carrying strings of bunting and the driver of a lorry which was stationary gave them some sort of a Christmasy greeting . . . I returned to the station, making on the way a brief call for local news the shop of a newsagent who is a member of a left wing organisation. He had decorated his shop with crowns and flags, as he must not insult his customers. I thought once more of the way in which the Coronation seemed to arranged [*sic*] to the advantage of everybody who had something respectable to advertise . . . I made a call in a street thickly populated with the kind of poor known in America as the 'Irish'. There were more flags in this street than I have since seen anywhere else or in any pictures of the decorations. In the middle of the road there was a Christmas tree in a tub, and the lampposts had been converted, illegally I am sure, into huge Belisha beacons. I asked questions about a tea party for children to be held in the street on Whit Monday . . . I found that a dance and sports had been held . . . The street had been saving collectively for six months, and as there were a few pounds over the mothers had celebrated when their children had gone to bed . . . I discussed with a police constable why these people had made more of the Coronation than anybody else and he said, 'These people know how to enjoy themselves. It is the same at Christmas.' The only reference I heard to royalty in the road was made by a lady. She said, 'I would like to be in at the wedding night of the Duke and Mrs. S-' . . . It was very funny to see the array of decorated lorries and pedestrians in fancy dress going over the hill headed by Police constable Smallweed and the scouts and guides with flags . . . Again the district seemed more important than the King in Westminster Abbey.[28]

On holiday in Beer, one Observer wondered about the relationship between the local and the national or imperial:

On the whole we had a most enjoyable day in perfect warm weather – hardly a threatening cloud. The people seemed quite satisfied that they had done their patriotic duty. They were greatly interested in one another and the cheering of efforts at entertainment was cordial on the whole, even if tinged with irony from brothers and 'friends'. England and Empire seemed to them to be the community – Beer. There was little evidence of any larger loyalty. If there was that larger loyalty, I missed it – yet it may be there.[29]

Classed sentiments seen in M-O directive responses across the mid-twentieth-century directives suggest an assumption that working-class communities seemed more enthralled by royalty and royal ceremony, seen in the following account by a male writer from Prestwick, Scotland:

I look out of a back window. Decorated lorry having finishing touches put to it by workmen. Very large Union Jack flying from roof of working class tenement. The most commanding flag in Prestwick. High pole. Very few people about. One or two working class visitors on holiday wearing sports jackets. A few rosettes – tricolour. From front window I see our plumber in his 'Sunday best'. I can see more flags now. Red Ensign from lower window of working class dwelling. Large Union Jack from upper window of working class dwelling. Majority of flags from windows. One or two small Scottish standards from windows or in gardens of villas.

This Observer also noted the importance of the local celebrations:

9.5-9.40 I go into sitting room and read the chapter on Lenin and the 1905 Revolution in the Ralph Fox memorial volume published by Lawrence and Wishart. While I read I hear kettle drums in distance. (The procession is forming up. Probably Boy's Brigade on way to join it.)

9.45 Church-bells begin to toll. I go out. Slight breeze now. The air is vibrant. Splendid day. Cool yet fairly warm. I notice that I am more 'extroverted' than usual.

At the Cross about 300 people waiting for procession. Chiefly shop-assistants on holiday – many girls – and visitors. Shop assistants seem better dressed than visitors.

Large Crown on G.P.O. Many flags on Town Hall. Three quarters of the shops (i.e. 3 of 4) decorated. Chiefly bunting – tricolour. Long streamers from standard to adjoining buildings. A good many decorations are inclined to be tawdry. Several illustrations of King and Queen in shop-windows.

It is now 10.5. Young boy scouts selling programmes. There are now about 1000 people waiting for procession. Shop-assistants and visitors predominate, but there are quite a number of upper middle class residenters and working men. Cheerfulness abounds. Some laughter. I do not hear the King and Queen mentioned. It's the local procession that's the 'draw'. Fairly strong breeze now. Considerable number of automobiles. The drivers do not heed the Belisha crossings. I did not see one car stop.

Later that evening, the Observer noted a shift in the festivities and the spirit of the crowds:

There is a decided drop in the collective barometer! Hundreds of people, nearly all working class, are pacing Main St. Many of them look tired and even dispirited. Dozens of cars, Glasgow bound, rush past the Cross. They are nearly all packed with families or men and girls. A policeman is on duty at the Belisha Crossing. He signs to me to cross and we exchange 'good evenings'. The people are nearly all 'cheap' and common-looking. Trippers from Glasgow. Their clothes are unattractive. About six motorcyclists tear up from the shore at great speed. There is a good deal of raucous sound – buses, cars, and harsh voices. Prestwick is like 'Saturday' Glasgow tonight. No Coronation spirit in evidence. Much colder. Almost like night in January. People arm-in-arm. One or two girls of the low type. Painted faces by the score and badly painted too! Young man tries to kiss girl. Both working class judging from appearance. Youths in waterproofs, some bare-headed. Girls in cheap furs. I see two intoxicated men. One, working man talks to a child (he doesn't know her). Another (upper working class) one pats an elderly lady – upper working class – on arm. I talk to woman tobacconist. She refers to process (the topic of today) and says that it was much better than she expected. She thinks the bonfire will be a success 'because it'll go up with a crackle!'[30]

A dental mechanic reported driving through the streets of Hereford in the morning of the Coronation and noted the decorations:

I proceed on my way – the little but rapidly growing town of Hoddeston is gay with decoration – they seem to have done it more intelligently than most small towns – having subscribed £180 or so and planned the business quite successfully instead of leaving it to private initiative as other places seem to have done. The Council Offices and War memorial have gas flames to light at night. The rest of my journey to Hertford is without event except for a tramp I saw with his few possessions in a sack – I wondered what his thoughts upon the Coronation would be.

He went on to report his experiences in a club where he and a friend had lunch:

Immediately after lunch the radio suddenly and rather unexpectedly burst into the National Anthem. Everyone stood pretty rigidly to attention – perhaps here if I had been a good observer I should have joined in and simulated an enthusiasm which did not exist in actual fact – as it was I incurred a certain amount of unpopularity by looking fairly unenthusiastic over the business – a ceremony which those Empire builders are a bit touchy about. After lunch the sports have started, little girls are running three-legged races, and potatoe races, I am irresistibly reminded of my own school days.[31]

The atmosphere of the day led people to remember past royal events:

> Looked up curve after curve of 'our moor', but our beacon is in the mist at 1300 feet, and so is Beamsley Beacon opposite. I remember George V's Coronation night, yelling round our beacon, after stumbling up the track past White Wells; and then tramping back with my bigger brother to Dick Hudson's to count bonfires down the dales. We put 'the flag' on 'the flagpost' and lit 'the beacon' in those days. All traditional stuff. No Woolworth's bunting.[32]

One Observer described attending church service in Norfolk on Coronation day:

> I got the car out and drove to church, arriving a little late. As I entered I was handed a 'Form of Prayer' (Form C) by the sexton at the door. The church was quite full which is not usual as the village is strongly dissenting and the church on Sunday is usually only 10% full. I walked up to the family pew where my Mother and Father and an aunt were seated. I looked round and noticed Captain H. and a number of British Legion ex-service men wearing medals. Another farmer Mr R and his wife (they regularly attend church). During the service the organ failed for a short time and we had to sing a hymn unaccompanied. I caught Captain H's eye and we grinned at each other. The service lasted about half an hour. We came out at 10.30. On the way out of church my Father stopped to speak to the vicar. My Father admired the service. The vicar said 'I did not like it when I first saw it, but I like it now. It went very well.' – the vicar is rather 'high' – My Father said 'It was so dignified. They have chosen the best bits from the Bible and prayer book.' . . . (Note on Capt. H – A Northern Irishman. During war specialised in escaping from German prison camps. Afterwards with the Black & Tans. Now farms and writes novels of adventure.)[33]

Many Observers expressed, or noted that those around them voiced, concern about the health of the Royal couple as they went through the gruelling Coronation day activities.

> My neighbours seemed very interested in the Coronation, but much more on the King and Queen as people . . . They wondered when the King and Queen would have anything to eat, and whether they would be very tired. They thought the anointing would be very messy, and wondered what the Queen would do with her hair. They talked a lot about the Duke of Windsor, most of them seemed to prefer him to the King. They wondered whether he was listening to the ceremony and said they were sure he was very relieved to be rid of it.[34]

One male teacher awoke that day with thoughts of the royal family:

6.30. Was woken by phone. Felt particularly sleepy, and disagreeably aware that I had to attend on duty, in charge of boys from my school. As I got up I thought how nervous the King and Queen must be. My wife and I supposed that the young princesses must be nearly off their heads with excitement. I decided to wear my old socks with a hole in the heel, rather than change them.

At breakfast, of tea and toast, we discussed my plans for reaching my view-point, and my wife's plans for spending her day. She had decided not to see the procession. It would make her too tired to do her house-work in the evening, and to get ready for the party we were going to have. If Edward had been King nothing would have prevented her going.[35]

This Observer's wife also contributed her observations about the day, recalling that after she fed her husband she fell back asleep and dreamt of a dagger under the King's pillow and a tramcar accident. She awoke later that morning at 11 am:

Furious to find how long I had slept. Got into the bath with the window open and listened to the radio from the flat above. Felt sorry that I hadn't gone to the Coronation. Decided to go to the next one. I wondered how old I should be and if I should have any children. Wondered if Edward was listening in. The maids from the house backing on to ours were beating carpets all the time. Dressed and read the News Chronicle for a bit. Tried to work out what a simplified Coronation service would be like . . .

1.0 pm Made off to the local pub to meet a friend . . . Pub almost empty. Radio going, but the few people there and the barmaid were not listening. No one took any notice when 'God Save the King' was played. As I had more drinks I began to feel rather sorry for George. When they played 'The King' again, I stood up and everyone else did too. Afterwards friend sat down and said indignantly 'My God!'. Then a parson came in and stood drinks to several men and drank George's health. My friend and I had more drinks. Noticed it was 2.30. What about the rest of that house-work and the party preparations? Went on drinking and talking Royal family personalities. More people in pub by now – everyone saying they were glad they hadn't gone. Several people said they were sorry Edward wasn't being crowned. One or two disagreed.

Drinking in the pub for another hour, the above Observer returned home 'very tight'. Later that evening, after the party at her house, she went to the cinema to see the footage of the Coronation.

Went to see News reel at Studio One. Place very empty. All disgusted with short Coronation film. Went home to bed. People dancing in a droopy way in the streets. Made me think of Job ballet. Felt atmosphere was v. flat. Went home and dreamed that I read that the King had died, from a yellow newspaper.[36]

Observations often included commentary about the abdication and the Observers' attitudes about who they believed was the rightful king. An eighteen-year-old publisher's clerk from Chelsea reflected upon how the abdication crisis negatively impacted her attitude not only towards the Coronation but also about politics in general:

If Edward VIII had been crowned, I would have gone, from the point of view of mixed curiosity and historical interest. The same, if present King and Queen had come to the throne in a normal way. I had very strong feelings over the abdication, and was highly indignant at the way Edward was more or less pushed by force off the throne because of a triviality which could easily have been settled. I was equally furious at the wave of Puritanism and narrow mindedness preached by Baldwin and the Archbishop of Canterbury, and promptly refused to recognize George VI as being King of England. At the moment I am an anarchist; as far as I'm concerned, Edward is the only rightful King. Otherwise, I think this whole system should have been brought to an end, and the country should have become a republic.

11.30–1.15 . . . I pity the King, and feel he is being ordered about far too much by the Archbishop; it is, after all his show, and he should be given a larger speaking part! Instead of which, he seems to be a puppet, herded from one corner to the other, told to kneel down, told to get up, with nothing to do or say, except give the right answers whenever indicated. The Archbishop is grabbing too much of the limelight . . . above all, it strikes me as being so painfully behind the times; this type of ceremony was quite all right in the old days, when elaboration, costumes and pomp were in keeping with the character of the age. But surely now, in these days of modern architecture, aeroplanes, speed and absence of unnecessary decoration, the coronation of the king of the moment should be automatically altered to match. Edward, I feel, would not have submitted to all this, or, at any rate would have had a sense of humour about it. The super-theatrical, artificial and rehearsed tone of the service begins to get on my nerves; I dash up to my room for a cigarette and a few minutes of peace and quiet, and return to the library just after the crown has been placed on the King's head, and in time to hear the Queen struggling through the same ordeal. The commentator's description of the Queen being supported up the steps makes me laugh, and I wonder exactly what is meant (if so, why? Although I should imagine she would be well in need of support . . .) or merely guided? Once more, I feel that owing to the complete artificiality of the show, I am incapable of any genuine emotions . . . whereas if it had been simpler and more in the modern tradition, I might have been impressed.

2.30 to 3: I return, faithfully to my post in the library chair by the radio. Their Majesties have left Westminster Abbey and are returning to Buckingham Palace; I am thankful that they have at least got crowned safely, without any bombs being thrown en route, or any fiascos taking place. Or rather, I am surprised, more than thankful, having been so keyed up in constant expectations of disasters . . . and I am glad that so far, all has been well, but somehow cannot think of the Royal Pair as being King and Queen of England. Whereas the first day Edward was proclaimed King last January, I immediately visualized and accepted him in his role. And, although I feel it is silly to be indignant, I am – that the Queen should be called Queen Elizabeth. The original Queen Elizabeth is one of my favourite characters in history, and I feel that her name should be preserved, and made to stand out prominently, instead of just being handed on to any Elizabeth who comes to the throne . . . On the radio, there is nothing of particular importance: more cheering masses, more descriptions of splendiferous attire, more music and rolling past of coaches.'

8: The King's speech. I felt sorry for the man, and vaguely uncomfortable. I sat there on tenterhooks, expecting him to stutter or dry up at any minute. It moved so hesitatingly and slowly, which gave me all the more time to guess at the Archbishop's helping hand in the writing of the speech. His particular philosophy and nauseating train of thought was only too evident; I wished somebody would drop a bomb on him! God Save the King, was played from beginning to end, including all the unfamiliar verses. We all refused to stand up. One of my friends gave the Communist salute. My mother, who is American by birth, and our Swiss housekeeper, both retaliated to the sounds issuing from the radio, by singing the words of their respective national anthems, both of which have the same tune. That, for the first time, strikes me as being so odd – that Great Britain, Rule Britannia should consent to sharing a tune with other countries!

8.30: The radio is turned off. We are all limp and exhausted by the non-stop excitement and general nerve-rackingness of the day. Extremely glad that it is over, and normal life in London can again be resumed, without stumbling over Coronation stands and lions and crowns at every step.[37]

The Observer on holiday in Beer noted conversations with locals regarding their feelings about Edward and Wallis Simpson:

Sat on the cliff and watched the sea and passing people – mostly villagers. One man – might be a visitor or local tradesman – came down with a dog. Dog decorated with Coronation ribbons – drew much attention.

Man looked pleased and basked silently in the admiration which his originality called forth.

12.40 Went to a café for lunch. We the only patrons (Cold ham and salad). Noted a portrait of Mrs. Simpson and a large black and white newspaper photograph of King George V in naval uniform. No signs of present King and Queen. After lunch got into conversation with proprietress of café. She was very busy making preps for afternoon – catering, etc. Casually drew attention to picture of Mrs. Simpson half-hidden behind some flowers. She said, 'Yes, I think her a remarkable woman. I know no harm of her. I have had that picture often turned to the wall and I had a beautiful one of her pulled down and burnt during the winter . . . I cannot talk to everybody like this for I have to be careful in business – but I do think we have lost a good king who had sympathy with the working classes and that is largely why he had to go. They got rid of him. If he had married a princess and lived with Mrs. S, he could have been crowned to-day. I cried when he abdicated. I think his farewell speech was splendid.'[38]

Radio enabled listeners to participate in the Coronation and feel connected to the crowds in the streets, as this housewife, who spent the day with her parents, demonstrates:

Father describes the last part of the broadcast which he heard in the other room – How the King and Queen came out on the balcony, also the Princesses and Queen Mary and how the crowd cheered when Queen Mary seemed to 'present' the Royal Family to the people . . . Mother remarks that 'They must be mad!' My father seems emotionally disturbed (pleasantly) by the broadcast. My sister and I discuss the fact that the King did not show much hesitation in his speech, compared to a speech we heard him make on a News Reel, we both agree that he has a pleasing voice. I then prepare to go home.

After the King's speech, the above Observer listened to the Coronation Party variety program, featuring comediennes Jeanne de Casalis and Elsie and Doris Waters (Gert and Daisy).[39] One Observer had a laugh at the expense of the BBC's commentary:

At one point the commentator used the word 'proceeding' rather often. I said, quoting the late John Tilley 'I hope that proceedings will proceed as proceedings have proceeded in preceding years.' Later we had 'The Queen is between the two bishops' and my wife said 'that sounds like chess'.[40]

For some, the BBC broadcast flowed through the day's domestic routines:

10.20 Listen in. Knit. Mother finished washing dishes but can hear. BBC technique excellent, their best broadcast yet we think. Conveys scene and colour of procession and one feels a bit of the thrill with the crowds. Can quite imagine being swept into a great emotion if one's feelings about monarchy and imperialism, etc. were not mixed like mine. To me it is both a wonderful ceremony and dressing up and playing dolls, but the music is glorious and we enjoy it without reservations.

11.30 Go upstairs and make the beds, can hear a fair amount. Listen in again. Very impressive but this gorgeous glitter of birth and wealth is set against background of distressed areas, war in Abyssinia and Spain. Wonder anxiously about Spain today.[41]

Some noted the fatigue of close listening all day:

I found the concentrated listening rather tiring. We sometimes passed numerous illustrated papers round, full of pictures of Royalty . . . Lunch was served round the wireless set and we ate and listened for another hour . . . A mention of the fatigue of protracted listening-in, of the fatigue of the people taking part in today's ceremony, of the feeling of Royalty after such an eventful day and especially the feelings of the Queen-Mother, of Princess Elizabeth and Margaret Rose and of the Duke of Windsor.[42]

At least one Observer felt the wireless broadcast was alienating:

wireless sets are giving off loud cheers – wish secretly I was seeing procession. Dash into house frequently to hear parts of Abbey Service and King's avowals – think the commentary boring. Drink sherry at midday meal, rest of family gloomy, decide broadcast of big events brings feeling of isolation.[43]

One Observer, a female psychologist, was clearly moved by the emotional drama she imagined playing out within the royal family:

something in me seemed to be saying distinctly and with all the force of my life as if to 'Albert' (as my instinct called him): 'It's Edward's or <u>no ones.</u> It's Edward's or <u>no ones.</u> Be loyal to your brother. It's his crown or <u>no ones</u>' and my voice rose in a crescendo. And I seemed to see him later in imagination refusing at the last moment in the Abbey to have St. Edward's Crown upon his head. 'It's not mine it's my brother's' he shouted, and again and again as he rushed down the chancel steps amidst the shocked, dumb-founded crowd. But the vision passed.

Throughout the morning of the Coronation, this Observer admits to feeling like 'a receiving set', picking up imagined dialogue between the royal brothers and the imagined internal conflicts of a usurping brother.[44]

The real drama of the Coronation procession and ceremony was played out for many on the wireless. Many Observers recounted listening to the day's activities. The wireless was a welcome way to participate in the day's events, but for some, it was intrusive. A 31-year-old male Observer reported not being interested in the Coronation but nonetheless took the M-O charge to heart and spent the entire day walking the streets of London to document the events for the organization. His walk through the streets was marred by the sound of the wireless:

At 12.20 pm, we go for short walk in vicinity. Every house seems to have a radio going at full blast, and all have opened their windows to give stray passers-by the benefit thereof. It occurs to one what it must be like to live under dictatorship, and be compelled to listen to frequent portentous addresses on the radio. This is more irritating than one had imagined.[45]

One Observer's terse response to the day survey was also a complaint about the wireless:

Suffered the tortures of the damned listening to the wireless from 10 am till 11.30 pm as my old housekeeper who was unable to go out to join in the fun! Was rebelling in all the fuss I was also trying to read and knit and answer futile questions as though I enjoyed it.[46]

In contrast, a 38-year-old female stenographer from Forest Hill, London, was irritated by others who complained about the radio:

Was definitely keen to hear the broadcast, so hurried over bath, breakfast, etc. As soon as I heard the announcement of the Royal Family entering their coaches, and heard the cheering, etc., I felt tears coming into my eyes. Especially when Queen Mary appeared on the scene. I had not had the radio on very long before the maid from below came up and asked me to tune it out a little, as the broadcasters' voices <u>vibrated</u>. Felt disgusted. My neighbours are frightfully reactionary, and profess to be very patriotic, judging by their condemnation of the Duke of Windsor which is positively venomous. The house was adorned with a few mouldy flags, survivals from Victoria's coronation, I shouldn't wonder. (All the same we must not have <u>vibration</u> on coronation day.)[47]

Observers who listened in tapped into the 'theatre of the mind', conjuring up images of the royal family from the BBC commentary on the wireless.[48] Some Observers wrote detailed descriptions of the mental pictures and thoughts that ran through their minds as they listened to the Coronation ceremony, like the stream of consciousness written down by a craftsman from Middlesex:

The sounds of the day enhanced the beauty, or the material value of the picture . . . The sounds which came to move over the radio on the return journey from the Abbey (in particular the descriptions given by the commentator at the arch close to the badly wounded ex-service men) caused me to glow with admiration, and I experienced a desire to be on the march with the soldiers swinging along rhythmically behind the band [. . .] It was not until Howard Marshall gave his graphic description of the Abbey that I felt any enthusiasm. That man is truly an artist in the matter of getting a picture over. The crowning ceremony I found most impressive. I actually found myself sympathizing with King George when his voice came over to me. Yes! It is indeed most difficult to give my thoughts coherently. One's mind had been filled before hand with so much pomp and splendour, riches and wealth, that it was well nigh impossible for me to believe my own ears . . .

The splendour and riches was beyond any description. I did my best to picture ladies dressed in priceless gowns and coats, precious stones scintillating from their persons at every angle, from their heads, their neck, their waists, their hands, and everywhere that ornaments and priceless wealth could be worn, there is was in evidence. The Abbey itself must have been a marvelous sight. In fancy, my hands went out to examine the wonderful collection of gold and silver, ivory, and wonderful articles placed ready for use in the ceremony. Here you will smile perhaps. My desire was to get close to the men and women who had brought all these wonderful things into being. If I could only have felt the crown, it would not have mattered to me in what metal it was made, I could have spent hours tracing the fine and delicate workmanship put into fashioning such a thing. Have you ever had the feeling of humble admiration for a superb craftsman? or artist? I am a craftsman, and I get a wonderful kick out of examining sculpture, and wood carving . . .

Let me get back to the point. The sympathy felt for His Majesty as his voice came to me. You will understand, I have never seen the King, in fact, I do not know him in the true sense of knowing a person, but it is possible for one in my position to judge the character of persons by the sound of voice: at least to some extent. If it were possible, I would have taken a part of his strain for him . . . The Bishop of London, in his reading, sounded to me, a hard man. The thought came, 'I hope I never come before him on judgment day' I have digressed. How difficult it is to think, and write coherently . . .

If we all stood by the King in times of stress, and kept the pledges made in the Abbey before us all the time, would it not be a safeguard against Fascism? The world must certainly depend on our empire to a great extent for good or ill, and in this time of unrest and secret striving after power, we must take up some side in battle. If we keep our promises of loyalty to our King, then I think it will mean goodbye to Fascism.[49]

REFLECTIONS ON BRITISH ROYALTY

In response to M-O's instructions, Observers commented on the value of the royal family and of the Coronation specifically. A museum assistant from Bulawayo reflected on the utility of the royal family:

> Of course it benefits a country to have a Coronation. On that scale any type of function stimulates trade. But it disturbs foreign relations. Above all a Coronation like this does not indicate progress. The Empire will fall if it does not evolve and the Coronation stood for everything that is static.[50]

This Observer also considered the complications of reporting on the royalty as if they were celebrities:

> It may be true as the London *Times* said in a leader that the Royal Family's private affairs are now the common possession of the nation, but I cannot agree that it should be so. The amount of powder and lipstick the Queen puts on her face for a public event is her own affair entirely and among intelligent people it can only be a matter of regret that the details are broadcast in the English press of the world. It seems to me like dragging the Queen down to the level of a film star.[51]

The young journalist who cycled through Kent on May 12th catalogued the responses of people he met along the way:

> I think it benefits some people to have a Coronation. It benefits not only those who wish to inspire respect for the status quo in Govt, but those who want to inspire local patriotism of some sort and also a great many people who wish to get some sort of advertisement or other out of it. They manage to further local or special interests by linking them with the national propaganda campaign. The Coronation is an obstacle to all those who wish to change things, as the emphasis is a traditional nationalism and tends to be hostile to the innovator and the foreigner. It is nice that most people enjoy the festivities, but they would enjoy them more if they were recording something gained in their way of living. The large fairy tale element in the festivities in England to-day seems to imply deceit somewhere.
>
> All the people who have spoken to me about the Coronation fall into five distinct classes. The most numerous are the people who are intensely interested because they put themselves in the place of the protagonists. They feel a sort of vicarious glory. The other classes are the people, chiefly schoolmasters, who think it is overdone and the public is tired of it; the politically active people of the right who say that the amazing loyalty of the people can only be explained by the people's thankfulness that things are better here than in Germany or Italy; the politically active people of

the left who say that it wasn't even well staged this time; and the polite who disliked it because it meant extra work.[52]

This 37-year-old male Observer from Southend-on-Sea took a negative view of the Coronation:

I did not see the Coronation, neither would I have done so had a free ticket been presented to me, plus a quite unlikely cash bonus, say of £5. Much to my surprise I had the day off. (My firm has made quite a good thing out of the Coronation, incidentally, and has broken out in a nasty rash of bunting and excess profits). I rose at 9 o'clock this morning, glanced through the paper, being much more interested in the news from Spain and the bus strike than the pages of 'historic supplements'. At 11 I switched on the wireless to hear the broadcast, but this was for the sake of others in the house, who, by the way, merely wanted to hear because they thought it an historic occasion than for any other reason. After that I read Voltaire's 'Candide' and at 12 o'clock adjourned for a pint at the local pub. Switched on the wireless again at 2-0 for the same reason as before, and off at 2-30. Reading Pat Sloan's 'Soviet Democracy' all the afternoon. This evening attending to my correspondence – including this . . .

My neighbours – or rather my workmates – will, like me, be heartily glad when tomorrow comes. They are tired of the Coronation, mainly because of the ballyhoo attached to it, and they realise how insincere so much of this is. The Coronation undoubtedly benefits certain sections of trade and it gives people an excuse for getting excited. I think the chief purpose it serves, however, is as a myth for the governing class by means of which they endeavour to bind the peoples of the Empire together. Whether, in this sense the Coronation is a good thing or a bad thing is, I suppose, a matter for future historians to decide. From my random notes, you will have probably gathered my opinions on the point, though I should like to point out that I hold these opinions without rancour either to the King and Queen personally or to the barbaric ceremony in which they have figured to-day. It all strikes me as faintly amusing.[53]

Another critical view reflected on why the royalty were popular but considered the cost:

I do not think that the 'benefits' of the Coronation outweigh the disabilities. Naturally, if we <u>must</u> have a King, he <u>must</u> be crowned with some show of pomp and pageantry. It is the custom, and the people want it because they have been trained to want it. It is colourful and stimulating like a technicolor film, and makes the King seem more than a man. That is how the people like to regard him, although they enjoy 'domestic' scenes and incidents connected with Royalty, because that makes them seem like themselves. In this way they can persuade themselves that they live in a true Democracy, forgetting that the King's domestic affairs are not connected with Parliamentary policy. I think that Coronation decorations have caused some increase in employment, but not much, and only for a short period. And, in any case, these decorations have given peace-time opportunities for profiteers – who wd. make similar profits in wartime. Those men who were not connected with the making of these decorations, and who are unemployed will be dissatisfied. They will wonder why money should be spent on flags when it might have gone for unemployment benefits. Certain big store-owners will spend money on decorations which wd otherwise have gone in Income Tax. Their patriotism is more apparent than real. It is true that a Coronation will bring many visitors to the country, and some trade. But all profits coming from such visitors and trade will go to the people who least need it. The state of the ordinary man will be as before; perhaps he will be a little bitter later on.[54]

I think the monarchy is to some extent a support in the maintenance of our political liberties but also it is the bulwark of class division and social privilege.

A great corporate act is a powerful national experience and is good or bad as it is used. The Jubilee drew the nation together in sincere admiration for a man who had lived up to a high ideal of service. Mass emotion, even if centered on a worthy object, is dangerous because it can so easily get quite out of control. For an unworthy object – e.g. anti-Jewish it can degrade terribly. I have heard the opinion that democratic Germany made a mistake in having practically no pageantry which the Germans love and missed (they have had their fill since!!)[55]

For some, international politics and events took precedence over national celebrations.

We talked about Spain – T. asked if Franco's success at Bilbao meant that he was going to win. B. Said he didn't think so, he believed the Government had taken Toledo. T. said they had won it and lost it before, and would they do so again. I talked about Franco's protest about the evacuation of refugees from Bilbao, and his complaint that the convoying of foodships was against the International law, and incompatible with the sovereignty of the Spanish government, saying it was absurd when his was not the legal govt. B. pointed out that the situation was complicated by the fact that some powers had recognised his as the legal govt., which brought the legal argument to an impasse. I then recapitulated a letter from Eleanor Rathbone which had appeared in a previous day's 'Manchester Guardian', showing how the Non-Intervention Agreement was not only operating against the Government, but securing that if it did win, it would be much more extremist and dependent on Russia than if we had recognised its legal rights. T. said she had always thought the N.I.A. was a bad egg – and that anti-Communist panic was being deliberately whipped up, when the Government were not Communists. B said he would like to point out to Eden that Caballero had been a minister in a Conservative Government. T., who has been reading history for her exam, says the peasants had to have the land, it's happened here and in France before now with no thought of Communism.[56]

2

Royalty in wartime 1939–45

The day survey method, originally employed in 1937 and used in the May
the Twelfth *Coronation day reporting, was designed to capture a day in
the life of Observers on a monthly basis. Over the course of 1938, the day
survey method was increasingly replaced by qualitative questionnaires
called directives, which '"directed" the participants into providing in-depth
commentary on various aspects of their lives'.[1] From January 1939 onwards,
the organization collected monthly directives until well into the post-war
period. The first 1939 directive asked respondents to write about their
strategies for savings and their attitudes regarding jazz music and dancing;
thereafter, topics range widely, for example: anti-Semitism, wartime
inconveniences, opinions about political leaders, reading habits, the BBC,
housing, religion and sexuality. Of the 260 subjects covered in wartime
directives, several were repeated across time, allowing for longitudinal study
of changing opinions and wartime morale.[2] No wartime directive asked for
the panel's opinions of royalty.*

*Some investigations regarding attitudes towards royalty were carried out
by Mass-Observation during the war years but resulted in only a handful
of staff-authored file reports. In 1939 and 1940, reports on royalty were
limited to audience applause of famous people in newsreels. Findings in
these reports tend to show a general apathy towards the royal family in
the early days of the war, though audiences tended to clap more for the
royal family than they had during the peace.[3] By the end of March 1940,
however, it was reported that the King and Queen received no applause
whatsoever and in May, royals received some applause, but it seemed that
audiences were bored with the newsreel footage that featured them.[4] June
reports on newsreels revealed similar apathy towards the royal family, and
Mass-Observation observed that military and political figures – both British
and French – were now far more popular than were the royals – likely a
result of the recent battle at Dunkirk and the increasing crisis in France.[5]
In the summer, audiences seemed to respond to those on newsreels who
were perceived to be 'doing their bit . . . All those applauded are <u>doing,</u>*

not merely saying or watching'.[6] *As the war came closer to home with the Battle of Britain and the beginning of the Blitz, Mass-Observation noted a perceptible change in audience reaction to the royal family that they argued:*

> . . . indicates a shifting from a <u>personal</u> attitude to a <u>patriotic</u> one. In the early days of the war when there were less surface signs of patriotism, the Queen was most applauded as she was the member of the Royal Family most liked. Now the King is clapped, not so much as a man, but as a symbol of the country.[7]

This point might underscore a shift away from the attitudes sculpted by the Abdication Crisis and the cult of personality built up around Edward in the media to a broader acceptance of George VI. Nonetheless, the 1940 newsreel reports showed that the Duke of Windsor's appearances were nearly always applauded.[8] *Negative attitudes about the Duke appear in the diaries in 1943 and are linked to judgements that Windsor is not doing his bit for the war.*[9]

Some of the overheards (Observers' recollections of overheard conversations) reported in the early stages of the war reflected a fear – or expectation – that the royal family would abandon their people in the event that war came home to Britain. One forty-year-old woman from Bolton responded gloomily to the June crisis in France, saying, 'I bet the King and Queen are packing to go – if they've not gone already. I bet the damn government's getting ready to fly too. They'll all leave us – as usual.'[10]

The only file report devoted to popular attitudes regarding the royals and based on 'indirect questioning and overheard remarks' written in the summer of 1940 demonstrates that the royal family was untested and seemingly unnecessary in times of crisis:

> The lack of interest [in the Royal Family] is quite marked. Besides a simple denial of interest, there were detailed remarks showing the same tendency, as that of a middle-class man of 20: 'I should think they're quite nice people, quite harmless, but redundant, – is that the word? – unnecessary. I'm not very interested in them.'

The file report noted a similar comment from a 45-year-old woman:

> I think it's all a bit silly – kings and queens in wartime. I don't think they're wanted. All them things are all right in peacetime – we like to have ceremonies, and royal robes, – but now it's up to us all – not Kings and Queens. That's what I think, anyway.[11]

Other comments offered some insights into how the monarchy was regarded more generally:

All the other countries have gone to pieces – and why? Because they didn't have a popular King to bind the country together. I think they give a feeling of national unity behind the idea of a King, and I think it's up to the Government to see that he's in safety, so that we can always look at him as a figurehead.' . . .

'They've had a pretty rotten time since they came to the throne, but they've done their job well. They'll certainly carry on when the war is over. Why shouldn't they?'

'I think they're wonderful. The King and Queen set a wonderful example to the whole country, though the King had a terrible job, suddenly being thrown into an office like that with his impediment.'[12]

Unfortunately, no other wartime reports regarding general attitudes about the royal family were made. Instead, file reports that included comments and observations of the royalty focused on events or specific individuals – for instance, a 1942 report on reactions to the death of the Duke of Kent and a March 1945 report covering the resignation of the Duke of Windsor from his post as governor of the Bahamas.[13]

Reflections on the royal family can be found, however, in wartime diaries. At the end of August 1939, Observers were asked to keep diaries for the organization.[14] Diarists continued to write throughout the war, and many continued posting their diaries to Mass-Observation well into the 1950s – a handful into the 1960s. Diarists often recorded their day-to-day activities and feelings, news of the day and their reactions to it and overheard remarks by neighbours and family. Despite the length of the war and the numbers of wartime diarists, mention of royals is rather thin and tends to cluster around certain diarists who made concerted efforts to bring them into the frame of the diary or those who commented regularly on news of the day. According to a file report analysing December 1940 diaries, royals and other famous personalities were rarely mentioned, 'unless some news items brings them to the public consciousness'.[15] Certainly the collection of diaries here is oriented around news stories that feature royalty. Additionally, royals enter diaries when there is a personal connection, such as a royal visit to the Observer's town. Still, there are surprising silences in the diaries. Given that Observers' thoughts and opinions of the royalty tend to show up in the diaries when featured in the news, it seems odd that few diarists comment upon the bombing of Buckingham Palace in September 1940, especially since many diarists do express concern about Londoners bombed that month. If the diaries give us a sense of Observers' day-to-day experiences and concerns, silence about the royalty may indicate important ways in which the monarchy is experienced and regarded in everyday life. The rest of this chapter gives a chronological accounting of diarists' mention of royals during the war, demonstrating moments when royalty become relevant.

1939

Ominous storm clouds gathered on the continent from March 1939, when Hitler annexed the entirety of Czechoslovakia, until August, when the Nazis and Soviets concluded a nonaggression pact. In anticipation of war, Observers began to write diaries in the last week of August 1939. Nella Last, a 49-year-old housewife from Barrow-in-Furness, noted a prophecy about the monarchy heard from her childhood that put her on edge about things to come that August.

Aug 31, 1939   when I was a small child I remember a prophecy dad heard – that little prince Edward would never be crowned King and that in 1940 a world war would start that would 'end things'. I'm no more 'scared cat' than the average but I have a cold feeling in my tummy when I think the first came true. Feel so tired I cannot keep awake but my eyes won't stay shut – wonder how the people who live on the 'edge of things' keep their sanity. Know I'll have to work hard to keep from thinking.[16]

The Germans invaded Poland on 1 September, prompting the British Parliament to urge Prime Minister Chamberlain to declare war. The declaration came on Sunday, 3 September. Many Observers noted their reaction to the news, some included reflections on the King:

Sept 3, 1939   10 am. An announcement comes over the air. An ultimatum, to expire at 11, has been despatched. Thus, finally, all our hopes of peace are destroyed. My sister is at home. Even now, she can't believe in what is happening. 'Yes but how shall we know? What will happen' Presumably there will merely be an announcement. There won't be any signs in the heavens and no air-raids. Not yet. No visible change at all.

11.15 Chamberlain speaks. He announces our deliverance into hell in correctly solemn tones. He claims to have done everything possible for peace, and I suppose he has, within his limits. He's not evil, just incapable of any large imagination or foresight. He's not directing events, he's just being shoved protestingly about. After the speech come announcements of the closing places of entertainment, about shelters and gas masks. And then, to leave no doubt in any one minds, to prove that we are fighting for the old loyalties and not for a new world, the National Anthem was played. To hell with the anthem, and the silly old Empire . . .

9.0 pm News. I had not heard the King at 6 o'clock, but here he was, or, anyway, his recorded voice. Although I am a staunch republican, as far as I'm anything, and thought the message was certainly platitudinous rubbish, he said it very nicely.[17]

42 REFLECTIONS ON BRITISH ROYALTY

Sept 3, 1939 we listened into King George – a speech which I heard unintentionally as I was reading a scientific periodical. General comments:

(I) 'Poor man.' 'It's a shame.' 'He is very courageous to do it.' 'Bless him.'

(II) Most agreed that considering his verbal shortcomings, it was a good speech.

(III) My own impression: The speech by one who has no direct means of ruling, can hardly be considered in the same light as some by the rulers. Generally the same strain, however, was present as in Chamberlain's speech and the same objections apply.

After this speech, during the playing of the National Anthem, no one stood up. A discussion then ensued as to what British Government would do, it and when, it had won the war. The general view was that Germany should be split up into little states.[18]

Sept 3, 1939 After a wild night of thunder, lightning and gale, there is a high, foamy sea and a blue sky. I see from someone else's newspaper that the issue of peace of war will be decided today, but I can't be bothered to hang round the wireless waiting for it. Hitler gave the only sort of answer he understands when he bombed Poland on Friday. I go off alone to the cliff and watch the magnificent sea. . . . I came up to dinner. I am told we are at war and Chamberlain has spoken. I'm glad I missed him. I don't want to hear him say 'God knows I have done my best.' I don't believe it. He could have secured Russian co-operation. And I don't want to hear the King tonight either. Sacrifice. Pull together. Justice. I'm willing to fight Fascism if necessary (and if we've treated Russia decently it wouldn't be necessary) but I feel tricked somehow. The National Govt has brought us to this pass by sabotaging collective security. They've not thought of justice until just lately.[19]

Though the conflict raged in Eastern Europe, inconveniences and uncertainties about the future punctuated the experience of home front Britain. Many of the Observers who mention the royalty in their diaries seem to do so after seeing them in newsreels or speeches heard on the wireless. George VI's well-known struggle with stuttering is often commented upon.

Oct 5, 1939 Churchill is my <u>darling</u>, his voice over the wireless pours vitality in me if I've even a sick headache. I think our Royal Family are REAL people.[20]

Oct 17, 1939 Last Wednesday . . . the Duke of Windsor got a good hand clap at the Forum (first class town picture house) when they showed pictures of him leaving home in his uniform. They very rarely clap at Town Picture house, it has to be something special.[21]

Nov 23, 1939 I can't say I was particularly gratified to hear that the royal princesses were the first to invest in the new war loan racket. However we were spared a description of their clothes![22]

Dec 25, 1939 King's Speech impressive. I am much interested in his efforts to master his weakness. He has improved immensely. But I feel sorry for him every speech must be an ordeal for him.[23]

Dec 25, 1939 Family lunch party – self, brother (18) and three maiden aunts aged between 44 and 60, their evacuee (80). Listened to King's speech. Everyone except myself stood up for 'God Save the King', though two of my aunts and my brother are pacifists.

Everyone wished each other a happy Christmas as usual. I don't know whether they realised the irony of it. Had very few Christmas presents in this household, but two other people said they had had more than usual.[24]

1940

With the spring, the Nazi offensive turned towards the Low Countries and France. For ten days at the end of May and early June, British Expeditionary Forces and French forces were evacuated from the beaches at Dunkirk. On 14 June, Paris fell, and a week later, France capitulated. In May, the Duke of Windsor, who had been living near Paris, packed up his valuables and unceremoniously left his servants behind as he and Wallis Simpson fled to Spain. On 2 July, Windsor was offered the governorship of the Bahamas.[25] The Battle for Britain kicked off in the summer, and bombs were dropped on mainland Britain for the first time at the end of August.

Feb 15, 1940 'The right king has gone', said the Cornishman (he was referring to the Duke of Windsor whom I found to have a loyal following down in the village where I have been staying. This is partly due I believe to so many of the men having come in contact with the Duke while serving on yachts.) . . . I could see . . . a conviction that had the Duke of Windsor been king – all this trouble would have never come about. I suppose people must find some excuse for the chaos into which their lives have been flung.[26]

May 24, 1940 Today we were discussing the rumour spread by the enemy about the King and Queen going to Canada. This is not believed, but it is nevertheless dangerous. One person summed it up in the following words, 'I should be disappointed in him if he did go. He might send the Queen and the children – but I don't think for a minute he would go himself.'[27]

June 8, 1940 In the afternoon I went to the cinema with a friend. It was as crowded as before the war in spite of the glorious weather and the higher price of seats. The audience clapped the pictures of the royal family on the news reel, clapping the Queen particularly loudly. There were roars of laughter and applause when a soldier of the B.E.F. said, 'We'll bloody well show Hitler.' As we went out of the cinema the commissionaire was saying, 'Standing for 2/6. Seats at 3/6 only.' And this was a suburban Cinema.

I went on to a small party to meet a newly engaged couple at one of my aunts' house. One woman at the party says, 'I wish my son (he's 18 years old) was a girl', and another answers her 'I wouldn't mind if I had seventeen sons. Then they could all go.' This reminds me of the woman in Noel Coward's 'Post Mortem' who writes newspaper articles 'I gave my son to England' and I create a bad impression by snickering maliciously . . .

We talk of the usual things – high prices of food, clothes, fares; of films, plays, books, family and connections in the forces. There is much speculation as to the reason why the Duke of Windsor has given up his post. Someone brightly suggests that he is a Fifth Columnist. This was indignantly refuted by his admirers among the company. However my own father, a man who is always hostile to any suggestion of rumour says there must be some reason. Speculation was stopped by the denial of rumours about the Duke in the nine o'clock news.[28]

June 14, 1940 Black Monday, blacker Friday. I have just listened to the Queen's speech. I don't know a word of French, but I was deeply moved by the Queen's tones, she has indeed a lovely voice. I suppose I was in the mood to be touched, the French national anthem never sounded more inspiring and appropriate.[29]

July 10, 1940 discussed the Duke of Windsor's appointment to the Bahamas. I thought it sounded petty to send him off there now but H. said it might be that he had Germanic sympathies & they felt it would be safer for the country if he was kept away. He still has a pretty strong following & his admirers might be led in any direction he chose.[30]

Aug 12, 1940 I wonder whether we are behind the Albanian revolt. We could produce Zog, of course, as we produced Haile Selaisse, after having ignominiously haled Victor Emmanuel as Emperor of Italy. We've got the Duke of Windsor out of Hitler's way so that he shan't produce the rightful King of England for us at a judicious moment, anyway.[31]

Aug 23, 1940 The King and Queen were clapped also the ARP, at a town cinema last week.[32]

The Blitz began on 7 September, with the bombing of civilian targets in London. Two days later, the first bomb hit Buckingham Palace but failed to detonate on impact. That night, the bomb exploded, shattering windows throughout the building, including the royal apartments.[33] Three nights later, bombs landed within 30 yards of the King and Queen. On that occasion, six bombs in total hit the Palace, two of which left massive craters in the courtyard.[34] The media reported on the event, yet only a handful of diarists mention the bombings or concern about the royal family.

This report was from an Observer who walked around Buckingham Palace after the second bombing:

Sept 12, 1940   Arrived outside Buckingham Palace just as the band (on parade) finished playing something out of Chu Chin Chow. The changing of the Guard ceremony was in progress watched by about a hundred people. When this was over and the old Guard had marched away to the band some fifteen people lingered about the railings for a minute or two but after four minutes no one was taking any interest in Buckingham Palace.

From this side (the front) no damage was visible but on the North side through the trees it could be seen that nearly all the windows were broken. Other damage could not be seen from Constitution Hill and there were no spectators.[35]

Sept 13, 1940   Friday the 13th but am I superstitious? Up about 7.30. Did not hear 7/0 news. Old man over slept. Pouring with rain. Heard 8/0 news . . . Went on duty. Fairly busy, dinning morning . . . plenty to do. Nothing from M/O so may post and chance things, in the hope that if you changed it will reach ya by being forwarded. Lay down during afternoon. Papers came at 2.30. Not very busy after dinner. Back on duty at 5/0. Not very busy. Heard 6 news. Buckingham Palace again. Will hit someone of importance one day. King and Queen to be honoured for not running away. This is an <u>entire</u> war in that respect. Bad psychological move on Hitler's part. So many people in America and our colonies interested in the ancient buildings. Perhaps he is getting desperate, but is such a wily devil that you can't take it for granted. Finished about 10 and got to bed about 11.0 after helping clean up dishes. At supper we were talking about the reported invasion and it was felt he may leave already, had a try, hence last week's rumours and Churchill's speech was only a cover up . . . Thought to go out during the afternoon, but – Just changed about 2/30 and was looking out of the window when down came some bombs. Saw the dust and pieces go sky high and shouted out and fell on the floor.[36]

13 Sept 1940   Buckingham Palace was deliberately bombed to-day. This seems completely absurd to me as it merely arouses people's anger. Bombing the East End caused misery and might have led to discontent and divided loyalty but with the King bombed we are once again united in one cause.[37]

Sept 15, 1940 Never heard sirens through night. Sunny but cool evening. Read Express. 1) John Gordon first, Lads! He raises my spirits and makes a proper fighting man of me weekly. . . . 4) Priestley – A joy to read!!! Them's my sentiments!! King's and Queen's Shelter? Not excessively elaborate? Say u? That must mean the big bugs must have them <u>more elaborate</u>!! And the real people, what have they?[38]

The following is a report from a journalist in Bradford detailing reactions to the bombings in London, including Buckingham Palace:

Sept 17, 1940 The chief topic in Bradford just now is the continued bombing of London.

Those whom I meet casually invariably remark – almost as soon as I've met them – 'Well, I see London's still getting it' – or words to that effect. People with whom I have business make similar observations. References of this kind are a feature of all conversation.

Sympathy for the homeless – particularly in the East End – in general.

With anger at German ruthlessness goes the hope that our Air Force will give Berlin 'some of its own medicine'. Without exception, everyone I've talked with believes that the bombing of Germany's civil population would stop these raids quicker than anything else.

Although everyone is angry about the attacks on London, no one seems very worried about them. People here are thankful that Bradford hasn't experienced a second raid, and I've heard a number of remarks similar to that of my tobacconist (a woman) 'So long as they don't get to Bradford again'.

Of the bombing of Buckingham Palace, most women have said to me, 'It's a shame, isn't it' – or something like that. No man has discussed this unless I've introduced it. Most men to whom I have mentioned the matter (I put it this way: 'Well, what do you think about the bombing of the Palace?') haven't said much at all beyond that 'it's a psychological mistake' – a phrase that, used in this connection, is rapidly becoming a cliché. A friend put this question to five of his employees (textile workers, men). To all five it would be a pity if the King or Queen got killed, but it would be of no more consequence to them than the death of Mr. Smith or Mrs. Jones. They didn't like to see anyone killed, but the King and Queen were just a couple of individuals to whom no symbolic significance attached in their estimation.

There were several men who comment a bit more:

<u>Station bookstall manager, about 50:</u> 'They're trying to destroy the hub of the Empire – the Palace. They think the effect of this on the Empire will be to their good. But it won't. It'll have just the opposite effect. It's a psychological mistake.'

Journalist, about 45: 'It they're doing it deliberately – and we don't
know that they are, though it looks like it – they're making a big
psychological blunder.'

Managing director of textile firm, about 40: 'If it's deliberate I'm
bloody annoyed about it. The King and Queen are nice people and
it's hitting below the belt to single them out. It would be different
if they tried to get at Churchill – we know they hate him. Though
the Palace always was an eyesore to me. But it's having good
psychological effect on the United States. We ought to send a Czech
squadron to bomb the Wilhemstrasse.'

Northern manager of London advertising agency, 39: 'I don't think
they're trying to kill the King and Queen. They regard Buckingham
Palace as a symbol, just as they regard the Houses of Parliament and
St. Paul's as symbols. They're going to destroy these symbols of their
culture if they can. All the same, these raids on central London'll
make Whitehall realise what we went through in Bradford a fortnight
ago with no defence at all. That's the only consolation I'm getting
from them – and I'm not the only one.'

Public library assistant, Socialist, about 28: 'I thought the first bomb
was a put-up job. It was so good for our propaganda. It certainly had
a lot of propaganda value – and we made the most of it. I know now
it wasn't, of course. But the more they bomb the Palace, the more
propaganda for us.'[39]

Sept 22, 1940 Unless [the King] is to speak to the people about the
bombing of London, I guess it must be serious to have to ask the
King to speak in order to soften the blow, but what I can't think.
Invasion, movement of the Government, King and Queen leaving
England, part of the Empire breaking away, it might be one of a
thousand things, all of them a shock, so I suppose all that is left is to
brace ourselves against it.[40]

Oct 7, 1940 I can't help being suspicious of the appointment of the
Duke of Windsor to the post of the Governor of the Bahamas. There
is something wrong about the whole affair from the start of the
French retreat, I am sure. I said something of the sort to my friend
Doris (31, married, w-c) and she agreed.[41]

Oct 17, 1940 I'd never have been one of those mothers who proudly
give her son's life for king and country – not all the kings in all the
world would be equal to my son. I'm not one of those loyal fools.[42]

Oct 18, 1940 London raid? I feel terrified when I think – days and
nights in shelters! The huge buildings in ruins – deaths and casualties.
It must be terrible. Then one can see that the people are not being
properly looked after. The power to see to comfy shelters is in the
hands of well-fed comfy people who take it for granted that 'the
poor will be always with us'. They have not learnt to 'put themselves
in Callaghan's place'. The people themselves must fight for right –

they'll get nothing by staying put and trying to look happy – that leads to official inertia. It may sound disloyal but I believe the king and queen are quite enjoying their 'bombing' and 'comfy shelter' and visiting the b-areas; sharing people's martyrdom.[43]

Oct 25, 1940 <u>News Chron</u> picture of Queen chatting with nurses all drawn up in stiff line gets my goat. I loathe to see men or women drawn up in lines to be inspected by 'superiors' . . . King's Speech – for goodness sake, stop it. It's painful to listen to. He doesn't even read with expression.[44]

Dec 9, 1940 One thing that I have heard a lot of people say, is that the King has visited everywhere else that has been badly bombed but Birmingham. Also, when they don't say we have had it bad, when we have had a heavy raid, annoys people. I think they get a kind of proud feeling when they are mentioned as having stood up to a bad raid, and feel slightly slighted because the King has not been to B'ham.[45]

Dec 25, 1940 Listened in to carols etc and to Britain under fire. We were much moved by the appeal from Coventry to put all thought of revenge. I noticed some slight improvement in the King's Speech but he still has the most awful struggle. Out to tea and for the evening, when we sang carols and talked – nothing else much. Back home early and listened in after I had got Peter to bed. Thankful to go peacefully to bed. No warning all night. One wonders why as Hitler has little use for Christian good will.[46]

1941

The Blitz continued to rage across Britain in 1941, with the largest raid hitting London on 10 May. Invasion fears began to ebb in the summer as the Nazis turned their attention towards the east and invaded the Soviet Union on 22 June. Pearl Harbor was bombed on 7 December, bringing the Americans into the war. The empire was now in mortal danger as Japanese forces began to muscle in on British holdings in the east. Hong Kong fell eleven days after Pearl Harbor, and British imperial fortunes fell drastically over the coming months. Comments on the royalty were few but coalesced around royal visits and speeches, though mention was made of the birth of the Duke of Gloucester's son in November.

Feb 13, 1941 A sister called in very early, to say that the King and Queen were coming to the stations during the morning. Having never seen them, or the Royal train, I decided to go. There was a small crowd, and the preparations were interesting; and a sister and I saw the King and Queen in their car; alighting; and in the train. It was a pleasant and unusual half-hour.[47]

Mar 31, 1941 The fifth column is no myth. There are times when I feel like saying, 'Why don't you allege that Glasgow was blitzed by the English?' What is happening to-day? People are coming up to you in subdued tones and saying, 'Is it not shocking about the King and Queen?' I in my innocence say, 'God Lord! They have not been hit!' And then it turns out that whereas they invariably send a message of sympathy to English towns they have given Glasgow the cold shoulder. Miss Smith, 'They have ill advisers!' Miss Bousie, 'Ill advisers! They fault's their own. They know what is going on.' And my memory can recall no message to Glasgow, either, though do recall messages to some English towns. I don't say that out loud . . . I think I serve the nation best by refraining from passing these stories on, for any attempt to stop them openly would I think drive them in firmer.[48]

Aug 10, 1941 On all day in the stationery canteen. We are getting a little tired of the everlasting 'browned off' complaint from the men. In their case it is caused by too much time on their hands, too little money to spend and nothing much to do. At 9 o'clock when the Queen broadcasted I was quite surprised to see that everybody left anything they were doing in order to listen – the place was completely hushed – this is something that only Mr. Churchill has been able to do. I had been looking forward to hearing Quentin Reynolds again and was not disappointed, his confidential manner of addressing his microphone-victims is effective.

The first night of the early black-out – and isn't it dark by 10.30. As we stumble home I am filled with thoughts of the winter – how quickly this summer has gone – I certainly have not appreciated these light evenings until tonight, and they are a thing of the past now.[49]

Nov 18, 1941 Duchess of Glo'ster has a son. Duke gets compassionate leave from army. Gercher. Do 'they' think anyone in the Empire or outside of it, believe he is subject to the discipline of the ordinary soldier? I am interested in any and all women and in any and all babies, but what interests me more is – why some have luxury and others nowt, and – heavens, what will this young Prince cost us, the ordinary people, before he dies? And will he be worth it or just a puppet. He wd have a worthwhile life but folk born in his set seldom do justify their existence. Everything round them from birth on tends to destroy what alone makes life worthwhile, breeds character and so on. I have no time for Royalty, but I do NOT hate them and I wd not like to see them harmed. But I do think they are out of date and I pity them. Theirs is such an artificial life. I expect, rid of the trappings, they are most of 'em, quite nice to know, and quite ordinary. But I also realise that my ideas are held by a minority, so Royalty look like staying put for some time yet.[50]

Dec 21, 1941 It is announced to-day that the King is to broadcast on Christmas Day – I wish he would not speak, I always spend a most uncomfortable quarter of an hour whilst he is on the air wishing the whole time that I could do it for him.[51]

Dec 25, 1941 <u>King's Speech</u> – 'Seemed to tell nobody nothin' rather poor thing to go out to the world. <u>Churchill's Speech</u> – How grand! Splendid old top! Just the kindly homely personal touch. Yes, he might have been President! Grand old boy how well you must have managed those old difficult Senators and all the critical World. Lovely to listen to you – Do hurry safely home. We worry for your return.[52]

Dec 25, 1941 Christmas Day this year was very like Peace-time ones, save that the families were not complete; some far away, we hope to have with us next year, others can never attend an earthly Christmas. To Them we owe more than we can ever pay. Still, the children helped more than anything else to MAKE Christmas this year. Rations have been eked out over the past few weeks and so we were able to make the table look something like pre-war days. This is a splendid achievement for Lord Woolton's Ministry. I wonder what people in Germany had! We all listen to H.M. the King this afternoon. I think it is a good thing that there should be such a broadcast, even if the subject matter is stereotyped, as it is bound to be.[53]

1942

By far the bleakest year of the war for the British, given losses in Burma and Singapore as well as unrest in India. The year 1942 also saw the retirement of Archbishop of Canterbury Cosmo Lang. Diary entries this year were the most critical of the royalty – perhaps a reflection of the lowered morale.

Jan 26, 1942 Am so glad the Archbishop of CANT is going. I have never forgotten his malice to the Duke of Windsor. That any follower of Jesus the compassionate could have faced a mike and said such cruel things about another human being, disgusted me for all time. I hope the Church will take this opportunity to put a worthy man into his place, seeing that we shall have to presumably go on having archbishops for some time yet.[54]

Feb 17, 1942 Duke of Windsor. It's funny how his name always crops up amongst the working people at a time of crisis. My official LCC helper (married, 45) talked to me while she peeled the potatoes for the school dinner declares if they only had a real leader like the Prince of Wales was, how different the feeling of the people would be. He, she declared, was a real man, and understood working people – what does a man like Churchill understand – really understand – of the feelings of the working people who are doing the hardest jobs of the war. She was certain that the enthusiasm that was lacking in the country would be here if only the Duke of Windsor were allowed to be King.[55]

Mar 8, 1942 Point values altered. Shall buy what is offering, no thought to spare worrying about such a subject. New photo of King – in RAF uniform, wearing decorations he has not earned and never could earn in his position. Why are the powers that be so stupid – such issuing of fraudulent photos only makes folk mad and piles on the hate of those who determine to kill off Royalty. They may think it unifies the Empire, but that is just where they are wrong. There seems to be some danger I may land a job this week.[56]

March 26, 1942 Our last night's suppositions about a Royal visit confirmed at 9.30 pm last night. Husband ordered to report at 9.30 am this morning in Lister Park. I hadn't time to join the crowds, but must have gathered in Town because this afternoon, at knitting guild, I have heard of lots of 'brushes' between husbands and wives because dinners weren't ready at mid-day. Most men argued that there was no reason why the King and Queen couldn't come on a visit without soldiers, policemen, and crowds thronging the streets. To stop or divert traffic, slow down transport, delay workers was hindering the war effort, not helping it. What the men really meant was that they were annoyed because their wives had had a morning out, so dinner was late![57]

Mar 28, 1942 Tom rang up to-day, he said it was hell on Thursday night and they came back with a terrific hole in their plane, he said however that it would be easy tonight, I wonder!! The King broadcast tonight – I thought it was his worst broadcast – and once I thought he would have to be faded out. It is a great pity because his voice, when he gets going, is very pleasant. I wonder if he realises the agony he inflicts on his listeners, every time he speaks.[58]

April 12, 1942 The Queen spoke on the wireless last night. She has a clean and very sympathetic voice, very attractive to listen to. I can recall the view I had of her driving to (London Bridge?) Station after her wedding, and how charming I thought they both looked. The King always looked so very much nicer than his photos . . . I have a great admiration for them both . . . I can't think of another word. But this is built upon respect and, in a way, gratitude I think.[59]

April 22, 1942 The papers say we have advanced 3 miles in Burma – the wireless says we have completed our non-stop withdrawal. Smacks of the Duke of Plaza-Toro![60]

What a farce! Princess Elizabeth inspecting the Guards![61] I am surprised at the King and Queen allowing it. Surely now is the time to stop that silly business. The men standing like cattle, while a chit of 16 passes along their ranks. It reminds me of the pictures of the late Czar's daughters dressed in the actual uniforms of the regiments of which they were colonels. The time for such imbecilities is gone.[62]

May 9, 1942 My mother, on hearing of the King and Queen touring the West Country said, 'What a wicked waste of petrol!' The feeling of people everywhere in this district at any rate is bitterly against the full rationing scheme. I have heard from several people that we are going to hear some bad news tomorrow. 'Prepare for a shock. Churchill never speaks unless he has some bad news to give us.' No one seems to trust the naval victory business, but there is a general feeling of suspicion about. My cousin says Lord Haw Haw announced at 1.30 that Norwich was bombed last night. It is funny how the Norwich raids have increased the amount of listening to Haw Haw . . . I have just been pushed from pillar to post and have spent my time in running and talking.[63]

June 13, 1942 When the result of the Derby was given out on the 6 o'clock News, it is revealed that the King and Queen have been present both days in order to see both the big races. Personally I don't blame him for seeing his own horses running, but was amused at one explanation of his visit to Newmarket – it was felt that if the King did not see the races it would give the impression that he did not approve and support the National Stud! I wonder if anybody swallowed this?[64]

June 14, 1942 Today is Allied Nations Day; London had a huge parade through the streets and the King and Queen and dozens of Allied royalty took the salute outside Buckingham Palace. I wish I had known, I enjoy watching processions, as it was we were on all day at the canteen. This week, however, for the first time for over 15 months we were relieved at 6 o'clock and was it a relief! I realise now that our day there from 9 a.m. till 10.30 has been too long and that as long as we were prepared to do it we were imposed upon. Edward Murrow's broadcast this evening was inspiring and I felt less depressed after it, particularly as the news from the middle East which preceded the postscript was far from good.[65]

June 14, 1942 As usual, a comparatively uneventful day. I wrote to my husband and went to post the letter. I have a cough, which is a nuisance. Down the town I met Mr. H, looking for someone who would look after his old mother. He feels quite bitter because the King and Queen went to the Derby – using petrol and 'if a man takes a day off, it is absenteeism, but they have time to go to races'. I gave my mother Cronin's Keys to the Kingdom to read and couldn't tear her away from it. My aunt came down after tea, feeling, as usual, depressed by the news.

June 15, 1942 I find the feeling expressed by Mr. H yesterday about the King and Queen and the Derby quite wide spread. Mr. W says the Libyan battle must be dreadful and can't imagine how the

ROYALTY IN WARTIME 1939–45 53

Commander can direct his troops. The feeling in the staff room seems to be that Tobruk is soon to be lost to us.[66]

Aug 10, 1942 On duty at the N.Z. club this evening. I met a young American who had just seen the King, Queen and princesses at Euston. He adores the Queen and said, 'We haven't a Queen of our own and she is the only Queen we will ever have. She is really beautiful.' He didn't care for the King – he was an admirer of the Duke of Windsor – in fact he was communistically inclined but he thought Princess Elizabeth, 'a honey, with her beautiful hair'. I was amused at these remarks from this tough-looking American, but the more I listen to men from the U.S.A. and Canada, I realise how completely Queen Elizabeth captured the hearts of everyone there during the official visit. Another told me that he had been introduced into the home of a family at the Elephant & Castle by a clergyman, and he was full of praise for the hospitality shown him. I think he was a little influenced by the fact that the family contained a marvellous daughter. Anyway I think a lot more of this sort of entertaining could be done and probably the hard-boiled appearance of most of these troops is no guide to their character and maybe many of them would enjoy this sort of hospitality.[67]

Aug 12, 1942 By the by – Announced to-day that the Duke of Windsor is to be Governor of the Bahamas!!! I see the last Governor got £3,000 – Population 66,908 'for the most part being descendants of liberated Africans' says Whitakers! This is really rather pathetic. I am sorry for the D. of W. . . . but of course Baldwin was quite right . . . the Simpson woman was quite impossible as a Queen with two husbands already living and one a British subject.[68]

On 25 August, the Duke of Kent was killed in an air accident in Scotland. M-O reported on the incident in one of the few wartime file reports to feature the royalty. A forty-year-old male was quoted as representative of many responses gathered for the file report:

There's no doubt about it, but the whole thing's a tragedy. But of course, he's no different to anyone else. There's hundreds of others dying in the same way every day, and nobody shares the grief of their wives and families, and at least the state will look after the Duchess and her children handsomely, whereas these poor devils have to bring up their children as best they can. There's that way of looking at it. Myself, I think the Royal Family are all right – they don't mix in with state affairs too much, and don't seem to lead extravagant lives. I don't think we've anything to complain of.[69]

Some diarists responded to the accident in similar tones to the indirects recorded in the file report:

Aug 26, 1942 Married 17 years ago today at Brisbane, Australia. No regrets from either of us even if I am an economic impossibility, quoth my old pot and pan. That is not his fault as he pegs away day after day to keep us both.

So, the Duke of Kent is killed. Well, the old queen has 4 sons so if she had come thru this war with all 4, she wd have been lucky. This will give the Royalty a leg-up as what with Buckingham Palace bombed and now a son killed, the ignorant will feel so sorry for the Royal family, unmindful of the fact that for 3 years now there have been women getting that news daily thousands of them now. I'm sorry for the old queen as a mother but no more than any other mother, and I'm sorry for the Greek wife with her so young baby, but hers will be fat sorrow, more easy to bear than thin sorrow. I reserve most of my pity for the widow who has to exist with kiddies on the widow's pension. This shd mean less money paid out of the national coffers surely? One hopes so.[70]

Aug 26, 1942 I hope they won't make too much fuss over the death of the Duke of Kent. It may be a sad event for his family, but to other people it is of little interest. I am no more moved by his death than by the death of any other complete stranger.[71]

Aug 26, 1942 It is with sorrow that we learn of the Duke of Kent's death. It turns out that Charlie has met the Duke several times in the course of business. He liked him and thought he had plenty of courage. There is much sympathy with the Duchess, but Queen Mary is picked out again and again. There are the usual types of envious remarks that are constantly getting levelled against the royalty, e.g. that Marina and the three children will have plenty to live on. I happened to say, with innocence, 'The Duchess will be entitled to a pension from the Ministry of Pensions', which I think would be a nice link between her and many other widows, but I was woefully misunderstood and the remark was received with peals of laughter as 'her pension will be able to pay for one dress a year'. And of course, there was the remark, 'if it had not been for the Duke no-one would have heard anything about the accident', and 'it is no different for the Duke and those he leaves behind than for the crew and those they leave behind'. Of course, the royal family don't feel any differently from other bereaved families, but the emphasis is always in a nasty sense.[72]

Aug 26, 1942 News of Duke of Kent's death – seemed general regret as he appeared to be doing a good deal for the war and is general popular. Good news of Churchill's doings – a great man not allowing ideological feeling to interfere with the desire to win the war.[73]

Aug 27, 1942 If half the things said abt the Duke of Kent are true, he was a nasty piece of work, and willing tho I am to make allowances, some of it must be true or so much mud wd not be thrown for some

ROYALTY IN WARTIME 1939–45

to stick. Thank God people are waking up and realising that Royalty are but human and not half gods, and one hears comments abt how worried we shd be abt Marina's future, etc. Sarcasm may not be lovely but it is better than apathy.[74]

Aug 28, 1942 The death of the Duke of Kent is sad but no more so than that of his fellow airmen. At least his family will not suffer materially and I doubt if his children will have known him as a man who sits at meals with them, who winds their toys and amuses them when they are ill. But then, I'm talking without knowing the facts. Perhaps the Duke did all those things![75]

August 30, 1942 Madge most upset over the death of Duke of Kent, said it so sad as they such devoted couple. I did not tell her all the tales Vi used to pass on when he worked at the F.O. No point in raking stuff up over the dead. I do feel they are making a bit too much fuss over him, H. said so too. How must people feel who have lost their own in flying accidents & on operational flights too, not joy riding. Madge reported a flying man told W. there sure to be a big enquiry into this crash, so many happen up there, usually due to pilot refusing to be gui[d]ed by navigator until they get to sea. Over confident pilot sails along & suddenly hits a mountain.[76]

1943

Allied fortunes began to improve with the victory in North Africa in November 1942. The Beveridge Report, which was announced a few days later, set a hopeful tone for the post-war future. The Russians began to hit back against the Nazis, forcing Germans to increasingly lose ground in the East while victorious Allied Forces in Africa mounted a cross-Mediterranean invasion of Italy, causing the capitulation of Italy in September. American GIs began to appear on British shores in droves this year as preparations for an invasion of France picked up. Diarists followed the King's travels to North Africa and one Observer found herself regularly explaining British culture to the Americans and notes Americans' commentary on British monarchy:

April 11, 1943 Enjoyed my slight lay-in this morning (9 o'clock) then got on with some Spring-cleaning. Joyce and I did a great deal and felt very pleased with our efforts. Pop as usual went to Trailer pump practise – absurd, because he knows more than the N.F.S. Instructors who take it, and has done it so often that he feels he could do it in his sleep. Anyway the other men from the road who go are awful muts apparently, old and doddery most of them, so they take a lot of teaching. The Queen's broadcast was quite interesting, we were most amused at her reference to the duty of wives to be faithful to their husbands overseas – it must be serious or she certainly wouldn't have referred to it.

June 16, 1943 It is announced this morning that the King is in Africa reviewing the 1st and 8th Army. I expect he is almost due to return or they wouldn't have given it out, considering the risk he is taking. Actually I should imagine that his visit to Africa means that invasion is not to come just now, surely they wouldn't start anything with him out there.[77]

June 16, 1943 Went for a lovely drive round Walter's district for Welfare Week. Right up to Farnborough in Warwickshire, still rather thundery and wet; at times, but awfully pretty in between the showers, a lot of the anti-aircraft sights are now empty, rather sad, so many have left little gardens, some with good looking vegetables, and so many looked quite pretty today, while in the winter when they were here, so desolate and ugly. I suppose a lot have gone abroad. Heard from Peter and Bay, Peter having a very busy time on the Wolds in Yorks doing intensive training, complains of his back, which he hurt going over a large fence and big ditch in his tank, also they are awful chalk pits they have nearly driven into. Bay seems very happy and was playing cricket at Ambleforth on Sunday. We hear the King has gone to N. Africa, to see the Armies there, lovely for him to have a change, and for him to have some of the cheers instead of Winston always having them.[78]

July 3, 1943 Suddenly realised why am so unpatriotic; the old sub-conscious suddenly threw up Edward 8, about which was terribly upset, though having a very gay life myself at the time. Felt then could never come to terms with British mentality after that.[79]

Sept 10, 1943 When I came into contact with the Americans, I thought the right and proper thing to do was to take them by the hand and instruct and guide them in British Institutions – I have not ceased to think so, but I have an idea that there is a counter process at work to change me from British ways of thought into American.

There are a number of subjects that never ceased being aired. The abdication of Ed. VIII is one. Nothing can shake Capt. Macgowan's belief 'he is a splendid fellow and she is a very nice girl'. This always leads on to derogatory remarks about our present King and Queen, for instance, 'This present King is a good King', he says. I say, 'Of course.' Then he goes on, 'He does what Churchill tells him. He does not rule.' I said, 'Naturally.' Then, 'He is just like Churchill's dog. Churchill says "Lie down dog" and down he lies, or "Get up dog" and up he gets.' There is some American idea that you cannot speak of the King and Queen in derogatory terms, e.g. Mr. Treckman in January said to me, 'If you walked into the Police Station and said that the King had committed adultery they would put you in jail.' I said, 'I don't see why they should. They would probably think

I was weak in the head.' He say, 'There you are. They would not believe you.' Today Capt. Macgowan, 'If you went about saying that King George VI was a bad character, you would get rounded up.' I said, 'No I should not. People would just not believe me.' Capt. Macgowan said, 'Well it is not like that in the States. We write letters to the Press saying that Mr. Rooseveldt [*sic*] is a blackguard, and our letters get printed for us, and everyone believes what we say.' I said, 'No one in their senses would say that Mr. Rooseveldt was a blackguard.' However, he then set out to explain that before he was struck down with infantile paralysis he was known to be a bad character.

The subject of Ed. VIII always brings up abusive remarks about the Archbishop of Canterbury. It used to count so little with me that I cannot remember whether that was Dr. Davidson or Dr. Lang, but I dare not say so outloud for I am constantly championing his action. It always goes on to divorce and associated subjects, about which Americans thought it very loose.[80]

Sept 30, 1943 Finished reading 'Must our children die'. I agree with Golancz mostly – but I imagine that hate is not easy to eradicate. Not that I <u>hate</u> Hitler and Mussolini but I do <u>hate</u> what they stand for – actually I can say that I don't <u>hate</u> anyone though there are certain people I dislike intensely – but they are people I know – I don't see how one can either like or dislike people one has never met. One can admire King George VI or Josef Stalin, but unless one came into personal contact with them, I don't see how one can either like or dislike them. One can love or hate the things they stand for and that is all – the feelings the great masses of people in England have for monarchy is I think mainly artificial – whipped up by the press and radio. Just a form of escapism.[81]

Oct 8, 1943 Went to cinema last night, our local. Saw Queen in news reel – what a stout matron she is getting . . . how obviously she draws her daughter into her conversation. Elizabeth seems unshy tho not forward but there is nothing gawky abt her so her training has been ok one imagines. King never seems to alter. Poor wretches.

Nov 10, 1943 Saw Louis Mountbatten arriving in the East for his new work . . . thought what a pity someone didn't swop him and his coz George in their cradles! Mountbatten has all the bearing of a king, a hero, a leader, looks and oh well, he doesn't stutter. I'm not running down our poor little King, but it is so obvious he is a poor do by comparison.[82]

Nov 11, 1943 Shocked hairdresser by saying I didn't think it mattered much if we had a King and Queen or not. . . . She said they were such an example. I said we had a similar example in the Churchill fam, the Edens, George Lansbury, and most back streets also. But they are so disciplined. . . . Yes I said, and how dull for them. . . . They have so much to do. . . . Most of it unnecessary said I. I reassured her that I wd not kill them off but wd give them some useful work. Expressed the disappointment I feel these days in Duke of Windsor. Instead of release him frm all the bumkum giving him the chance to show himself capable of a worthwhile job, he seems to be just frittering time away.[83]

Dec 4, 1943 Joyce came for luncheon and stayed to tea. Had a lot of good talk. She had had the Princess Royal to look at the Hospital, and gave her lunch. Said she liked her, and found her quite easy, as they talked about Bay, who was great friends at Eton with the second Lascelles Boy, and has stayed at Harewood twice. She was very nice to all the men, but very silent with the staff, etc. shaking hands, but not saying anything, such a pity as I am sure she is awfully nice if only she could 'get it over' better.[84]

1944

On 6 June, British, Canadian and American troops successfully invaded the beaches of Normandy, setting up the final stages of the war in Europe, as the Allies now pushed back on the Nazis on three major fronts. As they had done throughout the war, Observers commented upon royal visits and speeches this year. Rumours surrounding the Duke of Windsor are also noted.

Feb 14, 1944 I was at the N.Z. Club tonight, rumour has it that the King and Queen are going there this week, so there is much polishing and cleaning going on. I wonder if the King & Queen would get a shock if someone one day received them naturally – without all this cleaning, etc. They must think everything is very good in England, they only see that which is clean, attractive and happy – this is rather cynical, because neither of them seem to lack intelligence, merely opportunity to find out the truth.

Feb 17, 1944 Another girl has been attacked locally, so Phil came to meet us from the canteen this evening. I must say that I had never imagined that mass-emotion could be roused so quickly – even Mr. R., the manager of the Y.M.C.A., admitted that he was rather nervous – although I can't imagine that any man would mistake him for a female. The King and Queen went to the Club today I notice, so their cleaning and polishing wasn't in vain. The Government's plans for a national Health plan are announced today – takes the sting out of the Beveridge plan, and is certainly a clever move by the Tories, with a view to the next Election coming soon, I suppose.[85]

Mar 20, 1944 At lunch the two people I was with had heard that the Highland Division was at a certain place – that they were bound for

ROYALTY IN WARTIME 1939–45

the big jump, that Monty had seen them, also the King, and that they were not impressed with H.M. – 'Well, what do you think', said one of my friends, 'tough men like that, who've been through Dunkirk, Africa, etc. – you don't expect them to think much of somebody like that' with remarks abt. 'Degenerate stock, etc.' Personally I think our Royalties are nice respectable people, with a v. good sense of duty, wh. is more than can be said of all their critics – but I do wish the British habit of cant abt. Royalty cd. be discarded; the fiction of their 'graciousness', their social inability to do wrong; that is nauseous. Talking about thieving: shops, firms, sending things by rail who are resigned to having half stolen en route.

12 Apr 1944 Today's news is of the Russians sweeping on, enormous air battles over Europe, the Duchess of Gloucester 'expecting'. (However, the little Duchess seems the nicest of the lot . . . my Father, talking about Royalties at the weekend, said 'I agree with Wells, I haven't anything against our present King and Queen, but I believe in a Republic.')[86]

May 1, 1944 *This entry details the opening of Red Cross Offices by the Princess Royal:* Commandants in their red dresses lined the walk, and each one was presented to the Princess who was dressed in her A.T. uniform. She has changed very much since I last saw her, lost her nice pink cheeks, and looks delicate. After she had unlocked the house and made a little speech, fold by Lord Nuffield who has given money for the house I gather, we went in and found some nice people to talk to, and thoroughly enjoyed my tea. The Princes sat at a table in the window, various important people were taken up to her, suddenly the Duchess of Marlborough who was very much master of the Ceremony, said 'Mrs. Hodgson' and up I had to get and go forth with her to the Princess. She introduced me, and said I ran the Oxfordshire garden scheme, the P. looked very bewildered, so I thought it best to plunge and tell her I was Bay's mother. That went very well. She was so nice about Bay, and I liked her. Her eyes filled with tears when I asked after her Sons and she said the elder was in Italy. I remember the 'Mams' all right! Was afraid I might talk too long, but was moved off quite easily. Oh, dear it was a hot day, and we had such a long wait before she came, thankful to get back home and get into the garden.[87]

May 22, 1944 Rumour has it that Duke of Windsor is going to take American citizenship. Good idea. Never will I forget that awful talk the Archbishop of Cant gave on the air abt Windsor. That alone justifies him leaving the British Empire, and what more natural than that he shd take his wife's nationality. Whether such a step wd do owt towards consolidating friendship 'tween our countries one doesn't know. It is just possible, I suppose.[88]

June 6, 1944 We listened in company with the rest of the hotel to the Kings Speech (I was sorry for him – it was not inspiring – how different de Gaulle sounded) and we all stood up for God Save the King. Someone switched off the radio as soon as the Archbishop of Canterbury was due to come on, and I heard no one mention the Kings Speech though people had plenty to say about the rest of the news – What a good job of work the BBC had done – special praise for Howard Marshall who might have been at Lords he was so nonchalant etc.[89]

Aug 5, 1944 Lord Douglas Hamilton has been killed, husband of Prunella Stack, of whom there is very little opinion up here. I am almost amazed at the interest in the royal family up here, in almost every home the conversation turns to Princess Elizabeth or the Queen, I suppose it is because there is so much Scottish blood near the crown now. Felt so exhausted after yesterday that we decided to take things fairly easily.[90]

Sept 13, 1944 <u>Leopold?</u> The sooner royalty is wiped out the better for the world. The rulers should be the ruled what the heck use are royalties except to swank and waste money that poorer folks work for.[91]

Sept 28, 1944 The question abt changing the words of the Nat Ant made me chuckle inwardly. Malcolm Sargent wd say just what he did say, and poor Joad cd not cope with it as he wanted to say what I wd want to say – abolish the Royal Fam as well. If we must have the Nat Ant and Royalty, leave the words as they are. Why not 'frustrate their knavish tricks, confound their politics, on Thee our hopes we fix, God save us all'. Sounds to me o.k.[92]

Oct 4, 1944 Tribute in D.E. to Duke of Windsor yesterday puzzled us. Is there something behind it wh will be discerned later by us ordinary folk? If not, seems to us of no importance. Frm the bits we hear the Duke and Duchess of Windsor seem to live the life of their class; frequent trips to USA, staying at the best places with the best people, and so on. If he has done anything good for England lately, it is a light under a bushel, as the Bible has it.[93]

Dec 3, 1944 Today the Home Guard are standing down and there are going to be processions everywhere, the main one being in London, where most people seem to think the King will take the salute. This evening we heard recordings of bits of the march, as well as parades in various parts of the country, and it made one look back a long way to the first days of the L.D.V., as did the King's speech, and indeed we have come a long way since those days. I expect many H.G.'s (I know a few) will be sorry things have finished for them, but personally I would never be surprised if they weren't recalled, especially if the Germans start sending jet-propelled bombers over here. The seemed to have two or three bad patches in his speech, but goes on most valiantly where most others would give up altogether – I do think he is brave to speak to the Empire at all, as we are always looking for hesitation, whereas we don't notice it in others. Mr. Churchill's last speech was much worse than this one of the King's, but apart from a few remarks such as 'He seemed rather merry', or 'He seemed tired' it caused no other comment.[94]

Mass-Observation conducted indirect interviews regarding the King's speech in December, and while some interviewees were decidedly uninterested, others commented favourably, as can be seen in the following responses:

M50D, 'I didn't hear it – I didn't bother – I've got no use for all that. I don't think myself it would do any harm if we was to have a president instead of a king – then he could get sacked if he didn't satisfy.'

M40B. 'Royalty for this country is a stabilizing influence. Its function here is not to interfere with politics but to act as a unifying symbol for all the nations as represented in the British Commonwealth of Nations.'[95]

1945

As the war in Europe wound up in the spring of 1945, one Observer waxed lyrical about the demise of the royalty and another criticized royal reviews of the troops. The first general election in just under ten years took place in June, ousting the favoured Conservatives under Churchill for the Labour Party, which had promised to support the Beveridge Report's recommendations.

Mar 6, 1945 Such nonsense abt Princess Elizabeth joining the ATS. Anyway they haven't kidded us that she's starting as a private, and I bet her uniform came from Saville Row.[96]

Mar 16, 1945 I am unmoved by the news that the Duke of Windsor wants a change. It seems to me, in the absence of any news to the contrary, that those two have just joined the ranks of the idle rich – if they ever belonged anywhere else wh I guess they didn't when you come to think it out.[97]

May 1, 1945 Mussolini hanging in square! Yes it seems a quick end. Yet he need never have been had <u>ours</u> not toadied to him. Anyway, the Italians have a King (little beast) and a very wealthy one. What's he do for his money. Wish they'd hang him. Sed I to Tom 'We people have jobs, we cannot rule as well – so we pay well people to govern us – they <u>play</u> instead of working or caring for us, knowing if war comes <u>they</u> won't be held responsible.'

May 2, 1945 King's speech. Who cares? It annoys me to hear the piffling man jawing on about 'my people'. Days of Royalty are over. Among so many big things in this world a modern king is a piffling thing.

REFLECTIONS ON BRITISH ROYALTY

May 15, 1945 Royalties, no use to anybody except to the wealthy nobodies to uphold and head a certain <u>social</u> useless life. Cause more trouble than enuff and expense to peoples. Alright in days when they lead in battle, but now??? They shelter behind the fighters and take the countries wealth and have a good time <u>during</u> wars. Churchill did more harm than enough in Balkans by his love of royalty. Countries need men at their heads who can rule democratically.[98]

In June 1945, Mass-Observation reported on Victory in Europe Day (VE Day) celebrations and noted responses to the King's victory speech amongst those gathered at the celebrations in London:

'The four of us listened to the King's speech; it's always painful to me to hear his halting delivery, but I like the feeling of being one of so vast an audience . . .'

'The King's speech was the best I remember hearing him deliver. One felt the strength of the personality behind it; a brave and conquering personality overcoming natural obstacles . . .'

'At 9 p.m. the King. Most people that I know seem to feel the same about his speeches. Admiration for the way he faces the difficulties, fear that he shall trip up, and a kind of personal embarrassment when he seems likely to do so. I'm afraid this rather detracts from his matter sometimes, but it can't be helped, and, anyway, it gives an impression of common humanity which no oratory could do. Pity, though, for he has, otherwise, a fine resonant voice reminding one of his father's. A good speech, but necessarily formal. The occasion demanded it, and I expect he dare not allow himself the luxury of emotion.'[99]

Aug 15, 1945 V.J. Day. A happy day of rejoicing . . . Personally I can't of course begin to compare this day with V.E. Day the relief then and relaxing of the awful tension from one's own anxiety and anguish is a thing one will never forget, but today there is just the rejoicing for the <u>whole world</u> – and the glorious knowledge that the killing is over and the joy of thinking of those who have got their dear ones in the Far East – My brother Jimmy especially whose only remaining Boy is there . . . The King broadcast at 9 pm was quite the best he has ever made I thought, it really couldn't be improved on, and his delivery so extraordinarily improved.[100]

Aug 17, 1945 King & Queen seem to have had a day of it yesterday. I think Clem Attlee has acquitted himself well in his first appearances. King sounded much better last night. He seems unafraid now. When he gets stuck he goes to it and blurts it out. One imagines that before he used to sit in terror and the more fearful he got the more incapable. Sounded as if Muddlecombe's bucket was kicked over just before the King started.

I expect the next momentous event this nation will have will be the betrothal of Princess Elizabeth, tho who on earth can be a worthy consort is outside my knowledge. Husband says it shd be an American, to further bind the 2 nations together. On that argument, why not a Russian? There shd be a few of Royal blood knocking around if they prefer that, but maybe that wd not please the Stalinites, so wash that out.[101]

3

Princess Elizabeth's wedding 1947

Post-war peace brought little relief from the austerity measures that Britons had laboured under during the conflict. Wartime rationing continued, and even deepened, in peacetime as the need to feed and rebuild a starving continent fell upon Western Allied nations anxious to inoculate Europe against the revival of Fascism and the rising threat of Communism. Bread, never rationed during the war, was rationed in 1946 and potatoes were added to the ration list in 1947. That year saw further cuts to the meat ration and bacon ration; petrol for leisure travel was also forbidden, as was the foreign travel allowance.[1] Newlyweds and couples who hoped to marry faced post-war housing shortages, while food and clothing rations severely limited the options for celebrating weddings and setting up households.

Internationally, Britain faced a loss of standing as the fortunes of the Soviet Union and the United States rose to the status of superpowers. Further, 1947 saw the unravelling of the British Empire as India and Burma were granted independence and terrorist activities in Palestine forced the British to relinquish its mandate over the region.

Into this bleak landscape, it was announced on 9 July that the heir presumptive to the throne, Princess Elizabeth, was engaged to be married to Lieutenant Philip Mountbatten. Earlier that year, a Sunday Pictorial *poll indicated that 55 per cent supported a match between Princess Elizabeth and Prince Philip of Greece but 40 per cent did not. Many of those against the match cited their disdain for foreigners, while others believed it was time for royals to marry commoners.[2] Certainly, Philip's family name Schleswig-Holstein-Sonderburg-Glücksburg did not help matters.[3] Yet, as some* Observers *were to note, the fact that the British were mired in a civil war in support of the Greek monarchy complicated what some analysts might have taken as a knee-jerk popular bias against all foreigners. In the wake of the January poll, Prince Philip's uncle Lord Mountbatten pressed for his nephew's naturalization and in February, Philip dropped the Greek royal title and became Lieutenant Mountbatten of the Royal Navy.[4] The* Times *reassured its readers that this change was nothing uncommon, as many foreigners who served the British armed forces admirably, as Philip had done during the war, had a 'right' to take up British nationality.[5]*

The wedding was set to take place in Westminster Abbey on Thursday, 20 November. In recognition of the difficult economic times, it was decided that the day of the ceremony would not be declared a holiday.[6] Despite the awareness of the difficult times, many hoped that the fairy-tale wedding might lift the spirits of the nation. It was not a long-standing tradition for royal marriages to take place in Westminster Abbey but rather a practice begun after the First World War, beginning with Princess Patricia of Connaught in 1919 and Princess Elizabeth's parents in 1923; the Duke of Kent and Princess Marina of Greece married at the Abbey in 1934 – the first time Princess Elizabeth and Prince Philip may have met.[7]

The British public were to live vicariously through their young, photogenic Princess and her dashing naval fiancé, and the press indulged this need by reporting wedding preparations, household arrangements and gifts given to the royal couple. While many couples struggled to find housing, it was reported that the royal couple was to settle into Clarence House with £50,000 allocated by the House of Commons for renovations, and the King gifted his daughter Sunninghill Park as a weekend retreat.[8] The public was also treated to a display of gifts on view at St James's Palace, such as a picnic basket given by Princess Margaret, jewellery given by the royal family, various items of silver, gold and glassware. Imperial gifts included a full-length mink coat from Canada and a diamond tiara and necklace from the Nizam of Hyderabad.[9] More mundane domestic gifts, such as refrigerators, vacuum cleaners and kettles, were also sent to the couple, as were the quite generous gifts of women who sent in rare nylon stockings for the bride.[10] Perishable food items were donated to those in need, while twenty of the twenty-five dresses gifted to the Princess by the New York Institute of Dress Designers were given to women who were also being married on 20 November.[11] Despite many groaning under clothing and food rationing, the Princess enjoyed a gift of 100 clothing coupons given by the Board of Trade and, more importantly, gifts from the royal family of previously purchased cloth, for a gorgeous wedding dress with an impressive fifteen-foot train made of ivory silk tulle.[12] As with the gifts, the dress was made available for public view for an admission price of 1s. or 5s., to be given to charities of the royal couple's choice, after the wedding.[13] The nine-foot tall, four-tiered wedding cake weighed in at 500 lbs.[14]

Despite the fact that the wedding day was not declared a public holiday, crowds lined the procession route from Buckingham Palace along the Mall, through Admiralty Arch, down Parliament Street and around the east and south sides of Parliament Square to Westminster Abbey.[15] Schools across the country held parties for children to celebrate the wedding, and many listened in to the BBC's broadcast of the ceremony and commentary on the processions.[16]

Mass-Observers were asked about their feelings regarding the wedding in the December 1947 directive. The royal wedding question was posed as the last question in the directive, which included questions about the impact of the cost of living, jokes and humour and Christmas memories. Over 350 Observers responded to the directive, though most responded in more depth to the first three questions.

Observations

Many Observers commented on, or questioned, the media's emphasis on the fairy-tale romance and seeming attachment that the Princess and Philip showed for one another. Indeed, the Sunday Pictorial *poll mentioned earlier included the condition 'if the Princess and Prince are in love' in its query.*[17] *The following 44-year-old single female laboratory researcher wrote:*

> I was sorry for the bride and bridegroom because if it was a genuine love match, all the vulgar curiosity must have been a little tiring and nauseating to them. I made myself listen to the broadcast in the evening of the Wedding. I thought that it would be an education for me. All cheers and crowds make me wonder what was behind it all, to stand for hours, just to catch a glimpse of a carriage or two plus a few horse guards not even a decent procession with bands must have some deep significance behind it, but I leave the interpretation to the psychiatrists.

This Observer then reflected on the inextricable relationship between the heir presumptive's private experiences and her duty to the nation:

> I must say when I heard Elizabeth say the response in rather a trembling voice I realized for the first time that she is only just twenty-one, and the whole thing must have been a bit of an ordeal for her. I felt almost as if she was being sacrificed to make the nation . . . happy. Of course those of my friends which I could discuss the subject like me all thought of the first night and the sexual side and wondered how much Elizabeth knew or felt of these matters.[18]

Others also brought up the sexual side of the marriage under the harsh glare of public scrutiny and royal duty, such as this 55-year-old male engineer:

> My chief feeling about the Royal Wedding is surprise that it aroused so much enthusiasm. Secondly, it was regret that the young people could not be allowed to bed without all the publicity. Thirdly, disgust with all those who sought to pry into the private life of the wedded couple.[19]

Or this 51-year-old housewife, who considered the marriage nothing more than insurance for continuance of the royal line:

> I really have no 'feelings' about the Royal Wedding. It was an enjoyable break in the dull monotony of life as it is lived today where the only news is continued semi-starvation for this country and threatened atomic warfare for the rest of the world. The majority of people in the Brit. Isles prefer a Monarchy rather than any other sort of government. If we are to continue being a Monarchy we must have some prospect of a future sovereign. Elizabeth must produce an heir. She must be married. I think she and we are lucky to have found someone so presentable and not so foreign as Philip. (She might have had to have somebody like Alfonso XIII or Carol of Rumania). What <u>his</u> attitude is to his stud duties we can't tell – not knowing anything certain about the young man – but I should think he has weighed the pros and cons very carefully and considers that he is being well paid. I don't think he will have realised fully yet how close his wings will have been clipped and I don't envy him his job. He will have to walk delicately if he is to cause no offence in any quarter – there's young Elizabeth and old Elizabeth, to say nothing of Queen Mary and the Labour Party.[20]

In some responses, Observers identified with the common human experience of the wedding as a family event, thus underscoring a phenomenon that royal watchers and analysts have noted since Walter Bagehot remarked that 'a family on the throne is an interesting idea'.[21] The following comment from a 62-year-old unmarried female secretary demonstrates this imagined common bond:

> An admirably managed affair – well done ceremonially – not too hopelessly over-written by the newspapers. And just that heart-warming sharing of a natural and necessary stage in the life of Elizabeth and the Royal Family as to remind us of their humanness. All married women knew how <u>she</u> felt and all parents with married daughters knew how the King and Queen felt. The person I thought in a difficult position was of course, Philip. <u>Why</u> had he taken the job on? Would he find in the end that the job of being husband to such a prominent wife was too much a distortion of the usual husband-wife relationship.[22]

While some could identify with the royal family, there was also a very clear understanding that royal relationships were necessarily different, especially as it might upend the gendered expectations of society. Some Observers placed themselves in the roles of the royals, connecting with an imagined ordinariness, such as this male agricultural worker:

> I feel a bit sorry for both of them – especially Phillip – in having such a lot of publicity about the whole thing. I would have been a nervous wreck! I hope they are happy together.[23]

68 REFLECTIONS ON BRITISH ROYALTY

Or this thirty-year-old male shipping clerk:

I don't feel about the Royal Wedding. I think it is rubbish. There are plenty of serious things to do, without wasting time on archaic pageantry. Anyway, if I was a princess, I would far prefer to be married quietly. Probably Elizabeth agrees with me. I hope so, at any rate.[24]

A common refrain throughout this book, as well as in other studies that seek to understand public opinion about the monarchy, is an expectation that the immense wealth and privilege of the royals does not equate to happiness or independence of choice. The following fifty-year-old male insurance broker demonstrates what social psychologist Michael Billig calls 'ideological reversal', a concept Billig explains as when ordinary people imagine their lives as superior to those of the royalty.[25]

Chiefly a great sympathy for the participants being so much in the limelight. I wish I could know more about the Princess and her husband; is it really an arranged match? There is inevitably a thought that it is; if so, still more sympathy for them. I was far luckier, I chose my own wife.[26]

This female Observer similarly considered herself better off than royalty, who had to submit to burdensome public display:

I certainly don't feel any inclination to belittle the event by criticising the amount of money spent, and wished I could have seen it at close quarters. A Royal Wedding is such a rare occasion, that I feel it should be really well done and not skimped for the sake of a few pounds or dollars. The radio commentary made me feel incredibly sentimental but my final comment was 'Well, thank goodness I didn't have to go through such an ordeal at my wedding.'[27]

The following 33-year-old married male teacher questioned media narratives that encourage identification with the royal couple:

I am not a bit interested in how much was spent on the wedding, or how little, what the procession, crowds or presents were like. I cannot get enthusiastic about it, nor indignant except with stupid women who queued all night with little children to see the procession. BUT I would like to know one thing – if the Princess were just Miss Elizabeth Windsor, and her husband just any ordinary Naval Lieutenant, would they still have married. This essentially human side interests me very much. Do they when out of the public eye think of each other, and talk to each other, as my wife and I do, are they really in love. I hope so, and am inclined to believe so, but just because 'suitability' has to be considered so much in Royal marriages, I wonder. I think the Princess performs her official duties excellently, and I believe she will later be a ruler we can admire and respect, I would like to think that with a difficult task ahead she has in her private life the help of a husband who loves her and whom she loves – I do not feel any 'love' or 'loyalty' to the Royal Family, they are too removed from me, I only love people I know – but I am interested and have a Pauline love for all men and hope that these two persons will be very happy.[28]

Others leaned into the need to connect with royal couple, engaging in a parasocial relationship that projected feelings and character onto them, such as this 66-year-old widowed 'Provincial Lady':

I feel it is a genuinely 'good thing'. I feel that he and she are not pretentious, but mean the best, have a real sense of responsibility and will carry on the fine work of the two last monarchs. As for the 'show' I think it absolutely right. Something visual is needed as common ground throughout dominions. The simple folk appreciate the human plus royal set up. The money grant necessary in the circumstances.[29]

This retired 52-year-old female civil servant accepted the media narrative of a 'love match':

I was excited about the Royal Wedding, although I didn't make any effort to go up to see it and thought the people who stood for hours and even went up overnight were mad. I'm very pleased that it is a real love match and not a diplomatic one; and I think they really are a lovely couple. Both, from all you see (in photos only for my part) and hear of them, are fine personalities and worthy of their position . . . I welcomed this little bit of pageantry and public excitement, as a relief from the general drabness and monotony of public life generally. I wish more could have been made of it – a public holiday and celebrations of all kinds. The marriage of the heir to the throne doesn't happen more than once in a generation, and I think it should be properly celebrated – crisis or no.[30]

Austerity loomed over the commentary and opinions about the wedding. In the following Observer's response, it is clear that at least some young couples welcomed the wedding and experienced it as a celebration they personally could only look forward to when times were better for all. This young RAF lieutenant was happy to live vicariously through the royal couple:

Very happy – and envious. We can't think of it for 3–4 years yet! Glad they are happy. Most personal wedding. Seemed bad manners to be listening to someone's own wedding. Good for country, especially abroad. Gave us a breather – especially the women – too much austerity can have the same effect in long run as too little. I hope it keeps fine for Philip and Elizabeth: may they live happily ever after.[31]

Some Observers also believed that the ceremony projected a positive image of the nation to the world and felt that royal ceremonies were an important aspect of British identity. A 53-year-old 'farmer's wife' felt, 'The whole thing was so completely British and would only have happened here. It was so sane and human, so like things ought to be if people were decent and friendly and honest.'[32] This 57-year-old married male expressed pride in Britain's ability to stage royal spectacle:

I have nothing but praise for our Royal Family, and for the splendid arrangements that were made. I am very happy to think that after some weeks of muttered criticism – 'Why can't she be married like any other girl? Why all this fuss and upset to business? Why all this expenditure of public money?' – when the time came, almost everyone was caught up in the ceremony and the pageantry, and the prevailing atmosphere was one of cheerfulness and loyalty and goodwill. I am very glad too that the House of Commons voted the amounts recommended by the Sub-Committee. I am sorry that so many Labour members felt that they must vote against. I feel sure they must have been uncomfortable in taking this stand. For myself I am proud to belong at this time to the one nation in the whole world which can stage a Royal Wedding like ours, the nation to which all the world at this time looks up.[33]

Observers often compared the British constitution and royalty as favourable to the American system, like this 26-year-old member of the ATS:

More approving than I expected to – I think it was well managed, timely, and a great fillip to morale (sorry – not intentional) – <u>we</u>, Britain, could produce something lovely and fairy tale in spite of war and aftermath that the USA with all wealth and self-assurance just couldn't. Of course, the whole thing was lit up from within by the fact that Liz and Phil seemed so gorgeously happy and genuine about it.[34]

This young male trainee in the Forest Commission felt the royalty provided good return on investment in its projection of British values:

I'm flat out for the Royal Wedding. I liked it, admired the couple, was interested in the service, the pomp, the pageantry, the ceremony. I thought it must have been a terrific strain on Elizabeth, and I think she was absolutely marvellous and well earned her pay. I think these things tend to endear the Family to us, and that in turn, strengthens and supports the British way of life.[35]

Many Observers weighed in on the appropriateness of such an expensive spectacle while the nation faced deep austerity at home and conflict on the world stage. This female Observer commented on the positive aspects of the wedding, including a return to a sense of wartime unity:

> Very good idea. It gave everyone a break and some beauty and colour and excitement which is good for us when the conditions are so drab. It pulled people together and gave them the old feeling of solidity there had had [*sic*] during the war – took them out of themselves in fact.[36]

This 39-year-old single female schoolteacher also highlighted the positive potential in the day's events:

> As I lead a busy life, the Royal Wedding seemed very remote from me at the time, and I have never taken a particular interest in the Royal family, but I was very moved when I listened in to the broadcast, and when I had time to think about it, I could not help feeling a thrill of pleasure, at the obvious happiness of Princess Elizabeth and her husband. Since then, so many people were cheered up by the wedding that I think it is something to be thankful for, and I wish them all joy.[37]

This 59-year-old widowed teacher felt the ceremony and BBC coverage exceptional, and felt it a bright spot in an otherwise bleak landscape, but worried about the behaviour of the British public:

> I loved listening-in to the Royal Wedding. The BBC were grand.
>
> But, I was appalled by the mob-hysteria – it was such evidence of emotional starvation . . . of frustrations finding outward expression in the vicarious satisfaction of spectators. And such crowds and crowds of women, rather terrifying in the mass – so many looked hysterical in the photographs, I thought. But it was a lovely wedding, with a charming bride and a suitably handsome bridegroom, and the general feeling of goodwill to them from peoples all over the world was very stimulating and enriching. I know I felt full of happiness as I listened-in to that wonderful broadcast and I am sure it did the world good to think about something happy instead of all this appalling talk of war, and war's terrible aftermath. It was the light of happiness in a dark and unbalanced world.[38]

A number of Observers responded positively to the ceremony itself but felt that the behaviour of some of the British public reflected poorly on the nation. In particular, most Observers – regardless of how they felt about the publicized wedding – mentioned the spectacle that took place at Romsey Abbey on the Sunday following the wedding. Prior to the wedding, the press had announced where the couple planned to honeymoon and mentioned the Abbey as the place where they were to worship. Crowds turned up to the small village, lined the streets and sat through several church services in order to see the royal couple. The following housewife regarded the public attitude towards the wedding positively but believed the press went too far in advertising the couple's private plans:

> I thought the Royal Wedding was just as it should be, it allowed for so much spontaneous affection to be shown to the Royal Family and even people who affect to despise the Monarchy had to admit their own interest and excitement over it. The only mistake seemed to me to be the broadcasting of the fact on Sat evening that the Royal pair were going to Romsey Abbey to Church next day.[39]

This retired male civil servant was not particularly interested in the events but criticized the press coverage and the public's invasion of the couple's privacy on their honeymoon:

> I had little or no feeling about the Royal Wedding as a wedding and felt no excitement. I had sufficient interest to go see the film as a spectacle and piece of pageantry. I was amused and also slightly annoyed by the way the Press played up the popular feeling and thought it was overdone and overwritten, just in the same way as other Royal happenings have been. In fact the Press somehow at these times seems to overdo this sort of thing and overestimates the public appetite.
>
> I was disgusted at the way members of the general public invaded their privacy upon their first public appearance as I felt the young couple were as much entitled to privacy during their honeymoon as any ordinary citizen.[40]

This male Observer felt that royalty disliked the publicity and expressed admiration for the King and Queen:

> I do not believe that this couple or her parents wished for all the silly ballyhoo. I have too profound a respect for His Majesty to think that he could wish for the sickening idiocy perpetrated by the BBC and the Press. (I'm not very good at respect, and my bump of reverence was omitted – but George VI makes me feel humble. He's done a most difficult job in the most admirable manner. If we'd got half-a-dozen men of the same caliber at the head of our affairs we'd be better off.)

The Observer went on to criticize the parliamentary and press debates about changes to the Civil List and allocating allowances to the Princess and the Duke. The issue had been raised before the wedding, but the matter had not been settled until December. Ultimately, the Labour government decided in December to award Philip £10,000 a year and to significantly increase Elizabeth's allowance from the £15,000 she made upon reaching her majority to £50,000 a year.[41]

> The debate in the house on their allowances confirmed my increasing dislike for a certain type in the Labour Party. I look forward with apprehension to the dithering foolishness which will be our daily portion once the poor girl tells the Press that she is 'not accepting any engagements for some time'.

> And I'd love her and her husband to have the opportunity of telling the House of Commons what they really think of some of the members of the body.[42]

Others agreed that the bickering over royal allowances was inappropriate, like this female Observer:

> I felt happy for their happiness. Life grows more difficult for us all, more so for those in 'higher places'. Our princess will have a harder task than any previous ruler. She needs the security and background of 'personal' love and affection. It seemed turning back of the pages to a happier, more settled age. I'd have loved to be part of the pageant, even to stand and watch her go by. I've no patience with people who talk as if she should have been 'married in a sack' – in proportion to many weddings, her gorgeous fairy tale dress was not in any way out of place and it's dreadful to think of the income proposed being grudged and wrangled over, especially when I read it comes to a farthing a year per head.[43]

The debates made the following thirty-year-old single male clerk impatient with the Labour government:

> I felt that the government was against the wedding. The people had no holiday, and the decorations were truly meagre. This has been borne out since by the disgusting talk in the House on the Princess' salary. In spite of the adverse propaganda, the wedding was well supported and approved by the common folk. The government proved again that they are out of touch with the mood of ordinary people, who know what they want and are determined to have it.[44]

The following 56-year-old female teacher worried that the wedding might mar the nation's newly won socialist credentials:

> Of course when people like the Royal Family have been brought up to pomp and ceremony I suppose it is difficult for them to know what to dispense with. No doubt they did dispense with quite a lot from their point of view, but the time has come for these hereditary benefits to be

modified. I cannot see that Elizabeth's services to the nation, and still less Philip's, are going to be worth all the money spent on this occasion and now perpetuated in the money granted them. It must be embarrassing to a Labour Government to be caught up in a situation of this kind and indeed to many of us who want to adopt an international point of view – devoid of power politics playing one country off another. The show may appeal to America, but how can we expect Russia to believe that we are sincere in our Socialistic aspirations when they see so much wealth earmarked for a favoured few. That it helps our export trade etc is so much bunk. We were told that about the South African trip and we have yet to know that the returns outweigh the money spent then. Many of the things we get from SA we would have got any way. That the crowds which gathered were an expression of loyalty is bunk also. It was just being treated like a film show – a craze our young people have acquired from the trashy American literature they read. Crowds gathered on New Year's Eve too without any royalty.[45]

This 55-year-old male musician criticized the Labour government for supporting the allowance:

Mad. As a red radical republican socialistic agnostic I seem to have reason to be. All the cost, the smarmy writing, the religiosity, irked me to the top of my bent. The crowning distaste was in hearing a socialist govt. try to defend the money grant. This more nearly made me a Tory than anything that this govt. has done. The whole thing was to me revolting, enough to make a body frow up.[46]

This 51-year-old housewife supported the royal allowance but nonetheless criticized the couple's copious living arrangements when so many others went without:

Neither the wedding itself or the fuss about allowances troubled me at all. A future English Queen must have a traditional wedding – she is part of the historical jig-saw, and must have sufficient allowance to be able to carry out her job. After all the PM needs £10,000 or more a year.

I don't think, however, that there's any need for Elizabeth and Philip to set up any new establishments. Surely one of the suites in Buckingham Palace would be enough for the time they spend in London, and there are enough Royal residences scattered up and down the country without launching out in an entirely new estate.

I had no desire to <u>see</u> the wedding, but I would have liked to look at the veil. From the newspaper pictures of it, it must have been a 'thing of beauty'. But I don't want to stand in a queue for hours and then have a fleeting glimpse in the company of other women. Nor do I want to see one of the threatened replicas. The only part of the wedding service I wanted to hear was Philip's voice, to see if I approved of it. I do.

I am fully expecting Elizabeth to 'take after' her great-great-grandmother Victoria and have a quiver-full of offspring. My mother thinks I'm slightly indelicate, but agrees that Elizabeth knows how to hold a baby (inferring that I don't! Quite true!!).[47]

Some Observers took issue with the costs of the wedding and the allowances. Criticisms revolved around austerity and the value of the monarchy. This fifty-year-old single female teacher felt the couple should have waited for better days:

I feel that the Royal Wedding was a big mistake at this time. The luxury of the wedding presents alone, as well as the ease of obtaining houses to live in, was a great insult to people trying to bear with austerity living. I felt that if the couple had waited for two years until the nation were in better economic state, the wedding could have been made into a worthy occasion giving pleasure not only at home, but to thousands of visitors particularly from Canada and USA. These would have seen Britain cleaned up a bit, and would have brought over some welcome dollars.[48]

This male Observer wondered if the wedding was meant to distract the public from real issues that faced the nation and Europe:

The Royal Wedding was, I feel, used by the socialists as a political cloak. It annoyed me to think that any marriage ceremony could be so used. When half Europe is austere and starving, and not a few in England are starving, all the pomp and circumstance was galling to me . . . The Royal Wedding was to me a wedding, and – unless for political aims the sanctification of this marriage was neither more nor less than the poorest who can barely afford a registry office.[49]

The following Observer took the view that the wedding was staged to protect (and project) family values:

The poppycock fuss attending their wedding shows the low level of intelligence the masses apply to marriage. The whole performance is staged by Church and State to enhance the concept of family life, yet what relation the general standard of family life has to a couple who start with every circumstance of wealth and luxury is never questioned.[50]

This male Observer criticized the public reaction, the publicity and the Church, believing that the royals themselves would have preferred to give up the institution for a bit of privacy:

I am no more interested in Royal Weddings than in other weddings. I deplore the newsprint and public money spent on the event, I deplore the publicity given to the young couple's romance and to the prying, sightseeing and reporting carried out on their honeymoon. I did not see any of the newsreels of the event nor buy any publications concerning it. And as for the farcical 16th century ceremony in the Abbey itself – I am speechless! Some folk seem to live in past centuries, to glory everything that is old and pretty-pretty. What have we of the twentieth century to leave posterity besides Waterloo Bridge, the Mersey Tunnel, Battersea Power Station and extended cemeteries. To spoil the privacy of two young people – who probably would gladly be common citizens rather than royal personages, just for the sake of tradition and 'glorious' ceremony is cruel. Why not spend the thousands lavished on decoration on some research into cancer, silicosis, or even the common cold?[51]

The following 25-year-old single female typist lamented the waste and upheaval the wedding caused:

I got awfully fed up with the fuss made about the Royal Wedding but then I'm not keen on the Royalty. It seemed awful to make so much fuss at a time like this. When I read of traffic, bollards being uprooted for the procession, it seemed disgraceful to waste the time and money when they'd all have to be put back immediately afterwards. If it had been me, I should have been disgusted to have ears of wheat on a dress of mine as a symbol of fertility. We haven't progressed very far from the pagan, have we?[52]

The following sixty-year-old housewife criticized the cost of the royalty and felt that traditional gender norms should apply to the royals as much as the public:

Just another expensive show to please more than the poor folk. Yet there may be reasons I cannot understand – Diplomacy? I'm pleased with Philip – as far as I know. But in a country so poor and so short of necessities and a royal family who do no useful work and are paid too much – and a Socialist gov't – or are we? No, I'm sure it's a Tory-democratic govt – neither one thing nor another. So you'll see what I think of Royal Income. Wicked. Just keeping all sorts of stooges. They are too far apart from the people. We don't need Royalty – we don't live in Divine Right Days. Let Philip keep Eliz. We're fools. If they're in love, he'd be proud to do it and if he's the man I think he is he'll hate the pomp and nonsense of royalty.[53]

The following female office worker felt the spectacle interested only the royalty, children and Americans:

I don't particularly feel anything about the Royal Wedding. I'm neither for nor against the fuss. Reading in the newspaper about women spending the previous freezing night on the pavements of the route, gave me the impression that Londoners must be barmy or else all unemployed (to have nothing else, apparently, to usefully do). On the other hand, – while I am most definitely against having a veritable tribe of duchesses and children all being kept in splendour by impoverished Britain – yet I quite realise that the actual Royal family of King, Queen, and children is a worthwhile investment as a showpiece to endear us to the Americans (our rich cousins, so fond of their so-called 'freedom and non-imperialism', who are yet the most snobbish and monarch-worshipping people in the world). The wedding outfit was composed of gifts so didn't cost anything to the state, the bride enjoyed the fuss, the bridegroom also seems a nice lad, so whereas I could not care about the romance or even stir up any enthusiasm; yet I'm certainly not 'against' the fuss in any way.[54]

By contrast, the following male Observer felt that the spectacle held interest only for women:

Very mixed feelings. Strongest objections to the 100 coupons and all that while those urgently needing them are refused all concessions. Appalling waste of money, time and manpower. But such display 'lets off' a vast amount of suppressed emotions which needs a vent from time to time (in the masses I mean) and by 'projection' a vast number of the 1,864,396 women in this country for whom there can be no husband (short of polygamy) were able to enjoy a phantasy nuptial. I hope the day is not far off when society will allow them real motherhood even without a husband.[55]

Gendered responses were also registered by a number of male Observers, like this 71-year-old married male draughtsman:

It would be surly to try and deprive the 'riff-raff' of a great source of enjoyment, but what a lot of nonsense! How utterly preposterous and idiotic! Fancy women in thousands remaining on the route all through the night! I have nothing against ROYALTY: it must be a rotten sort of life; I blame the stupid fools who allow themselves to act towards Royalty in such unintelligent ways. It all makes me feel how far I am from being an Englishman! I rarely chat with folk, and so do not know whether anybody agrees with me. My wife does not; she was excited and keen, and wanted to see all pictures in papers, and especially visited Cinema (which she rarely does).[56]

The following male civil servant commented on the gendered nature of the event but felt that many enjoyed the affair:

This was of course primarily a woman's occasion and most of the crowds and interest were women and woman fostered. The men were interested as much by their women's folk interest as much by the occasion. The great demand for evening papers in the City, long queues of men indicated their desire to take home the first pictures to their wives. It has demonstrated once again the people's love of pomp and ceremony and free spectacle but more than that an exhibit in our strength, our inherent dignity and refinement. I think all classes, whether great or small and whether consciously or unconsciously, received some kind of mental uplift from the occasion and a factor on which cannot be ignored our political and social life, despite all the good solid republican talk.[57]

As much as the day was thought to be about a supposed womanly love for all things weddings and romance, there was also the sense amongst some Observers that they stood above those who, they thought, were mindlessly caught up in the festivities. The following male republican Observer is indicative of this attitude:

I am a republican and loathe this pomp and ceremony due to royalty, in fact I would not like it in a republic. Royalty and what is termed Society, petty snobbery chiefly found in the middle and working classes, and due to a large extent because of Society – classes tending to climb into the next one above; all this I detest. I do not fool myself into thinking that all this would necessarily disappear if a republic was announced, that in itself would do little.

There is another angle to all this, how about the Royal Couple and the effect on them. I pity them for not being able to really have the maximum of free choice in choosing their life partners, and when they marry, it is regarded as a public entertainment; and have to live a 'Royal' life – poor devils, perhaps they would prefer to be like the Duke of Windsor married to one he really loves and freely chose to marry, and retired on a pension. All this pomp and ceremony is a healthy outlet for the majority of peoples' love of this sort of thing, due to a large extent to their environment and education.[58]

The following 45-year-old housewife disparaged royal supporters but also demonstrated that she felt alone in her attitude:

A terrible waste of money at a time we should not be wasting. But I realise that there are lots of nitwits and halfwits about and that Royalty must pander to all, and maybe the girl herself liked all the todoment. Who am I to object or even have an opinion? I'm told she costs us only a farthing a head or something footling, so what am I grumbling about?[59]

A 75-year-old married male retired teacher took a similar view:

> Repulsive. Interest by idle people in the wedding of a rather dull person, of whom no kindnesses are recorded, to a doubtfully dynastic outsider is in itself unwholesome. The details of expenditure, and labour on tawdry show, can only gratify the thoughtless. The example of an effort to get back to a spending and self-displaying regime isn't at all helpful to other dull women.[60]

Some used the royal occasion to put their understandings and criticisms of the British monarchy on paper. Those who expressed criticism, or stated republican convictions, often tempered their answers in a spectrum of ways, from enjoying the pomp and circumstance of royal events to a feeling that though imperfect, the British monarchy was the best alternative to other forms of governance. For instance, this male Observer commented, 'My sentiments are republican . . . although I regard the monarchy as a useful piece of constitutional machinery.'[61] These responses offer exquisite insight into opinion polls which regularly show little appetite for a republican option. This female Observer felt caught between her socialist thinking and her enjoyment of pageantry:

> As a Socialist I don't really approve of Royalty! Here reason and sentiment clash. The colour and pageantry, which go with Royal events rather appeal to my sentiment, a little oasis in the drabness of life, but my reason condemns them as useless, out-of-date and unjustifiable. I should thoroughly enjoy seeing the procession, the wedding dress and the presents, and yet I can't see any sense in them. In the same way I disapprove of large landed estates to benefit one family; yet it gives on a pang when I see them sold up for building estates. And it seems to me terrible (if true) that the wedding dress cost £2000. Who benefits? Remembering the rags, hunger and misery in Europe, if not in England, I feel perhaps it would have been in better taste to have had austerity.[62]

Many Observers who expressed republican or anti-monarchist feelings seemed resigned to their minority position, and the inevitable endurance of the British royalty, like this male Observer:

> I am strongly against any form of monarchy and any form of National Sovereignty. These things are, in my opinion, the direct cause of all Wars. But, so long as we have a Monarchy, a certain amount of pageantry is essential to keep the thing going. So, although, in a way, as a believer in some form of World Government, I strongly deprecated the fuss about the Royal Wedding, as we still have a Monarchy, I think it was a good thing. Or, if not a 'good' thing, at least a fairly harmless sort of jollification.[63]

The following male Observer also seemed a bit resigned to a royal reality but strenuously objected to their cost, especially when others went without:

I have no objections to the marriages of members of the House of Windsor, any more than I have to the marriages of any human beings. I object strongly, however, to having to pay for them. Being a republican by sympathy I object to our established order of royalty. However, I realize that for the masses of people some sort of figurehead is apparently essential, and certainly the present king and queen perform their duties adequately. My real objection is to the unnecessary expense involved in the presence of the touts and hangers-on who seem to be essential the royalty as it is organized in Britain. In any case, while there are people in the country who do not get enough to eat, and although they are less in number nowadays they still exist, I think it criminal that people such as kings, queens and princes (equally with others, of course) should have not financial worries at all.[64]

The following 54-year-old housewife objected to the royalty, its cost, and questioned whether the public supported the institution or just the spectacle:

The average person does NOT need a royal family to look up to. There are enough great men and women, who have done service for humanity, for us to revere. To idealise royalty is an artificial reverence. We do not admire the Royal Family for special qualities – they may or may not, be worthy of our admiration. Royal blood has no virtue whatever. I do not think royalty binds together the Empire. Colonials love the pageantry connected with royalty, but I do not believe they would withhold their help in our time of need, even if royalty were done away with, nor would they feel less tenderly towards 'Home'. We can have pageantry without royal family as the head of society, as we can appreciate the plays of Shakespeare without living in the conditions depicted in the plays. When people cheer royalty it is not really love of such an institution that they express. It's just an excuse to let off steam. They'd enjoy any glorified Punch and Judy Show just as much . . .

I dislike intensely the idea of blue blood being something superior. It is akin to racial discrimination, caste, class distinction as we have in England, all of which lend to hinder man's development. I am all for 'hitching or waggons to stars' in order to draw inspiration from great people, but let our heroes and heroines be truly heroic and not merely 'blue blooded'.

Then, of course, there is the financial aspect. To spend so much on the upkeep of royalty, to use so much manpower and woman power on ceremony when every industry is short of man-power, to squander on useless luxuries where we are crying out for necessities, all are galling to anyone with an economical soul, or a sense of fairness. I think it would have been a great gesture on the part of the Royal Family if they had insisted that no presents, other than small family ones, should have been given to Princess Elizabeth and her husband . . .

I repeat that I have no personal animosity towards the Royal Family, neither have I any special liking or admiration. I think the system is not even fair to <u>them</u>. How can any of them develop naturally in such an atmosphere? No wonder Edward VII and the Prince of Wales went off the rails . . . As a Socialist, I can only hope that some day, we can do away with royalty without causing pain to anyone. But can we?[65]

The following male Observer resented the monarchy and the assumption that everyone supported the institution. He also underscored the relationship between the royalty and British imperial subjugation:

I feel that the Royal Wedding only serves to show the decadence of the monarchs and monarchists throughout all the world. Thousands of pounds and hours of labour have been wasted in perpetuating a useless relic of the Middle Ages when it could have been utilized to rehabilitate our economic stability to that value. Our monarchy binds together a colonial empire in subjugation and forces them to rightfully claim their emancipation as has been the case in India. The peoples of Africa have been utilized as slaves to the colonial creed of British imperialism for the past hundred years, and to attempt to perpetuate this state of affairs will only bring the day of downfall to this capitalist society nearer and nearer. The Royal Wedding in itself has been a glorified exhibition of the so-called 'divine rights of royalty' – a princess who has received £200 a week from the day of her birth accepts 2d from a weekly pay of 16/- from every soldier of the West African Frontier Force who was compelled to give this amount as a subscription for a Wedding present. Among 20 soldiers (5 of them officers) in the British Army Unit in which I served, a circular was distributed calling for a subscription of 6d a head. There was no response – until the General sent a circular this time with a <u>personal footnote</u>. Our C.O. was thus intimidated into paying the whole amount <u>himself</u>. Such is popular feeling – and not the hysteria of the crowds who thronged the façade of Buckingham Palace on the eve of the Royal Wedding.

Personally, I wish the couple themselves a happy and long life – and longer life than I wish for the system of even 'limited' monarchical government.[66]

A few Observers cited Philip's Greek connections as reason for criticism. The following 42-year-old female married domestic worker wrote:

Disgusted. Bridegroom is a Greek of the parasitic classes. Because of him and his relative Marina, Duchess of Kent, this country ranges itself

82 REFLECTIONS ON BRITISH ROYALTY

against the Greek patriots. The royal couple will be over-paid and under-worked and live luxuriously; also they will breed child parasites who will be granted huge allowances and reared expensively.[67]

The following 67-year-old unmarried female nurse seemed supportive of the British monarchy, only if it eschewed foreign blood and kept itself to a high moral standard:

Damn the Royal wedding. I don't want to think about it. I hate the thought of our future ruler having married one of that Greek family with its history of unhappy marriage and separation and divorces. Even the Duke's parents were separated, and although his father only died a short time ago, the young man was brought up by his uncle, and, apparently, never saw his father after they left Greece. I think it was a shame that those women spent all those work-hours on that elaborate wedding-dress and veil, when such workers are so in demand for our factories. And why did all those foreign, deposed royalties have to come over here for. A fine family for the King to entertain. Why wasn't she allowed to meet some of our young aristocrats, and not this young man? . . . I don't believe in cousins marrying, but [it] would have been better than marrying, as she has done, a man related to her through both his mother and father . . . There would have been no need of a new, ill-omened dukedom, nor of a grant from public funds, not the ill-omened name Phillip as the future prince consort.[68]

On the other hand, the following 31-year-old single male journalist supported Philip and questioned the line of thinking expressed earlier:

We are monarchist by tradition . . . and 'Time and Tide' was right in proclaiming the danger of Communist 'cashing in' if there was any popular objection (I didn't hear any at all) to Royal extravagance. I might have felt there was something in the Daily Worker Greek Royalty line if Philip was in any sense a Greek, or a reactionary. No one who has come under the influence of Lord Louis Mountbatten as much as Philip apparently has could be anything but progress in the best possible sense.[69]

Support for the British monarchy, either residing in a positive view of character and morality or in the benefit of a constitutional monarchy, was also found in Observer responses, such as this male hospital stretcher-bearer:

The Royal Wedding involved a great deal of expense and took up a great deal of time and energy that might well have been used in other directions more usefully – on the surface – but even so I think the pageantry which is loved by so many is a very necessary feature of life so far in Austerity anyway. The Royal Family as it now exists as an institution in Britain today is one of the nearest ways of maintaining a more sane form of Government in Britain than either Communism (as it is in Russia now) or Fascism can offer. My enthusiasm for Royalty goes no further than this but by all means let this – the sanest or at least – least harmless form of man-worship continue as long as necessary.[70]

The following male Observer was ambivalent about monarchy but felt it the best system for the present circumstances:

On the whole I think that it was a great occasion very fitly organised and managed. I have a great friend who thinks that the Monarchy and all that goes with it are a waste of time and quite ridiculous, and we had quite an argument about it. I see his point of view, and from the strictly logical angle there is something to be said for it. But Life isn't logical. Men (and to of course a much greater extent women) are not logical beings; and this has to be taken into consideration.

Until we arrive at a World State, each Nation must have a Head, and I consider that the hereditary Monarchy provides the best solution for this Country and of course the British Commonwealth of Nations. I cannot visualise an elected President giving that continuity that is so essential.

There is no doubt too that people like pageantry and this is a good thing in that it brings to mind the history of the Country. It is of course a bad thing if, as in Germany, it degenerates into jingoism.[71]

The following male researcher considered the positives of the wedding and royalty, even if he seemed ambivalent:

I haven't got very strong views on the subject. The whole idea of a monarchy is a bit off and illogical, but regarding royalty merely as a symbol of respectability and permanence and family institutions seems the most sensible attitude. From this aspect I am glad if the Princess has married someone decent and reasonably English in characteristics, and the Duke looks from pictures very typical of the young man often met in the Navy (and fairly respectable public houses). If she likes him, good luck to them both. They've got a lousy job being gaped at by the common herd, and I hope they get some fun out of life.

One aspect I liked was a full church wedding, a reminder to the form-filling devotees of what marriage should be, and what a Registry office isn't. I was very glad that the pageantry was impressive and carried off well, and I was very pleased that so many people went to see it all and cheered them, whether they knew the reason for their cheering or not. This popularity does indicate a solid adherence to something permanent and very English and is a good one in the eye for the stinking Communist types. The only grumbling I heard was from a Communist.

Summing up:

1. I approve of Royalty as a personification of good characteristics in life.
2. I was very pleased that so many people liked the Wedding, which meant a fondness for tradition and nationalism (in a decent sort of way) and respectability.
3. I am glad a good pageant was put on.
4. I think the Duke looks a decent chap and will make a good Prince.

   N.B. If the Royal Family had been a fast set of good-for-nothing wrecks, you will appreciate that my views would be rather different.[72]

The earlier Observers' comments reflect a sentiment noted by participants in Michael Billig's study of attitudes to royalty that 'those who perform badly or uneconomically, should face redundancy. Once the institution of monarchy fails to deliver the goods, it becomes exposed.'[73]

A few Observers commented on the relationship between the royals and celebrity. In the following case, the Observer thought that the ceremony and attendant gatherings felt more like red-carpet film star events and did not fit the royal couple. The following 45-year-old housewife was indicative of this feeling:

I got heartily sick of the Royal Wedding and thought I had never read so much lummy rot in the press. The whole affair seemed to me to be particularly ill timed and irritating. All very personal and petty, but I got bored with the description of the dresses, presents, etc., and the attempt that was made to glamourize the whole affair and at the same time try to make people believe it was just an ordinary wedding and that the royal Family practically had to make do and mend like other people. I don't grudge the Royal Family their extra clothing coupons if only people would be honest about it. If you are going to have a monarchy, you should be prepared to pay for it and to accept that they are not as others are. I am sure that there is sufficient feeling of loyalty and affection for the Royal Family in the country to make all the press bally hoo quite unnecessary. Though not a royalist myself, I thought some of the letters in the papers which beefed because the Princess was having a 'nice wedding' when so many girls had'nt the coupons were just petty and spiteful, but they were the logical outcome of the press campaign. The whole affair was too like Hollywood and the young couple though pleasant enough just could'nt compete with the 'stars'. God forbid that they should try, but why make the attempt. The whole affair struck me as very vulgar ... However, if it cheered up the country, I suppose it served its purpose, though I should think it would have been pleasanter for all concerned if the wedding could have been celebrated in the summer.[74]

PRINCESS ELIZABETH'S WEDDING 1947

Meanwhile, the following 60-year-old housewife took a different view, interpreting the occasion as above Hollywood celebrity and offering the public a chance to participate in a genuine love story and connect personally to the couple:

I think the Royal Wedding demonstrates a hunger for something beautiful and <u>real</u>, as against the eternal phoney sentiment of films. A real princess, really in love with a real prince, married with a real service, with real royalty for parents and relations. We can't all have gorgeous silk wedding dresses spangled with pearls and go to church in a glass coach, and have a long train – so what? For goodness sake let's have one real good one for anybody to see who likes that sort of thing. And thousands <u>do</u> like that sort of thing. I got a sort of impression that even the King and Queen were a little taken aback at the enthusiasm, so ungrudging and unjealous, left-wingers notwithstanding. I personally am left quite cold by royalty, I don't quite know why. We use to see the King and his brothers and sisters quite a lot as children, when we lived in Soho. Later, too, in adolescence I got a burning indignation at the horrible contrast in that part of London between riches and poverty. Carriages and pairs used to wait for the 'Drawing Rooms' in the Mall, with the Debutantes playing cards inside and every sort of hunger and dirt outside. I went rabid socialist and it has left its mark, I suppose. But colour and beauty and art are deep seated needs to people one or two generations from living in the Country and the country people have not got far enough away from squire tradition to lose interest in Royalty. Anyway the need is obviously there, and in particular royalty deserves its popularity. We can still be socialist if we like, and democracy should presuppose that if we elect to have a royal house we can. And we do, it seems. The main grouse revolves round the money it costs . . . In any case, most of the enthusiasts were under the impression that they were paying for this wedding and even then were more than willing. I think there was a talk on the BBC on the money question, but I didn't hear it. Our vicar was most amused at the congregation at Romsey Abbey going at 8 am to communion and staying on through Matins, having to give to both collections![75]

Finally, the following 46-year-old housewife took the wedding as a portent of better things to come – imagining what would be called the Second Elizabethan Age upon Princess Elizabeth's ascension to the throne five years later:

I feel the Royal Wedding has put as back where we were in the world's estimation, before the Duke of Windsor threw his crown away. I feel it was the beginning of a new era. Already the impetus to do better, to create, to start, to live, not exist from day to day has begun to manifest itself.[76]

4

Coronation of Elizabeth II 1953

George VI passed away in the early hours of 6 February 1952. The King had been ill for some years, enduring surgery in 1949 to help ease ailments associated with thrombosis and another in November 1951 to remove a lung. By 31 January 1952, the King's health was improving well enough for Princess Elizabeth and Prince Philip to embark on a Royal Tour of East Africa, Australia and New Zealand. Less than a week into their tour, while in Kenya, the royal couple were shocked to learn of the King's death. Princess Elizabeth was now Queen. In haste, the royal entourage flew back to London for the formal ceremonies investing Queen Elizabeth II as monarch and to attend the services marking the passing of her father and his funeral.

Two months later, the Coronation of Queen Elizabeth II was set for 2 June 1953. The Coronation Committee was comprised of representatives from the UK, South Africa, Australia and New Zealand, Canada, Pakistan and Ceylon and chaired by Prince Philip. Preparations for the Coronation steadily mounted over the ensuing months, while necessary changes took place to mark the new reign, such as the Queen's choice of her official cipher. Proclamations were made to announce the Coronation, with thousands witnessing the event in person in London, while many more watched on television. The question of televising the Coronation service in Westminster Abbey, however, sparked debate for much of the autumn of 1952. Mobile television units had been used in the Coronation processions in 1937 but not in the Abbey Service.[1] The Earl Marshal, the Archbishop of Canterbury and Churchill were initially against televising the proceedings in the Abbey but changed their minds after witnessing a demonstration of the positioning of television equipment in the space.[2] By December, it was announced that most of the service – excepting the anointing – would be televised. The decision to televise the Coronation service underscored the modernity of the new Elizabethan age, offering unparalleled visual access to the proceedings; the excitement generated by this led to a huge increase in television sales and licenses. Viewing parties were planned across the nation as many newly minted television owners invited family members, neighbours and acquaintances to watch the day's broadcasting, while towns and villages set up large-screen viewings in communal spaces. Still, reception was uneven and spotty in 1953: those on the Sussex coast had only recently been able to receive transmissions, Brighton erected a special antenna in order to receive clear transmissions of the Coronation broadcast and some in coastal towns were disappointed by poor reception.[3] Thus, television had not yet eclipsed radio by 2 June 1953, and many listened to the Coronation activities on the wireless. Newspapers, magazines and souvenir Coronation programmes carried images of the royal family, procession route maps and orders of ceremony to inform those watching on television, listening in on radio or waiting along the parade route. Cinemas carried newsreels of the day's activities, and many ended the day watching the big screen.

In March 1953, Mass-Observation began preparations for gathering observations of Coronation-related activities in the lead up to 2nd June. As Mass-Observation prepared to get investigators out onto the streets, an announcement was posted to its panel urging Observers to take down their observations of the Coronation, its preparations and local activities. Additionally, it published an advertisement to the general public requesting their participation in the collection of Coronation observations, which received good response (Figure 1).

Mass-Observation collected a vast archive of varied materials including newspaper clippings and local guides to Coronation activities, as well as surveys and reports made by paid and volunteer investigators. Volunteers and Observers described local displays and the extraordinary number of souvenirs regaling shop windows and shelves and noted the arrival of tourists and dignitaries; they took note of local efforts to organize all manner of Coronation events and commemorations; as in 1937, Observers also recounted their activities and feelings, as well as overheards, on the day itself. This chapter focuses on volunteer and panel observations and begins with pre-Coronation activities and preparations, followed by day diary observations and commentary about the Coronation and the monarchy.

In response to the March call for observations of pre-Coronation activities, Observer and writer Naomi Mitchison offered a rare perspective as the wife of a newly elected Member of Parliament. Here, she records how Scottish Labour MPs and their wives worried over their anticipated attendance at the ceremony in the Abbey:

I did not go to the last coronation, largely on political grounds, but decided to go to this, as I would, as MP's wife, get a seat in Westminster Abbey and I like seeing all types of anthropologically interesting ceremony. I am also reporting it for the *Manchester Guardian*. I am wearing a semi-evening dress with three quarter sleeves, of a kind which will be most useful later, of tawny peach coloured rough Chinese silk, which will wash. It has a high collar. I have a crocodile handbag which I got cheap at a sale (I need a new bag), but crocodile shoes far too expensive, so I have bronze,

REFLECTIONS ON BRITISH ROYALTY

```
W H E R E   W E R E   Y O U   O N   J U N E   2nd ?
MASS  OBSERVATION  WANTS  YOUR  STORY.
* * * * * * * * * * * * * * * * * * * * * * * * * *

        On JUNE 2ND, a Queen is to be crowned.  We may have
different feelings about the Coronation and we may be doing
quite different things on the day.  But it is the sort of day
that many now living may not see again.

        Many books have been written about the Coronation and
about the Royal Family.  Mass-Observation wants to bring out
a different kind of book, a book about what ordinary people
will do on Coronation Day and about what they think of it all.

        Will you help by sending us an account of your day ?
Tell us what you saw happening around you, what you thought
and felt and what you heard said.  Just put it all down in
your everyday language.  You don't need ever to have written
anything before in your life.  And, if you prefer, you need
not even tell us your name or address.

        If you would like to help, please send your account at
any time that suits you (giving your sex, age and occupation)
to:
                    Mass-Observation,
                    7 Kensington Church Court,
                    London, W.8.

There is no age limit.  We are just as interested to hear from
you if you are 9 or 90 and we shall be most grateful for how-
ever much or little you write.

        Mass-Observation is an organisation which has written
a number of books about everyday habits and ideas and which
also conducts public opinion surveys.
```

FIGURE 1 "Where were you on June 2nd?" Mass-Observation advertisement for participation in coronation survey. Mass-Observation Archive, University of Sussex Special Collections, Royalty Topic Collection, Coronation Surveys and Questionnaires, 69-1-B.

also brown nylon gloves. Had no lace of the right length, so borrowed a very pretty bit of Carrickmacross. Labour MPs wives a bit worried about clothes, some of them will look very funny. A bit torn between old republican principles and a desire not to let the Labour Party down! Men in very mixed clothes. [Mitchison's husband] will be in an ordinary suit, but various others have gone to Moss Bros. Also anxiety about sanitary arrangements! In fact the latter was the thing most talked of at the House! We have breakfast and lunch there, and go back afterwards for fireworks. We got two members tickets for Speakers Green for the girls, but [one] can't come; it seems a shame that the *Guardian* haven't let her off, and goodness knows where [the other daughter] will be. She is entirely on reporting royalty for the *Daily Mirror*. Her immediate boss has had a nervous breakdown, I don't wonder at all. If one hears any young woman speak of our dear Queen as 'that bitch', one may be fairly sure she is a reporter.[4]

Preparations

Several panellists and anonymous members of the public responded to the early call for pre-Coronation observations. They described preparations for local celebrations, decorative displays and souvenirs. Respondents in London recorded the arrival of tourists and Commonwealth officials. Parents and teachers noted how they explained royal events to their children and students, and some charted the ebb and flow of excitement and oversaturation in this period. The following month-by-month survey includes snapshots of the lead up to the Coronation:

March As soon as the earliest preparations were being made we talked to the boys about them: eg, the Court of Claims,[5] the spinning and weaving of the silk for the Queen's train. Items of historical interest were specially appreciated, newspaper items, pictures, advertisements of souvenirs and so on were eagerly bought and discussed, and we all liked the National Savings Calendar of which we had one for the school.

Gradually, coronation ideas began to increase, from pictures of decorated china to boys' sock turnovers with a knitted pattern of crowns, and so on.

Then we began to feel satiated, so we dropped all mention of the Coronation for some weeks. So, when official programmes, souvenirs, and decorations appeared, we were fresh for them, and enjoyed pictures of Gog and Magog,[6] and the various Commonwealth visitors in strange dress.

A visitor gave me a stick of rock with the word Coronation in it. Boys brought model Royal coaches, medals and buttons, pencils, and pencil boxes and toys of all kinds for us to see.

The indoor decorations centred mainly on pictures of the Royal children, and shield patterns rather than flags; and the oldest boys designed and painted large shields with coats of arms, and emblems of the main Commonwealth countries.

No one that I spoke to wished to go to London to see the Coronation procession; they did not want to cope with the crowds. Many preferred the chance to see the Television pictures.[7]

April A rather unusual, but unattractive, display has appeared in a show window at the front of an engineering works. A model of the Coronation procession has been made from unsuitable coloured cardboard, which through not being strong enough, bends in several places. In front of the model at the letters EIIR worked in small, square metal nuts. These would be improved if they did not include several which are going rusty. This display is an eyesore.

Much more praise is deserved by the taxi driver, who has emblazoned his cab by flying three small Union Jacks on the front of the roof, above the centre of the windscreen . . .

In the middle of Bradford City centre one departmental store has devoted an entire window to coronation mugs, cups, saucers and other crockery, offset by streamers. The overall result is pleasing to the eye, and gives the impression that the window dresser tried his best to capture the dignity of a great state occasion.[8]

I suddenly felt I would like to buy a Coronation souvenir either for myself or for someone in my family. Something really nice, possibly lasting, not too expensive. But the important thing to do seemed to be to buy it now and I spent about half an hour going all round Derry and Tom's ground floor. I looked particularly at a small, satin-covered cushion, ash trays, tea trays, all things we need or would like to have at present. But in the end I didn't buy anything after all, nothing nice enough at the price I could pay. I remember looking at Wedgewood mugs and china at least a month ago and thinking if I had any souvenir I would like something like this but of course I would never be able to afford it. But the impulse to buy wasn't really there then.[9]

American Invasion. The arrival of the Americans in force is generally a sign that something untoward is happening. They always join us on our great occasions. Shop windows are beginning to show Coronation souvenirs of all kinds. Indeed, there seems already a feeling in the air that something exciting and unusual is soon going to take place. Perhaps it is the youth of the Queen or perhaps the obvious happiness of her family life with her handsome Consort and two charming children that gives this extra feeling of interest, and anticipation for her Coronation. Miniature Union Jacks are appearing on private cars. Window boxes are displaying red, white and blue flowers and expectant wooden boxes are showing themselves outside Whitehall windows. The Gurkhas arrive – the first contingent of Commonwealth troops to take part in the Coronation. The most untroubled of all, perhaps, are the starlings in Whitehall who refuse to still their chattering or interrupt their activities for King or Commoner.[10]

May Coronation biscuit tins are being bought decorated inside with red and white with tiny sweet biscuits in every section. On the blue lid is painted a picture of the Queen and the Duke with the inscription: Coronation of H.M. Queen Elizabeth II. June 2nd.1953. Pictures painted on the sides of the box show Windsor and Balmoral Castles.

The *Sunday Express* announces articles by the Duke of Windsor entitled 'My Coronation Thoughts'. Evidently he intends to make money out of an event whose responsibilities he was not himself prepared to shoulder.[11]

I find that Coronation has by now soaked into everyday life so much that it is quite impossible to notice and remember for record all the references to it. Nearly everywhere you look there will be a crown or a bit of red white and blue or a picture of some member of the royal family, it is impossible to notice; also the subject wanders in and out of conversation like the weather, and only the more memorable sayings are remembered.[12]

Elizabethan banquets are to be a feature of London this summer, 2-pronged forks, 2-handled beakers, trenchers, pomanders and all![13]

There is keen rivalry between the many stores and shops to advertise and display Coronation wares and commodities and there is a tremendous display of flowers on, in and around almost every shop, building and street, in addition to the profuse artificial decorations and flags.

Cinemas are vying with each other to advertise in original and novel manners their programmes specially arranged for Coronation Week. The people of Bath, after a slow start, now seem to have caught the spirit and are, generally, becoming most enthusiastic.

It seems that many people are going to London to see the procession, most of whom seem to have booked seats on the route.

There has, since Easter, been a most determined attempt by the people of Bath and the Corporation to tidy up some untidy corners, and by the liberal use of paint. The result is indeed most pleasant. Several historical buildings are being floodlit.[14]

There have been many unfavourable comments about the Town Hall decorations, Yellow and Red are the predominating colours and most Tories are shocked that the Labour Party colours are displayed in preference to Red, White and Blue. (Burnley has a Labour Council). In the poorer areas, the streets are thick with bunting and there is much enthusiasm for street parties. Out of town, there are rows of undecorated Semis. It seems that if one starts on a row, or block, most of the others seem to follow suit, another pointer to this 'better than the Jones's attitude'. In the better class areas, many houses are very tastefully done. There is usually a flagpole as a centre piece on the lawns.

Street Parties. Arrangements for these are now almost complete, and are nearly all being held in the poorer areas of town. Raffles and collections have been held for several weeks now to raise funds, and inside accommodation has been arranged in case of wet weather. Several are using Church Halls, and one street are so wealthy as to hire a Marquee.

Children are the main reason for these parties, but old age pensioners are also invited. Souvenirs have been purchased to be distributed, Pot Mugs are the most common of these. The children will be given sweets, minerals, and iced lollipops, and many groups have arranged to be photographed. The focal points for organising these street parties seems to be the local grocer's shops, and people with retail businesses near have all contributed to the funds, many offering goods to raffle.

There have been many petty squabbles between women about allocation of duties and petty jealousies flare up about street parties invitations. Many are holding TV parties, and here, it's a case of, bring your own food. Hostesses don't wish to be missing the show whilst in the kitchen.[15]

Joke 1:Made by lecturer [Age 45, male, no sense of humor, rotten lecturer, 1st class demonstrator, loves himself above everything, but good man in his line] – 'The new alphabet: A, B, C, D, E to (two) R'. (Corny isn't it?)[16]

Overheard:'What does the Queen do during the singing of the National Anthem? Does she sing, "God Save Me" or does she look coy and pretend she's not listening?'[17]

The traffic is becoming unmanageable. 'Long live the Queen' is being shown in all the buses. Even the latrines in the parks are showing gay colours as if to hide their real purpose . . .

Paddington area, except for the station, no decorations are shown. It is said that the Council is hostile.

It is remarked that not a workman had been heard to complain of the long hours during the Coronation preparations . . . A Coronation flame is to burn for 10 days at Bexhill. It will be kindled by runners. [18]

June   The night before the Coronation. In the evening I went round by the Abbey and to the bottom of Whitehall where it was difficult to move without stepping on a human being, as the crowds were settling down for the night. Some were lying on rugs and mats. Some who had pillows were already asleep. Others were laughing and talking and signing 'It's a long way to Tipperary'. Street sellers were shouting their wares – red, white and blue favours, programmes. One man was displaying plastic mackintoshes for 5/-. Barrowmen seemed to be doing a fairly brisk trade in fruit, sweets and soft drinks. The Queen's Beasts were still covered. A slight drizzle was falling but it failed to damp the spirits of the enthusiastic crowds.[19]

Coronation week events

Some Observers sent in programmes of local community events which underscore the variety of ways in which community members might participate in the celebrations. Moreton, Merseyside, for example, staged a week's worth of entertainment finishing with events aimed at bringing the entire community together for street parties, a 'Grand Coronation Fete', celebrity concert, 'Coronation Street Party' and finally a town meeting. The new Elizabethan age lent itself to many mock Elizabethan displays and costuming: Moreton residents could witness the Union Jack being 'carried into the village by a mounted escort in Elizabethan costume and raised by the British Legion' to mark the beginning of the week's ceremonies and watched the escort in costume ride out to signal the end of the momentous week.[20](See Images) In Corley, a television was set up in the 'new Festival room' and a fancy dress parade for children took place in the afternoon of the Coronation, followed by 'a very full sports programme'. A children's tea was to take place in the school, while meals for the rest of the residents took place in the Village Hall (though they were instructed to bring their own cutlery). The day wrapped up with a bonfire in the evening (Figure 2).[21]

The following Observer, from Pontypridd, Wales, discussed the organization of local Coronation celebrations and connected the experience with memories of prior royal events:

When the date for the Coronation was fixed things started to move in our Village like in all other towns and villages. A meeting of the people was called to form a Committee to arrange for the Celebrations and I was invited to be the Honorary President since I've lived here the longest and am the oldest inhabitant. On Coronation Day there was a Television set put in one of our Chapels to which anyone would go and watch the service and the Procession but I was unable to go and stayed at home listening to the Wireless.

People are fortunate today in being able to see and hear the actual service and so the Queen is brought nearer to us, which is different to the old days when we only read about these things. I remember Queen Victoria's Golden and Diamond Jubilees and I also saw her when the Royal Train taking her to open a new Dock in Swansea and broke down near our farm near Llanharan and the Queen got out of the train and sat on the bank. I am very interested in our new Queen because four years ago she

CORONATION DRAMATIC FESTIVAL

A FEAST OF DRAMATIC ENTERTAINMENT IN TUNE WITH THE SPIRIT OF CORONATION WEEK.

Each evening at 7-30 p.m. at the Sacred Heart Hall. Admission 6d.

Tuesday 2nd to Thursday 4th June:

"ONE WILD OAT"

A Comedy by Vernon Sylvaine.

Presented by Moreton Coronation Dramatic Sub-Committee.

Each Evening at 7-30 p.m. at the Sacred Heart Hall. Admission 6d.
Friday, 5th June and Saturday, 6th June:
Matinee at 2-30 p.m., Saturday, 6th June:

"LOVE IN IDLENESS"

A Comedy by Terence Rattigan.

Presented by Moreton Coronation Dramatic Sub-Committee.
Joint Producers: B. Collins and K. Freeman.

FRIDAY, 29th MAY, 1953.   Admission Free.
7 p.m. at LINGHAM PARK.

DISPLAY OF PHYSICAL EDUCATION

by over 400 children from Moreton and Leasowe.
Organiser: C. D. CLARE.
with the help of teachers of all local schools.

Music by the Band of Gorsedale Secondary Modern School. Salute and march past. European National Dances. Country Dancing. Gymnastics. Free Standing Movements and Skipping. Mass Assembly.

CORONATION DAY

TUESDAY, 2nd JUNE, 1953.
10 a.m.—12-30 p.m. and
12-45—3-30 p.m. at SACRED HEART HALL.   Admission 3d.
TELEVISION SHOW on Enlarged Screen.
There will be two separate periods for which tickets will be issued in advance. Maximum ticket issue 700.

2 p.m.—8 p.m. at the PARISH HALL.   Admission Free.
ARTS & CRAFTS EXHIBITION (see page 9).

3—5-30 p.m. TRAVELLING MARIONETTE SHOWS.
Each performance about 20 minutes.

No. 1. 3-00 p.m. Curlew Way.
        3-30 p.m. Lingham Primary School Yard.
        4-00 p.m. Furze Way.
        4-30 p.m. Borrowdale Road/Briscoe Drive.
        5-00 p.m. Meadowbrook Road.
        5-30 p.m. Saughall Road/Hoylake Road.

No. 2. 3-00 p.m. Wallasey Grammar School Playing Field, Leasowe.
        3-30 p.m. Wallasey High School Playing Field, Leasowe.
        4-00 p.m. Yew Tree Green.
        4-30 p.m. Coniston Green.
        5-00 p.m. Chadwick Street.
        5-30 p.m. Ely Avenue.

CORONATION STREET PARTIES.

Felicity Grove.	Swan Road.
Fernway (Lingham Primary School).	Oundle Road.
Burrell Drive (Victory Hall).	Curlew Way.
Ivy Lane.	Briscoe Drive.
Orchard Road.	School Close.
Sunfield Road.	Murrayfield Drive (Wallasey High School Playing Field).
Pasture Crescent.	Twickenham Drive (Wallasey Grammar School Playing Fld).
Eastway.	Carsdale Road.
Yew Tree Road	Fairoak Road.
Westway.	

CORONATION DAY—continued.

3 p.m.—5 p.m. at LINGHAM PRIMARY SCHOOL GROUND.   Admission Free. Seats 3d.
FODENS PRIZE BAND.

2-45 p.m. at LINGHAM PARK.   Admission Free.
CRICKET MATCH.
Arranged by Moreton Cricket and Social Club.

7-30 p.m. at the SCOUTS' FIELD, Upton Rd.   Admission Free.
SCOUTS' DISPLAY & CAMP FIRE COMMUNITY SINGING.

7-45 p.m. at LINGHAM PRIMARY SCHOOL GROUNDS.   Admission Free. Seats 3d.
CORONATION REVUE (see page 3).

7-30 p.m. at SACRED HEART HALL.   Admission 6d.
"ONE WILD OAT" (see page 5).

WEDNESDAY, 3rd JUNE, 1953.
2 p.m.—8 p.m. at the PARISH HALL.   Admission Free.
ARTS & CRAFTS EXHIBITION (see page 9).

3 p.m. and 5-30 p.m. at BLACKHEATH DR.   Admission Free.
Two performances of "CORONATION CAPERS"
A Travelling Variety Show, introducing Children's Competitions.
Arranged by the Wallasey Corporation.

7-30 p.m. at the SACRED HEART HALL.   Admission 6d.
"ONE WILD OAT" (see page 5).

7-30 p.m. at LINGHAM PARK.   Admission Free.
EXHIBITION OF SCOTTISH DANCING
Presented by Moreton and District Caledonian Association.
MODEL AIRCRAFT RODEO
including Team Racing, Stunt Flying, Balloon Bursting and Streamer Clipping. Arranged by Wirral Model Aero Club.

7-45 p.m. at LINGHAM PRIMARY SCHOOL GROUND.   Admission Free. Seats 3d.
CORONATION REVUE (see page 3).

FIGURE 2 Pages from Coronation Week Programme for Moreton, Merseyside. Mass-Observation Archive, University of Sussex Special Collections, Royalty Topic Collection, Directive Replies from Panel, 69-7-E. DR676.

CORONATION OF ELIZABETH II 1953

passed very close to me at a big agricultural show held in Cardiff and I shall never forget her kindly and friendly smile. Our old age Pensions day was Thursday and buses came to pick us up and take us to the tea party where we were given a wonderful time with plenty to eat, a souvenir and all joined in community singing. On Saturday we had a Carnival and Sports followed by a grand tea free to all. The weather was lovely, most likely this is the last Coronation I shall see but it was the finest I've ever enjoyed because I am 92 and retired from Cavalry work when I was 65. I say 'Long life and happiness to our young Queen'.[22]

Ox-roasting

Mass-Observation was particularly interested in traditional local celebrations, especially ox-roasting, and asked members of the panel to reach out if an ox-roasting was planned in their area so that staff could advise panellists on how best to record these activities. Several responses were collected, though none share whether they were advised on their observations.[23]

Combe Hay is a very small village, consisting of church, manor, post office, pub, about 25 cottages and a few farms, very scattered. There is no transport service of any kind either bus or train available.

The ox, which was given by . . . a local farmer, was sent to Bristol to be dressed. The fire was lit at 7am and the cooking commenced at 2 pm.

When I arrived at 8pm there were about 22 cars, mostly belonging to local people and their friends and about 80 people in the field watching the ox being cooked. By 8.15 when the cutting-up commenced there were about 150/180 people. Beer was provided for grown-ups, lemonade and crisps for the children.

Men and women were in about equal proportions and about a third of the total were children.

While the meat was being served more people arrived in cars, making the total about 200/250. These people were not local and it was thought that they had seen the details in the newspapers and had come from distances. They seemed mostly youngish (under 40) men and women without children and mostly looked lower-middle class agricultural type.

Almost all the inhabitants of the village were there, mostly cottages and their older children.

The weather was cold and looked as if it would rain, though actually it did not during the eating of the ox. People wore raincoats over cotton frocks and blue suits (ready for dancing in the village hall afterwards) the main attitude appeared to be rather amused interest when the meat was cut and put into sandwiches, the younger people packed around to get theirs, the sandwiches were served on individual cardboard plates decorated in red white and blue.

There were lots of jokes about the meat ration, housewives saying they could do with a joint that size: a man complimenting the roasters and saying it was the nicest bit of meat he'd had since meat rationing etc.

Most of the people took the meat eagerly and appeared to enjoy it, commenting that it tasted wonderful and was well cooked etc. . . . I noticed several people holding the paper plates in order to put the bread in their pockets . . .

On the whole the spectators took it all very quietly. There was scarcely any excitement except just before the ox was removed from the spit, when people feared that the meat would fall from the bones into the fire as it was very well cooked.

As they started to cut it up the young people crowded around and got the first sandwiches; the older people stood back and had theirs when there was less of a crush.

The whole thing was over by about 9pm though I noticed some of the young people were crowding around by the fire later in the evening.[24]

Coronation day

As Britain and the Commonwealth prepared for the Coronation in the spring of 1953, they were also closely following an unfolding drama half a world away on Mount Everest. A team of climbers reached Camp III at 20,500 feet on 25 April, and British newspapers regularly kept track of the climbers' progress and the weather conditions on the mountain. The Times *carried reports that included detailed descriptions of the experiences on the mountain from the expedition team. To underscore the excitement of the new Elizabethan age of discovery, reports included both a sense of adventure and daring as well as explanations of the cutting-edge technologies that allowed climbers to reach to the heavens.[25] When news came in of a successful summit by Edmund Hillary and Tenzing Norgay, the first Elizabethan age was rapturously linked with the new: 'Seldom since Francis Drake brought the Golden Hind to anchor in Plymouth Sound has a British explorer offered to his Sovereign such a tribute of glory as Colonel John Hunt and his men are able to lay at the feet of Queen Elizabeth for her Coronation day.'[26] Many Observers mentioned learning of the news upon waking, which seemed to add a special buoyancy to the day.*

The following observation of the day highlights some of the main themes seen across directive responses for those who stayed home on Coronation day. Everest starts the day and everyday life is punctuated throughout by the Coronation broadcasts. Even those who were not inclined to be interested in the Coronation found themselves drawn in by aspects of it – especially the service in Westminster Abbey. Special mention of the Queen of Tonga – who laughed and waved to the crowds from an open carriage despite the rain – appears in many observations of the day. As with Everest, which had been summited by a Nepalese Sherpa and a New Zealander, Commonwealth added lustre to the British crown.

I thought I was immune, but I awoke this morning with the feeling that this day was different, like Christmas or one's birthday.

The weather however is quite unpatriotic and one feels sorry for those foolish people who have spent the night on the procession route; those who took children should be punished.

The bright spot this morning is Everest, that really is something to enthuse over. Great chaps those climbers. I got some amusement from the efforts of my newspaper to connect this achievement with the Coronation.[27]

The following married male hearing aid technician sketched out the day's events, starting with the Everest summit:

8.50 am Awakened by my wife calling upstairs 'Everest's been climbed' when the paper arrived.

8.55 Got up to hear 9.0 am news in (vain) hopes of hearing later information on Everest

9.0/10.15 Breakfasted, leisurely scanning Newspaper and Punch

10.15/11.30 Listened to Coronation Broadcast rather disinterestedly, whilst adjusting two front doors, and chasing birds in garden.

11.30/12.45 Cleaned and adjusted Electric fire, whilst listening to the Abbey Service with gradually increasing interest

12.45/2.0 Leisurely lunch, whilst continuing to listen. Thought Queen very sincere, D of Edinburgh carried himself well, D of Gloucester badly, D of Kent poorly and D of Norfolk redeemed them. Wondered if D of Norfolk required Papal dispensation to attend, and whether such dispensation would amount to de facto recognition of Henry VIII's action, recognition that the Queen was head of the Anglican Church which is Catholic. I was struck by a consciousness that the past is by no means as past as we're inclined to think – that WE stand as upon the shoulders of our remotest ancestors.

2.0/6.0 Addressed 150 postcards while listening with occasional interest to the Procession. Thought the BBC and the Queen of Tonga made a wonderful job of it. Tea.

6.0/7.0 Listened to Irish Radio (German Dance Music) <u>for a change!</u> (From Ireland) News of Mt Everest and report of 3000 Coronation casualties with 114 in Hospital. (Fed up with Nat. Anthem and Cheers. God help the Queen!) I may be made all wrong, but I hate people in the mass. They say and do such stupid things. Yet I could, but for restraint, fall for the hysteria of the herd. However, Britain is now no doubt secure as a Monarchy until the Jubilee, and will I think be good for the Conservative cause. Anyway, I have little doubt that the French, American (and perhaps Italian) Republics were envious of our heritage of tradition, and I could not wish for a better focus for the Commonwealth (at the present stage) than an hereditary Monarchy. India's decision has created an admirable precedent. Will Pakistan follow? There is nothing I would change, but I would hate to be amongst the cheering mob (wonderful how they get the time!)

7.20 Heard Gillie Potter,[28] who summed up wonderfully

7.30 Heard Jimmy Shand[29] (a favourite of mine)

8.0/10.0 Third Programme and bed.[30]

Naomi Mitchison reported the view from her unique position in Westminster Abbey.

Go over covered way to Abbey about a quarter to eight, find seats in middle gallery, facing peeresses (north side), can just see throne and glimpse of King Edward's chair, look for the stone[31] under it with feeling of resentment.

Plenty to look at, specially peeresses' diamonds. From 8 to 9.30 watching and talking to friends and acquaintances: the air of a part. Identifying peeresses, Argyll handsome in silver lame, Devonshire in a seventeenth century dress. Music muted, mostly percussion and horns. The four guinea coronets better than many of the family ones with real stones. Many Labour wives looking pretty awful with a few Parma violets and a punch of gauze sort of thing. Only saw one other woman with lace like mine, looking equally odd. Many with saris all looking ravishingly beautiful, the tiny diamond in the nose so becoming.

At 9.40 a procession with the regalia, one didn't see very well, only the whacking great crown.

At 9.50 the queue via the Peers to the Ladies. Everyone still in a very frivolous mood: is it a party or a religious occasion? At 10.10 a large cross goes by. At 10.25 we stand for an invisible procession; from where we are we don't see the main procession route north of the throne. Most of the interesting people have sat down in the aisle before they get as far as the throne. But various odd people wander about the ceremonial space apparently aimlessly. The Earl Marshall stalks in front of the peeresses like a short-horn bull.

At 10.40 there was a bit of sunlight, one hoped it was clearing. Then came the main procession, with the comic heralds, who stood round the pillars and various other people who seemed equally pointless. One was suddenly aware that Monty had got into the middle of things as usual. Also Churchill, who got a corner seat from which one could watch him watching. After the procession a broom and vacuum cleaner. I thought these were magnificently like the House of the Interpreter in the Pilgrim's Progress, but they were really because foot prints on the carpet show up so much on TV. We wondered where the TV was. I was taking notes, a girl in front of me was sketching.

I couldn't see much when everyone was standing as I am too short, could not see the Queen go by at all but did get a glimpse of her at the Recognition which was extremely impressive. She was in a very simple dress which looked from where I was like a sacrificial victim, the lamb white maiden dear in the circle of mute kings. We all shouted with real wholeheartedness, but it could have been louder.

Then the oath business was out of sight. We heard the Queen over the loud speakers; she has a rather nasty voice, I think, very Londony and with a bit of sneer in it. Then came the various prayers, Gospels, etc. A few people joined in as though it were a real religious service, I had never been to an English communion service before. The music was awfully good, but I always find the Creed pretty odd.

Then the golden pall was brought. We couldn't see much of what was going on, though after it was taken away one could see her in the fitted dress of cloth of gold which was really stunning. One could just get a glimpse of the next bit, all the magic things being brought and touched. Finally they brought that enormous great crown and put it on. The peeresses did a good ballet movement with their crowns, lifting them and putting them on but spoiled it all by fidgeting with them afterwards. In general they fidgeted a lot. The Kings at arms put on kind of cracker crowns, and the Lord Chancellor looked very silly with a coronet over his wig. We all shouted but again not very loud, I thought.

It was dark again though there had been a moment during Zadok the Priest at 'All the people rejoiced', the sun came in and set the diamonds on the peeresses twinkling like mad. I kept worrying about the poor people outside getting wet, including my daughter. Where I was we couldn't hear anything from outside except the guns. There was an impressive moment when the Queen was helped to the throne apparently bowed down under the weight of the golden royal robe, and carrying her odd things; the crown looked enormously too heavy for anyone to wear, but it reminded me of Alice's crown in Alice through the Looking Glass.

Then there was the homage. Prince Philip has a nice voice and of course that bit was too, too breath-catching, but a bit bogus. Then the various others and a lot of coronet play. I now kept on seeing the coronets as red cakes with cake trimmings round them and feeling very much that none of these people were the real leaders of the country in any sense. Many of them were thoroughly bad people, others nonentities.

However we all shouted God Save Queen Elizabeth, Long Live Queen Elizabeth and (with a certain embarrassment) May the Queen Live forever. Then there was All People on Earth, but I didn't think it was very fully sung by the congregation. They could have made much more noise. Then there was the Communion; I felt it was all a bit embarrassing. Some people were treating it as church, repeating the General Confession, etc. [My husband], I noticed, joined in some of it. I did with the Lord's Prayer which always strikes me as unexceptionable. Otherwise one listened to the music. I watched the peeresses fidget, attend to one another's straps, whisper and cross their legs. Churchill watched intently. I was also thinking what I would say in my Manchester Guardian article.

Then people began to gather for the next procession. I saw Nehru looking incredibly distinguished, talking to the Pakistani Prime Minister. Also magnificent Queen Salote [of Tonga] and several people in odd clothes. But it was impossible to see the main procession from where we are, at least for me . . .

There was a good moment when Churchill walked into the centre of things flaunting his robes and looking impatient as though to say what is this girl keeping me waiting for? . . .

We started for the car a bit after four, having some difficulty, but the crowds were clearing quickly and we got down the Embankment. I ran up to the *Guardian* Office, got there about 5.30, got a typewriter, and had it finished shortly after five [I think six?] They said I was the first to get my piece in.[32]

Mass-Observation asked its respondents to compare the last Coronation with the new. Those who remembered both tended to feel that 1953 was more exciting, more commercial and more expensive than 1937. Certainly the bleakness of the economic depression and uncertainties caused by the abdication crisis and international conflict shaded the memories of 1937, while the exciting potential of the new age amplified the experience of 1953. While 1953 was by no means without its uncertainties and conflicts – nuclear threats, the Korean War and the unravelling of empire, for instance – few Observers mentioned them explicitly in their writing on Coronation day. In her account, a sixty-year-old retired married schoolteacher remembered the economic dislocation of the 1930s and worried about its return:

I remember the 1937 Coronation which seemed a very tame affair compared with this, or it may be that I was too busy with my four young children then

CORONATION OF ELIZABETH II 1953   101

to notice outside events. All I remember is taking the older children to see the fireworks. People in Lancashire were very poor at the time (the slump period) and could not have afforded the decorations, etc. that are evident everywhere now. Many thinking people fear a return to unemployment in Lancashire now that the Coronation orders are finished.[33]

The following 34-year-old female secretary felt that the 'disappointment' of the Abdication Crisis marred the 1937 Coronation as she contrasted it with the more colourful and exciting 1953 celebrations:

I think the atmosphere at this Coronation was entirely different from that in 1937. I wasn't very old at the time, but I remember the disappointment that was felt in 1937 that the sovereign to be crowned was not Edward VIII, who, I think, was much more popular than George VI <u>at that time</u>. He proved his worth, however, and there is no doubt that he was one of the best-loved monarchs our country has ever had. This Coronation sees a young woman on the throne, and I think most people have sympathy with her because of the burden of responsibility she has to bear, and admiration for the dignity and sense of dedication that she has brought to her high office. There seems to be much more enthusiasm this time than there was in 1937. I don't remember seeing so many souvenirs in the shops in 1937, and I can't recall all the special Coronation biscuits, cakes, and so forth. Much more money seems to have been spent this time, but I think it has been worth it, and given the nation a real tonic.[34]

The newness of television access framed many of the responses, such as the following:

I should be able to remember the 1937 Coronation but I do not seem to recall more than decorated streets, and some boxes of food at school. I do not feel that it was anything like such a great occasion. Someone said to me that there is more fuss this time because a <u>Queen</u> is being crowned. I think this may be true, and also because she is young and the family appears romantic. She is confident, too; we all worried about her father having to endure so much. He was a sincere but not a romantic figure. The last Coronation was an anti-climax after the Windsor affair. We're also still trying to enjoy ourselves after the War. Television has made the greatest difference. People are in on the inside although only nobility took part. We seem to me to be trying to make a comeback as a great nation. 1937 appears as nothing compared with this, but perhaps the Records of the time tell a different tale.[35]

This married 37-year-old male lecturer mentioned the television experience as a significant difference:

So far as I can judge, the 1953 Coronation was head-and-shoulders better than 1937. Probably because there was a much greater national unity on this occasion . . . One other comment: judging from many accounts, this was the most dignified and best-organized of all Coronations. Could this be due to the presence, for the first time, of the 'common herd' (in the form of TV)? It seems to me that what used to be a pretty rough old peers' outing has been turned into a most wonderful and deeply significant ceremony. Altogether, I would describe June 2nd as a great day for the British![36]

Television parties were central to the experience of the 1953 Coronation. While television sales increased in anticipation of the televised broadcast, the majority did not have a set, and watching television – what is now often a solitary or household experience – could be intensely communal. This 45-year-old single female teacher reported loneliness returning home after spending the day with watching the ceremony with friends:

I got up at 6.20 am and ironed before breakfast. After preparing a sandwich lunch, I gardened for an hour, then went to a friend, who had invited me to watch the Coronation Ceremony on her television set. We were 6. Up till then, I had felt very cold, and wished it had been a warmer and pleasanter day for such an important occasion. While we watched the ceremony, I forgot it. We watched till 2 pm then again at 2.30 pm till 5 pm. I found myself getting bored with the continuous procession of soldiers, but was interested again at once, when personalities came into view.

Coming home to tea in an empty house, I felt rather lonely, for this seemed an occasion when one ought to be with others to celebrate. I felt this specially when some houses in the road had special 'fairy' lighting and generally the people seemed in holiday mood. However, I forgot all about this as I worked – staining floors most of the time, and was thankful for wireless which enabled me to hear the Queen's speech. Also, I was interested to hear what people thought throughout the country, were doing to celebrate the Coronation – again through wireless . . .

It did seem a special day, and I felt united to other people in this crowning of the Queen, but was emotionally different: I did not want to eat different food, or wear different clothes. In fact, as it was such a cold day, I wore a green skirt and woolen jumper with a navy cardigan – my everyday working wear![37]

This married 29-year-old male recounted preparing for guests to arrive. His account then described the day's events, including the experience of watching the televised broadcast:

Just before 10 am we discovered that the couple downstairs who were to have gone over to watch their sons TV would not be able to do so as their son had just phoned up to say that their set had broken down so we invited them upstairs to see our TV together with her sister who was staying with them, my wife and I spent an anxious ten minutes trying to arrange the room to accommodate 7 persons comfortably. We moved the TV set first this way and then that trying to find the best position, finally as is so often the case finishing by leaving it in its original position. The dining table had to be moved, more comfortable chairs brought up from downstairs for we have not enough easy chairs to seat seven and dining room chairs feel rather hard after two or three hours and this was to be an all day session. I began to worry lest our set should let us down also but it served us very well and my fears were unfounded. Our guests from downstairs came up and we all settled ourselves down, Mother and sister in law were late as usual and the procession had started when they arrived, so it was ten minutes of twelve before we were all settled again. It was very cold and we had left it too late to light a fire without disturbing anybody so we put the electric fire on but naturally it was some time before the room warmed up and so we all sat with coats and woolies on. I feel certain that we were all impressed by the procession to the Abbey and even more so by the service that followed inside. My wife and I were deeply grateful for the opportunity to see the actual service of Coronation. It was a wise decision we think to televise it and it surely proved itself against its critics, for very few people in this country had any idea of what went on inside the abbey except from photographs and printed matter and these alone could never convey the majesty and significance of the service, but the TV camera did for we were right amongst the great and noble from start to finish. We were all impressed by the whole procedure and seeing our young queen so composed and confident throughout that long ordeal for her made us all feel a little more patriotic.

Our small group consisted of 5 women and 2 males, not very much was spoken between us at first then a cup of tea warmed us all up and thawed the ice and comments on the robes jewelry etc flowed fast. Prince Phillip was the ladies heart throb as usual but young prince Charles stole the show in the two glimpses that we were given of him in the abbey and again on the balcony at the Palace later on and at the window of the palace looking out at the returning procession. Our day was spent completely indoors for we are going up to see the decorations and floodlighting later on in the week for we felt that we would see more by staying at home today and the decorations and floodlighting would keep until later. A quick lunch was had after the service was over and we all set about the washing up clearing it all away in record time so as to be ready for the return procession in the afternoon. There had to be a cup of tea of course before we all settled down again and a second cup for me. We all remarked on the rain and it was agreed that the weather had let us down rather badly. Our guests from downstairs stayed until the end of the ceremonies at 5-30pm when we all had tea. A farther friend of my mother arrived then for tea and it was planned that we should all go up to the local recreation grounds to see the display of fireworks but the cold wet weather made us change our minds and we stayed indoors and watched the TV again instead. This was very nice for our last arrival who was able to see a repeat of some of the scenes as her husband having to go work at an awkward time was not able to come earlier, though she had listened to the ceremony on the radio.

We listened to Mr. Churchill's speech and then the Queens speech, saw her majesty switch on the floodlights and then viewed the beginning of the firework display.[38]

Another married Observer recounted hosting guests for 'televiewing' and described an evening of washing up, more visiting, wireless listening and watching fireworks:

On 2nd June I got up about the usual time and tidied up the flat and prepared food for 2 visitors who were coming to teleview the coronation ceremony. It was cold and my visitors were elderly so I lit a coal fire. Guests arrive about 10 am. We had tea and biscuits out of a Coronation assortment in a special tin. I dressed in a red white and blue overall, having realised that I happened to have one with those three colours. I put up a portrait of the queen near the entrance to my sitting-room door. I made the room gay with flowers – blue anchusa – red roses and a white rock plant (name not known).

10.15 am. We started to Teleview. Between noon and 1 o'clock at a less exciting moment, I quickly heated and brought in soup and dry toast. We continued to watch T.V. – all thrilled and deeply moved by the ceremony.

During the short interval in the proceedings I served a cold lunch . . . Then the processions began about 3.30 and I served hot coffee made with milk to keep us going. We continued to watch.

Then about five we had a pot of tea – a trifle and some cakes. My visitors had to go at 5.55 to catch a bus. They were so happy to have seen so much and I was very happy that I'd been able to share the experience with these two kind friends – kind to me after I had been bombed out.

I did a grand washing up. Then went on a short walk about 6.30 to 7 pm with the neighbour of the downstairs flat. I visited her and her sister to see the telerecording of the Coronation. Before it began I made some sandwiches for refreshments. The neighbour came upstairs about 8 pm. Her sister had gone out earlier to help with a street tea-party but we left a note for her, so she came eventually about 8.55 pm.

We ate sandwiches and had coffee and cakes about 9.10 pm (and we ate sweets at intervals throughout the day) – or smoked cigarettes – I did not smoke.

CORONATION OF ELIZABETH II 1953

We listened to Sir Winston's speech and the Queen's speech, which we thought was so sincere and direct, that our hearts were warmed more than ever towards her.

We watched newsreel and then went on to watch the fireworks on South Bank. I washed up again – and went to bed about 11.30 pm tired out, but so happy to have had the chance to follow a coronation.

I dreamed the ceremony over again and I remember being struck once again with the perfection of ritual. Every part had been well rehearsed.

Everything had been very quiet outside. During the day, I forgot the whole world, I forgot everything I usually do. I lived the Coronation Day as a special day, and nothing else at all mattered.[39]

Some Observers had a quiet day watching the day's events on the television with family, such as this 37-year-old assurance officer:

On Coronation Day my wife my son aged 6 and I took the easy way out and confined ourselves to our TV set. From the time the program started at 10-15am we three with my mother and a friend remained mesmerised by the screen until the very end of the ceremony and procession etc. My son went off to an organised children's party at about 3 pm; my mother and friend left after tea. From then on, except for a short break when I collected my son from his party my wife and I followed the TV programme right round to the end of the firework display.

During the latter the boy woke up and was allowed a quarter of an hour or so of viewing before going back to his bed. We thought to go out and join the crowds somewhere but found the weather too damp and chilly and accordingly went straight to bed.

I hadn't expected the TV programme to be very brilliant and didn't think I would spend too much time viewing, but in fact I found the . . . presentation beyond criticism. The ceremony in the Abbey was for the most part awe-inspiring and the procession and the other comings and goings fascinating.

In addition to the charm of the Queen I was very impressed profoundly by the deportment of the Duke of Edinburgh and was delighted by the impishness of Sir Winston Churchill and the . . . laughter of the Queen of Tonga.

Prior to Coronation Day I had become thoroughly cynical about the whole business but by midnight having seen several scenes as many as three times all my acidity had been neutralized and to me it will remain a wonderful and memorable day.[40]

The television experience was impressive and memorable for many, but some offered a critical view, feeling that television could not measure up to the moment, such as this 46-year-old married male shopping clerk:

REFLECTIONS ON BRITISH ROYALTY

<u>Criticism of television programme:</u> Technically excellent, but <u>no</u> feelings of '<u>dignity</u>' or <u>excitement</u> got over; seemed rather unreal, both the ceremony and the processions were shown far <u>too long. Television is too small for an event like this</u> and the whole thing could have been a puppet show.[41]

And the following single female secretary:

Thoughts – Mostly admiration for the Queen and the Archbishop – BBC Commentaries – London Crowds – RAF Fly past pilots and THE QUEEN. And amusement at myself being glued to the wireless hardly daring to move in case I missed anything. At night watching television (I preferred the sound broadcast in the morning but this may have been the fault of the set. I found the pictures restricting and not clear. It's only my third viewing of Television, so perhaps I'm not 'up to it'.) I felt sad – the Queen looked so . . . weighed down.[42]

Some Observers recounted their experiences among the crowds who watched the Coronation procession in London. As is seen here, Observers might listen in to the wireless broadcast over loudspeakers along the route and then make it home in time to see the ceremony in Westminster Abbey on television. This female social worker got up early:

I got up at 3 am dressed, and then made breakfast for myself, and my 2 relatives. We left the house at 4 am it was not light, and not warm. We took a . . . bus to Finsbury Park Tube. There we found a number of people on the platform, but managed to get a seat in the train. We alighted at Leicester Square, and walked down Charing Cross Road, through the barriers at St Martins, and along Northumberland Avenue to the Playhouse Theatre, where we had booked accommodation on the roof. In the Theatre, which we got to through a fair crush of people, we were asked to go and sit in the Dress Circle. We found people there who had obviously slept the night on the floor covered with blankets. The Wireless came on at 5/30, and at 6 am, we went out on the roof. We found one of our party was already there, and had secured a nice seat (we had taken stools) on the front row, looking right down Northumberland Avenue. We noticed that already the pavements were full, that many people were lying partly covered in blankets, and newspapers. The crowd was continually being invaded by St. Johns Ambulance men who with stretchers picked up the casualties. I noticed through my glasses that they were more often men than women, and not old men either. Undoubtedly we are the stronger sex. At 7 am, the Navy came to line the streets, and how the crowd cheered, and sang 'All the nice girls love a sailor' etc. Soon the school children started arriving on the Embankment, girls and boys bearing banners with numbers where they were to stand. By 8 o.c. the

Embankment was full of them. They cheered everything police on bikes, dustcarts, etc etc. At 7 3/0 we went down into the Theatre, and had a meal we brought with us, hot tea in Thermos, and sandwiches and cakes. We also had a tidy up there being a Theatre plenty of facilities.

About 8 oclock the Lord Mayor's Coach rumbled along the Embankment with the Pikemen in front . . . Then came the long procession of motors with foreign potentates. Followed by the Prime Ministers all with escorts except Mr Nehru of India; all were cheered, especially Mr Churchill. All this time the ambulances were literally running about and the St Johns men very very busy, and very kind. We all felt so sorry for the folk and for their relatives who had to go off with them, it did seem a shame. Then came the Procession of the Royal Family, we couldn't see the people in the cars and coaches, but got a general impression of great splendour. Then quite capturing the crowd came the Queen of Tonga in an open carriage dressed in traditional dress of lovely pale pink, and I think bare footed. Then the Pakistan people, and other Asiatic rulers. We all felt amused that on this bitter day they were in open carriages!!! We were all very cold . . . mainly we were too thrilled to feel the cold. Then at 10/30 came the grand procession of the Queen, the marching men in red, and the yeomen of the Guard, and at last the lovely fairy like Golden Coach. This ended the procession except for the BBC recording van following slowly after. To our amazement we were able to get away at 11/30, and returned home again via Leicester Square. We noticed the litter on the streets, they looked as if papered with rags!!!

On arrival home at 12 oclock, we went upstairs, and watched Television, saw the Crowning of the Queen then came down and had a meal, and I to rest for 2 hours until 5 oclock, when we again watched Television. Then a meal at 6/30, and a little more rest. Feelings I can't describe wonderment at so much beauty of colour, admiration at the good humour . . . of the crowd, and the helpfulness of the Police. Oh we are a grand people, this sounds self-praising, but we are.[43]

Another female Observer caught up with friends for the procession:

Four of us joined up on Monday evening and spent the night outside the Carlton Club – Pall Mall – we managed to get into the second row of spectators – we had a rug which we sat on – newspapers galore to keep at the cold, woolen vests . . . short sleeved jersey and long sleeved cardigan, thick tweed skirt, big coat, nylons, pair of men's ¾ hose . . . gloves and headscarf, and I was still frozen! And before the end of the day, the water had run down my neck and I was wet through. We took sandwiches, sausage rolls, biscuits, chocolate ovaltine tablets, barley sugar, boiled sweets and Vitorange glucose thirst quenchers. We ate very little not fancying any of the food except the apples. We had a flask of rum which we gulped neat at long intervals in an effort to keep warm and act as a stimulant. It was too cold to sleep but we did shut our eyes. The noise also made it impossible to sleep. The night passed very slowly indeed. We managed to stretch our legs by walking to the toilet facilities in Trafalgar Square just before dawn – the queue was very long and we abandoned all hope of ever getting there again – so resisted the temptation to go for a cup of coffee or to have a sip from a friendly neighbour – (those who went were away for more than three hours in the queue.)

4.30 am we had to put away our rug and stand. This soon proved an agonising business and the thought of twelve hours solid standing sent my husband and myself to the back of the spectators where we could lean against the Club stand and sit occasionally. Here we were able to hear and follow the whole of the Abbey Service through the Club's radio (we had no loudspeakers on this part of the route).

Although very wet and cold I managed by standing on tip toe to see everything and everybody, and wouldn't have missed any of it, but next time, if there is a next time, it's T.V. for me.[44]

Listening in was a common experience, even for those who had access to a television or who had decided to watch the processions from the streets. For those without a television, the wireless could offer the immersive experience seen in the television parties earlier or form the background to holiday and everyday activities. Even still, many paused to listen at critical moments in the ceremony, like the anointing. The following thirty-year-old housewife recounted her day:

I got up late, but got the washing up and other chores done in time to listen in to the Broadcasts. I started listening in as the Queen left Buckingham Palace. From then on I continued listening in while doing all the other things, such as nappy washing . . . My husband and small daughter treated the day as an ordinary holiday and went gardening. I called them in when the actual anointing was going on and from then on they too listened. I had prepared a cold lunch the day before, but my husband shaped he mashed potatoes with a crown for the amusement of small daughter (aged 2 ½) I switched the radio off when the procession from the Abbey started, as I was tired of listening by then. In the afternoon we went to the village celebrations.[45]

This thirty-year-old single male civil servant offered his critical take on the day and the wireless broadcast:

Between 10 and 11 had a breakfast of corn flakes in hot milk, and then had a shave about 11 am, having heard half an hour of the radio commentary (we have no television nor consider it worth the money at its present stage of progress). After that listened to the Ceremony without comment; however, when the Archbishop (as was his duty) invoked the name of God I could not help remarking to myself mentally that the name of God hides far more than it reveals, and from my own philosophical standpoint stood aloof from it all as being all rather barbaric and paganistic in its ritual. In fact between 12.0 and 12.30 it was so pagan and barbaric to me that I could not help remarking to my family that the Anointing seemed to me just a pagan rite, and especially the affirmation that Christ himself gave his blessing to it, since to my Buddhist mind such an utterance of blind faith is mental barbarism pure and simple, however elegant the words uttered or the learning of those who utter them, for they give no proof that they themselves have actually realized such an affirmation from Christ within themselves. After that I let it pass, and listened to the Communion Service. After 1.0 pm, the whole proceeding began to bore rather than elevate me, and towards 2.0 we began dinner. Between 2.0 and 3.0 we finished dinner, which for me (being a vegetarian) had consisted of cheese, new potatoes, greens and Yorkshire pudding (according to my memory – for I had forgotten to write notes of this meal and of other meals, but it was a perfectly ordinary meal such as I might have at home any Sunday). . . . Between 3.0 and 4.0 and indeed between 4.0 and 5.0 just sat listening to the procession, studying it on the Radio Times plan and pointing out the various points as the procession arrived there. Between 5.0 and 6.0 found me still just listening, and towards 6.0 tea began to be go ready. At 6.0 we were at the table settling down to a salad . . . Between 7.0 and 8.0 took the dog out for a walk in the fields nearby, and between 8.0 and 9.0 typed off a letter or two. Between 9.0 and 10.0 came away from my typewriter to renew the flowers on my personal shrine, and felt a little annoyed because I had forgotten to listen to Sir Winston and the Queen on the radio. However, we had supper and had the 10.0 pm News on the Light Programme, and up to 11.0 prepared for bed.[46]

Barrow-in-Furness housewife, Nella Last, was impressed by the wireless broadcast, commenting favourably on the Queen's voice and presence:

I was grieved to wake to wildly fluttering curtains and no gleam of sun peeping through and any flags in sight were draggled and twisted . . . I took the paper from the letter box and got one of the best 'thrills' of the day – to see we had achieved the seemingly impossible task of climbing Everest – such a wonderful gift for the Queen, one to remember. I looked anxiously at my husband's face. He looked so nervy and complained of a bad night. I often feel of late I'm a goldfish in a bowl – never 'achieving' anything in my round of days, the bowl a little 'wall' that shuts out every outside interest or dims and distorts. I hurriedly cleared the table, made beds, and dusted, decided to put a new band and left on my tweed skirt, the suit needs cleaning and rather to my surprise my husband kept the wireless on most of the day. I fried bacon and eggs, and we ate bread to them – I'd enough soup from yesterday for my husband for mid-morning, and we had custard and dates and a cup of tea. He had a little rest in the big chair instead of lying down. I felt so sorry when it rained in London. Many people would catch colds. I felt as I listened to the full throated cheers it was the answer to weary criticisms of 'Britain's being tired'. Such a serene 'confident' voice has the Queen. I feel she had the 'God bless' of millions listeners. She would be every man's ideal sweetheart, wife, daughter and behind her mere 'glamorous' beauty there is a miner strength and beauty – so much beauty, purpose, faith, and just honest 'goodness', makes me want to cross my fingers as I feel it's too much for any one person and look with gratitude at Phillip's strength, his kindly face and read of his gallant 'independence' and refusal just to be a 'Queen's husband'. I marvelled as I listened to all and every detail and thought of the planning and rehearsals, the hard work that has to be behind all such pageantry. I felt too I shuddered at the 'litter' to be cleared away.[47]

While many reported excitement over the day, or being won over by the brilliance of the festivities or the gravitas of the proceedings, others were unmoved and voiced their criticisms of monarchy and/or the extravagance of royal events. Some mused over the value of the monarchy as well as the pomp and circumstance of royal occasions. This sixty-year-old married male lecturer was unimpressed:

Some conversation regarding the mentality of those who waited overnight in such weather; my wife said she would have liked to have seen it as she would never have another chance to see all that pageantry, but would not pay such a price. I observed that in my lifetime I had missed three coronations without perceptible ill effects, and had better things to do with my time than to support this commercialised racket.[48]

The following retired schoolmaster listened in but did not let the day's events intrude too much upon his day:

I did exactly the same things on 2nd June last as I do on any other day, except that I was obliged to have my mid-day meal at home instead of getting it out, as the shop was closed.

I got up at 6.30, bathed, shaved and lighted the fire and had breakfast. I never went out in the forenoon except to buy a newspaper. I did the household chores, as usual, and listened to the Radio until the Service started in Westminster Abbey when I switched off as I find all religious services extremely distasteful. Just as I was getting my lunch ready the phone rang and it was a friend whom I had not heard of, or seen, for nearly 5 years. He was staying in Edinburgh and for some reason wanted to come and see me. I think he imagined I should ask him to stay with me. I did nothing of the sort and said I was busy and rang off. I had fruit, bread and cheese for lunch followed by a cup of black coffee . . . I thought all the fuss about the Coronation was extremely silly, vulgar and ostentatious. Exactly the sort of thing I detest. So far as I know, I thought the same thoughts, did the same things, and behaved in exactly the same way as I do on any other day. About 4 o'clock a friend came for tea. He, like myself, was fed up with the whole Coronation business. I know so few people that it is hard for me to tell you what other people thought about the Coronation, but my charwoman said it was all a lot of drivel and a great waste of money. In the evening I went to a Coronation Concert which I enjoyed. The Queen's Speech and Mr. Churchill's were relayed to the Hall. It was the first time I had ever heard Mr Churchill speak. At least it was the first time I had ever heard a whole speech of his. It was the sort of stuff one would have expected him to say. The same applies to the Queen's Speech. Quite harmless, but quite meaningless. Just a string of common-place sentences. I thought her voice quite untrained. I mean I had, perhaps, imagined she would speak like a well-trained actress. She didn't. But she spoke distinctly and, after all, the main thing was that everyone should hear what she had to say. Which, I should think, apart from the deaf, everyone did.[49]

The day became an occasion for this 67-year-old married female to observe the day's events and ponder the monarchy:

Even on Coronation Eve there was an atmosphere of unusual tension, of the kind one feels just before going abroad, or on the eve of an examination, starting a fresh job, or taking part in a special performance. One felt a blend of the feelings common to all times of crisis, together with some of the excitement belonging to Christmas Eve . . .

I had envisaged the day as a sort of ordinary Bank Holiday, as far as I was concerned, and had planned odd jobs, such as cutting the hedge. But these just didn't come off. In any case the weather was not favourable for gardening, but apart from that, there was something compelling about the day which seemed to carry one along as irresistibly as the surge of an outgoing tide.

About 11 am I turned on the Radio. I can lay claim to no great transports of loyal emotion, but the service had beauty and dignity, the music being for me especially impressive. I did not listen to quite all of it.

About 1 pm I went out to see if many people were abroad. A few rather furtive looking cyclists were on the main road, possibly enjoying the unwonted freedom from traffic. Some cars went by at intervals, though much less frequently than usual. The Common was almost deserted. A few keepers were at work, but apart from them I saw only two fathers wheeling prams, and a man exercising an elderly dog . . .

I had had various invitations to see the evening television broadcasts so at 8 pm I took a visitor from the country to see the shortened Abbey ceremony and the following newsreel, and to hear the Queen's speech.

Comparing Sound Radio with Television, I found the former more impressive though the latter certainly did not lack interest. I could not help thinking however, in common with the experience of others, that the unavoidable dwarfing of the screen could not but detract from the splendour of the occasion, reduced as it was to the proportions of a marionette or puppet show, conveying an atmosphere of unreality.

My thoughts during the day were more for the waiting crowds out in the wet, than for the pomp and circumstance of the Queen's progress. So far as appearances went, the heavens did not smile on the occasion. Had the sun shone no doubt this would have been acclaimed as its due recognition, as Queen's weather. As things were nobody seemed to suggest that the converse held good, that the Heavens were in mourning. But this is perhaps a curmudgeonly thought for a day of national rejoicing . . . But apart from the urge to see the show, and get the best view, it is incomprehensible to me that so many were willing to endure so much discomfort and misery. Why this enthusiasm for a social set-up, of which the Monarchy is the Peak, which in no substantial way benefits them? – A social order which puts the emphasis on Birth and Position rather than on Brains and achievement? Perhaps it is just that the Monarch has existed so long as the Established Order that their acceptance of it is instinctive as an inevitable factor in their lives. Or perhaps they find their satisfaction in realising vicariously the triumphs and splendours of High Estate, in the enjoyment at second hand of the sumptuous fare, and the splendid trappings of others.

Though the presentation of the Abbey ceremonial did not lack beauty and dignity, underlying my appreciation of this I was conscious of a sense of resentment, not only for the extravagance of the whole proceeding, the loss of time for much-needed work, and the general dislocation, but mainly because of the atmosphere of something near idolatry. Is anyone human being, of however exalted rank, entitled to so much adulation and homage? – symbolic though it may be? I found especially, the spectacle of the kneeling Archbishops somehow distasteful.

The outstanding fact which cannot be ignored, however, is the will of the people as a whole; they like it. The day for most people was a happy one – in which the peace and goodwill of Christmas day seemed to be combined with the spirit of co-operation of the War years. This spirit of Unity is undoubtedly good, but must there always be a state of emergency or some special national event to evoke it? If only this spirit could be used constructively in everyday life, to campaign against its ills, what a really wondrous new age might be the result . . .

Royal personages seem to win their laurels with a minimum of effort or actual merit. Their role is fool-proof. They really have no need to DO; they only have to BE – just themselves, to win acclamation. The only price they have to pay is that of frequent boredom, and fatigue. A smile becomes a miracle, the most banal utterance is treasured as if it were a gen of scintillating wit, the use of a nick-name is front-page news. Their success transcends that of the greatest genius, the most brilliant actor, musician or statesman. When one thinks of the long strivings of genius, often never recognised at all, one is just overcome by the preposterous unfairness of it all.[50]

5

Townsend Affair 1955

In November 1955, Mass-Observation issued what would be its last official panel directive until the Mass Observation Project began in 1981. Not counting the correspondence collected for the Coronation in 1953, four years had passed since the last directive was sent to the panel. Since the late 1940s, and especially after 1949 when it became a limited company, Mass-Observation became increasingly involved in using its methods for market analysis and directives were issued with less regularity than before.[1] Observers were told in the letter accompanying the November 1955 Directive that the organization was busy researching commercial and industrial issues, but events in the autumn of 1955 spurred Mass-Observation to reach out once again to the panel. 'Two Coronations and an Abdication are in our files,' the letter explained, 'and we feel it essential that this most recent royal crisis should not go unrecorded.'[2]

The royal crisis that captured the attention of Mass-Observation and the press – British and foreign – was the question of whether Princess Margaret would marry royal courtier Group Captain Peter Townsend. Townsend was a commoner and a good deal older than the young Princess – sixteen years her senior – but he was also a dashing war hero who acquitted himself bravely during the Battle of Britain and became a favourite of the King and his family after his posting to the royal household as equerry in 1944. With the King's death in 1952, Townsend featured ever more actively in the lives of the Queen Mother and Princess Margaret. Concerns about age and rank may have been surmountable – all accounts suggest that the Queen and the Queen Mother were fond of Townsend and keen to support Margaret's happiness – but Townsend was a divorcee and the Church of England rejected divorce and remarriage while one's spouse was still living.

Townsend was granted a divorce as an 'innocent party' and given custody to his two children on the grounds that his wife had committed adultery; however, remarriage to a member of the royal family was nearly impossible. Since the British monarch is the head of the Church of England, the Queen could not support the marriage without precipitating a major crisis for the monarchy. Further, Margaret was third in line to the throne; should tragedy befall the Queen and her children, the young Prince Charles and Princess Anne, those who advised the Queen shuddered to think that the next sovereign might be Mrs Townsend and her consort, the divorced Mr Townsend.

Even if the Queen wished her sister happy, the question of Princess Margaret's marriage was a constitutional matter and the Queen had to consider the Royal Marriages Act of 1772, which stated that a member of the royal family under the age of twenty-five could not marry without the consent of the sovereign, and such decisions were to be discussed with the government. Nonetheless, when Townsend and Princess Margaret approached the Queen and Queen Mother about their relationship weeks before Elizabeth II's Coronation, it seems that they were not discouraged.[3]

Though the situation was complicated, Princess Margaret must have felt that the atmosphere was at least somewhat favourable, for after the Coronation service, the couple were seen by an American journalist in a 'half-embrace', followed by a loving gesture in which the Princess brushed away a piece of fluff from Townsend's uniform.[4] The New York Daily News *broke the story several days after the Coronation, which brought on indignation by* The People, *which strenuously denied the possibility that the Princess was in love with a divorcee and howled that 'the good name of the Royal Family, a distinguished Court servant and Britain itself [was] dragged through the mire'.[5] As the story developed in June and July, it seemed that the relationship was, indeed, a distinct possibility. Aneurin Bevan's weekly,* Tribune, *came out in support of the marriage and called out the hypocrisy of the British cabinet for standing in the way, since some cabinet members – namely Anthony Eden – had recently divorced and remarried.[6] In July, the* Daily Mirror *polled its readership and found that a whopping 96 per cent of those who participated in the poll supported the marriage. The poll brought condemnation down upon the paper from a number of fronts, including the Press Council, which admitted 'the great interest of the public in the lives of members of the Royal family' but 'strongly deprecate [the poll] as contrary to the best traditions of British journalism'.[7]*

With the story breaking in the media, the situation became ever more complicated for the couple and after some palace intrigue, Townsend was posted to Brussels. The hope was that time and distance would help the couple see reason – or, at least, kick the can down the road until the time when Margaret, as per the Royal Marriages Act, could counter the Queen's objection at the age of twenty-five. With Townsend packed safely away on the continent, the press quieted down until the spring of 1955, when a possible hasty marriage in Scotland was mooted in the Sunday Pictorial. *Soon after, another newspaper reported that Townsend had suggested he might run away into exile with a 'certain lady', a comment he strongly denied.[8] After a few weeks of speculation, the British press was once again quiescent on the matter, until days before Margaret's twenty-fifth birthday in August, when questions began to arise as to her potential decision. Answers would have to wait until mid-October, when both the Princess and Townsend met in London. The tabloids exploded with the story, urging the Princess to decide, while reporters and photographers hounded the couple wherever they went. Amid much speculation, Princess Margaret finally announced her decision not to continue the relationship on 31 October. The papers carried her announcement the next day:*

> I have been aware that subject to my renouncing my rights of succession it might have been possible for me to contract a civil marriage, but mindful of the Church's teaching that Christian marriage is indissoluble and conscious of my duty to the Commonwealth, I have resolved to put these considerations before any others.[9]

The announcement went on to assert that the decision was fully her own and that Townsend's 'unfailing support and devotion' gave her strength throughout the ordeal.[10] The reaction in the British press tended towards support and sympathy for the difficulties Margaret endured and appreciation for her personal sacrifice. The Manchester Evening News *was indicative of the response: 'A deep sense of sympathy and admiration follows Princess Margaret's announcement . . . She has made a hard choice with courage and a sense of duty that sets a shining example.'[11]*

The rules were undoubtedly different for the royal family: royal duties and obligations cut across individual choice and inclination, tradition was expected to prevail over modernity and individualism and adherence to a higher sense of morality and conduct than was expected of others in British society was paramount. Princess Margaret's struggle was emblematic of the nation in that moment: the 'royal crisis' played out within a larger landscape of social change, and intense anxiety about that change, in post-war Britain.

Responses to the November 1955 directive highlight attitudes towards the British royalty and notions of its role in British society, demonstrating how, for instance, the ways in which the Windsor Brand qualities of royal self-sacrifice and duty played out in the minds of the British public. But the directive goes far beyond mere royal scandal. Given the nature of the affair, notions of love and marriage animated directive responses, as did anxieties regarding divorce and the state of marriage. In addition to Observers' feelings about Princess Margaret's decision, the directive plumbed attitudes about religious leaders' responses to the crisis, providing insights into the decline of established religion in Britain. The directive also sought to gather statistics on religious and political affiliation, which can assist in understanding Observers' responses. Finally, the directive sought Observers' opinions on the actions of the British press over the reporting of the affair. The reactions to this question engage with questions of royal prerogative, privacy and the newsworthiness of the royal family in the age of celebrity. Unrelated to the Townsend Affair, but very much a part of the landscape

1. How do you yourself feel about Princess Margaret's decision not to marry Group Captain Townsend?

2. On the whole, do you think she has done the right thing or not, or don't you know?

3. (If Yes or No): And why exactly would you say that?

4a. How do you feel about the way the newspapers as a whole have handled the matter of Princess Margaret and Group Captain Townsend?

b. And how about the religious leaders?

5a. Do you think these events are likely to affect peoples' feelings towards the rest of the Royal family in any way at all?

b. (If Yes): In what sort of way do you think it may do this?

6a. When did you last go to church?

b. (If within last 6 months): What denomination was the church?

7. And which political party do you most sympathise with yourself?

8. How do you feel about the advent of commercial television? We should like to have your opinions on any specific programmes or advertisements you have seen.

FIGURE 3 *Directive Questionnaire, November 1955, page 2. Mass-Observation Archive, University of Sussex Special Collections.*

of British culture in the mid-twentieth century, the directive's final question provides researchers with information regarding opinions about commercial television (Figure 3).[12]

Observations

Over 230 Observers responded to the directive, and while the attitudes towards Princess Margaret's decision were mixed, a majority of Observers supported the Princess's decision, often echoing attitudes published in the press. Observers often employed emotional expressions that were also seen in media reporting, expressing 'sympathy', 'sorrow' and 'admiration' for the Princess, 'disappointment' or feeling 'angry' or 'miserable' about the decision: one Observer reported hearing a woman declare, 'I feel furiously. I'm boiling with indignation about the whole thing. I felt terribly unhappy and weighed down all yesterday, thinking of her.'[13] The heavily contested and mixed public reaction to the story 'was revealing', Claire Langhamer has argued, 'of a nation at a point of emotional transition'.[14]

Reasons for supporting Margaret's decision tended to cluster around her position as a member of the royal family. Some Observers felt 'relieved' that Margaret had done the 'right thing'. The following male, married 37-year-old master printer, expressed a common argument seen throughout the

118 REFLECTIONS ON BRITISH ROYALTY

directives that royals are, and should be, fundamentally different than other Britons:

> Partly because one tends to regard members of the Royalty as 'public' property they are in effect our servants in the realm of pomp and ceremony and no matter how much they mix with the more humbler person they can never become one of them. Frankly I don't think we would like them to become so. And so with Princess Margaret, feel that if she married Group Captain Townsend bang would go another symbol of our devotion – or respect – and so begin to crumble the very edifice they have built up and which helps to make the country so unique in this respect.[15]

Imagining royalty as a public good can also be reason for the public interest in what might ordinarily be considered private matters for private citizens. The following male, married 45-year-old cost accountant, explains his right to weigh in on the matter but takes a more cynical view of the decision, which he assumes was correct only in the fact that the Princess had no other choice. In thinking about the role of the press during the whole affair, this Observer also asserts the public's right to know about the private concerns of the royalty. In doing so, he contrasts this moment with that of the relationship between Edward VIII and twice-divorced Wallis Simpson in 1936:

> I liked the straightforward nature of her statement. The marriage of a Royal person is public business and one is entitled to form one's own opinions as a member of the public which supports the Royal family and is entitled to look to them for leadership. As far as a member of the public can tell Group Captain Townsend is a most suitable person for a Princess's Consort, having a war record for courage of the calm responsible kind. I would have thought him more suitable than the night-club habitués with whom we used to see her depicted in the papers, or than some foreign prince . . . Even if she does not marry in 5 or 10 years' time it may then be too late to produce an adequate number of lusty little princelings . . .

> The elaborate ritual fictions which surround the Royal family justify themselves by providing a personal focus for loyalty . . . and to destroy at a moment's notice one of the chief pillars of the ritualistic structure, the Crown being head of the Church, even though this pillar will have to go sooner or later, might well bring the whole lot down . . .

> I think it a good thing and an important thing that the newspapers have kept the public informed of what was going on. This contrasts very favorably with the conspiracy of secrecy about the Abdication, when the whole population were made mugs, being required to switch their assiduously fostered loyalty at a moment's notice. We got a good King,

probably a better choice than the one he replaced, but the fact remains that he was not divinely chosen, not by heredity, not by public selection or acclamation, but by the personal decision of one Stanley Baldwin made behind our backs. This time representatives of all classes of opinion were able to express their views in public and the Princess was enabled to make her decision in the light of all shades of public opinion on this matter of public concern.[16]

Others reacted favourably to the difference between Princess Margaret's behaviour and that of her uncle's, underscoring royal difference. This married 51-year-old male telephonist, who reported that he didn't think much of the story 'Until the Press made such an unholy fuss' about it, argued:

It is my contention that the Queen, her sister is overworked. This being the case it behooves other members of the Royal House to rally round and do something. If we are going to play at Kings and Queens in this country (and Empire) for heavens sake lets do it to the rules. Despite the wailing housewives and the sort of Press that panders to these subnormal types, either do the job for which we pay some £6000 a year or follow your heart and leave the country. After all a king did give up his throne for love. This is England and we do not go in for Playboy Kings or comic opera crowns.[17]

A number of Observers linked the affair with the Abdication Crisis, highlighting royal difference, for instance, this unmarried 58-year-old female:

I feel glad that the Princess has at last made a decision if only to stop the appallingly bad taste of the newspaper campaign of the last few months, the inventions, surmises, guesses and other means of filling columns and the spying of photographers. I understood that Princess Margaret is somewhat self-willed, and I wondered whether she would insist on marrying, flouting the law of the land, and of the Church, and causing turmoil not only in England but in the Commonwealth.

The Princess belongs to the royal family, and cannot behave as any ordinary girl. She is well paid for any work that she does and she should not do anything to lower moral standards. She is young, but not too young to set an example. I am glad to feel that she has shown more strength of character and loyalty to strong convictions than did Edward VIII, who, to my mind, ran away in a difficult situation, and, incidentally, was the cause of the Princess's dilemma.

In my opinion the behaviour of Townsend is most reprehensible. He is much older than the Princess, and he had already failed in a marriage, and he should have kept away from her years ago and not allowed the affair to develop. He must have known of the difficulties which would arise.[18]

This 59-year-old housewife employed similar reasoning of royal difference and highlighted an expectation that the royal family act as exemplars of family life:

Agreeably surprised. I must have misjudged her, as I have always maintained that she is too much like her Uncle Windsor, and I expected her to do as <u>she</u> wished, no matter what befell.

I think she has done the right thing. The answer to this question depends on one's conception of 'royalty'. My conception is not of a privileged family with wealth, palaces, jewels, clothes, cars, etc, etc, but of a family, the head of which is the Queen, set apart from the rest of us by the very act of Coronation. It seems to me that the rest of the family should also share in that 'apartness', which entails duties and standards not demanded from the rest of us – to such a degree, at any rate. There should not then be the slightest suspicion about their morals or their conduct – their example must be perfect. I believe, too, that laxity in marriage strikes at the root of family life, which is the only stable foundation for national life. For a princess of the Royal family to strike a blow against that foundation would have been unforgivable. Women ought to be only too thankful that she has stood out for the sanctity of marriage, even if there has been 'subtle pressure' put upon her, for women and their children are the chief sufferers from divorce which has become all too easy.

When the marriage was mooted some years ago, I was quite prepared for her to go on with it, provided she became plain Mrs. Townsend, and gave up her privileged position in the Royal family. I am still of the same opinion, and I quite expected that she would do so. I can't decide whether she didn't think 'her world well lost for love' and couldn't bear to be out of things, or whether she realised that if she gave up her Royal position she would be letting her sister down, in that she would not be able to take her share of the burden which rests on the Queen's shoulders . . . I should have had no objection to marrying Townsend had he not been a divorcé. Great emphasis has been laid on his 'innocence' in the divorce. I don't believe that there is 'innocence' on either side in these cases . . .

I feel sorry that Princess Margaret should have chosen an 'ineligible' and – something I never thought would happen – I admire her for her decision.[19]

Royal difference was also on the mind of others, who connected the affair with Hollywood and an Americanized, sensationalized view of romantic love, as did this married 42-year-old male architect:

TOWNSEND AFFAIR 1955

In the existing circumstances it was the only thing that she could do without damaging the traditions of 'duty first'. One can regret very much the circumstances in which all royalty find themselves. As long as the British royal family is set up as the syntheses of proper living and an ideal of a family these tragic decisions will have to be made from time to time . . .

I think it is right. To do the other thing would be to accept the America film ideology that love is the only thing that matters. If the American idea spreads widely it can smash society, destroying all normal sense of duties and loyalty to social unit or nation.[20]

For the following 45-year-old single primary teacher, it was difficult to ascertain the facts from the overwrought media reporting, but, she felt, it was likely the best decision overall. This Observer felt that the incident may undermine the distance between common and royal:

I suppose I would say that considering the circumstances she has been wise, but as I do not know exactly what has happened it is difficult to decide. It will never be easy for a member of the Royal Family to please himself or herself and I would say acceptance of one's lot is the most sensible solution. It doesn't seem to me to be her task to alter the situation but the duty of the country as a whole through Parliament. The Church should not be able to exercise such power . . .

I think the newspapers have 'played up' the situation to such an extent that in many cases they have alienated sympathy as people grew weary of seeing photographs and headlines on the front pages. They tried to outdo each other in sensationalism. This was particularly true of the Sunday papers. When they had no news they made up some. This went on far too long, largely of course because no statement was forthcoming from official quarters, and once embarked upon a race, the papers seemed unable to stop . . .

It may bring the Royal Family down to a more ordinary level. So many people have been inclined to think of them as 'different', to put them on a pedestal and it may give them rather a shock to realise that they have the same problems as their own neighbours and themselves. On the other hand it may promote some sympathy for them. Other people may realise that they are real, and would wish them to be able to live a more natural life.[21]

The following married 35-year-old male philosopher believed that the episode should undermine the difference between royalty and ordinariness:

I admire the decision but I think it was wrong, it will do good but, that facet should not be eligible for consideration.

I am speaking something in the light of a paradox, but, what I am driving at is this: Princess Margaret is a human being, a delightful person and a member of the most wonderful family in the world, she is in the line of succession to the British Throne. All these things (with the exception of the human being portion) are not the burden of the common folk, we can do as we like. Princess Margaret however, although endowed with the same feelings, emotions and abilities, cannot under the present system, be as free as we are. It is said often that what is good for the goose is good for the gander, one might well ask 'Why should Princess Margaret be denied the freedom of the common peoples'. The answer is 'The Church' 'The State' and the 'Religious and Traditional claptrap of dictatorial idiots'. The system should be altered, Monarchy should be able to marry whom they please, they should be allowed to follow the desires of their own hearts and the Acts, Rules, Regulations, Protocol and other traditional rubbish should be taken down off the shelve and rejuvenated to measure up to the modern concept of life and living.[22]

Others expressed anxieties about social change and the risks inherent in such modern individualism, feeling that Princess Margaret's decision was an important expression of conscience and example of duty in a society that seemed to have lost sight of such values. This 34-year-old single male cleric weighed in on the matter:

I am thrilled and delighted at the decision.

First, because she has recognised essential Christian teaching on the indissolubility of marriage; secondly, because she has put this duty before her private wishes and inclinations; thirdly, because in her exalted position her decision will carry great weight with many people in humbler walks of life, and is therefore a big step forward in reviving a sense of duty in a generation which has been in danger of forgetting the concept . . .

When all the fuss has died down, I think there is likely to be increased admiration for the Royal Family as a whole. Unlike King Edward VIII who put personal inclination before his duty. Here is a young and popular member of the Royal Family whose sense of duty is paramount. This is bound to carry weight with thoughtful people, and will gradually permeate to others as well. The dignified restraint of all the other members of the Family, too, is bound to reflect to their credit in due course.[23]

This married 41-year-old male school teacher agreed:

An excellent decision. Probably very hard to make. The Princess deserves our sympathy and prayers but has without question acted wisely, bravely and rightly.

Marriage vows are far too lightly regarded today, the same attitude is apparent in other ways, 'An Englishman's word is his bond' appears all too often to be true only as long as it is not difficult to keep a promise. Our stock of fortitude seems to have been used up during the war and we are now far too anxious for ease in every way. The Princess has publicly and dramatically (though this drama was not I believe her choice, but forced on her by newspapers) made a stand for keeping promises and displaying fortitude and she has shown that these are linked with the Christian Faith. All this is good. Keeping promises, showing fortitude, and realising that Christianity is a demanding faith calling for strength from its adherents. I greatly admire her for what she has done.[24]

The following 64-year-old single female retired civil servant agreed but showed some flexibility in thinking about divorce:

I was very glad to hear of Princess Margaret's decision. I admired her courage, felt that she had upheld the traditions of our royal family in putting what she conceived to be her duty before personal satisfaction and I felt deep sympathy with her in having to make such a difficult choice – and in the sense of loss which she must be feeling. It would be hard enough for any girl, but must be much harder for her, with all the publicity and no respite from public life . . .

I do think she has done the right thing. Quite apart from my personal views on divorce and remarriage in general (and I believe that except in special circumstances it should not be [allowed]) what might be right for any ordinary person would not in the present state of law and custom be right or a Princess. It would have caused many difficulties, probably 'wrangling' of rules to get out of them; it would also have set a bad example (and be claimed as justification) by the many people who nowadays consider that 'right' is what one desires – and that personal satisfaction should not be sacrificed to any ideal. Now instead Princess Margaret has given an example and encouragement to all who are trying to uphold the primary claims of duty.[25]

The earlier mention of 'wrangling' points to a common theme throughout the responses, which underscores an appreciation of the constitutional and democratic nature of the British royalty, recognizing the power which might have been wielded to please a member of the royal family. While royalty were clearly set apart in the public imagination, restraint was also key and underscored the limits of difference in a democracy.

Other Observers supported Margaret's decision, even if they did not personally agree with Church doctrine or divorce. A 64-year-old Observer who gave her occupation as, 'In addition to being a married woman, which is an occupation in itself, I am a RD Councillor, Parish Councillor, and general

odd-jobber to my husband who is a poultry-farmer and a St. Dunstaner',
saw the matter in this way:

> Princess Margaret's decision not to marry Group Captain Townsend is
> entirely her own affair, and it is an impertinence for other people, who
> are not her personal friends, and have no access to her mind, to have
> 'feelings' about what she does or does not do. Interest, of course, in so
> charming and popular a Princess there is bound to be, but for heaven's
> sake let the vulgar public now leave the poor girl alone.
>
> Of course she has done the right thing, <u>given her personal beliefs and her
> principles</u>.
>
> Although I do not personally happen to agree with the Church's teaching
> on divorce (or indeed on a great many other questions, mainly doctrinal),
> I recognise that Princess Margaret does. She is a devout and believing
> member of the Church of England. Given such beliefs, what other course
> could she take, whatever it costs her personally? . . .
>
> I think the prestige of Princess Margaret herself and of the whole Royal
> Family will be enormously increased as the result of a young woman of
> 25 being brave enough to put principle above personal desire. At least she
> has saved the Royal Family from falling to the level of film stars.
>
> I detest the way in which the cheap press has handled this matter. It has
> been not merely impertinent, but abominably cruel. Anyone who thinks
> otherwise should ask herself or himself 'How would I like it if my young
> and pretty daughter were faced with a problem such as this, and the
> whole world gaped and goggled at her while she made up her mind?'[26]

*A married 55-year-old male inspector disagreed with the Church on divorce
but again fell back on royal difference in the matter:*

> If a Royal family is to be maintained – a question on which I have an
> open mind – it is imperative that its members should have 'royal' not
> 'commoner' standards of behaviour . . .
>
> The Royal Family are leading members of the Church of England and
> profess loyalty to its principles. These include the belief that marriage is
> indissoluble. I do not share that belief but I do not think that it is right
> for a member of that Church to contract a marriage which the Church
> condemns. Apart from Captain Townsend having a divorced wife still
> alive the marriage was an obviously unsuitable one. I doubt if Princesses
> normally make suitable wives for commoners. I do not think marriages
> between men over 40 and girls of 25 are normally successful. It is rarely
> wise for a woman to marry below her. The Princess would have had to
> give up her position in the limelight and retire into obscurity. Once the
> novelty had worn off I am doubtful if she would have liked her new role

TOWNSEND AFFAIR 1955   125

...

I disagree with the Church of England's views on the remarriage of divorced persons but I don't see how the religious leaders in view of their beliefs could have done other than oppose the marriage.

It will probably lessen the respect in which the Royal Family is held, while I regard the decision not to marry as right and think it most unfortunate that Princess Margaret allowed the situation to arise. She was wise not to choose the wrong course but she would have been much wiser if the need for such a choice had not been required.[27]

The following unmarried 63-year-old retired schoolmaster, who responded 'Couldn't care' to the question of how he felt about the matter, also cited royal difference as his reason for thinking Princess Margaret's decision appropriate; his answers, however, are more cynical, pulling down the veil of royal mystique.

As we have a Royal Family which has got itself raised to positively idolatrous heights, they must observe some sort of conventional behaviour to justify the immense amount of money they cost . . .

Considering all the mysterymongering the Royal Family itself made of the whole matter, such lunatic behaviour could, in present-day conditions, only result in the way the newspapers, as a whole, reacted.

The religious leaders handled the matter in their usual humbugging manner. A lot of cant and hypocrisy.

. . . I should think Princess Margaret's reputation, in most people's minds, will be enhanced. She will be looked upon as a martyr. The Duke of Edinburgh, who is supposed to have been very much against the match, and who is, I should think, much disliked by quite a few people, will be looked upon as a prig. Otherwise the Royal Family will escape any sort of censure or praise.[28]

Nella Last, a 66-year-old housewife from Barrow-in-Furness, regarded the situation on personal terms, identifying with the connection between the young Margaret and the dashing older man:

as one who has had a lot of 'interference' one way or another by others, I'd have said feelingly, 'let her go her own way.' However, as the papers seem to print running commentary, with <u>no</u> regard for privacy, I grew more and more annoyed. She should have been well spanked – though 16 <u>is</u> too old for that perhaps – when she developed a 'crush' on a married man with children and are so much older. On the other hand, few 'sensitive' girls in their teens haven't idealized some male – my own at 15 or so was for a fanatical curate, who later gave his life and health in the mission fields. He was poor, did a lot of sick visiting and passionately loved flowers – thought they gave a message of hope. When I look back to the way I ruthlessly plundered relatives and friends gardens, I smile, but while it lasted it was a 'flame'. Why didn't the Family see this 'pash' as girls used to call it, and was it wise to put a halo on him by banishment. Yes, she did do the right thing at a belated hour when she had made herself and family food for gossiping tongues throughout the world . . .

What else could she have done? When she finally made the decision, circumstances were exactly the same. All her wishful thinking wouldn't and couldn't alter the fact of Townsend's divorce and the fact that the Queen as head of the Church couldn't countenance a marriage. Margaret has the same way of feeling 'above the law' that took her uncle the Duke of Windsor into exile.

Usually a supporter of the royalty, the episode shook Nella's confidence in the difference between the royal and the ordinary:

Candidly speaking at the present moment I feel slight contempt where before, I'd have said I had 'admiration'. To see 'our fairy princess' could act like a spoilt adolescent at 25, and be let do so has shaken me somewhat.[29]

While the foreign and British tabloid press made much of a romantic love match, some Observers questioned this narrative and believed marriage would have meant unhappiness for the Princess. These responses lean towards an emotional attachment with the Princess and her plight. Townsend, as the worldly and older man, usually suffered much criticism in these responses, as is seen in this 65-year-old married woman's response:

It was right. One day it will be realised (by the Princess) that she was right – apart from any religious scruples . . . Because it is always right to do right. Because I think there is a younger, fresher, real 'lover' she will meet later. If this man, Townsend, had loved her truly he would have kept right out of her way and realised that to her he was the comforter and helper in her time of stress when her father died.[30]

The following 64-year-old female regarded the matter as personal and considered her own life experience in her response. As with many Observers across the directives, royalty and celebrity were incongruous:

I have no opinion concerning Princess Margaret. I looked upon it from the start as a purely personal affair and I refuse to look upon the Royal family as film stars or such to be exclusive subjects of my conversation – in fact I hardly ever discuss them. I am ready to concede to a girl of

25 the right to decide to marry, who to marry, and a right I demanded myself at 21!

There are silly people who will persist in treating the Royal family as deities as long as they are ignorant of a Higher Being.[31]

A 41-year-old female considered the problem from all angles, citing age and the negative impact the marriage would have had on Margaret's family. She also worried about Margaret giving up the world she knew for a man this Observer was uncertain loved Margaret. In the end, this Observer concluded, 'She has taken the course I think I should have done.'[32]

The following 63-year-old married man engaged with the couple's situation as if he were an uncle, imparting advice:

Entirely approving. Not being personally acquainted with either party, my opinion, if demanded, can only be on the most general lines and with all reservations. On the score of age the success of the marriage is not too easy. As for social differences, I gather that Townsend is of satisfactory stock and probably – as a person – vastly preferable to most of the Socialites Pr. Margaret seems to have chiefly met. Townsend would have required great tact and modesty and I would have been sorry – for him. But all these considerations are entirely for the protagonists themselves. As an uncle to either I would have pointed out the difficulties which arise where there is any great difference in age, tradition, social habits or outlook but ended by agreeing that goodwill, patience and affection can overcome all of these and given an avuncular blessing.

In handwriting, the Observer added to this typed response: 'Except, of course, for the . . . divorce'. *He went on to discuss his feelings about divorce:*

The difficulties in the way of such a marriage would have been many but I am romantic (and experienced) enough to believe that a sufficient degree of 'Love' could conquer all these. But the divorce objection is, in my eyes, on a different footing. This is not a matter of taste or of convenience but of honour. And honour has precedence. This is old-fashioned I know – but – 'Think not that Morality is Ambulatory'.

In the remainder of this Observer's response, he chastised the Queen's management of the affair in a diatribe that questioned women's ability to rule:

I <u>do</u>, however, think that the 'Palace' . . . meaning the group of persons (if any) who advise the Queen in private handled the situation badly. My own private deductions (all guesswork) are these.

This has been entirely a woman's affair. The Queen, as Queen and as elder sister must have the final authority. I imag[in]e the whole affair as entirely between the Queen, her mother, and her sister. How trying, as a person, P. Marg. may have been, but from observation of not dissimilar situations in everyday life, I expect she was very trying indeed . . .

But I do consider that, when the balloon blew up, two years ago or so, the situation was handled very badly indeed . . . that here the responsibility rests on the three women, and chiefly the two elder ones . . . The Duke of E., who is no fool, would certainly confine himself to the barest minimum of expressed opinion and a complete refusal of decision. As a husband, and as a Consort he could also be counted out . . .

'When a woman kills a chicken

Dynasties and Empires sicken.'

'There was an old woman who loved animals so much and had a heart so tender than when, on one occasion, she absolutely had to kill a chicken herself she went about it so gently that she took an hour over the doing, and when she had finished it had to be given to the dog.'

That was my breakfast-table summing up.

I do not think that Churchill (if consulted) would have advised such tactics. In my opinion, whatever and whomever they consulted, the management has all the marks of having been entirely in the hands of the Queen and her Mother. As mothers and elder sisters often do, they underestimated the tenacity of will of the younger sister. With the best of intentions they tried to kill the chicken by inches . . . instead of saying, 'My dear girl! You can't marry him he's got a wife already and we don't accept divorce.' They went about it the other way on.

My reason approves the result but deplores the methods used. My sympathies are entirely with the Princess and especially with poor Townsend.[33]

Some respondents answered that they had no way of assessing the situation and therefore felt unable to answer whether Princess Margaret's decision was the 'right' one. Observers who felt unable to respond with certainty about the decision often cited the fact that their knowledge of the matter was refracted through press reporting of the matter. The following 49-year-old single female was uncertain about the Princess's real feelings on the matter but questioned the double standard that seemed to apply to Margaret but not to Anthony Eden:[34]

In spite of myself I admire Princess Margaret for making a martyr of herself but I don't think she should have been faced with only the 2 courses. The antitheses were quite artificial. I think she could so to speak have had a morganatic marriage and kept her jobs. I don't see why we can admire a divorced and remarried Prime Minister and not a

Princess married to a divorced man. I just don't know whether she has whether she has done the right thing <u>for her</u>. This depends on her own feelings and her motives for acting as she did.

I say this because I don't believe in absolute rightness and wrongness of certain actions considered apart from their context. Whether an act is right depends (for me) on the circumstances and the attitude and motives of the action. I find that most acts are not clearly right or wrong (it would be simpler if they were), but the lesser of many evils or the least bad in the circumstances – a matter of calculating the consequences.[35]

Many who disagreed with Margaret's decision cited the importance of romantic love and individual agency, expressing concern that undue pressure was put upon Margaret to decide against personal happiness. As in many of the responses, regardless of their position on Margaret's decision, veiled or outright criticism of the monarchy is common. One 48-year-old married shipping clerk wrote, 'I feel that she has been <u>coerced into refusal</u>.' The Observer went on to explain why he disagreed with the decision:

I) Everyone, Royalty included, should be perfectly free as regards to his or her private life. II) If Princess Margaret had become a private citizen, it would not have been a great loss to the community, and would have been a certain amount of financial gain. III) Laws regarding Royalty, and perhaps Royalty itself, seem an anachronism in 1955.[36]

The following 80-year-old widow also disagreed and criticized the Church and the Queen for their roles in the affair:

The papers said Princess Margaret showed great courage, but she would have shown <u>much</u> greater courage if she had stuck to her guns and held out against great odd and married the one she truly loves . . . She is only a very weak third from the crown and had no right to give up her chance of a happy marriage . . .

It made me wild to read excerpts from peoples all around the world. Excerpts, if you please, practically only from speeches by Bishop this or that, this Dignitary from Rome, etc etc. I believe that our religious leaders of the Church of England saw the red light some time ago and have sold millions of pounds worth of property, against the day when disestablishment is in force – the whole status of the C of E is a farce, when high places are given by a Prime Minister who had the courage to marry again, while his first wife is alive, and who like Mrs. Townsend, was divorced and has married the man with whom she went away. Not all C of E clergymen are so hide bound by the laws of the A of Canterbury, who says they are Christ's laws. I would gladly

130 REFLECTIONS ON BRITISH ROYALTY

marry the lovers. I have only come across two women who disagree with me – one a church bound devotee and the other who holds the Royal Family sacrosanct and Margaret must'nt lower herself by marrying a commoner . . .

It's selfish of the Queen to demand (if not in words) that her sister should give up the man she loves, in order to assist her in the various duties which devolve on Royalty – suppose Margaret died; she and the Queen Mother would have to do without her help. No one has the right to demand such a sacrifice . . . Could not Peter Townsend be made a Duke? What's to hinder? He is a gentleman and I wonder whether all our dukes are as well bred? and not just very wealthy.[37]

A 62-year-old married man who had served in colonial administration and was now a lecturer and author felt that Margaret should have followed in the footsteps of her uncle and let the British public down when she bent to pressure from above:

I assume in this answer that the princess is or was seriously in love with Townsend; but where such powerful forces exist to prevent the public from knowing the whole truth, it is important to remember that good reports are just as suspect as bad . . .

Nevertheless . . . I regard her decision as indicating lack of moral courage. In saying this, I ought perhaps to allow further for her 'conditioning', an education aimed consistently at making her submissive to counsels provided that they come from certain, viz., royalist and ecclesiastical. I greatly regret her decision, but can hardly say that I was disappointed, as I expected little else; but my mind goes back to the time of the abdication of Edward VIII, – the only king for the past hundred years who came near to creating some respect or the throne; then a friend of mine remarked to me: A victory for the powers of darkness! . . .

To make the institution of royalty palatable to those not readily suggestible and requiring some logical reason in support of existing political systems, it is usually urged that the king is above politics or partisanship, a focus on loyalty or those who agree in little else. The princess's decision, which is not hers alone but unquestionably that of the royal family as a whole, gives the lie to this fiction; it shows the monarchy to be technically neutral, but neutral against the majority of the British people, let alone the Commonwealth as a whole, who do not share the funny ideas of the Churches of England and of Rome; it proves beyond doubt that neither the churches concerned, nor the royal family, are anything but hypocritical in their adherence to the principles of democracy, they having made no effort whatsoever to ascertain the views of the country generally . . . The princess failed in her duty to the country and to humanity in that she had an enviable opportunity of standing up publicly for common sense and kindliness, but through superstition and weakness gave instead an example of phariseism . . .

It may induce some socialists to reflect seriously that no progress towards democracy or socialism is possible until we democratise the monarchy, which is probably cheaper than getting rid of it.[38]

Naomi Mitchison agreed that a different outcome to the affair would have meant a positive remaking of the monarchy:

I wasn't interested at first, but after the Times leader, and after realising how much was actually due to the revolting stuffiness of the Queen (this being based on 'informed' Fleet Street gossip) I became more interested and pro the marriage, though I felt they were both rather stupid people, but Princess M at least more human than her sister. No, I think she should have stuck out. Because it would have been a step towards the democratisation of the royal family, on the Scandinavian and Dutch lines, which seem to be the only reasonable ones. I am slightly in favour of a monarchy, because it is more fun and gaily coloured than a President, but not if it is going to assume semi-divinity, of the kind which appears to suit the present Queen. She seems to have put very severe pressure on her sister, but I think if the sister had stood out against it, she would have gained in popularity and so, in the end, would all the family. She could certainly have gone on doing useful things (if opening bazaars and reviewing troops <u>are</u> useful things) . . .

Muggeridge's article in the New Statesman summed it up . . .[39]

I am sure this will make the Queen less popular. People will say she is a heartless bitch and quite right too. If her sister was a horse she would have kinder feelings.[40]

The following female Observer expressed similar sentiments regarding democratization and modernity:

It seems to me to be a difficult and complex question. In my opinion divorce seems to be completely rational where good cause for divorce exists – and once divorced there can be no valid reason against re-marriage. Following from this it therefore appears that the Church's attitude towards both marriage and divorce is irrational . . .

My personal feeling of course is that it is highly regrettable that in the 20th century we should be overruled by medieval ideas. The C of England and the RC Church simply fail in the 20th century to understand the fundamentals of life. They hamper progress in refusing to recognize new sets of values, they bring discredit on themselves which reflects adversely on the Royal Family. Some people say the whole affair adds prestige to the Royal Family, but many more only see that they are hidebound by tradition and are failing to be progressive. The fact that he is 15 years older than P. Margaret is the one and only reason against the marriage . . .

She should have taken this opportunity to break down some of the out-of-date conventions which surround Church and State. This would have been a democratic move in a democratic age. She has clung to medievalism.[41]

One married 50-year-old accountant felt Margaret's decision 'discreditable' because 'she either submitted to ecclesiastical and Court influence knowing that she was thwarting her own conscience, or else she wouldn't sacrifice £15000 a year'. *This Observer also felt that the royalty enjoyed being treated as 'Hollywood stars'.*[42] *The following 55-year-old housewife from Leeds felt that Townsend was at least as good as any other upper-class or royal option and questioned political and religious arguments against the marriage:*

To me it seems that the arguments for the marriage outweigh the arguments against it. He seems to be a decent man – true he is not a peer or a member of any royal family, but once you allow your Princes and Princesses to marry anyone who is not of the blood royal, I can't see why they forbid marriage to a man whom even the Times describes as a very gallant gentleman . . . If there had been a Swedish Prince available, no one would have objected. But if one is going to be snobby I imagine Townsend's ancestors were a cut above the founders of the present royal house of Sweden. The divorce of course is a pity . . .

I don't see that the succession matters either. As things stand Margaret is third but if she renounced her claim to the throne and Charles and Ann came to a sticky finish before providing heirs there are a whole tribe of Gloucesters and Kents who would no doubt be able to grace the throne as adequately as Margaret. And even if she didn't, I feel sure that Townsend would be an improvement on the Duke of Edinburgh. The only thing I can see against the marriage is that a lot of stuffy but important people object – some on religious grounds, some on political – it might hurt the dignity of the Throne and weaken the Commonwealth. I can see their point, but, I just don't think they are going about it the right way. If you treat them as film stars and fashion models one minute, then as good democrats 'just like you and me – or rather I' and then switch over to a high priestess and vestal virgin mumbo jumbo you may be pleasing some of the people all the time but you aren't achieving dignity . . .

I may be dense but honestly I can't see how marrying a divorced commoner can make her unable to open new schools, give away prizes at the Royal College of Music, attend charity concerts and go through all the dull civic chores that seem to be the life work of royalty nowadays. Royalty nowadays don't seem to <u>start</u> things – they just declare them open once the spade work has been done. George VI did start playing fields or boys clubs or something, and the Royal Society was started by the Stuarts and even the Prince Regent took an interest in art, but I'm dashed if the present lot do anything except getting photographed.

I don't think the events will affect people's feeling towards the rest of the Royal Family beyond deepening whatever feelings they already have. The abdication crisis was different. People felt insulted I think (though they wouldn't admit it) that their idol preferred a twice divorced woman to <u>them</u>. But though lip service is paid to the fact that she is third in succession, no one really thinks of her as the future Queen and no one I've met who thought she shouldn't marry him because of her position hasn't agreed tho' usually somewhat half-heartedly – that her renunciation doesn't <u>really</u> matter, because if worst came to the worst there are all the Gloucesters and Kents to fall back on.[43]

The following Observer, a married 63-year-old male musician, felt 'Pretty miserable, because it is not a really free decision'. He went on to disparagingly discuss religion and royalty in contemporary Britain:

I have been struck by the quoted remark of GKC,[44] that when people drop religion they take to <u>any</u> myth or object of devotion. It may be that royalty has taken the place of religion: tho' I see big snags in that argument. I am a good deal alarmed at the whole business, tho' – not seeing how to fit in with any sort of democracy we are supposed to be moving towards. I have boiled a good deal at most of the newspaper work on this business. No wonder the more realistic USA press sees how very bad ours is.

I have no words too bad for the bishops and other persons, in general: but as noted above, I hold no supernatural beliefs, and consider religion a deadly evil. I detest the power of the Church, and its fantastic connection with the State. BUT given the strict teaching of the C of E., I fully understand that its parsons could find their hearts to tell her not to marry him . . .

I wish the affair would make people think about the game; but that seems impossible. There is a deep seated myth and glamour (in the strict sense) which seems to make most people incapable of straight thinking in any matter concerning royalty. I often despair of the British because of that – among other things. A few waverers might perhaps think less about royalty, and be less inclined to revere the system; but I have no real hope of any radical change in the bemused and bewitched attitude of our people.[45]

Observations: Reflections on divorce

Divorce rates were on the rise after the war; many of those divorces were the dissolution of hasty wartime marriages, which were four times more likely to end in divorce than those couples married in the late 1930s.[46] In this section, Observers' responses engaged deeply with the question of divorce, as well as the role of religion, in deciding the outcome of the Townsend Affair.

The following divorced 47-year-old male bank cashier respected Margaret for deciding according to her 'principles' but explained his position on divorce, arguing that there are some scenarios where divorce was perfectly reasonable:

I admire her for keeping to her principles. If anyone has genuine beliefs then I admire them for sticking to them and despise them a little if they fail to live up to the standards they hold out for others, this is quite irrespective of my opinion on the validity of their principles. I am not ashamed to enjoy a drink but I should have a poor opinion of a temperance advocate who was a secret drinker. This is my view on divorce and as she, I believe freely, has decided to do what she believes right I think all the more of her for doing it. I cannot on the other hand see much Christianity in the Church of England view on divorce. I believe people should think very deeply before marrying and, having married, should do their utmost to make a go of it and remember that they too may have faults. Nevertheless being human we err and people do make bad marriages and I can see neither sense nor reason in two people making their own and other people's lives miserable by continuing to live together neither can I see any sense in either remaining lonely, single and unloved forever once the marriage has ended . . .

On divorce I consider it wrong to lay down any hard and fast rules and it is certainly dangerous to talk of 'guilty' parties. How often has a man run off after some other woman because his wife took no effort to share his pleasures or hobbies? Divorced parents may well foster juvenile delinquents and one cannot give a marriage up as one would resign from a club, but when all is said and done there are people who marry, who find themselves most unhappy and their constant bickering and strain will be equally bad for children. It is no good trying to keep a completely broken marriage going and if separation occurs I see no reason to condemn people to loneliness.

My own divorce was secured on the grounds of incurable insanity. For ten years before the divorce she had been certified and for the last two of those ten had not said one intelligent remark. What earthly point is there in keeping such a thing going?[47]

Some Observers worried that Margaret's decision would make it more difficult for ordinary Britons to secure a divorce, such as this married 43-year-old male scientist, who worried that the media's reporting 'reduced the Royal Family to the level of the cheaper sort of Hollywood star.' He wrote:

> though the spectacle of the Princess doing her duty is highly edifying, the decision is likely to make it harder rather than more difficult to get a sane legal approach to divorce in this country. It is fair enough that those who think it sinful to divorce and remarry should abstain from doing so; but it is a gross interference with personal liberty that their attitude should be reflected in the laws that apply to a majority who do not share their attitude.[48]

This 38-year-old divorced and remarried male civil servant also worried that the decision imperilled access to divorce:

> I think it is impossible to know whether she has done the right thing or not. What would be right for me (I divorced my first wife and have re-married) would not necessarily be right for her ...

> From the point of view of thousands who have re-married after divorce the decision is unfortunate in that it may be used in the future to strengthen the opposition to easier divorce. (Of course, there is the faint possibility that Princess Margaret has taken a dislike to Sir Anthony Eden and has stage-managed the whole affair to convey to him an elaborate insult. Much as I should like to think so, I doubt this.)

> Obviously to a convinced republican there can be nothing interesting in reports on the Royal Stud. I must admit, however, that I had a flicker of hope when the story went round that Princess Margaret might renounce all claims on the royal family and become a commoner. For a blissful moment I thought that her keep might become a charge upon her husband and not upon the state – but it was only wishful thinking.[49]

The following 37-year-old married male journalist took the opportunity to criticize the Church and its doctrine:

> She has put herself in the right, which is always a good thing to do ... My views on the church are on the whole anti-conventional. The marriage vows are ridiculous. Solomon is not excluded from the Bible because of his number of wives. Divorce should not be regarded as a crime, either by church or state ...

> Religious leaders acted with the stuffy pomp and self-righteous sanctimony that can be expected of them. Heaven, I fear, will be a very dreary place.[50]

136   REFLECTIONS ON BRITISH ROYALTY

Finally, a number of Observers made clear their position against divorce.
The following '50+' widow joked about the situation but underscored her
anxiety about the future of marriage:

> Is the glow of romance enough? Of course not – or only in novelettes.
> Would she have liked being a stepmother, and a declassee princess? Not
> Margaret!!!

> More seriously, my view is that divorce is a bad, bad thing, only to be
> considered as a remedy for utterly disastrous bad relationships. If mar-
> riage is to continue to be regarded as a life-partnership, as I profoundly
> hope in the name of decency and civilisation it is, the Royal Family must
> make their views on this clear. If they all think the law and social code
> should be altered to make any and every marriage a trial job then set up
> the new marriage-contracts now on that basis. (But can anyone imagine
> the Queen sponsoring this?) [51]

A married thirty-year-old Catholic made his position against divorce clear:

> I feel that Princess Margaret's decision not to marry Group Captain Peter
> Townsend was the only correct one for her to take. I feel very sorry for her
> and even more sorry for Peter Townsend. Nevertheless I quite definitely
> feel that any other decision would have been unthinkable. On the whole
> I definitely think that Princess Margaret has done the right thing. Because
> I am quite definite in my belief that marriage is indissoluble ('What God
> has joined together let no man put asunder') I have no other objection
> to the marriage whatsoever. I do not care that Peter Townsend is older,
> nor that he is not of the nobility. Neither do I worry about his being
> previously married (had his first wife died). What I do base my objections
> on is that, in my view, he is still married to Mrs. Townsend. [52]

A 47-year-old unmarried female expressed anxieties about the state of
modern British society in this response that underscores a sense of relief
that Margaret's decision confirmed her hopes that the royal family were the
nation's moral and religious leaders:

> I do not claim to be at all original in saying that I admire the stand which
> Princess Margaret has made in regard to Group Captain Townsend.
> Previously, I had heard that she was religious, and really cared about
> spiritual matters. I am so glad that this rumour now seems to be correct.
> I admire her very much, and respect her . . .

> I think she has done the right thing, even though it must mean much un-
> happiness for her (apart from the satisfaction of doing what she believes
> to be right.) . . .

> I think Princess Margaret has done what is right for two reasons . . . it

would seem desirable that at least some people should have the courage to refuse to countenance divorce. It would seem that many of our troubles with young people today are due to broken homes. It may be that I am reading too much into her decision. Perhaps she does accept divorce in certain circumstances, but it seems that she may take the stricter view. (I am prepared to admit that as a middle-aged spinster, I am narrow-minded about divorce. Yet I do not accept the Church's teaching without a good deal of questions. Even if I myself were ordained, I believe it might happen that sometimes I would have to advise two people to be divorced as the lesser of two evils.)

The second reason for my believing that Princess Margaret has done the right thing, is that she is in the line of succession to the throne. If she accepts hers responsibility in that respect, she cannot wholly please herself. She could, of course, withdraw from the line of succession (following the necessary legislation) but her sister would still be the queen. To contract a civil marriage as with Group Captain Townsend, would mean that Princess Margaret could not unite as closely with the Royal Family as at present . . .

Many people . . . will think of the Royal Family with even greater respect because even if rather lax in their own principles, people like to think the Royal Family set a good example. And there is at least a superficial regard for religion today, and this latest decision from one of the members of the Royal Family, supports the best traditions of religion.

I think that many people will urge the Church to change the law on divorce; that, perhaps, divorced people may be 'accepted' by the church. Some of these may be thoughtful people who would urge the Church to be more human, but many, I feel, would do so because we live in an age where people want an easy life, and are less ready to accept discipline than perhaps people were before 1914.[53]

PART II

Mass Observation Project, 1981–2022

Fiona Courage

Mass-Observation redux

The archive of material from the original surveys, including diaries, directives and ethnographic work undertaken by Mass-Observation, was eventually brought to the University of Sussex in the early 1970s, following negotiations between Asa Briggs, the University's vice chancellor and professor of history, and Tom Harrisson. Harrison's intention was to make the archive publicly accessible and to write a series of books based on the original material collected. Unfortunately, Harrisson and his wife were killed in a motor accident in Bangkok in 1976, leaving his intended books unwritten but with the beginnings of an accessible archive established. The University continued to support the housing and cataloguing of the archive, enabling researchers to access the treasures within.

This access sparked new interest in the methods of Mass-Observation and its use to record the opinions and experiences of people in 1977 around the celebration of Queen Elizabeth II's Silver Jubilee. The success of the 1977 Silver Jubilee project suggested that there was appetite for this kind of project and in 1981 under the direction of Professor David Pocock and Dorothy Sheridan a new Mass Observation Project was established to collect data on everyday life in contemporary Britain. A panel of volunteer writers was established and a set of questions, or directives, was sent out to them on specific themes.

Amongst the themes that were included in the 1981 Directives was the wedding of Prince Charles to Lady Diana Spencer in July of that year. Although never envisioned at the start as a long-term exercise, the Mass Observation Project has run continuously since 1981 to the present day, spanning a much longer period of British life than its original foundation and royalty continues to be a thread running through the project.

About the project

The Mass Observation Panel of Observers has remained a voluntary collection of participants. The number of members varies through time; at its peak in the 1990s nearly 1,000 writers were on its list, the number now being around 400. The number of responses received over the years has ranged from 100 to 300 and now sits at around 120. Mass Observation Project Directives are currently sent out three times a year, with each directive normally comprising three themes. The themes can range greatly, for example, alongside commentary on the royal wedding in 1981 Observers were asked to reflect on Britain joining the European Economic Community (EEC), whilst the 2011 Spring Directive carried questions on donor conception and gambling alongside the request to keep a day diary of the wedding day of Prince William and Kate Middleton. The questions are designed to be open to encourage in-depth qualitative responses rich in opinion, belief and experience; they become biographical narratives written through the lenses of the topics being asked about. As such we can use them to discover the 'confusions, ambiguities and contradictions that are play in everyday experiences' enabling an understanding of society in terms of the individuals that it comprises.[1] These contradictions illustrate the complexity of social opinion; they highlight how society and its response to events is not a uniform or even bilateral discourse but 'messy' with multiple layers of interpretation and intersecting reactions.

Appreciating the depth of insight that this messiness gives us, we can also see how commentary on an institution such as royalty can give us insight into broader societal values and how these might shift over time. The Mass Observation Project Directives covered within this part touch on almost every major royal event since 1981, including weddings, divorces and deaths. They punctuate the project's life span with enough regularity to provide an insight into how British society interacts with monarchy over a period of vast social, cultural and technological change. Comparisons of how the Silver and Platinum Jubilees of Queen Elizabeth were celebrated can provide an appreciation of how local communities have changed over forty-five years.

6

Jubilees and weddings – 1977 and the 1980s

The Silver Jubilee 1977

The year 1977 marked the twenty-fifth anniversary of the accession of Elizabeth II to the throne. The jubilee included extensive tours throughout the year by the Queen and Duke of Edinburgh around the UK, Australia, New Zealand and the Pacific Islands. Official celebrations in the UK culminated in June 1977 and included a procession of monarch and consort in the Gold State Coach to St Paul's Cathedral for a service celebrating the anniversary. Communities around the UK were encouraged to organize festivities including street parties, parades and fetes that were often months in the planning.

A publication on royalty was originally proposed by Tom Harrisson as part of his return to the helm of Mass-Observation following its arrival at the University of Sussex.[1] Following the sudden death of Harrisson, Philip Ziegler continued the work of pulling a publication together.[2] In addition to the material already available on royalty in the archive, a decision was made to revisit the Mass-Observation tradition of asking members of the public to record their reflections on Queen Elizabeth's Silver Jubilee celebrations. Participants were asked to start their reflections on the events from early 1977, recording the impact that planning events for the jubilee was having on their communities.

Reflections came from all around the country, with respondents recording both their own thoughts and the opinions of others. The responses are much more akin to earlier Mass-Observation responses, with a more objective form of ethnographic observation and interview, contrasting with the later Directives that encourage a more subjective self-reflection. The responses provide us with both an on-the-spot record of events being held around the country and a reflection of attitudes to monarchy that illustrates the role, if any, that monarchy played in everyday life across Britain in the 1970s. (The nature of the original call means that we do not have much biographical data for individual Observers in comparison to later Directive responses.)

Opinions on monarchy

Many of the Observers took it upon themselves to record how others in their locality responded to the jubilee plans earlier in the year, providing an interesting snapshot of levels of enthusiasm that can then be measured against those of a few months later.

In February of that year, one male respondent, a retired member of the colonial administrative service, sent in his report on attitudes towards the jubilee from Cornwall, a place whose population he described as not thinking of itself as English and having 'little time for London and all its works'. His own feelings were that the celebrations should be a thank you to the Queen for her services to the nation but instead it would become

an occasion for us to get something out of it. By us, I mean the public at large . . . the children who will no doubt as usual gets mugs that few will cherish, the old folks who will expect and get a free tea, the young who will expect prizes at the sports, the shopkeepers and manufacturers who will use it to make a profit, and all the charities and do-gooders and pet-projecters who will hope for something to come their way in celebration of the Jubilee and who will complain bitterly and bitchily if it doesn't . . .

my main sources of information from questioning are the milkman (also chairman of the parish council), the postman, the vicar, the head-master of the local infant and junior school, my wife, the postmaster, the staff of the village shop and of the nearest garage, a few expatriate artists, writers and potters and the nearest we have to a squire and his wife.

Most people, and this included the majority (15 to 6) of the schoolchildren between 8 and 11, have heard of the Jubilee and know roughly what it means but this is probably more a tribute to the power of TV than to any special feeling for the monarchy. Public attitudes i.e., opinions expressed at public meetings and when talking to strangers, are of course not the same thing as private feelings, although people in this part of Cornwall do not think of themselves as English and have little time for London and all its works ('Bugger me, I don't think nothing of she!'), the generally adopted public attitudes to the Queen is one of respect and even affection, and one hears little in the open of the sort of sophisticated and intellectual criticism that would probably be voiced by some in a rural community of the same size in Kent or Sussex. For this reason almost the only view expressed at meetings (see local press cuttings attached) and in public discussion about the Jubilee is 'Yes, of course , we must do it proper – mugs for the children, sports for the young people and a feast for the rest', 'Can't do less than they did last time can we?', 'Wouldn't want it said they did it better down Mousehole way, would we now?'

In private however people tend to regard the Jubilee as a bore. 'The best thing about it will be the day its over' as the village post-master put it.

JUBILEES AND WEDDINGS – 1977 AND THE 1980S

Although he is a middle-aged and very amiable queer, he was only saying what most of the more orthodox males and females of all ages think in these parts. Another opinion voiced by our by no means militant or reactionary milkman is that people are not happy about Prince Charles' appeal on television for money of which, so the milkman says, this area's allotted contribution is £10,000, only half of which will come back to Cornwall for local projects. He also complains that this is just another case of the same old people – the hard-workers and the savers – being asked once again to shell out for the benefit of those who are always getting something for nothing – the overfed and underdisciplined children, haired mannerless youth and the already over-cushioned elderly.

Although no one will say so in public, thoughtful people wonder whether children will cherish Jubilee mugs. 'Even in our day,' the middle-aged tend to say, 'when as kids we had little enough, we put the bloody thing away in a cupboard and forget we ever had it before the week was out. Now half of them won't even bother to take it home.'[3]

A 25-year-old lecturer at a technical college in Ayr questioned around sixty 16-17 year olds either in the building industry or commercial training course students.

Only a handful had actually heard of the jubilee, and after I had explained briefly what it was, the immediate questions were about the possibility of extra holidays next year.

Most of the males were antagonistic towards the royal family and the queen, making comments like 'she's never done anything for me', and 'she's paid to do nothing'. Once we had discussed what the queen actually does do, and considered the possible benefits the country could derive from royal visits abroad etc, the antagonism turned towards the other members, or 'hangers on'. Few could see that there was any possible justification for the Civil List.[4]

In Brighton, a 55-year-old female literary agent considered herself an anti-monarchist but still recognized benefits in terms of the tradition and continuity monarchy provided. She believed that the jubilee should be celebrated, albeit not on a lavish scale. The following are opinions gathered from those she met in January and February of 1977:

24.1.77 Male, dentist, 40: 'I would prefer not to have a monarchy but as it exists it would be churlish not to celebrate the jubilee.'

6.2.77 Female, 60ish, middle-class (housewife): 'All these books are going to be such a bore.' 'Why don't they pay taxes?' In our present economic circumstances why can't they be prepared to give up something. 'The jubilee is going to be too commercialised, isn't it?'

Male, 35, freelance builder: 'I do stand for the national anthem. I think they perform a useful function.' Wouldn't want to get rid of them because so many people like them. Doesn't want to spend so much money on jubilee. OK to use jubilee as a peg for anything that was going to happen anyway but it shouldn't be used as an excuse to spend extra money.

7.2.77 Female, 40ish, middle-class: Queen and Prince Philip are OK, but not hangers-on. Shouldn't spend any money on jubilee except (this was an after-thought) it might bring in more tourists.

68, Female/ Scottish accent (had just paid over £100 for a second hand fur coat), casual meeting in a cafe: In answer to a question about whether we should celebrate the jubilee: 'She'll (the Queen) make damned sure we do!' General tone was that her sister was a whore and her daughter was a bitch (her words, not mine!)

Female, 50ish, middle class: Jubilee money spent may be justified if it brings tourist into the country. 'We'll be able to make a pile of rubbish and sell it to the foreigners.' Monarchy does represent continuity.

Male, 55ish, working-class: thinks monarchy is very important. Keeps out the dictators.

Female, 55ish, ballet teacher: Adores the monarchy.

Female, 50ish, middle class: Queen performs very difficult duties with devotion. Admires her very much. Loves to see her on television.

On the same day, I attended a Spanish conversation class, where a discussion on the monarchy was provoked by the teacher. The class is predominantly women, predominantly middle-aged, mostly lower middle class, some middle class. Out of approximately 20 people 1 was the only one to voice anything remotely approaching criticism. It aroused great personal hostility and an accusation from one woman of being a communist. This particular woman (middle class, 40ish) also said (translated from Spanish!): 'Of course there isn't the respect there was 25 years ago.'

9.2.77 Husband & wife, 70ish, working-class: Monarchy very important. Helps to maintain standards which we're in danger of losing.

11.2.77 Male, 60, retired personnel manager: would do away with the lot of them if he had half a chance.

13.2.77 Discussion over dinner. Male, female, 30ish, actors (previously unknown to me) very scathing in their general tone about members of Royal Family and people surrounding them.[5]

At the opposite end of the country, another Observer interviewed individuals from different age groups in her town, providing an insight into how residents of Gilsland, Northumberland, felt about the jubilee in February 1977.

JUBILEES AND WEDDINGS – 1977 AND THE 1980S

From the Under 25s:

M. 17. A-B 'I'm pro the monarchy, although I find it a defunct institution. But I feel in this present time of economic crisis, painting the pillars gold in Fortnum and Mason is really hardly going to boost the confidence of foreign investors in Britain as a viable proposition. The cost of keeping the monarchy going is minimal – when you put it against the fact that an extra 1000 civil servants are being created simply to deal with the mess left by the devolution bill in Scotland. But this Jubilee is costing everyone far too much.'

'You cannot divorce monarchy from economics. Or politics. Monarchy until the death of Albert was very largely political. It always has been. It is a historical fallacy to refuse to accept that economic conditions are irrelevant. Who are we trying to con with all this bunting? The I.M.F? Besides, it's making us too much of a cuckoo clock country; it's demeaning – we're getting like Princess Grace and the Rose Ball in her toy kingdom.'

'There's nothing like having a puppet on a string – is there? They're briefed before they go out to dinner, and they do it very well – but it's all just to puff up the pride of some silly little mayor in a suburban town. Who has just spent the rate payers money on some filthy dinner to entertain her that should have gone on that which his town really needed.'

(The above is an amalgamation of remarks made by three highly educated, upper class, pre-university boys. In my house, over New Year – No marks for guessing who one was, Philip!)

F15-16. C-D. (The following quotes are from the school children in the typing class locally. They are more D. than C. because, for some reason I cannot fathom, there is an 'only if all else fails' attitude in the North to getting your child to learn shorthand-typing. Therefore not v. articulate – but the message is clear.)

F. 15-16. C.-D. 'Yes – celebrations would be fine, if she invited us all to the Palace.'

'Too big a fuss. It's alright if you have a nice booze-up – but all the do's in our area are going to be for the hob-nobs.'

'All she does is wear big hats and wave.'

'I've got a friend who's a clairvoyant and he says there's not going to be a monarchy by 1990.' (General applause.)

'She opens new buildings. – but you can get Pop Stars to do that, and they're better.'

(Only two came out in favour. The only reason was : 'She's a canny' bird – so why not?' 'Canny' in Northumberland means nice – not mean. It's praise.)

Children:

M.12.C. 'Boring ads on the tele about it, aren't they?'

F.9.C. 'I don't think I want to meet the Queen – she's pretty to look at but she's not real, is she? Still I'm getting a new dress for the do because Mum's so worked up about it. And it'll be a holiday.'

M.14 .A-B 'Does that mean Prince Charles is illegit? I read he was 27, and the Jubilee is 25 years isn't it?' (This is a popular misconception I have found. And not just amongst Northern working class people. Until recently lots of people who had not become aware there was to be a Jubilee, immediately thought it was their silver wedding anniversary and their evil minds leapt to Prince Charles's age. Note: this means that her silver wedding did manage to stay out of the lives of people who werenot interested; unlike this Jubilee.)

Middle-aged and Oldies:

F.70s.B 'I started a movement round me because nothing was being done and no mention. So I held an open meeting to find out if anyone was interested. They're a funny lot you know (N.B. "Here" is about 10 miles from Gilsland.) I don't know yet how it will go. I think it's a good idea. because people will get to gather, work together as a community, and it will brighten up a drab time. I'll spend money – my husband won't because he's too mean. But he likes the Royals. Just doesn't want to pay for them.'

F.40s C-B. 'I'd feel very insecure without a monarchy, so I think the Jubilee is a good idea because it's an excuse to do something traditional.'

M .50s . B. 'I have no feelings. No feelings whatsoever. And I'm not even going to waste my breath on it.'

M.30's.C. 'I'm a right grass-root Socialist. But if I can trot out the old chestnut, the Monarchy is a harmless industry. And I'd not be so churlish as to stop people having celebrations – let them waste their money if they want to. But don't involve me – I can't be bothered.'

M.25.B 'The Queen is a respected politician (???? – V.M.). And we all know she works hard. It's a good tourist attraction. And it'll be everybody working together. Why is that a good thing? I don't know why, but . . .' (N.B. A lot of the middle-aged middle-class people I spoke to had this feeling that the main advantage was that the Jubilee would bring communities together again. Query; Is this a particular feeling to isolated country places?)

F.35B. (On the local committee, mother of two children, extremely nice; part-time teacher.) 'Well, I'm only doing the committee because I'm the sort of person who gets involved in everything. I get dragged into the lot – dustbins

JUBILEES AND WEDDINGS – 1977 AND THE 1980S   147

or Old People's Homes. You name it. I'm not crazy on doing all this work for the Jubilee. If it wasn't that this is my village I wouldn't give up all this time. If I was away, I'd go to the celebrations on the day – Yes. Because I sort of approve. But the main reason this lot is giving me any pleasure at all is that I am head of the Brownies. And it's what's in it for the children that appeals to me. I can remember what a good time I had at the time of the Coronation. I was 10 and I decorated my doll's pram. I want my Brownies to have fun. I'm going to dress them all up and we're getting a float. Oh yes, the Brownies are keen. They're the right age 7-10 . Besides they have to be keen on the Monarchy to be a Brownie. It's one of the regulations that to be a Brownie you have to know about the Queen and promise to serve the Queen'.

Writing in May 1977, a Scottish Observer encountered little interest amongst his fellows on the Scottish Islands:

Through the islands (Lewis Harris Miss Skye Islay) there's been a feeling that the Jubilee is some thing that the '*daoine more*' (the 'big people) are concerned with – it's not much to do with us the Gaels. It's come up in conversation extraordinarily rarely usually only when I bring it up, or when it comes up as something objective like the weather that's going to happen to us.[6]

He goes on to recount what he describes as

Further cynical and probably libellous comments are made about the Fund . . . the gist being that none of it would be spent on doing the things Uist needed anyway.[7]

Other Observers also reported cynical responses from those they spoke to about the fundraising around the jubilee. Writing in March about her small Norfolk village, one woman describes:

People don't seem to talk about it much unless the subject is specially raised. There also seems resentment that some villages are trying to raise so much money for the celebrations. Money is pretty short in a lot of families around here, and I think some people really cannot afford the £1 – £2 being asked for . . .

Endless requests for prizes, donations, sponsors etc. for fundraising for Jubilee events. There seems more thought going towards the Fund Raising than actually what it is for.[8]

Jubilee day

As jubilee day approached, there seems to have been a significant increase in interest and activity, with accounts of planning, fundraising and communities coming together throughout the country. The residents of Ryhope Village in Sunderland held coffee mornings and raffles whilst each mother whose child would attend the street parties contributed 10 pence per child per week in the weeks running up to jubilee day. A grand total of £309 was raised with some left over after the party costs were covered, suggested to cover a coach trip for the mums and children in the school holidays. Meanwhile, the £1.10 left over from the party held in Cleveland and reported on by an Observer was donated to the Prince of Wales's Jubilee Fund.[9]

Many of the responses to the Silver Jubilee call include narratives of how the jubilee was celebrated within local communities. The jubilee celebrations focused on the weekend of 7 June 1977, and many communities organized events similar to the account of the jubilee party in a small Norfolk village recounted here.

Jubilee Day: I woke up to a cold, grey drizzling morning. Mrs. X arrived at 9.15 to collect the chocolate cake I had made – she was going round the village collecting everyone's contribution towards the Jubilee tea. At 10 a.m. went to relation's house in the village to watch her colour T.V. and saw the Royal procession to St. Paul's. The Queen looked beautiful, but solemn and one felt very moved seeing her. When all the Royal family arrived on the steps of St. Pauls the wind blew their coats and dresses which were all different colours, and the impression I got was of flower petals fluttering in the wind – what a pretty sight they were in yellows, greens, pinks and blues.

We watched the T.V. until about 12 o'clock and then dragged ourselves away to get a hurried lunch. After lunch we changed into tidier clothes, collected various neighbours and set off for Wimbotsham, our next door village with whom we were joining up for the celebrations. By now it was raining hard, and we all met under a lime tree on the village green for a short service led by the Methodist Minister. With umbrellas dripping we clustered together and sang and prayed for about 15 minutes. There was a happy feeling of togetherness under the lime tree. Next was the children's fancy dress parade in the school yard. By now it was really pouring with rain and the children were arriving from all directions. What was to be done? It couldn't be cancelled and there was no room in the school or village hall as the teas were all laid out there. The fancy dress parade took place and frozen and shivering Brittanias, cave men, tramps, St. George's and gypsies walked round. My husband and I had to judge the different classes which was an impossible task. Such trouble had been taken over the various costumes and all seemed to be home made. Also we had to hurry as the children were on the verge of catching pneumonia by the looks of them. One little boy was a dragon with lovely home-made cardboard feet which were huge and made marvellous squelching sounds as he stepped in the puddles.

JUBILEES AND WEDDINGS – 1977 AND THE 1980S 149

By now the rain had eased up a bit and we went onto the playing fields for the sports. There was every sort of race ranging from the toddlers race to the one mile for men. There was something for everyone and spirits rose as the rain eventually ceased. I took part in the ladles egg and spoon race – I was so nervous of dropping the egg that I went much too slowly and came last much to my family's embarrassment! The final event was the tug of war, various pubs and the two villages had teams. Feelings ran high as we all shouted for our different teams to win. Our village didn't fare too well – the tie man was the shepherd's large son who was wearing fancy high heeled boots. After a few pulls off came one of his heels which quite spoilt his concentration on tugging. Our team consisted of the said shepherd's son, the blacksmith, the cowman, the farm manager, the tenant farmer, the forester, the farmer's son and the mechanic. The eventual winners were the eight brothers of the Goodings family who run the local haulage firm. They are nearly all over 6 ft. tall and nearly as broad – a crate of beer was their prize for winning.

Tea was the next item of the afternoon. 700 people had been catered for at a sit down tea in the village hall and school. We sat down at long tables and each person had a plate full of delicious homemade scones and cakes put before them and a piping hot cup of tea. It was more than welcome and warmed us up.

After tea was the presentation of the Jubilee cups and mugs in the school playground. All the children of 16 downwards queued up and were given their mugs and cups . Looks of eager anticipation on all the children's faces as they waited for their presents.

Back home about 7 o'clock and then off in the car to some friends who live an hour away. Then dancing in the street in their local small pilgrimage town of Walsingham. It was dry now but bitterly cold and we all wore our warmest clothes. There was a disco in the market square, and everyone joined in the dancing. There were free cups of coffee and biscuits given out by the Women's Institute.

I think the general feeling about Jubilee Day seemed to be that it brought people together. There was an atmosphere of friendliness and happiness which some people said hadn't been felt since the celebrations at the end of the war.[10]

Alongside the street parties, there was significant interest in street decorations and the dressing of houses and shops in celebration of the jubilee festivities. One Observer described how her home town of Lewes in East Sussex was swamped with red, white and blue merchandise in all the shops from hardware to women's clothing, whilst the South Eastern Gas Board shop advertised the offer of a free jubilee mug with every kitchen stove purchased.[11] The jubilee mug played a significant part in almost every narrative of a party, seemingly every child being given one as a memento of the occasion. One writer from Stoke-on-Trent, also known as the Potteries, felt the impact from a professional standpoint.

> The most striking feature has been the demand for Bone China Jubilee Beakers and Loving Cups. I am a consultant to a group of Stoke Potteries and the demand for these and other Jubilee momentos has exceeded our expectations. Whereas we expected demand to cease by Jubilee Day, we have now repeat orders which will keep the lines going for several more months. On a personal note, I have supplied locally nearly 200 beakers and loving cups admittedly on favourable terms![12]

Despite the earlier lack of engagement reported by respondents in February–April of 1977, by the time they were recording events around jubilee week, interest appears to have increased significantly. It should be noted that the nature of the request from M-O was to record events for the jubilee, and therefore anyone not involved in an event or within observational distance of one was unlikely to have contributed.

For those who were involved, the overwhelming reflection on the events was one of success. One Observer, perhaps coloured by the success of sales of jubilee mugs mentioned earlier, stated that 'from wide ranging contacts . . . I have not heard one word of opposition to the jubilee celebrations, in fact they seem to have acted as a sort of antidote to the general despondency of the nation in its present economic depression'. Another commented that despite enthusiasm for the jubilee being slow to get underway in his town in Cambridgeshire, in the event the response was 'tremendous':

> I reckon that at least 800 people out of a population of 1100 took part in some way, publicly. And yet, there was no mass demonstration, no cheering, no frantic flag-waving, no excitement. All was remarkably quiet, orderly and well-behaved. There was no more alcohol consumed than on a normal day (possibly a good deal less – I didn't have a 'drink' all day.)
>
> What was the point of it all? Just this I think. At a time when so many divisive issues confront us in all directions, here was something which prompted people to get together in a spirit of friendliness and co-operation. I have never seen anything like it before (and I have lived in the village for over 30 years). It seems to me that, if one were looking for an answer to the questions, 'Why Royalty?' (as Willie Hamilton[13] and his like seem to be doing) then the answer is that Royalty is the only positive unifying agent in our society today. The affection for the Queen is so real, so deep and so universal that it can be, and mostly is taken for granted. The London millions, quite rightly, got together and cheered. The Foxton hundreds, quite properly, got together and everybody was nice to everybody else.[14]

In recollecting the jubilee celebrations a teacher from the London Borough of Bromley also observed what she perceived as the unifying power of the jubilee celebrations on a local and national level.

I did not expect the Jubilee celebrations to be as successful as they have been. It was as though groups and individuals had created whirlpools of interest in the Jubilee into which people are sucked, while those who had no real enthusiasm were not unaffected by the ripples. (Excuse the metaphor). I've read of an anti-Jubilee campaign in 'The Guardian', but that appears to have got nowhere. Certainly I've seen no signs of the 'stuff the Jubilee' stickers which were supposed to be selling well. Those who disagreed with the Jubilee appear to have been completely swamped by pro-monarchist sentiment . . .

Whatever political and economic troubles there are, I felt that certainly during this week the British people were united in celebration. Perhaps the success of the events was partly due to the Queen remaining as an essentially non-political figure. Today (12 June) I read somewhere that the Jubilee celebrations demonstrate that Britain is still United Kingdom and I fully agree with that.[15]

Summer Directive 1981 – Royal Wedding Special

On 24 February 1981, the engagement of the 32-year-old Prince of Wales to nineteen-year-old Lady Diana Spencer was announced following a short relationship. The wedding took place on 29 July 1981 at St Paul's Cathedral in London. It was estimated that 2 million spectators came to London and another 750 million watched it worldwide, making it one of the most watched and, at £57 million in 1980s prices, one of the most expensive events in British history.[23]

The UK was in its second year of recession with over 2.5 million people unemployed, whilst inflation was slowly coming down from its 27 per cent high in 1979 but still standing at 10 per cent. Riots took place throughout the country, most markedly in the areas of Brixton in London and Toxteth in Birmingham in April and July; the root cause of this civil unrest lay in racial tensions, intersected by high unemployment and economic and social deprivation. Tensions around the situation in Northern Ireland were high; the UK prime minister Margaret Thatcher took a clear stand against the Provisional IRA whilst IRA prisoners were embarking on highly publicized hunger strikes, with Bobby Sands being the first of ten hunger strikers to die on 5 May.

The British media was also entering a new era, with Australian tycoon Rupert Murdoch purchasing The Times *and* The Sunday Times *in February 1981 in addition to his ownership of* The Sun *and the* News of the World tabloids acquired in the late 1960s. Murdoch, a staunch anti-monarchist, did not believe that the British royal family should enjoy any special immunity or respect from the British press as the headlines of his tabloid papers illustrated in the years following Charles and Diana's wedding.[16]

The Directive

Following the success of the 1977 Silver Jubilee Survey, M-O decided to launch a similar survey in the summer of 1981 with questions relating to the country's economic situation and the royal wedding. Observers were asked to record reactions to events leading up to the day and to keep a diary for the day of the wedding.

M-O received around 280 responses to its Special Directive, around 200 female and 80 male responses. The oldest responders were over eighty whilst the youngest was eighteen. The writers faithfully stuck to the request, keeping diaries of their day, recording meals and activities as well as opinions on the events regardless of whether they were involved with or ignoring the celebrations. Responses covered both the factual activities of the day and a broader response to the event. Both types of responses revealed the writers' views on the monarchy, media and the state of British society at that time. The nature of the accompanying questions in the Directive meant that the impact of high unemployment and economic constraints and civil unrest was already in the consciousness of those writing and appears to have tinged some of the responses in a way that may not have been so apparent at a more prosperous time.

The Day

The diaries for 29 July 1981 include accounts of how people celebrated the wedding as well as illustrate how daily life continued around the royal events. For many, it was an event looked forward to and enjoyed, one signalling a new era of the royal family. A 51-year-old woman living in the East of England recorded that she did little more than watch the ceremony and associated processions that day, providing a detailed reflection on her experience of the event:

We switched on the TV about 8.15 and kept an eye on the preliminary programmes until we had breakfast at 9.30. We kept switching from ore channel to the other, trying to deride which one we preferred, and about 10 a.m. settled on BBC 1. We liked the way the commentary was informative without being intrusive, and that the occasion itself was allowed to unfold. I particularly noticed Prince Charles expression as

JUBILEES AND WEDDINGS – 1977 AND THE 1980S

the landau first came into view (how many other bridegrooms also wear that 'Oh well, THIS IS IT'!), the delightful dresses of the bridesmaids, they looked like the Flower Fairies from a book I had as a child, the sideways looks of the police men and women watching the crowds, who were able to be alert yet catch a glimpse of the carriages as they passed; the thoughtfulness of whoever planned the details so that when the carriages reached the bottom of Ludgate Hill, they alternately passed to the left and the right of a traffic bollard so that the crowds on each side of the road got an equal number of closer and further away views of the occupants; the care everyone took of Earl Spencer, and his brave effort to keep going through the ceremony though I wouldn't be at all surprised if it cost him a few days bed rest afterwards); the anxious look on the Queen's face throughout the ceremony, and the way 'Queen Mum' looked round Prince Charles to see how Diana was getting on halfway through the address by Dr Runcie; how quickly Diana had changed her lovely engagement ring back to her left hand sometime during the ceremony, and the sad look which came over Princess Margaret's face from time to time so that she stopped singing – was she recalling her own wedding, and regretting it's unhappy ending? . . .

We all watched the honeymoon departure, and loved the heart-shaped balloons and 'Just Married' notice. Everyone liked Di's outfit, and thought the style and colour were just right for the occasion, and for her colouring. Her impulsive kiss on the cheek for the gentleman at Waterloo Station (probably someone she has known all her life anyway), was very endearing. I can't help thinking that whilst Queen Mum no doubt smilingly approved as she watched on the Royal TV, the Late Queen Mary would NOT have considered it proper for a Princess of Wales to behave in such a fashion. This wedding certainly has shown how Royal attitudes have changed during this reign, and I believe the changes have all enhanced the Royal status among the people. We no longer see them as doll-like glittering symbols, but as a family who have a very difficult and often arduous job which they do very well. Comments on the rest of the Royal family were that Princess Anne's outfit, though quite unlike anything she has worn before, was really a knock-out, she looked more elegant and pretty than she has ever looked before; that the Queen Mum's change from her usual blue to a pile green was a wise choice in view of the number of blue outfits one saw in St Paul's, and that Sarah Armstrong-Jones has grown.[17]

Several writers experienced events in person whilst in London, including a 31-year-old male who headed off to work a twelve-hour shift at Temple in central London on the wedding day with no intention of getting involved.

I finished work at 9 pm on the eve of the Wedding and London's Underground was as crowded as it is in the weekday rush hour except that instead of office workers the trains were full of parents and children eager to see the firework display in Hyde Park. There was a definite carnival atmosphere and souvenir sellers were everywhere making a killing, after all, this being a one-off event meant that the goods on sale could never be sold, again . . .

I work in Central London and only a couple of minutes from the Royal route. When I arrived at Temple, which is the station opposite my building, it really did seem as though something very big was about to happen. Soldiers and airmen were standing to attention and practising marching. Lots of policemen wearing dress uniform milled around and the coachloads of bobbies were parked everywhere.

I had been studiously ignoring both the preparations and the torrent of media publicity leading up to the Day but this concentration of troops aroused my curiosity. And at last, the crowds began to stream up towards the Strand to see the procession of Royalty and especially the Happy Couple. The air of excitement and anticipation was infectious – I had told my wife that I would not even bother to look out of the window, preferring to seek sanctuary in the bar we have annexed to our canteen, but when my colleagues suggested we leave our telegram work and stand and watch the pageantry, I happily agreed. Americans and tourists were lining the route and children watched the parade of horses ridden by gleaming helmeted guards through periscopes which some enterprising trader had been selling. My workmates were standing on milk crates, waste paper bins and anything else which would elevate one off the ground. But the police disapproved saying that if the crowd surged back there would be an accident. Spoilsports!

Even I, someone who had not concealed my anti-monarchist views in previous weeks, craned my neck and had a splendid view of the passing dignitaries. When the Queen, followed by all the other senior members of the Royal Family went by they received deafening cheers.

Only Lady Diana, who was not yet to be accorded the National Anthem which was being struck up as soon as a crowned head approached, had a bigger roar than the Queen Mother.

One American lady had tied herself to a lamp post and was visibly overcome at seeing the Royal Family in the flesh. The Yanks had certainly made it their day as well; the scaffolding surrounding St. Mary's in the Strand was adorned with a massive Stars and Stripes, beneath which was the legend 'Love from America – Ooh la la'. It had all the whimsical irreverence the States gives to an occasion like this – almost a whiff of Times Square at presidential primary time in the middle of sober and dignified Strand, WC2.

I had my lunch, washed down with a couple of pints, and returned to the spot where ninety minutes earlier I had watched the First Citizens go by in a blaze of heraldry and pomp. The half dozen or so Filipino girls who work in our canteen giggled and snapped away with their Instamatics. They had been watching the service from St. Pauls on a portable black-and-white television whilst attempting to serve meals and as soon as the commentator announced the Couple leaving the cathedral, they shed their aprons and headbands and ran up Essex Street to watch the royal newlyweds.

Back they all came, this time of course, headed by Prince Charles and his new Princess of Wales. Tumultuous cheers filled the air and subsided only as other dignitaries, looking very important in braid, be-medalled with scrambled egg on their peaked caps (although no-one knew who they were) passed by in Rolls Royces.

When the British Royals had gone I decided I couldn't be bothered to wait and see the crowned heads of Europe. It was back to work where I phoned my wife and told her what I had seen. She told me that Charles and Diana had fluffed their lines and how magnificent was the wedding dress; clearly, she had enjoyed the ceremony immensely . . .

On reflection the atmosphere was infectious; even the most ardent anti-royalist was loathe to make any hostile comment during this carnival time and I personally felt that it was a pleasant change from the riots which had been raging in Liverpool and other areas of Britain. It showed another side to our way of life and pushed the street violence off the front pages. Somehow the wedding served to throw a ray of hope on a society despairing of the rising crime rate and sporadic mindless rioting and looting which had had the nation wringing its hands in anxious dread for the future. It gave an assurance that the fabric was intact after all and lifted much of the gloom of the recession, unemployment and general melancholy prevalent in these times.

To a cynic like myself it may have been a jamboree the nation. Could ill afford and a display of ostentatious indulgence more appropriate to the days of the Empire. But at least I can tell my grandchildren that I looked down my nose at it while I was actually there![18]

The surprise that he expressed in becoming caught up in something that he had been 'pooh-poohing' for weeks was shared by others.

Parties

Many of the Observers commented that enthusiasm for street parties was markedly less than had been visible during the 1977 Silver Jubilee. A Londoner born in 1918 went even further back, as he drew a comparison with the Silver Jubilee of George V in 1935 and the Coronation of 1937. Despite both dates experiencing equally high employment as 1981, 90 per cent of the houses around his home in Fulham were still decorated and 'Each street had a party that went on late in the night, but these activities were noticeably absent around this area on 29 July'.[19]

But parties were had, including the event described by this female living in London:

> Did not see later events as from 2.30 p.m. I was involved in getting the tables ready at the dead-end junction of ours and the next street. Slight breeze made things a bit tricky and we had to Sellotape the paper table cloths down and cover up the plates of sandwiches from drying out with the hot sun. Whatever would we do without the universal ever present Sellotape!
>
> The children started arriving and about 80 per cent were in fancy dress and we had a parade of the before the Spurs players Chris Huyton and Paul Miller came to judge them. Signs of the times the winners of one age group were a pair of punk rockers!!! All the food was donated and masses of cakes and sandwiches were prepared augmented by ice cream. After eating the tables were stacked at the side and the children's disco began. Funny when we had the Coronation party it was all sorts of races egg and spoon, sack, three-legged etc. This time it was a horde of John Travolta's gyrating around and trying to convince us they were the winners. Where did all the energy come from??
>
> About 5.30 I slipped away and [*her husband who had been working at a local hospital that day*] and I had a little rest and time to talk about the day's events. He was terribly disappointed not to have seen much of it. And later as we joined the adults' party he also missed the repeats . . .
>
> The tables were rearranged for the grownups by putting them in a rough circle with a space for the disco to go on until a few minutes before midnight. We had great fun with a knobbly knees competition won by a seventy year old man, and a wibbly, wobbly walk for the ladies won by one of the organisers. There was a couple of large bowls of punch, and various wines but some brought their own to supplement the supply. One person made a beautiful square iced cake well decorated with C & D flags etc. About ten o'clock the fish and chips arrived or chicken and chips for some. Unfortunately 12 long French bread loaves were forgotten so they had to be stored in someone's freezer. As [*husband*] was again due to get up for early duty we left the party at 11.30 not realising it was intended to close just before midnight so we lay in bed and listened to Auld Lang Syne and cheers for various helpers.[20]

Opinions on the wedding and monarchy

Some Observers criticized the extravagance of the wedding, including a Scottish female Observer:

JUBILEES AND WEDDINGS – 1977 AND THE 1980S

The actual viewing was quite compulsive. But nevertheless the whole show seemed to me totally irrelevant, not to say in bad taste, when one thinks of the (nearly) 3 millions unemployed, social security and NHS cutbacks, Brixton and Toxteth (etc etc), compared with the fabulous sums of money spent on wedding clothes, hats, banquets (etc etc)? 'Bread and circuses'??[21]

For a thirty-year-old clerical worker in the South East, the timing of the wedding was problematic:

I myself felt that the wedding came at an unfortunate time when so much money was obviously spent on the occasion and the country with such high unemployment and poverty in a lot of areas. A lot of older people did not think of it in the same way and felt it was what the country needed to bring itself out of the doldrums. It attracted a lot of attention from the Press but the Street Parties did not seem to carry the excitement as of Jubilee parties . . .

Most reaction to the Royal Wedding came afterwards from most of my friends as to the length of the honeymoon at Balmoral, the wedding presents and residences etc. Most were quite disgusted as to the 12-week honeymoon and how they seem worlds apart from ordinary working people and many felt bitter about this particularly with regard to the difficulties many people are having at present. As I have said before I felt the wedding came at a not very happy period in the economy of the country.[22]

Opinion on Prince Charles's choice of bride was also expressed, both in terms of her position and the age difference between the two. A single male in his forties observed that whilst 'most people were pleased that he had finally made a choice even if there was some cynicism about his actual choice and her age in relation to the "need" to produce an heir to the throne'.[23] A 28-year-old teacher from London discussed the wedding with her thirteen-to fourteen-year-old students whose general opinion was that the Prince was 'cradle-snatching'.[24]

Sentiments on royalty amongst the home nations of the UK have always been mixed, and the investiture of Prince Charles as the Prince of Wales in 1969 had received a mixed reception from the Welsh. His wedding appeared to have a similar effect as noted by a 56-year-old living in Cardiff:

As you probably know, there was a division of feeling in Wales between the usual 'British' loyalty to the monarchy and the anti-Prince or Princess of Wales faction, which is largely confined to the younger, more radical element. I was travelling a great deal at the pre-wedding time, between rural Wales and Cardiff. The picture was much the same everywhere in Wales – patches of loyalty expressed by flags and decorations, contrasting with areas of no display at all. My inner-city area put up its house decorations very quickly just a day or so before the wedding day. Personally, I watched almost every minute on TV and listened to the radio commentaries as much as possible, switching from channel to channel, weeping copiously throughout, as many of my friends confessed to having done. I hadn't intended to watch at all and certainly did not share the devotedly loyal feelings of some friends who were not prepared to let anything interfere with their viewing. We were agreed that as much as anything we were weeping for lost values, for the fact that the Royal Family were expressing the kind of affectionate family life so many of us have lost; that the young people were kind and respectful to their parents; for the fact that everyone involved was conforming; for the obvious happiness of the crowds in the streets engendering much the same feeling as does the last night of the Proms.

My elder daughter (29) said she hadn't made up her mind how she felt about the wedding, the younger (24) said she hadn't bothered to watch at all, and those reactions I found typical of those age groups. There were some street parties in Cardiff and elsewhere, but not as many as for the Jubilee.[25]

Modernizing the royals

The fact that the bride was not of royal blood (although still from an aristocratic family) seems to have added to the representation of the wedding as a modern-day fairy tale that enabled not only the bride but also those watching to transcend the everyday. This is well illustrated by a 29-year-old from Reading who found herself caught up in the romance of the event despite being a self-confessed 'anti-royalist':

I remember thinking how funny it was to see Michael Foot sat amongst all this pageantry, but in a way it was comforting, if he could forget some of his principles then so could I!

Of course the Prince looked dashing and his bride beautiful, it wasn't just the things of which fairy tales are made, it was the very fabric. She walked slowly up the aisle on the arm of her Father just as I had done eight years ago, and somehow, I wanted to believe they were truly in love as Dave and I are. They did sound as if they meant their vows, particularly him, but who knows or ever will know? Blood determines Royal marriages rather than Heaven. All the same I felt a tear threatening, but a man died in troubled Toxteth last night and I remembered just in time . . .

[*writing at the end of the day*] Well it was all over. Diana and Charles were man and wife at last and the world will still be in a mess tomorrow just as much as it was yesterday. Today though I felt happy, most people

JUBILEES AND WEDDINGS – 1977 AND THE 1980S   159

found a smile from somewhere and it's been such a long time overdue. We are all living in such a joyless world, where so many people have lost all hope and frustration runs rampant in our streets, that most of us welcomed this little bit of magic, as temporary as we all knew it would be. It's an ugly world, and today we had a ray of sunshine, clouds were gathering almost before the last coach disappeared, but it was sunshine, and I for one felt the warmth.[26]

Some took a more cynical note, including a 32-year-old woman from Cornwall who considered the notion of a fairy tale as being outdated in a modern world:

Perhaps the wedding was a folk celebration of every mother's eldest son marrying every father's youngest daughter. The wedding caught the popular imagination, capturing the folk memory of what a wedding should be like and justifying the pale imitations that are acted out at local churches a few times each month.

Nearly everybody has been prepared to believe the image that was presented in the newspapers and on TV – that the wedding was a fairy tale – and it certainly looked enchanting and romantic. However, both partners were from similar rich and sheltered aristocratic backgrounds. (Had Prince Charles married – in St Paul's Cathedral and with the Queen smiling benignly – a 20 year old, black, unmarried mother from Brixton, it could have been described as a fairy tale. But that, of course, would have been impossible.)

The media image of the Princess of Wales seems to be similar to that of Mary in the Catholic Church – the Virgin/Madonna: the virgin bride becomes next year's Diana and child, thus providing excellent – but vapid – copy for the tabloid newspapers and the women's magazines and ensuring the continued popularity of the monarchy. I wish people could take a more honest view of the event and examine their own attitudes to it, rather than gladly accept everything as it is presented to them.[27]

The next royal event recorded by Mass-Observers signalled another step away from the traditions of centuries, as the Queen's second son, Prince Andrew, married Sarah Ferguson, an event celebrated for its move to less formality but that also sparked the beginning of some of the most targeted and personal critiques of members of the royal family by the British press.

Autumn Directive 1986

The year 1986 was a quiet year for M-O Directives with only one being issued at the end of the year. The Directive comprised a request to keep a diary over the Christmas holiday and a separate question asking Observers to reflect on major events that had happened over the year both public and personal. Writers were asked to note down the events that happened and then to comment on them and discuss with others to help M-O 'record what people really what people experience as opposed to the media assessments'.[28] *The 720 responses received are therefore interesting in that they reflect what Observers felt was important, or what merited remembering in national and international affairs, and how this may have measured up with their own lives.*

The national and international events of 1986 recorded by Observers comprise a wide range of events, and the nature of what is recalled can be seen as reflecting the interests of the Observers – the Football World Cup being one that was barely referenced whilst other events including the Challenger Space shuttle, which exploded shortly after launch killing all seven members of its crew, were mentioned by many. The explosion at the Chernobyl Nuclear Power Plant in the USSR (now in Ukraine) on 26 April caused great concern over contaminated food and environments. Other events often mentioned included the launch of the UK government's information campaign on the AIDS virus and the US bombing of Libya.

In the context of the British royal family, three events were mentioned. The Queen's sixtieth birthday in April of that year was noted by some Observers. For a 65-year-old from Yorkshire who was born six years before the Queen, the event sparked nostalgia for her childhood as she remembered her grandmother sharing the newspaper announcement of the then Princess's birth with her.[29] *A fifty-year-old female Observer from the South East recalled the events as being a happy day for the Queen, and that she herself would 'remember for a long time that picture of her, all smiles, in that yellow outfit, surrounded by all those children . . . and the daffodils. A real breath of spring.'*[30]

For a 45-year-old from the North West, it was a point at which she reflected on the future:

> Now that she has reached this age, should she hand over to Charles, or should she let him carry on as he is until his family is a bit older, thus giving very slightly less 'limelight' life? Has she already decided when she'll hand over, or is she waiting for the right time?[31]

Observers also made note of the state visit to China made by the Queen and Prince Phillip that autumn. Around a fifth of the Observers mentioned the visit, the first to the country for twenty-five years, but the royal event that garnered the most comment was the marriage of the Queen's third child, Prince Andrew, in July. As third in line to the throne, Prince Andrew had attracted public interest for several years in both his official duties as a naval officer and a member of the royal family and in his private life as 'among the

JUBILEES AND WEDDINGS – 1977 AND THE 1980S 161

world's 10 most desirable bachelors'.[32] *In 1985, he started a relationship with Sarah Ferguson, daughter of Prince Charles's polo manager and friend of Princess Diana, and their engagement was announced on 19 March 1986.*[33] *The wedding itself took place on Wednesday 23 July 1986 at Westminster Abbey, and on the day of the marriage the newly married couple became commonly known as Duke and Duchess of York.*

Observers were not asked specifically about the royal wedding, but many referenced it as a significant event without prompting, with reflections on the event ranging from anger through disinterest and into enthusiastic celebration. For this 35-year-old male it was

the most hyped event of the year so it's not surprising that it immediately springs to mind. I found the whole thing nauseating (I'm probably in a minority of 1:99), but appreciate that a lot of people enjoyed it. We didn't even get given a day off work![34]

A 35-year-old woman was also surprised by the fact the royal wedding stood out for her but suggested that it was 'a bit of light relief in a very sombre year'.[35] *A 45-year old woman agreed, observing that*

for a day one could forget the cares of the world and enjoy the happy atmosphere . . . A bit of bad feeling because the day wasn't declared a national holiday. Funny really how such an occasion fills everyone with patriotism, sadly forgotten the week after.[36]

Some Observers welcomed the new Duchess as 'a happy girl, a breath of fresh air',[37] *whilst another liked her because she 'has lots of personality and seems to radiate with laughter'.*[38]*Meanwhile, a 55-year-old female went so far as to state that:*

I have never particularly liked Prince Andrew, especially as he seems to live up to his nickname of 'randy Andy' and was inclined to think that Sarah Ferguson was far too good for him.

However, this Observer concluded that having seen them both being interviewed on TV, 'I was rather won round. I think they are very well matched.'[39]

Another 55-year-old male also commented on the favourable impression the interview made on him:

What did create more comment that anything was the television interview with the young couple before the wedding. I'm sure most of us had Sarah Ferguson listed as an inelegant, frumpish girl with a figure like a badly packed parcel and damn-all dress sense, but she came across as a very nice girl with a huge sense of fun.

162   REFLECTIONS ON BRITISH ROYALTY

We talked about the interview in the office next morning . . . agreed that Sarah had made a much more favourable impression than Princess Di at her pre-marriage interview. Sarah was outgoing and open, wasn't frightened to laugh out loud and seemed down-to-earth and self-assured, whereas Di had been irritatingly coy and terribly naive.

W said that Sarah, in fairness, was older than Di, but our future Queen doesn't improve with age. The media raves about her, but I am filled with apprehension. Given a change of roles I would be more prepared to swear allegiance to Prince Andrew and his wife than the two oddly-matched pair we have lined up for the throne.[40]

It was perhaps inevitable that so soon after the marriage of the Prince and Princess of Wales the comparisons would be made of both the couples. One 64-year-old Observer was 'glad that Andrew could be allowed to choose his own bride and that she didn't have to be free of a "past" because presumably she will never be a queen'.[41] This reference appears to hint at contrasts with the marriage of the Prince and Princess of Wales five years earlier, a comparison that was made by several writers. A 57-year-old woman reported on an overheard comment that claimed:

She is no young innocent. Certainly not a virgin. But of course, it's not as important as it was for Charles. He had to marry a pure English rose whose character was impeccable.[42]

But not everyone made such a favourable comparison as one 36-year-old woman observed:

Everyone shared the young couple's happiness and wished them well, as we do any young couple getting married not that we are necessarily patriotic or particularly like or know the couple involved. From comments, especially by older people, it would seem that Andrew (Randy Andy, the Playboy Prince) and Sarah (lumpy and awkward, a lady with a past) are far less popular than Charles and Diana.[43]

Comments on Sarah Ferguson's 'past' were also made by other Observers highlighting the media coverage that her previous life and relationships was beginning to receive. A 39-year-old clerical worker wrote that her friends discussed the wedding the day before, and that whilst they thought the new bride was 'quite nice' they were amused by the papers' references to 'her former lovers as "close friends"'. [44] For a 61-year-old, this 'past' contributed to what she perceived as:

In the case of 'Fergie and Andy' there was probably more rapport between ordinary people and the Royals than ever before. This was mostly due to the fact that both he and she had 'been around' as the saying goes. She was

JUBILEES AND WEDDINGS – 1977 AND THE 1980S

no dewy eyed innocent awaiting a knight in shining armour and he had even gone as far as being practically engaged to a girl who was slightly notorious as opposed to being famous. At one time the nick-name 'Randy Andy' was bandied about. Both, however, were very personable, outgoing people, and the British public quite clearly approved of their match.[45]

A 32-year-old Observer also focused on the life experience that Sarah Ferguson brought with her, writing that her 'female friends seemed to feel that Sarah was the right choice for Andrew and they liked the fact that she had a job and seemed relatively independent and very articulate'. [46]

Not everyone claimed to be a fan of the new Duchess's non-traditional air; for a 73-year-old male Observer Sarah Ferguson's persona was not a breath of fresh air:

As someone who admires those of the Royals who work hard and earn their keep I was still finding it hard to swallow the acceptance of Fergie as a wife for Prince Andrew, not that he could be accused of being a novice in the game of amour, but remembering the crisis over Mrs Simpson and the Prince of Wales one is left gasping at the change in the moral climate both amongst the Royals and the establishment, especially the Church.

Maybe the [aura] of the King Teddy era and the history of successive amours of other Royal Princes have tempered the climate.[47]

Whilst not so openly critical, another Observer commented on the contrast of old tradition against the new social mores that the arrival of Sarah Ferguson in the royal family might bring:

Amazed that the Queen accepted this woman into her family, as her previous (live in) boyfriend's associates were involved with drugs and 'fast' living – she is supposed to be so straight laced. Expect she knows that this girl will give her son tit for tat!! Now the girl's career will be successful because of position.[48]

Comparisons were not only made of the Queen's daughters-in-law but also of their wedding ceremonies. Watching the wedding at a friend's house on a colour television set, a 36-year-old female Observer thoroughly enjoyed the ceremony but agreed with her fellow group of watchers that the 'Charles and Diana wedding had something more solemn and important about it'. [49]

As no holiday had been declared, some Observers accounted how they experienced the wedding whilst at work. A forty-year-old administrative worker described how workers in her office adapted to the day:

The Royal Wedding in July seemed to be a very exciting event for everyone. I remember being doubtful when the Royal couple got engaged as to whether Miss Ferguson was right for the Prince. Many people I spoke to had their doubts. But as the day got nearer people got more caught up in the excitement. Lots of people found the news up to the Wedding very boring and I must admit it did seem to be the sole topic of newspaper and television. By the time the day arrived many people were heartily sick of the whole thing People were disappointed that it was not to be a public holiday and a lot of workers booked a day's holiday just to watch the wedding on the television.

On the day itself, because I had to work, I set our Video Recorder to record as much as possible of the ceremony. I was eager to see how all the guests where [*sic*] dressed the ladies outfits and hats and of course Miss Ferguson's wedding dress. Everyone hoped it would not be the let-down the Princess of Wales dress had been. In our large office at work we had three or four portable TVs and many people did no work at all that morning. Most of my work is done over the telephone, and surprisingly it was very busy that day. My calls normally come from the public at home, so I was amazed by how people were telephoning me right through the ceremony itself, seemingly a great many were not interested at all in the Royal wedding. I contented myself with the knowledge that I could watch all this at my ease that evening. I did notice that as the couple gave their vows our office was very quiet, everyone was glued to a portable screen, if you could get near one. The silence was broken by a huge sigh all around the office. Everyone seemed to enjoy it and most people were not disappointed at all with Fergie's dress.

I unfortunately had set our Video Recorder for the wrong time, for which I will never forgive myself, but there was certainly no shortage of television coverage. I think I was fed up of seeing that wedding by the time the day was over.[50]

Others also enjoyed watching the event. Despite complaining about the cost of the event, a 32-year-old admitted that she still loved to see royal events on television.

I love the coaches and the costumes and the pageantry, and to see the crowds lining the streets. In the hairdressers Rochelle and Wendy agreed that the Princess of Wales wedding dress had been a disaster and that Sarah's was much better. They said that Sarah Ferguson is a person of real character and fun, but wonder how long it will last and whether she will have to toe the royal line.[51]

One Observer's enthusiasm for the event echoed the sentiments of others who responded to the 1981 wedding, namely that the British had a talent for putting on a royal show:

The best Royal Wedding ever. NO other country can do such an occasion as well as we British.

JUBILEES AND WEDDINGS – 1977 AND THE 1980S

Sarah Ferguson was like a breath of fresh air, and turned what is usually a stuffy and predictable occasion into a day to remember. Never before have we seen the Royal family so relaxed. Sarah infected them all. Her bubbly personality and natural charm reached out to everyone. Our young people felt they could identify with them. Prince Andrew has made a wise choice. He'll have to stay on his toes, Sarah's no Shy Di. She will do things her way. Although I think she will respect her position as a royal. She will not let it overwhelm her.[52]

Another Observer reflected that the new Duchess made things 'human':

Beautiful, I cried tears of happiness for them both. The Duchess of York has somehow made everything human for me concerning the Royal Family. Many of the people around me were upset that they couldn't have the day off. Some took a day's holiday specially.[53]

One important shift in the relationship between the younger royal family, the public and the press is evident in the widespread usage of 'Fergie' instead of the Duchess of York. The Observers' writing in this Directive signals this change in the way the younger royals are described. A 40-year-old who had enjoyed watching the wedding with her young son, commented:

Lots of fuss in the press about 'Fergie' as the tabloids called her – not known if she thinks of herself as Fergie.[54]

This 58-year-old Observer watched the ceremony with the elderly patients at the hospital where she worked and recalled:

we were able to get all the patients on our ward up early and spent most of the day viewing the event and had sherry and 'wedding cake'. One patient concerned to hear the bride say 'I, Sarah . . .' as up to that day she had been referred to as Fergie – thought he was marrying someone else.[55]

Summary

The 1977 celebrations seem to mark a transition point in the relationship between the royal family and the public and as such can be seen as a useful baseline to examine how the relationship has evolved over the last decades. The new generation of royals began to become more active in public life with their lives coming under more critical scrutiny than previously, in part due to a change in its relationship with the media and increasing tabloid interest in private lives and foibles.

The extracts in this chapter show how royal events were judged as being mired in tradition, not only upholding the values of continuity and stability by linking the monarchy with its history but also showing signs of change as tradition attempted to come to terms with a modern world. The jubilee, celebrated with a familiar ceremony, was followed by the Wales wedding as the meeting of modernity with tradition. With hindsight, the subsequent failure of the Wales's marriage could be recognized as one of the first signs that royal tradition in a modern world could no longer work. The marriage of the Duke and Duchess of York was commented on by some Observers as representing an even clearer break from tradition with Sarah Ferguson being contrasted to Lady Diana Spencer as being someone equal to the job of becoming a 'modern royal'.

M-O accounts provide evidence that these events were largely celebrated within the context of community. Communities raised money together, organized together and celebrated across the generations contrasting with reports from later Directives in which celebratory interaction with the royal family became increasingly centred on family and eventually individual and social media.

Despite the optimism of the royal events that took place in 1977 and the 1980s, the following decade proved to be much harder for the royal family in terms of their relationship with the media and the public. Neither the Wales nor the York marriage provided the fairy-tale endings promised, demonstrating that the break with tradition was harder for the British royal family than might have been hoped. The break up of both marriages was covered extensively by the British press through the 1990s, with the press's relationship with the royal family coming under extreme scrutiny following the death of Diana, Princess of Wales, in August 1997. The events of the 1990s had a visible effect on public perceptions of the family, particularly around the events of early September 1997.

M-O continued to chart the opinions of its Observers around royalty with two Directives on the subject during the 1990s. The first of these, issued in late 1992, asked Observers to reflect back on the year that Queen Elizabeth dubbed as being her 'annus horribilis'.

7

Divorces and funerals – the 1990s

Winter Directive 1992 – a looking back at 1992

Mass-Observation continued to chart the opinions of its Observers around royalty with two Directives on the subject during the 1990s. The first of these, issued in late 1992, asked Observers to reflect back on the year that held little joy for Queen Elizabeth.

On Wednesday, 25 November 1992, The Times *led its front page with the headline, 'Sad Queen dubs 1992 her "annus horribilis"', accompanied by a large photograph of a sullen-looking Queen Elizabeth taken the evening before. The Queen had used the phrase during her speech at a lunch given in honour of the fortieth anniversary of her accession by the Lord Mayor of London at Guildhall. The paper described her as 'sorrowful, a mite hurt, but essentially philosophical' when describing the year that had been 'a catalogue of persona; sadness and misfortune'.[1]*

The year 1992 saw the divorce of her daughter and the very public disintegration of the marriages of two of her sons. News of the separation of the Yorks broke in March amid claims that the Duchess was having an extramarital relationship.[2] The shock of having the family's 'dirty linen washed in public' was further exacerbated by the publication of the Princess of Wales's biography, in which her marital problems were detailed, including the Prince of Wales's affair with Camilla Parker-Bowles.[3] The revelations in the book were followed by the leaking of transcripts of recordings of intimate conversations between Charles and Camilla (commonly termed as 'Camilla-gate') and Diana and James Gilby (dubbed 'squidgey-gate'), neither of which left either Prince or Princess in a particularly good light with the public.

Finally, on 20 November fire destroyed part of Windsor Castle whilst the Queen was in residence, burning for seven hours and causing extensive damage that had posed a threat to 'one of the world's greatest collections of artworks'.[4] Restoration costs were estimated as being in the tens of millions of pounds, and by 23 November 1992, only two days before the Guildhall speech, fierce public and political debate was taking place on how the repair bill would be covered. The day after the speech, it was reported that the Queen had agreed to pay income tax, making her the first British monarch to do so since 1930.[5]

The Directive

It was against these revelations and conflagrations that the M-O Panel were sent a Directive in November 1992 asking them to look back over 1992 and note their reactions and feelings to events of the year, from national and international happenings to work and family occasions. As with the 1986 Directive, the Observers were not prompted to mention any royal happenings, so it is notable that so many did mention the troubles of the royal family at this time, possibly due to the very recent and widespread reporting of the Queen's 'annus horribilis' speech at the Guildhall that month.

Unlike previous Directives around weddings and jubilees, Observers interacted with events through the media rather than participating in activities, so responses concentrate on opinion and observation of unfolding events in the royal households. As ever with the M-O Panel, responses to events ranged from sympathy to anger demonstrating the complexity of the relationship between the royal family and individuals.

A retired seventy-year-old male from Kent observed:

This last year must have been the worst in many years for them. It shows that they are like any other family and can have break up and wrong doing by members, and today it is as the Papers say a news story. In the past it would not have had so many lies etc printed, and only printed as it was best for us to know, said by a high civil servant and the Church.

The trouble with the Royal Family is that like any other family things go wrong. In the past as in a lot of families it was kept within the family and people did what they could to stay together. But now it is so much easier to break up and even divorce.[6]

Sympathy or apathy?

The sympathy of several Observers lay with the Queen, in some instances stretching to empathy as the familiarities of ordinary family life were recognized. A 72-year-old housewife from Dartmoor agreed that the events showed the royal family to be like any other but referred to the difference the media made to this.

DIVORCES AND FUNERALS – THE 1990S

What can one say about the Royal Family? I feel very sad for the Queen who has to carry on regardless of her feelings which must be tumultuous. Of course the family are like any other family when it comes down to human relations and then are affected by the current epidemic of marriage break up. But I can't find words to say what I think of the press and the intolerable intrusion in the lives of these poor people, already traumatised by their inability to resolve their problems.[7]

A 74-year-old from Yorkshire whose husband had died in 1992 still found space to sympathize with the effect press intrusion could have.

I feel sorry for the Queen, yes she has had a bad year, indeed she's not alone in that. I think the newspapers should stop making news where there is none and stop besieging the younger members of the family every time that go out. Divorce and operation are the in-thing of this age. What people really want from life is happiness.[8]

Others were less patient with the situation the royal family found themselves in, such as one seventy-year-old female from London:

I really don't see what is so new about Royal scandals. Why does anyone suppose that they aren't normal humans like the rest of us? If what the Nation wants is a perfect tribal symbol why don't we make do with a Totem Pole?[9]

A fifty-year-old housewife from London experienced a feeling of being let down, understanding that members of the royal family are human but expecting a standard of behaviour deemed appropriate to their role:

The unrest in the Royal Family has also upset me. We don't expect them to be angels but why couldn't they have carried on and preserved the status quo for the country I really do not know. After all mistresses etc are not unknown. The same for male lovers etc. Their houses are quite big enough to keep away from each other and new establishments were hardly necessary. Still what is done is done. I have no idea what the outcome will be. Personally I feel Diana should make herself scarce and leave Charles to dedicate himself to trying to hold the monarchy together. They have a pretty poor record at the moment.[10]

This feeling was echoed by other Observers with responses comparing the lot of the royal family to the troubles many others found themselves in. A retired library assistant from Yorkshire felt that

the troubles of the royal family are insignificant when compared to the lot of many. At least they are cocooned against the harsher realities of life.[11]

A 61-year-old from the North West agreed, feeling that:

> Apart from the economic situation, last year seems to have been dominated by scandals among the royal family. Coverage of the Royal Family seems to have been at the expense of real investigations into more important matters such as the state of the Health Service, Education, Transport, Energy and industry.[12]

Scandal

The scandals referred to largely centred around the breakdown of the Princes Charles's and Andrew's marriages. Many Observers referenced media coverage of the scandals as a reason for losing respect for the royal family, citing the behaviour of individual members as contributing to showing its loss of worth. A 42-year-old housekeeper from Derbyshire described her disillusionment and disgust with the family, in particular citing the transcripts of intimate phone calls between Prince Charles and Camilla Parker-Bowles that were first published by the Sunday People *and* Sunday Mirror *in January 1993.*

> I read the transcript, hardly love talk is it? He says 'I wish I could be reincarnated as your TAMPAX!?' Well if a man said that to me I would think he was a pervert! The whole tape shows Charles to be very childish in his language, rather reminiscent of the babyish language his great Uncle David used when creeping up to his wife Wallace [*sic*] Simpson . . .

> Now this young man, Charles, is hoping to be our King one day and as such, Head of the Church of England. We all know what the bible says about adultery and Charles in his unique and privileged position as the eldest son of a sovereign, he should have taken his position more seriously (even a common man would have behaved better Charles he had the moral of a tom cat). He deserved a good telling off from his mother, we all know the Queen has a temper, well, she should direct a few sharp words in green, naive Charles's ear.[13]

Some Observers focus their criticism away from the royal family and towards those joining it, commenting on the struggle they may have had to adapt. A seventy-year-old retired chartered engineer from Hampshire compared the behaviour of Princess Margaret's ex-husband to the younger generation as she writes:

> I think too of the Lord Snowdon, Margaret's forgotten husband. He has carried on with life-after-royalty in a dignified manner, showing much more stature than many of his former in-laws.[14]

In a similar vein, a 76-year-old retired clerk from Nottinghamshire believed that:

There is also the fact that Royals used to marry Royals all of whom were brought up to a certain code of practice but none of the children of our present Queen has done this and difficulties have appeared which makes good news for the media but becomes very damaging to themselves. I wonder if there are signs here that the monarchy is breaking up or at least signs too changes from the way we know it.[15]

A 46-year-old oil exploration worker from Aberdeen also commented on the difference between royal and non-royal backgrounds resulting in turmoil for the family, recalling sentiments expressed in the 1981 Directive about reasons for Prince Charles's choice of bride:

It does not really surprise me about the break up of Charles and Diana, sad though it is. It is very difficult to know who is to blame given the copious leaks, supposition and claim/counterclaims. A marriage made in heaven it most definitely wasn't. It appeared to me a matter of eugenics in choosing Charles' bride. She had to be young, good breeding stock, healthy, reasonably intelligent and docile to be acceptable to the Palace, and that's what they got initially. By all accounts Charles' appointment calendar revolves strictly around his polo fixtures! So how would any marriage survive that. And then there is the barking mad Prince Phillip, I don't blame any bride for wanting to get away from that! I rather like Charles but he really is an old fogey at 44 years old and clearly does not like his wife upstaging him.[16]

A 59-year-old retired radiographer from Gloucestershire also drew attention to what she saw as the consequence of non-royals joining the family, laying the blame squarely at the feet of Princess Diana and the Duchess of York:

As an ardent royalist I have been so very saddened by events this year. Well, I never have had much respect for the Sporks (and gather the children are not well behaved), but I have admired Charles and Diana. So their separation was a blow to me.

I had thought Diana had behaved so well and with such dignity when A. Mortens's book was published. Then it gradually dawned on me that she was in favour of the book – she may not have instigated it, but I'm sure, if she had wished, it would not have been published. I was furious at the tabloids for the photographs of Charles and Diana on their Korean tour, where they had looked so solemn and the tabloids had only shown head and shoulders and the full photo later published showed they were at a war memorial.

However my sympathies now lie completely with the Queen and P. Charles who have behaved with dignity and as one would have expected. Andrew has also been most discreet and behaved well over the whole episode. Sarah has certainly made a fool of herself. As for Diana, I feel she has been disloyal, spiteful and manipulative. Her official jobs she does well, and no doubt it is not easy to be married to someone who appears to have so little in common with her and if they are often apart. However her actions have rocked the monarchy. Many working women live fairly separate lives from their spouses. I would have thought the Wales' had enough houses to live fairly operate lives and not get to operation/divorce. Diana must have known that whatever the difficulties their marriage was meant to be forever. I do wonder if her father had still been alive whether all this would have happened. He might have instilled a spark of loyalty into her ...

Having discussed this with various friends (who all feel let down by Diana) I was interested when one rather blamed 'B.Palace' for sanctioning the marriage in the first place.

I feel so let down that no way would I support any charity connected with Diana (though I would not go out of my way to discover which she did support).[17]

A 41-year-old clerical worker, who had her own troubles in 1992 with the deaths of several close relatives, observed:

I did wonder if Diana had engineered the whole thing in order to force Charles to abdicate and her son to rule with her guidance, either in order to gain power which she wouldn't have had if she had been discreetly shuffled off to the sidelines, or as revenge for him having an affair with Camilla Parker Bowles.[18]

Other writers appeared to revel in the royal family's difficulties that year, seeing the events as the arrival of a new era phasing out what they described as outdated institutions. A 39-year-old woman from Yorkshire wrote:

There was all the fuss over the Royal Family of course, which lightened some of the bad news. Andrew Morton and his book could prove the downfall of the British Monarchy yet – I rather hope so. I've never been that Republican, but the Royal Family as it stands has been shown as a completely fossilised creation. I'm extremely glad the Queen is now paying some tax; I thoroughly enjoyed Morton's books; think Prince Charles has been shown up like his adulterous predecessors; think the Duke of York is a dork and his estranged wife very much a commoner; and think Diana should be the next Queen, because she is easy on the eye and has glamour, if no brain.[19]

Evidence of a changing society

Whilst a 75-year-old retired insurance officer regarded the royal happenings as evidence of an emerging problem with governance within the UK:

1992 has been outstanding to me, and I take no pleasure in making this claim that my strong convictions over the years have proved so right. These, in particular, are that this country is and has been quite appallingly governed for ages, and that our so-called Royal Heritage is constituted of a bunch of worthless parasites and hangers-on, and that this lack of leadership and example from the top has reduced this nation to third-class status. Furthermore the greed and poor service of the business world particularly in the city has helped to contribute to this sorry state of affairs and these factors combined with the ineptitude by the police and law officers has indeed rendered 1992 an 'annus horribilus' [*sic*] and it is ironical that those very words were uttered by a person whose family and influence has contributed significantly to the lowering standards, both in morale and behaviour of the public at large.[20]

Many Observers laid the responsibility for the personal troubles of the royal family at the feet of its younger generation; a 64-year-old housewife from London felt that the queen should shoulder some of the responsibility:

I have become increasingly dismayed and disillusioned over the past few years as successive scandals about the royal family come to light. I have, up to now, been a staunch supporter of the Queen and her family, but first the split of the Duke and Duchess of York, closely followed by that of the Prince and Princess of Wales have tasted that support to breaking point. The publication of the photos of the Duchess of York, the book about Princess of Wales by Andrew Morton, and finally the text of telephone conversations between Prince Charles and Camilla Parker-Bowles, destroyed any respect I had for these people. I know the Queen is not responsible for the behaviour of her children, but i do think that one or two remarks from her, disapproving of this behaviour might not come amiss.

She also reflected on the Queen's agreement to start paying income tax from 1993 in order to cover the repairs to damage caused by the fire at Windsor Castle, observing how the change had only come about as a response to public and political criticism to the family's financial commitments:

There was also the controversy over the Queen not paying income tax. It's true that she has finally offered to pay this tax, but the offer was a very long time coming. After the fire at Windsor Castle, there was no

174 REFLECTIONS ON BRITISH ROYALTY

immediate offer from her to contribute towards restoration. If she had done this, I think the people's respect for her would have been given a badly needed boost. It was only after the consternation expressed at the Government's shouldering the financial responsibility for making the repairs that an offer to contribute was forthcoming. It seems to me that the Queen could do with the services of a good PR man![21]

With a facetious tone, a 65-year-old male from Wales highlighted the contrast of the royal family's financial situation with that of many people in the UK at that point:

The two Latin words 'Annus Horrubilis' [*sic*] uttered by THE QUEEN in an end of year speech (God bless her and all others who depend on the public purse for subsistence), sums up the year according to her. Some public sympathy has been shown for her 'suffering' – and miles of newsprint have been used to discuss her family's plight. What with her two sons' marriages going on the rocks and Windsor Palace catching fire, the hearts of those whose houses were repossessed (due to mortgage repayment defaults) must have missed an extra beat or two as well!!

THE QUEEN'S delayed decision to pay tax like the rest of her subjects must have caused her some sleepless nights, – even though she will most probably not miss the money.

On the positive side that nice Home Secretary who so eagerly and promptly after the Windsor fire declared that the taxpayer (you and me) would be delighted and honoured to pay for the repairs to the castle must have cheered up the Royal Family no end with no need at all now to cut back on the Xmas shopping. Others, with the same basic problem as that encountered by a section of the castle, who also have no roof over their heads and are sleeping in cardboard boxes in our cities must have been rather envious of the anxiety expressed over the burnt roof of Windsor Castle and wondering how long it will be before the Home Secretary does something positive about putting a roof over their heads. Anyway, it's nice to know now that the castle is really ours (I hadn't realised that before the fire) and as that is so it being our duty to keep it repaired . . . they say!. What about repairing all those schools and hospitals which are also ours? As we use them every day shouldn't they have priority?![22]

The events of the year caused some Observers, including a 69-year-old female from the West Midlands, to reflect on the future of the British Monarchy and their faith in the institution:

I'm afraid like a lot of people, I have become disenchanted with the Monarchy although I must say the Queen has acted through it all with great dignity, as she always does. It is assumed that the Queen will begin

DIVORCES AND FUNERALS – THE 1990S

to contribute to the Treasury and not before time but I for one have destroyed all my scrapbooks about the Royal Family! It can never be the same but I would not like the system changed.[23]

For a 67-year-old housewife from Scarborough, disillusionment came in the form of an increasing 'classlessness':

Classlessness seems more noticeable now that the Royal Family's marital troubles are on a par with those of the 'common people'. I have always been a keen royalist but during the latter part of 1992 I have begun to question my own loyalty and to wonder whether the monarchy should continue after Elizabeth II. I suppose it shouldn't really concern me personally as I am only a few months older than the Queen.[24]

One area that provoked marked criticism from several Observers was the role of the press, in particular around the marital troubles of the Prince and Princess of Wales and Duke and Duchess of York. This criticism of the press echoes that of Observers' writing during the Townsend Affair and would increase over the 1990s, particularly in the stark spotlight of events surrounding the death of the Princess of Wales. In 1992, a 76-year-old retired clerk from Nottingham observed:

the press and TV have been given more opportunities to enter their private lives and this has revealed to the public more of their way of life whereas years ago the monarchy was considered to be beyond reproach in many ways so the newspapers if they were aware of any misdemeanours were not permitted to publish it or not until years after it had taken place.[25]

A 65-year-old male from the West Midlands also felt that the royal family had been 'hounded' along with other public figures such as Members of Parliament:

But how about Royalty? They have been hounded, I feel very sorry for the Queen, no mother at her age deserves what the Press have thrown at her what with divorces, fire at Windsor . . . Oh! of course she pays no tax – did Hitler pay tax? Or Bush? or Saddam Hussein? No I think I'll stick by her Majesty, at least she brings millions of pounds to our lovely country with tourist trade.[26]

A 63-year-old woman from the South West felt sure that the issue lay with a new republican leaning direction of some of the major newspapers:

There are two aspects of this campaign to denigrate the Royals which are particularly worrying. The first is why? And I believe the answer to this lies in the fact that Murdoch is a republican. So here we have a foreigner

176   REFLECTIONS ON BRITISH ROYALTY

with the power at his disposal to destroy our monarchy. And he might succeed.[27]

Similar concerns about the power of the press were raised by B89 who was less concerned about how the family led their private lives and more concerned 'about the fact that telephone conversations can be listened into and recorded. The spectre of Big Brother impinging on anyone's civil rights looms ominously.'[28]

A 38-year-old female teacher from Manchester could 'remember being fascinated but their wedding – she with her "look at me I'm wonderful" attitude and her lapping it all up. To me their life epitomised the empty glass if the 1980s and their separation was a sign that that had ended.'

Suggestions were also made on possible alternatives including a slimmed-down version of the family:

I used to be more Royalist than otherwise but now feel that the only real reason to retain the monarchy is the dread thought that otherwise we might have Mr T as President. Certainly there is the feeling that we could with a much less expensive Head of State, far too many hangers-on, too many paces, privileges etc; the past twelve months has seen a diminution in respect for royalty as such, though role models like the Spanish, Dutch and Scandinavian monarchies have received favourable comment.[29]

Summer 1997 (special) – the death of Diana

The press fascination with reporting revelations and chasing stories on Princess Diana appeared to escalate in the years following the separation of the Prince and Princess of Wales. Diana's developing independence from the royal family appeared to give her the confidence to disclose her own side of the story, culminating in a now infamous interview with Martin Bashir, broadcast on the BBC in 1995. The revelations made by the Princess about the adulterous relationships of her husband and herself were shockingly revealing for watchers.[30] During the interview Diana claimed that she wanted to be remembered as the 'queen of hearts' and much of the subsequent coverage and, possibly as a result, public sympathy was with Diana as the wronged party. This balance of sympathies came to a head two years later when the tragic events of 31 August 1997 thoroughly tested the relationship between the Monarch and her subjects.

On the morning of 31 August 1997 the world woke up to the news that Diana, Princess of Wales, had died in the early morning, following a car crash in Paris. The events of the following week took on an almost mythical tone as the UK witnessed a process of mourning across the country that culminated in a funeral watched by around 32 million in the UK and over 2 billion around the world, whilst around a million people gathered in London along the route of her funeral cortege. Millions of bunches of flowers were laid at venues around the country, the late Princess's home of Kensington Palace being the largest focus of this phenomenon where the carpet of bouquets spread 30 feet from the gates, sometimes reaching a depth of 5 feet.

The media reported scenes of mass public mourning with people openly weeping and comforting each other and others waiting, sometimes for hours, to sign books of condolence that sprang up in venues ranging from cathedrals and local government offices to supermarkets. During that week, the British royal family were subjected to a significant level of criticism as media channels reported unhappiness and even anger towards the Queen and her family for attending church as normal on the Sunday morning of the death, for not immediately returning to London, for not ordering the flag at Buckingham Palace to be lowered and, perhaps most of all, for remaining silent.

The 'Special Directive'

Within a few days of Diana's death, it became clear that the volunteer writers were already recording events for the Archive. Whilst staff had not initially planned to send out a Directive on the subject, the unprecedented reaction of the media and the public in the wake of the death compelled M-O to put out a Special Directive. The Directive was issued on 8 September 1997, with an acknowledgement of M-O's 'long-standing interest in national events and the significance of the Monarchy'.

Whether you are a royalist or a republican, please send us your feelings, opinions, observations. Feel free to discuss whatever you think is important, including the media coverage and any other issues you think may be relevant. If you change your opinions and feelings please chart the change.

The Archive received around 250 responses, most of which numbered several pages of in-depth reflections on events. Some writers kept a diary or sent in extracts of their personal diaries detailing the events as they occurred. Others reflected on the events of that week from a distance, sometimes months later, thus providing contrast to the immediate responses gathered by M-O.

The responses were wide-ranging, from highly emotional reactions akin to losing a close personal friend to sheer dismay over the extreme displays of public emotion being relayed by the media. Alongside their own personal reactions, many took the opportunity to analyse public mourning or to reflect on the royal family, particularly in light of the volume of criticism levelled at it during that week.

Personal reactions to the news

A recurring theme of polarization in terms of opinions and feelings expressed is present in the directive responses, ranging from attitudes about the Princess herself, the level of emotional connection felt by Observers or expressed by others, the opinions on the levels of public mourning witnessed, the speech of Earl Spencer during Diana's funeral or the response of the royal family to events.

In the initial response to the crash, some Observers expressed a deep connection to Diana and felt her loss as intensely personal, whilst others responded in a depersonalized way, simply recording events as they watched others grieve.

Writing on 31 August, a female, 49-year-old clerical worker, was one of those overtaken with emotion writing sixteen pages to Mass-Observation over the week following the Princess's death.

> What a waste of a lovely person who had the common touch, the people's princess. I haven't done a thing all day except cook the dinner because I have just felt so stunned and shocked, and I have cried several times because she did not deserve this.

> I have never seen anything like this before and it has taken the palace and the media by surprise. I knew she was popular and a well-loved princess but I had no idea that everyone felt as I did and even more strongly than I did. All those people, all those flowers, all those people waiting seven hours to sign the books, it's unbelievable and very, very moving.

> If I had lived in London I would have taken flowers but instead I took some to the Princess of Wales Hospital in Ely because I heard other people had and I lay them there this morning. Also today in Ely they have opened one of the chapels in the Cathedral for people to sign a book of condolence. I will go and do that on Wednesday, my day off. I have never felt the need to lay flowers like this before but something inside of me wanted to do it and so I can understand that need in other people all over the country because almost every town and city has got somewhere to lay flowers and books to sign.[31]

Meanwhile, a 53-year-old factory worker from Suffolk first heard the news whilst on holiday with her husband in Cyprus from another holidaymaker and responded in an almost physical way:

> I asked my husband to ask this lady if what I heard was true. He waited until we had got onto the boat, and when she said that what I had overheard was true I felt like hitting her. I felt as though she was telling me that somebody in my family had died.

> When I first heard that she had died, the first thing I said was that I blamed Prince Charles. If only he had loved her she would have been alive today.

DIVORCES AND FUNERALS – THE 1990S

I still feel that and after being a royalist all my life, I now see them all in a different light. I think all the Royal Family chose Diana just so she could bear the next King of England. They all knew that he was seeing another woman, who's name I can't bear to mention. IF only Charles had given her love, that lovely lady would have been alive today.[32]

For others the level of upset they experienced surprised them, including a 67-year-old ex-school secretary from Exeter who wrote:

As I have said, I was very upset at the death – more so than I would ever have predicted. I have wept often to think of the manner of her death. I don't understand why I find it so upsetting – after all I felt no particular interest in Royal affairs. I can only think that I saw her as a very unhappy and badly done-to woman. If my sympathies lay anywhere it would be with Diana, rather than Charles and family.

Writing on the day of the funeral, a 37-year-old teacher from Stockton-on-Tees found himself becoming more interested in the public response to the event rather than in the death of the Princess herself.

I knew the World would be Watching and I felt quite proud that 'we British would do it Properly' and that the public in London would play their part in this amazing show (Shades of Evita here?) . . .

In conclusion, I felt the funeral was an amazing show of public and Royal display, where I was proud to see that Britain could do it so well. I honestly believe that the media, unintentionally perhaps, orchestrated the hysterical response. Despite the blame that was thrown their way – the ordinary public's demand for Diana stories, both when she was living and dead were being delivered to feed a basic need. The public killed Diana. Were they mourning for her or for the realisation that they had all played a part in that tragic loss? A cynical response perhaps, but I would still admit that the week was very unusual and I doubt I will see another like it – not even the Queen Mother will get such a send off.[33]

For others the initial shock and sadness gave way relatively quickly as exemplified by this 35-year-old male administrative manager living in London.

So yes, I did feel sad. On Monday. And then on Tuesday. But not after that . . .

After all I didn't really know her. I'd not met her. She was neither friend nor family. So the sadness one can feel for someone who is ultimately a stranger is finite. Yet the public grief was astonishing. As each day passed, became worrying. What was this outpouring of grief all about for a nation best known for its reserve? What national catharsis was taking place? I saw some of the testimonies people wrote and thought, 'get a life!' On reflection, it seemed an extraordinary drama had taken place, one of such magnitude that there may not be another one in our lifetime. Everyone wanted to be a part of it. I suspect many of those who got very involved were those whose lives were perhaps coloured by sadness and loneliness. Her death gave them the opportunity to display the grief they felt for their own lives . . .

I felt frustrated by everyone's unquestioning sadness.[34]

A female writer aged forty-one was similarly frustrated with the public's grief, writing:

I would like to stress that no one in my family, and no friends to my knowledge, have shed one tear for Diana. We didn't like what we knew of her, weren't taken in by the PR job. What has brought us close to tears is the constant boring slushy, saccharine harping on about the unremarkable fact that a bimbo got killed in a drunken car crash. I DO NOT think she was a wonderful, loving mother, nor an inspiration to single mothers everywhere (what an insult to single mothers!) She was a rich woman who had her kids looked after by a nanny and packed them off to boarding school to be bullied by strangers at the age of seven, when any loving working-class mother would still be protecting and cuddling her sons. She never had any of the work or struggle involved in being a mother. She and her children were kept at the expense of tax-payers. I DO NOT think she was a bloody living saint, drooling compassion in her wake like a snail leaves a trail I think she was a shining example to anyone who wants to work the press. I am sick and tired of being told that she's my icon, and that I adored her.[35]

Reacting to public mourning

Another area of contrast within the writing was the response to the public mourning that took place in the week following Diana's death, including the laying of hundreds of thousands of bouquets of flowers at the gates of the Princess's home at Kensington Palace. Some described participating in the public response by laying flowers or signing of books of condolence. This Observer found solace in sharing their grief with others:

But this past week has been a unique nationwide collective experience of togetherness such as I have never experienced before.[36]

Others also noted similar feelings of unity. A 64-year-old female from London travelled to Kensington Palace to lay flowers at a point where the carpet was still only 10 feet wide:

DIVORCES AND FUNERALS – THE 1990S

From subsequent pictures in the media you will recall how the sea of flowers became an ocean of love and joy. Yes, joy. There was a feeling of kinship amongst the thousands of people and a quiet of joy and togetherness. We were proud that we loved her.[37]

Some, however, could not understand how a level of grief could be shown for someone they did not know personally, including a 45-year-old civil servant from London:

I was surprised by the public hysteria over Diana's death reflected in the extensive media coverage. Perhaps the populace need to express adoration for someone following the decline in religious belief (or maybe it was always so). Her lack of perfection seems to have made the public identify more easily with Diana. However it seems absurd to call a woman brought up in wealth and privilege the 'people's princess'. I am not a royalist but I did not expect so much antipathy towards the royal family. It is hardly surprising that people brought up in an isolated environment do not react in the same way as other members of society. The nation needs a head of state and the King or Queen seeks as good as any. I am not convinced that another system would identify more suitable candidates in Britain at present. The 'great and good' tend to be rather self-satisfied while politicians appear self-seeking.

Other people told me they felt the reaction was excessive but were in a minority. Some said they felt like outsiders in society during the period up to the funeral. Private Eye maintained a critical stance towards Diana and the media attracting a number of positive reactions from subscribers.[38]

The nature of the grief surprised some Observers, including a Welsh 76-year-old who expressed surprise at the general outpouring of grief:

Indeed we all ask ourselves WHY? Why such grief, why so widespread? During the week, culminating in the funeral, I look back in amazement at the sheer personal, deep sorrow and have come to some conclusions. Here was a beautiful, available, flawed human being whom we all saw continually on screen and in papers. A consummate performer, manipulating and being manipulated by the Press and YET someone 'up there' in the Royal circle who was seen loving and enjoying her boys, and touching, affectionately, other people who obviously responded to her needs and yet found great solace in her interest in them. Reading the copious reports and seeing all the interviews, I am still amazed at how many hard hearted people were all overtaken by the sheer magnitude of the feelings her death evoked. One cynical friend in London rang and said 'we are not Monarchists are we?'

Yet I went out in the crowds tonight and saw young, burly men clutching flowers and crying. On examination I think that we all genuinely felt assaulted by the manner of her death, and all our own past and present sorrows were amalgamated into one huge concerted feeling of horror at the 'if only' syndrome – if only we'd done this or that when someone died and so on.[39]

For some Observers the contrast of their own feelings with the extreme emotions they witnessed, and that were being depicted by the media of a nation united in grief, left them feeling like an outsider in their own country, including this 43-year-old male teacher from Norfolk, who wrote:

In the week between the death and the funeral I sometimes felt as if I were living in a foreign country. I thought I understood something about the British people but perhaps I don't.[40]

A 44-year-old secondary schoolteacher from Bolton also expressed a feeling of alienation, especially feeling strong social pressure to publicly participate in the mourning. Even though she had no intention of watching the funeral on Saturday, this Observer felt it would be inappropriate to be seen outside washing her windows during the ceremony. Her new partner arrived later that day having had a similar experience and they agreed that:

I feel as if I am the only person in the whole country who never shed a tear over the death of Diana, and who never watched or heard a moment of her funeral. I wasn't making a particular point of this and had no strong feelings one way or the other about her as a person, apart from mild irritation when she did things like taking her underage sons to a 15-certificate movie. But her death coincided with major events in my own life and I hardly gave her a thought except when discussing the phenomenon of the nation's grief . . .

The day of the funeral was the day W was coming to my house for the first time: our second weekend together. Even Radio 3 was covering the funeral or having some special music on in Diana's memory, so I cleaned the house from top to bottom in silence. The street outside seemed unnaturally quiet, and I remember trying to finish cleaning the outside windows before 11 o'clock. I think I felt some kind of pressure to be inside by then, not to be seen to be ignoring the event. I did ignore it, however.[41]

Whilst the perception of a mass response to the death reminded one 71-year-old woman from Wales of scenes from Red Square in Moscow following the death of Stalin. She wondered if this demonstrates that a country needs more emotion from time to time, writing:

DIVORCES AND FUNERALS – THE 1990S

The local radio station has a daily review of the papers and on Friday the guest the presenter had in was a young man who was defending the Royals. The presenter said she thought someone was stirring things up – I wondered if she knew that Rupert Murdoch who owns most of the papers is very anti-royal and it was probably his doing. We were amazed at the person who said they cried more over the Princess than over their parents death. I did wonder if they and many of the other weepers were actually depressed anyway and this was some subconscious emotional catharsis. Letters in the Telegraph made us feel that maybe we were right in thinking people should be getting things in proportion and be a bit more rational.

I also feel that if I had said to anybody what I have written here, last week, I would have been made to feel callow and cruel. It is sad that so many have such shallow emotions and seem to wallow in grief.[42]

Other Observers also commented on media coverage, attributing the wall-to-wall coverage as being responsible for whipping up heightened levels of grief and public mourning. Even those who admitted to being glued to their radios or TV screens on first hearing about the Princess's death professed to feeling tired of the frenzy of reporting as the day and indeed the week progressed. The extent of coverage on radio and TV caused a 64-year-old retired dispenser from Somerset to refrain from joining the public mourning, despite professing to be a royalist.

As that Sunday progressed I became irritated at the continuous radio coverage (and T.V), with 'top' presenters being called in to talk, in hushed tones, about the life of Diana (which surely by now everyone knew). The only facts known at that time could have easily been included in extended news bulletins. Over the next few days this coverage – by then the newspapers too printing little else – became so intense that I am positive it whipped up hysteria among the population. At that point I decided I could not join in this hysteria and would not be signing any book or laying any flowers.[43]

In May 1998, a 51-year-old male from the South West reflected on the situation with the benefit of hindsight and wrote:

It has been my impression that the BBC is prone to go overboard when a big news event occurs. This surprises me because often these 'events' do not have so many ramifications and often gave little political significance. In fact this was largely true in this case: Diana's death was primarily a family tragedy. She was a peripheral figure following her divorce. She was not a significant reason for shifting other news stories off the front page for a whole week. The whole thing was magnified by the media, although there was widespread and demonstrative grief (I myself signed the book at Bristol Cathedral and wrote personally to Prince Charles). That national mourning was astonishing, but was it really news?[44]

But not everyone was critical about the volume of coverage that events received that week. Some writers felt that it provided a sense of community with whom they shared their grief. A 36-year-old freelance decorator from London stated that she 'needed the media coverage over-load to meet my own response to it all'.[45]

The outpouring of a public grief caused some writers to reflect on the spiritual aspect of the response. The Archbishop of Canterbury claimed that the response of the British public to the Princess's death was proof that the country was still very spiritual,[46] but for some Observers the public response demonstrated a lack of traditional religion, countered by a need for an alternative spiritual outlet. A retired analytical chemist born in 1924 reflected on this feeling:

This adulation fascinates me more than all other aspects of the phenomenon (other than the arranging of the actual funeral with all the problems that poses, there will be many senior police officers and others glad to see Sunday!!) It does seem to me that her death has unveiled some form of spiritual need amongst many people. I do not expect that many of those who feel the need to express this great loss could tell you why. Partly maybe it is the violent end of a Fairytale turned tragedy. Maybe it is a focus for personal griefs and difficulties (including loneliness) from present or past, and the knowledge that Diana had suffered too. Then there is the possibility that it is a reaction against those wicked Windsors who gave 'D' such a terrible life. Also maybe they think she was a commoner standing up to the establishment (forgetting her very privileged background). So one's mind goes on and one asks why this mass expression of outward sympathy, feeling of a personal link with someone never met or even seen in person and spiritual longing, has not been ignited by the ministry of we Christian folk and our Churches. Where have we failed?[47]

A 64-year-old from the North West also pondered on the idea of the public grief being a substitute for traditional religion but also saw elements of what she described as the 'bandwagon effect':

The wholly unprecedented display of national grief took everyone by surprise, and no one quite knows how to interpret it. Our culture is rapidly changing; attitudes towards death are changing; the way we express our emotions is changing. I am convinced that one of the strands in the public grief over Diana is the loss of traditional religion, and the search for substitute. The multiplication of little shrines centred round a

DIVORCES AND FUNERALS – THE 1990S 185

picture of Diana, and surrounded by flowers and candles, is a strongly religious phenomenon, suggesting the danger of a Diana cult being almost an alternative religion.[48]

For a 53-year-old from the South East, writing a week after the funeral, the scenes of public grief were about creating a community that she felt had been lost in contemporary society:

My reactions to the public response to her death was I think 'they are mourning for themselves' because society has become such an atomised and alienated place people have been grieving for a lost sense of community in private up till now. Diana's death represented to them the loss of someone who publicly at least displayed humanistic characteristics . . . she publicly cared but also in her approach to people, eg touching them, crying with them, identified with their suffering. I believe her death unlocked a whole raft of public grief about the loss of community, the loss of collectiveness. I do not believe all those people laying flowers were laying them for her, they were laying them for themselves and their own communities. Having said this I think it was an amazing spectacle and people clearly enjoyed being together as a group united (for once which is rare) in a common endeavour. I suppose these responses are those of a sociologist but they are personal, not derived from any other source.[49]

'Speak to us Ma'am'

The royal family, and the Queen herself, came in for unprecedented criticism around the way they responded in the immediate aftermath of Princess Diana's death. In the days following, the Queen was silent about the death and stayed in Balmoral with other royals, including the Princess's two sons, rather than returning directly to London.

Headlines seemed to fan criticism of these actions, for example, on 4 September 1997, The Daily Mirror *carried the headline, 'Your people are suffering: speak to us Ma'am'* [50] *with a photograph of distraught mourners. As with the wider public, some Observers also expressed anger against the Queen and royal family, in particular Prince Charles, echoing the sentiments appearing in much of the press. This 32-year-old from Yorkshire and Humber wrote:*

My anger towards the Royal Family has been one of the stronger emotions I'd felt during the morning [day of death]: how they'd treated Diana, how Charles had cheated on her, how she was never appreciated for the work she did, how they'd taken away her HRH title. I blamed then for Diana not being sufficiently protected against the Press and that she wasn't surrounded by special protection people . . . I'm not convinced of the sincerity of these gestures.

[4 Sept 1997] All of this week, the reaction of the Royal Family has been totally out of step with that of the public and it seems that everything they do is only because they feel obliged to because of public opinion and not because they want to. Maybe the Queen is being very poorly advised, maybe it's just become obvious to us that the Queen belongs to a very different generation of Royals with an approach that is no longer appropriate.[51]

Others also criticized, but with less anger, instead resigned to the bad decisions that the royal family seemed to make. For instance, this 64-year-old retired banker from the South East:

I believe that she [the Queen] did mishandle her public relations (yet again) in this situation. I consider that for the first couple of days, before it had become clear that a huge public reaction had begun to develop, she behaved reasonably in remaining at Balmoral. But by, say, the Tuesday, she should have recognised that a tidal wave of emotion was passing over the country, especially demonstrable in London, and she should immediately have gone there and delivered some expression of gratitude. You really cannot have people delivering flowers and queuing for hours to sign commemoration books – and the Queen apparently taking no notice. Even if she was personally distracted by her grandsons' distress, her advisors should have got her on track.

Sadly the monarchy has in the last 10 years or so, frequently botched its public relations. A stark example was the Queen's maladroit re-action to the public demand that she should pay income tax. Instead of immediately saying she would pay, leaving the detail to be settled later, she let the controversy drift on for nearly a year, stoking up unpopularity. No large company would so badly mis-handle its image – it would not last long if it did.[52]

But other Observers had sympathy with the family's actions, recognizing the need for the family to personally have time to come to terms with the shock of tragedy before being able to respond publicly. A 41-year-old author from Watford wrote:

They [the public] could not recognise genuine stunned shock, disbelief, grief and suffering displayed by the sombre and withdrawn Royal Family but had to have their own melodramatic demonstrations of extreme mourning for a woman they have never even known personally. Could it be some sort of guilt complex, projecting onto the Queen and Prince Charles the blame they ought really to have turned on themselves because

The funeral

The funeral of Diana Princess of Wales took place on 6 September. Although not accorded a state funeral, the Princess did receive a royal ceremonial funeral at Westminster Abbey, preceded by a procession through the streets of London and accompanied by Princes William and Harry, her brother Earl Spencer, Prince Charles and the Duke of Edinburgh. The two young boys walking behind the coffin, along with the public act of showering flowers on the hearse that drove the late Princess from the Abbey to her final resting place, provided highly emotive images that seared into public memory. A 74-year-old retired teacher travelled from her home in South West London to the centre of the city on the day of the funeral to witness events for herself:

The forecasts had been that there would be thousands of people up in London. I decided that I would aim for Hyde Park and watch the giant TV screens. I caught an early Underground train. There were a lot of people, mostly families with children of all ages and bearing flowers. It was noticeable how warm and friendly the atmosphere was. We were advised to alight at Knightsbridge and walk from there because Hyde Park Corner Station was too congested.

In Hyde Park the crowd was already five deep lining the route from Kensington Palace. Further into the Park there were thousands of people settling down on the grass in front of the two giant TV screens. They were quiet and friendly – chatting to those nearest them. As time passed more and more and more people came. When I stood and looked around there were people as far as I could see. What was so impressive was the silence – hardly a cough – even the small children were quiet. The commentary started. Still it was quiet – but there was applause when the Union Jack was put at half-mast on the Palace (there had been ill feeling that this had not been done earlier). During the Service in the Abbey there continued the amazing quiet in the Park. People quietly showed their feeling, wept, comforted each other. There were no cameras – it was all very personal. It seemed to me that many people were, perhaps for the first time, expressing their sorrow for losses and families. At the criticism of the media's intrusion into the Princesses' life, there was totally spontaneous, unprecedented applause.[54]

The speech by Earl Spencer during his sister's funeral divided opinion. One 54-year-old housewife from Bedfordshire expressed support for the Earl's speech, but once her initial sympathy had subsided she questioned whether the sentiments expressed had been appropriate given the circumstances:

Then Earl Spencer's speech made me weep again. Such a brave speech to make, being critical of the press but also of the royal family with them all sitting there. The press had said during the week that he wasn't afraid to speak his mind so his speech would be 'interesting'. I sort of assumed that it would have had to be vetted by the Palace first but apparently not. According to the paper the Queen was not pleased. The public were though and applause ran through the crowd outside, then amazingly through the Abbey itself At a funeral! (Although at the time I applauded his bravery, on reflection I felt that it probably wasn't the right time to say what he did. The family were hurting and it must have added to their hurt. Confusing for the young princes too, who must have divided loyalties. I suppose he felt that if he didn't say it all then he'd never again have such an opportunity. Despite his assertion that Diana's 'blood family' would ensure that the boys were brought up as she would have wanted, I feel now that that was an emotional and unthought out response to the tragedy. He lives in South Africa, there's little he can do. Diana didn't seem that close to her own family.)[55]

Writing to the Archive in early 1998, a 72-year-old retired office manager from Bridlington agreed:

The one jarring note in the service came from Earl Spencer when he implied that he, as Diana's brother would ensure that her two sons William and Harry were brought up to fly free, subject, of course to the constraints of Royal duties and protocol. By implication he seemed to be saying, that the Royal family are not fit and proper people to be trusted with that side of the boys development. Well, if they aren't why should anyone accept that he is. In recent months he has been revealed as a serial adulterer, among other nefarious things, as was revealed in the proceedings in the divorce court in South Africa. The sound of the applause for the Earl's speech, as it swept across the thousands in Hyde Park and all along the route, and up to the doors of the Abbey, and finally through the doors and into the Abbey to be taken up by the congregation, was by itself one of the most remarkable things about the whole day. I said to my wife when he finished. 'Well he seems a straight talking kind of a bloke'. On reflection after about half an hour I came to the conclusion that taken in the context of a funeral service with the Queen sitting opposite him, although not on camera, and unable to make any reply, constituted a deliberate and unfair attack upon Her Majesty, especially coming from a man of his rank.[56]

A turning point for Britain and its royal family?

Following the death of Princess Diana discourses in the media and M-O often discussed the need for the British royal family to reflect the societal changes that were highlighted during the days following 31 August. For a 68-year-old retired legal professional from Shropshire, the events illustrated how the royal family no longer represented what it meant to be British:

> Their stiff upper lips freshly starched they showed the world the British way to be in the face of grief, not to portray the slightest hint of emotion, let that guard drop for a split second . . . But what was happening on the streets spoke volumes. The royals don't represent the British anymore they are not the ideal family firmly placed on top of the representational tree of the British way to be and react. We were crying in the streets, we were hugging, comforting and consoling each other, men and women showed and shared emotions like never before. Was this New Britain that had eased out of the mould along with New Labour? I thought so at the time. Blair was there . . . as he should be the elected head of the country expressing grief joint collective grief a tear in his eye a tear for us all . He appeared genuine I am sure he was but there was some wonderfully stage managed scenes to come. He played a role that helped to save the Royals even more embarrassment than they deserved and he ensured that the nation got to grieve this special person in a special way like no ever goodbye that had been seen before and I doubt be seen again.[57]

For a 72-year-old retired librarian from Nottingham, the protocols that had dictated the Queen's actions, and which had come in for so much public criticism, were a symbol of the royal traditions that made the family no longer fit for purpose in the modern world:

> The difficulties, the failure of protocol to meet them adequately, all arise from one thing. The age-old custom in dynastic families to protect the succession by arranged marriages between partners of appropriate rank regardless of personal feelings. Generations have accepted the custom until now in spite of evident misery or sometimes resignation by the consort to the extra-marital behaviour of the monarch to the extent of acknowledging royal mistresses. This time, a wife has spoken out about her treatment and has shown herself to be enterprising in retaliation. The modern world has made it possible, for the first time, to do so without social ruin. With the aid of the media she has rallied people to her support and gained their sympathy against her husband and his family – indeed against the system on which the continuation of the dynasty in its old form depends. At the same time she has branched out and changed the usual royal state and charitable visits into personal crusades, thereby

obtaining great and deserved personal popularity through her efforts which put those of the other royals, past and present, in the shade and on the side-lines. Suddenly, through this tragic accident, it all comes to a sudden end, with agonising difficulties, not to mention guilt for everyone involved while the public assembles en masse to pay tribute but also to offer opinions on the situation in the most vociferous way. I do not know what will be salvaged. Perhaps the long term effect on the Royal Family and its protocol will not be great but there may well be some changes or adjustments.[58]

A 43-year-old teacher from Norfolk also discussed what she expected of royalty, but rather than demanding change she reflected on what monarchy symbolized to her and what would be lost should it cease to exist in its current, or any, format:

As a preface to what I am about to write, I should say that I believe that the institution of the monarchy has a function. It provides cohesion and continuity. Even though the royal prerogative is nowadays exercised by executive government (and more often than not in its own interest) its existence is a reminder of the power the monarchy once had. We know that the monarch has a role to play in the law making process and that the services swear an oath of allegiance to the king or queen. We do not expect the monarch to intervene in political matters and neither would most people welcome it. The monarchy is symbolic of a ordered and stable society that has evolved without any revolutionary upheaval for three hundred years. As far as I am concerned, the monarchy is not about personality. In a hereditary monarchy the throne can never be vacant because there is always continuity. Despite what I have written I would never call myself a 'monarchist'. I appreciate that in a modern democratic society the existence of a hereditary monarchy is anachronistic. But whichever political party is in office there are always going to be areas of public life which defy public scrutiny and accountability. The monarchy is one of these. I believe it was Bagehot who wrote that too great an exposure – 'letting the light in' – would prove to be its death knell. The events of the past week have certainly compromised certain personalities within the royal family. I am really not Interested in the personal foibles of the Queen, Charles or Diana. I am more concerned whether the institution of the monarchy has been damaged beyond repair. Of course it is far too early to make any sort of judgement.[59]

Summary

The 1990s proved to be exceptionally difficult years for the royal family at a personal level and in terms of their increasingly fractious relationship with the press. Inevitably public opinion of the family was reported as being at an all-time low. The public response as reported in the media accentuated the notion of sympathies lying with a wronged Princess whilst the royal family, and unusually the Queen herself, were subjected to vocal public criticism and demand for change. The M-O responses to the death of the Princess, however, reflected a wider range of reactions demonstrating a far more nuanced response than the press portrayal of a nation united in grief. M-O provided a forum for those expressing opinions that they felt would be unpopular or contrary to what they perceived as the dominant discourse of the population.

Events over the two next decades were to demonstrate changes in the royal family's approach to interacting with the public; however, they have also shown how tradition and protocol retain a strong place within the monarchy. The Windsors reinforced their image of continuity through ceremony and tradition whilst also conceding to modernization. Royal events covered by Mass-Observation in the 2000s exemplify this paradox of old and new – the ceremonial traditions of the Queen Mother's funeral and marriage of the Prince of Wales to Camilla Parker-Bowles. That marriage alone underscored the profound changes which had taken place in royal norms and expectations by the turn of the twenty-first century: a marriage that was impossible for both Edward VIII in the 1930s and Princess Margaret in the 1950s.

8

A tentative recovery? The Royal Family in the 2000s

The 2000s began for the royal family with the celebration of the Queen Mother's 100th birthday. For a family still recovering from the personal tragedy and public ramifications of the death of Diana, Princess of Wales, the first years of the decade would test the public's reaction to the concessions to change being made by the family whilst also testing its tolerance for maintaining tradition. Two years after celebrating her centenary, the Queen Mother died, only weeks after her youngest daughter Princess Margaret. Despite losing her sister and mother, the Queen went on to celebrate her fiftieth jubilee later that year, each event demonstrating that traditional royal protocol lived on. In contrast, 2005 saw the marriage of the Prince of Wales to Camilla Parker-Bowles, the union of two divorcees whose relationship had been so publicly outed the previous decade.

Mass-Observation's first directive on royalty used the birthday of the Queen Mother to test how Observers felt about the royal family in 2000, only three years after the events that appeared to rock the monarchical relationship with the public.

Summer Directive 2000 – Queen Mother at 100

The Queen Mother's 100th birthday was celebrated with a service of thanksgiving at St Paul's Cathedral in London on 12 July 2000. This was followed by a procession down the Mall and balcony appearance at Buckingham Palace on 4 August 2000, accompanied by her two daughters and watched by a crowd of what the Guardian *newspaper described as 'respectable if not ecstatic dimensions' estimating around 30,000 people.[1] A birthday 'pageant' was also organized for 19 July,[2] of which coverage, or the lack of it, sparked some controversy when the BBC announced they would not be covering the parade in full.[3] The event was eventually televised by ITV, stepping in for the 'wrong-footed' BBC.[4]*

The Directive

M-O included the birthday as part 2 to its Summer Directive in 2000. The Observers were asked if they had plans to celebrate the occasion and to comment on the controversy over the BBC's decision not to broadcast some of the celebrations.

The question received 208 responses, the majority of which expressed little or no interest in the celebrations and a markedly apathetic response to the royal family as a whole. The opinion, and length of response of many writers, was reflected in the short paragraph submitted by a 23-year-old female postgraduate student from Manchester.

> I was aware from items in news programmes that it was the Queen Mother's 100th birthday, but I haven't watched any of the programmes about it, or her.

> Although I don't have any strong views on the Royal Family, I am not at all interested in anything that concerns them. I slightly begrudge the amount of public money (through tax exemption etc.) they receive, and don't believe that they should have any role in government. Otherwise I think the immediate family (Queen, Prince Charles, and Charles' children) perform an important function as ambassadors for the country, but the rest should lose their privileges.[5]

Many shared the opinions expressed by a retired senior business executive from the South who was seventy-nine years old and whilst acknowledging that 100 was a milestone age, the Queen Mother had led a comparatively easy life:

> Reaching the age of 100 is a matter for congratulation by family and friends (provided that the person concerned is happy to have survived so long – if one's quality of life is low some might well have wanted to leave it.) But as for the Queen Mother; I am not in the least bit interested. She chose to marry into the royal family – granted she did not expect to become queen, she expected a very comfortable if somewhat restricted life – and apart from the war years when she had an energetic round of morale-boosting engagements (but suffered none of the physical hardships and loss that many of the people who cheered her had) she has never had to do very much. I expect she missed her husband when he died but it enabled her to retire into the background as her daughter took over the throne.

> She has had a very comfortable life – never any worries about money, few responsibilities for many years other than sinecures like being Honorary Colonel of a regiment, or Patron of a charity, pleasant homes (note the plural) to live in and people to look after all her needs. She illustrates the

nonsense of having a family who by birth alone demand the loyalty of the rest of us as 'subjects'. I fought for 'King and country' but over the years I have become a republican. Parliament has just been discussing the 'Privy Purse' which will ensure that the Queen will receive £10m of our money every year for some years to come. Part of that is passed on to her mother – I hope she is duly grateful for our generosity.[6]

Others displayed more marked anger at the royal family. The events of 1997 affected some writers' opinions of the family and its place in contemporary Britain, tempering their interest in the Queen Mother's centenary. For a 38-year-old male living in Oxfordshire, the response of the royal family to the death of Diana, Princess of Wales, had a lasting effect on his belief in them as individuals as well as an institution.

Personally I have no plans whatsoever to celebrate the 100th birthday of the Queen Mother. I have begun to think that the Royal family is nearing the end of its time. In this day and age it seems silly to me to have a Queen and all her hangers – on living off the state and their antics over the past few years have really put me off them. It all began with the death of Diana, Princess of Wales. I think they all behaved abominably keeping themselves shut away in Balmoral when all the country was grieving for a beautiful young woman cut down in her prime, who had been so shabbily treated by the Royal family.

I think all of the Royals are completely out of touch with society. They don't live in the real world, so how can they have an understanding of what it's like to live in England today. They are remote, hard and some of the Royal soil should be done away with.

I think the Queen is a very-hard working monarch, and in some ways I do admire her. But I cannot forget her face when she appeared after the Princess of Wales's death, and I really think she was jealous of all the attention that Diana had got. I can't imagine the country in the same state when she dies or any other member of the Royal family, including the Queen Mother.

I used to think that the Queen Mother was a wonderful old woman, but now I think she has got a nasty, petulant side, as have all the other Royals. The Queen mother has led the life of Old Riley, never having to lift a finger to do anything for herself, and when I compare her life to that of my grandmothers, now sadly dead, there's just no comparison.[7]

This final sentence from another Observer is echoed by others who increasingly compared the status of the royal family to that of ordinary people and questioned their right to the privilege that comes with their titles. The level of criticism aimed at the Queen herself is harsher and much more personal in some of these responses when compared to those in the pre-1997 Directives on royalty.

The role of the Queen Mother in preserving a family that seemed to many as out of touch with contemporary society was summed up by a fifty-year-old housewife and language tutor from West Sussex who reflected that it was the insistence on maintaining a certain set of values and traditions that resulted in an outdated royal family:

I feel that the institution of the monarchy and the royal family in particular are more unpopular than they have ever been, and that this is in part the responsibility of the Queen Mother. Her reluctance to relinquish an expensive and privileged lifestyle, one which has ceased to exist almost anywhere else in this country and which is alien to the majority of us, together with a determination to retain her matriarchal position have helped to maintain artificial barriers.

At any other time she would have been pensioned off and sent to the dower house, but, by skilful use of the media and, no doubt behind the scenes manipulation has created a unique position for herself. This has enabled her to retain her influence, which is based in standards and traditions that are outdated and hypocritical.

Historically it seems that the general public was accustomed to and accepted the royal family as having their weaknesses and peccadilloes. However, the influence of 'Victorian values' required a respectable and responsible royal family, to whom the idea of duty came first, and divorce was unacceptable. The creation of the cosy image of the royal 'happy family' is a 20th century one, which has been blown apart by the behaviour of the younger royals in recent years. The reaction to the death of Princess Diana showed that the public accepted the fact that their idols were deeply flawed human beings.

The creation of the Queen Mother's image as a cuddly grandmother shows someone with an astute awareness of how to manipulate the media. Her influence on the rest of the royal family may have prevented a more modem socially aware royal family, and entrenched traditional elitist attitudes. This has contributed significantly to the accusations that they are out of touch with modem life and attitudes, a view with which I agree. I am not sure what the Queen Mother is actually supposed to stand for, but I feel that, at the very least she should now be allowed to retire to her castle in Scotland.[8]

But for some, the general lack of interest in the celebrations was a sign of concerning societal changes. An ex-shop manageress, aged seventy from Essex, recalled the past events that she had enjoyed and now rued their passing and what it signified in terms of loyalty to the country:

It is surprising to me that there are no plans for any 'street' parties. In my younger days the public were much more enthusiastic about any sort of loyal celebration. We would all wear our red, white and blue clothes and hang out the Union flags. But we were taught in our schools to, be proud of our Country and sang the anthem with gusto! Many of today's children don't even know the words or our anthem and associate the Union flag with National Front.

I am definitely a Royalist, I still believe the tourist attraction, brings a lot of money into the country. Where else is there such pomp and ceremony? And besides, who wants a president?[9]

As one of the only Mass-Observers to actively participate in the celebrations, she decided to go to London to see the celebrations for herself.

Well, we stood in the crowds for hours on a beautiful sunny day, with a magic atmosphere. Thousands of tourists were around us and all languages were being spoken. Cheer after cheer went up as the Queen Mothers carriage came by. She looked lovely in pink and with a smiling Charles at her side in the open carriage, it was perfect.

Those magnificent horses, and the ultra smart guards wearing silver helmets with scarlet plumes was something to be proud of. Colour and pageantry abounded, while a thousand voiced choir sang all the old songs from year ago. MAGIC!!

The wonderful parade had such varying themes such varying that one could never write about them all with enough praise.

The different regiments of soldiers from kilt-wearing Scotts to old fashioned guards wearing, beat-skin hats were immaculately turned out. Proud horses in jingling harness carrying huge kettle drums looked superb. Then there was the fly past of the famous red-arrow planes and the release of one hundred white doves. Nothing was forgotten, and throughout it all the Queen Mother stood and smiled and waved. Altogether a magnificent day and well worth the effort to go there Later, some Americans said to me 'Honey – only the English could put on such a magnificent pageant. Don't ever get rid of your Royals or your history.'

Later we went to Buckingham Palace to see the Royal family come out onto the balcony. There were still thousands of people and I did not see any nasty disturbances. In fact the opposite feeling was all around, and everybody seemed very happy and friendly. If only we could always have this feeling around us, wouldn't it be great. I did feel proud to be English again, something I have found lacking for years.[10]

The BBC's decision not to televise some of the celebrations highlighted a shift in modern programming as it sought to fulfil contemporary audience

A TENTATIVE RECOVERY? THE ROYAL FAMILY IN THE 2000S 197

interests rather than traditional assumptions. An adult education tutor in her fifties from Birmingham wrote:

I'm afraid I don't have much to say on this subject, I don't mind the Q.M. having a party or even a bit of a public celebration if that is thought appropriate, it doesn't really concern me. She is even older than me, a different generation, not a part of my life. I haven't registered what plans have been made as I will not be taking part. I am aware that there has been some controversy about what is televised and by which channel, but as I have no desire to watch any of it I haven't taken much note, I know from friends in the BBC that they need to broadcast what people want to see. Too much coverage will result in an outcry that too much time and money has been spent, to the detriment of the rest of the broadcasting programme. A lot of debate about this or very low viewing figures could be an embarrassment to the Q.M. as well as to the BBC. In this context I also hear that the broadcasting of possible future royal events in some cases will be curtailed, for instance it may involve not particularly popular members of the Royal family. The BBC also makes money by selling its programmes, I can't think of any other country which could have more than a passing interest in the QM's birthday-a small mention on the news perhaps. Also, all the retrospective programmes, articles etc will be done now: what will appear as an obituary? All the same? What more will there be to say, unless she runs off with the milkman in the meantime![11]

Spring Directive 2002 – the royal family in 2002

Two years after its last royal question, Mass-Observation continued its tradition of documenting responses to royal celebrations and events with Queen Elizabeth II's Golden Jubilee, celebrating fifty years on the throne. Three other events also spurred the call to record Observer's opinion: the death of the Queen's sister, Princess Margaret, on 9 February, followed quickly by the death of the Queen Mother on 30 March 2002, and Prince Harry hitting headlines with tales of his experimentations with alcohol and drugs being covered by many papers.[12]

Despite the celebrations of the Queen Mother's 100th birthday two years earlier, the British royal family was dogged by negative feedback from press and public alike with plans for the Golden Jubilee events receiving headlines such as 'Palace plays down fears of jubilee flop'[13] and 'God Save the jubilee'[14] appearing in The Guardian *in January and February, whilst the Murdoch-owned* The Sun *reported on 23 January 2002 that the race was on to 'save the Queen's Golden Jubilee from being a flop'. The paper reported that only 300 applications to hold street parties having been made in comparison to the 12,000 for the Silver Jubilee in 1977 and that an Opinion Leader Research poll revealed that only one in twenty Britons believed the jubilee*

198 REFLECTIONS ON BRITISH ROYALTY

would have the greatest impact on the UK's mood whilst one in four believed that England winning the football World Cup would – all evidence that the jubilee 'has failed to capture the nation's imagination'.[15]

The Directive

The questions on royalty were sent out to Observers as the second part of the Spring Directive. The panel was asked about plans to celebrate the Golden Jubilee and whether the events of the last decade had affected how people felt about the Queen and the constitutional monarchy. They were also asked to reflect on differences between the mood of the Silver Jubilee in 1977 and that of 2002:

> The papers seem to be suggesting there is less loyal feeling now than in 1977. They also suggest that all the regulations and insurance liability problems of the 'compensation culture' are going to hamper party organising and may spoil the fun. Do you agree?[16]

The Directive also asked Observers to comment on the death of Princess Margaret and the media response to reports of Prince Harry's experimentation with drink and drugs. The Directive was posted shortly before the death of the Queen Mother. As a result of Observers returning their response at different times, those writing before 30 March sometimes referenced what they thought would happen when she eventually died whilst those writing after often included a response to the event even though there was no reference to her in the Directive.

Princess Margaret

The death of Princess Margaret at seventy-one was commented on by around half of those responding. Some respondents expressed sympathy, whilst others saw her as a hanger-on with no relevance to contemporary public life, with some references to a hedonistic lifestyle.

The sympathetic responses were often tinted by nostalgia, portraying the Princess as a romantic, sometimes tragic figure, whose happiness was affected by her position as a member of the royal family. Some Observers of the same generation as the Princess seemed to share a sense of empathy with her and having experienced her life in tandem with their own. A 72-year-old retired primary schoolteacher from Newcastle was explicit in acknowledging the generational aspect to their emotional response to her death writing:

> I think this was an age thing. I was sad. I thought of the passing of Margret Rose, my age exactly, remembered the pretty child – she was a princess to

me and she died a princess. Yes I was sad and it was right to be low key. After all the publicity she had to put up with, the family gave her back her privacy and mourned for her in private, in her family.[17]

It was identification with aspects of the Princess's life that gave a 67-year-old retired shop assistant from Manchester a sense that she understood the Princess:

My husband was born on August 30th 1930, the day before Princess Margaret, and as I am the second sister, we both felt affection for her. We sent a birthday card to her on her 70th birthday. The papers printed some very cruel things about her and I don't think she should have had such a low-key funeral. Following in the Queen's footsteps must have been so hard for her, all she wanted to find the love that she had lost when her father, King George VI, died.[18]

This reference to finding love might be assumed to refer to the Townsend Affair (see Chapter 5) which is referenced by around a fifth of the Observers responding to this Directive. The events from thirty years prior appears to have struck a chord in collective memory, even for those later, and indicating how much of an impact the affair had on people's view of the royal family. The affair certainly seemed for many to create the image of the Princess as a victim of tragic romance, as suggested by a female 55-year-old personal assistant based in Paris:

Still she was not all that old but she to me always portrayed a woman who had loved passionately but was not allowed to follow that love as she desired. We know now that [if] the situation had arisen today it is likely that she would have ended up marrying Captain Townsend. However at the time, and particularly after the abdication of the King, court advisors could not allow this marriage to take place. I definitely believe that she married Lord Snowdon on the rebound, that theirs was not a happy marriage and that she was always searching for love. After her death we saw so many clips of her with Capt. Townsend and she seemed to be so much in love.[19]

Whilst several are sympathetic to the notion of lost love, many counter this with a reference to the Princess's personal choice. A 48-year-old teacher living in Bolton observed that as a child her mother had 'sold us the line about Margaret's tragic and romantic love for Peter Townsend'; it was now 'more fashionable to see it as a hard-headed un-willingness to give up the privileges she had been born to'.[20] She went on to observe that the Princess probably 'meant little to people under thirty'; however, there is evidence to the contrary, for example, from this 40-year-old nurse:

I didn't agree with the media coverage of her as a 'tragic Princess', she made her choices. If she had really loved Peter Townsend then she would have given up her Royal status to be with him. People do make enormous sacrifices for love. She chose the lifestyle of a Princess, not 'Duty' over love. Or perhaps she knew it was a love that would not last and so it was not an appropriate choice.[21]

An 85-year-old retired administrator from Surrey admitted that although he had sympathized with the Princess's experience at the time of the affair, this feeling did not endure:

I had a fleeting sense of sympathy with Margaret when she was prevented from marrying a divorcee, but that evaporated very quickly; she made up for losing him by having plenty of other consorts and living a hedonistic life.[22]

Many responses that referenced the Princess's death stated they were not personally affected by it, pointing to heavy smoking and drinking as contributing factors in her poor health and, particularly, a series of strokes recently suffered. One Observer wrote, 'when she did appear in public in a wheel-chair she looked nothing like the former Princess Margaret.'[23] A sense of her not being relevant to the contemporary public was shared by some, even those of a similar generation. A 66-year-old retired quality engineer from Berkshire, himself only four years younger than the Princess, felt that 'she had been out of the limelight for years and had little relevance to today'.[24] It was perhaps because of his generational position that he did reference her past life stating, 'I felt sorry for her some years ago when she was treated badly by the establishment.'[25]

The Queen Mother

The death of the Queen Mother at 101 years of age did not surprise Observers, and reactions to her death were largely framed in terms of the effect on the Queen and the response of the nation. A 38-year-old IT consultant from Edinburgh reflected on his surprise of the public response to the event. He suggested this was due to a diffusion of news as a result in the rise of the number of media channels, the power of media to influence interaction with royal events and a significant reduction in the respect in which royalty was held in contemporary society:

Dreading [Queen Mother's death] because I assumed it would herald an orgy of compulsory patriotic grief. Rather unexpectedly this did not arise. In all seriousness, I expected that the country would have been brought to a halt and there would have been nothing else on television for days.

A TENTATIVE RECOVERY? THE ROYAL FAMILY IN THE 2000S   201

I think if this had happened ten or fifteen years previously, that may not have been the case. There are a number of possible reasons why this didn't happen: we are no longer huddled around only three British TV channels. There are hundreds now, they are more diverse, if not better, and crucially they matter less. There are always cartoons on another channel. Another factor is that it is far easier and safer to express republican sentiments in public, and the Royals are much less respected and apparently 'popular' than they seemed to be when I was growing up in the seventies. I'm sure that they, and the powers that be, realise this, and realised that the kind of spectacle of mourning presented in days gone by would be all too vulnerable to ridicule.[26]

Some felt that the response to the Queen Mother's death and the ceremonies surrounding her lying-in-state and funeral showed that the public were in fact more pro-monarchy than the media made out. A retired librarian in her sixties from East Sussex felt that the events had 'caught the media in a lie' and that the media's 'subversive campaign to persuade us that we were all becoming anti-monarchy' had in fact 'fallen spectacularly on its face'.[27]

Sympathy for the Queen was repeated by many writers. Several commented on how this would 'increase support for the queen as people will sympathise with her losing her sister and her mother within weeks of each other'.[28] As mentioned earlier, the Directive was issued shortly before the death of the Queen Mother, and for some Observers, this enabled them to reflect on what they had written before her death and how the event changed their response. One such example is a 55-year-old personal assistant who wrote:

The perception of the Royal Family since 1977 has changed, the majority of the Royals are no longer held in such high regard with the exception of the Queen Mother and also the Queen but to a lesser degree. The Queen has had a hard job trying to preserve the monarchy whilst at the same time, moving with the times. She may have been ill advised and has not always handled her family in the best way. I still think of her as someone who has done the best job she could.

I wrote the paragraphs above prior to the death of the Queen Mother and I feel now that there appears to be a change in people's attitudes towards the monarchy. To see the Queen walking by herself into Westminster Abbey for the funeral really tugged at my heart and she seemed so very sad and alone. To see how much Prince Charles was grieving over the loss if the Queen Mother who had been like a mother to him in the early days of the Queen's reign and who had played such an important part in his life.[29]

A 36-year-old Observer unemployed due to long-term illness and living in York recorded how the royal family's reaction to the death of the Queen

Mother had helped people identify with their loss, something that she attributed to lessons learned in the previous few years:

> It helped us to feel more involved in the Queen Mother's death that members of her family actually showed emotion and spoke quite openly about the Queen Mother in the days before the funeral. It's one lesson at least that they seem to have learnt from Diana's death – the apparent coolness and detachment and lack of emotion was greeted with horror and disapproval, and they now seem to appreciate we need to see a human side to our royals.[30]

A 68-year-old retired banker from Surrey agreed with this, sensing that the royals were now more 'in touch' with public sentiment:

> [The queen] might be guided by her son Prince Charles, who in recent years, since the death of Princess Diana, has succeeded in projecting the required image. I have the impression he is in touch. Only this week he was photo-ed leaving a farmhouse where he had stayed for bed & breakfast. He has obviously had good advice, because I feel he is approachable, even perhaps, ordinary.[31]

A 55-year-old personal assistant felt that the death of the Queen Mother had altered the public attitude, believing that this might have an effect on public appetite for the jubilee celebrations.

> The death of the Queen Mother just over three weeks ago has I think changed people's attitudes to the Royal Family as a whole, and especially the Queen. Being somewhat sceptical of the results if surveys and other opinions portrayed in the media, especially some of the press, it was rather satisfying to see proof that people do not aways behave as they are expected to do.
>
> The outpouring of grief and affection for the Queen Mother, and sympathy for the Queen was very moving and in a way uplifting . . .
>
> Because of this, I think that the Queen's Golden Jubilee will have much more support from the public. There is obviously a strong feeling of sympathy with the Queen, losing her sister and her mother so close together, and admiration for the way she has behaved.[32]

The Golden Jubilee

The majority of Observers stated that at the time of writing they had no plans to celebrate the jubilee for a variety of reasons ranging from having not heard of any local plans through to an outright refusal to be involved

A TENTATIVE RECOVERY? THE ROYAL FAMILY IN THE 2000S   203

as they did not support the monarchy. As mentioned at the start of this chapter, there was significant media coverage earlier in 2002 that suggested little public interest in the events being planned at a national level. Writing on 23 May, a 66-year-old retired secretary from Surrey had her own theory as to why this was.

> According to the press and television programmes the Royal Family has lost some of the affection the public once had for them. It may be less due to what they have or have not done but that times have changed and people have less reverence than they once had. It may be one of perception. I have a theory called the Git Factor which goes thus – we are a git nation. Going to be a Royal celebration? Can't be bothered, not interested, can't be arsed. Nearer the day – well, we might as well see what's on, take a look. Not bad eh? In fact quite good. Glad we came.[33]

Three days later on 26 May, only a week before the main events taking place in London, the earlier Observer wrote:

> The pace is hotting up and press and news programmes have shown that we are indeed a nation on the threshold of enjoying ourselves and let's not forget, it is no mean achievement, reigning for fifty years, celebrating a Jubilee. Deep down we must have at least a grudging admiration.[34]

Some Observers planned on attending events, including a 77-year-old living in Wales who saw the jubilee as an opportunity to celebrate during what had been a trying year for many rural communities, such as hers, that were reliant on pastoral agriculture.[35]

> Our small hamlet has been planning for quite a full celebration for the Queen [Golden Jubilee]. We all feel we need something to bring us together after foot and mouth isolating us for far too long.[36]

As well as commenting on the events themselves, the nature of the questions around the jubilee caused many of the writers to reflect on change, both of society and of their own attitudes to monarchy. An Observer living in York reflected on changes since the Silver Jubilee which she had celebrated as a thirteen-year-old:

> It's a completely different world to the one that we lived in in 1977. As kids, we were quite excited about going to a party up the road. It was a sunny day and there were lots of flags and red/white/blue and loads of people we didn't know. People aren't really into that kind of thing any more. I was worried that Buckingham Palace wouldn't have updated its ideas, so it was kind of a relief when they announced the 2 concerts in the grounds of the Palace. I think there's a lot of interest in that.[37]

Another Observer who experienced the Silver Jubilee as a fourteen-year-old also agreed that the response to the Golden Jubilee reflected a change in society over twenty-five years:

> Today is different I think because there isn't such a sense of community. One of the reasons for this is the way people just don't interact anymore, as children we knew each other and played in the streets together but that doesn't happen anymore.[38]

Others laid the blame for these changes on the royal family themselves, with this 67-year-old retired clerk citing the events of the previous decade:

> The royal divorces have lessened the respect we once had. We still hold the Queen in respect but the rest seem the same as us now. No better, no worse. We used to look up to them now we feel equal. We still want the Queen and the monarchy even if tarnished a little. A few weeks ago I may have said that people were less loyal but since the Queen Mother's death at Easter the country has shown it does remain loyal.[39]

Writing from her home in Shetland, a 44-year-old single mother suggested that public respect for royalty had been reduced by the realization of the power of the people:

> The royal divorces and the annus horribilis make the Queen and Royal family appear more human. I think there is less loyal feeling now than in 1977. The world is a different place now. Since the fall of the Berlin Wall people feel more empowered to change things for themselves. They don't feel the need for an all powerful figurehead.[40]

Others, including a 67-year-old retired clerk from London, observed that the changes made by the royal family to increase their relevance to contemporary life might instead spell the end of the monarchy:

> I don't think the royals have ever really recovered their position since Diana firstly because they handled the whole thing appallingly and looked so cold and uncaring in their response. One part of me is exasperated by the whole lot of them and the other part can see some good things. I think Charles has come into his own and the boys are a credit. At least they seem normal even if we will never know if they are or not. But it is perhaps that normalness that will eventually finish them off altogether. I mean why would anyone want to keep them on the manner in which they live now if they're just like any other kid. I can't see the monarchy existing in say 50 years time but whether or not what replaces them will be any better we'll have to wait and see.[41]

A 35-year-old from the West Midlands agreed that the family had damaged themselves through the events of the 1990s, but she also believed that the change in respect for the royal family was a symptom of a less patriotic society, fuelled by media coverage:

There has definitely been a change in people's feelings towards the monarchy in recent years for the worse but I would not necessarily say it was due to the divorces and the annus horribilis. I think the reasons are many and more complicated but include media overage being more intrusive these days covering the Royals personal lives rather than their work. I think Diana was instrumental in encouraging this e.g. her interview on TV where she ran down Charles. I personally think she has done a lot of damage to the monarchy though I know this is not a fashionable thing to say especially as many people have martyred her after her death. Also, people are not brought up or educated to be as patriotic like they were in my parents' time. I cannot remember the last time I heard the national anthem let alone saw people stand to attention when they heard it play. I think since the Queen Mother's death there has been a slight swing back in favour of the monarchy and the jubilee and the world.

This idea of a changing society was also shared by a 57-year-old retired teacher from Hampshire who believed that increased emphasis on individualism was beginning to replace reverence:

The country has moved away from adulation of those with rank, wealth and privilege, however much power these people still retain. We have all been encouraged to value individualism and self-achievement, through greater emancipation of most women, more spending power or youngsters, media influence, an education system which has tried to embrace egalitarianism, and the dominance of idols from sport and entertainment, rather than the echelons of society. These are irreversible changes, and the effects on royalty are also irreversible.[42]

For a 32-year-old male local authority worker living in Lancaster, it was a case of society moving forward whilst the monarchy had not:

Back in 1977 we were still in the grip of Victorian and Edwardian morals in the 'Gawd bless you Maam' school of thought. Now the number of people who think this 25 years later has diminished greatly. I don't think the divorces helped but as Bob Dylan said 'the Times they are a changing' and the commons after hundreds of years of forelock tugging are waking up and realising that the only difference between us and them is money not breeding.[43]

206   REFLECTIONS ON BRITISH ROYALTY

The alternative to monarchy

As in other Directives on royalty, the responses often included reflections on republican alternatives to monarchy in the UK and their desirability. An eighty-year-old retired senior business executive from the South of England had witnessed three generations of royalty during which time his attitude had changed:

As a boy of 16 I caught a train to London at about 3.00 in the morning and stood in Trafalgar Square until about 5.00 in the evening to see the coronation procession of George VI.

As I was on leave from the tropics in 1953 I was able to obtain tickets from the colony where I worked and sat in The Mall to watch a similar procession. Nothing would persuade me to go to any trouble to see any member of the royal family now! I think the last time I saw one close to was when the queen came to my cathedral to give the royal maundy money, and I was on duty as a steward. I took part in the VJ Day parade in 1995 and saw the queen and many of her family as we marched passed the saluting base in The Mall.

By that time I had been a republican for quite a few years. I think the whole idea of one family having a heredity right to hold the highest place in the country and church is an anachronism. People say 'it works – what else could you have?' To take the first part of the question, it really doesn't work if you take the cost to the people involved – I don't think anyone could claim being a member of the royal family brings the kind of normal happy family life that most of us aspire to. What kind of life has the Prince of Wales led – his job only begins when his mother dies?

He was forced into a marriage which inflicted great unhappiness on the young girl whom he (along with others) chose, when he really wanted to continue an affair with a married woman. He now sees his mother-less sons growing up and facing the huge, unnecessary burden of being 'royal'. Anyone who wants to be head of state with that kind of baggage attached to the job is unfit to be a head of state in the first place![44]

Some Observers were critical of royal family's wealth and position whilst still recognizing their unifying potential for the nation. For a 73-year-old retired journalist from Gloucestershire, the opportunity for the monarchy to refashion itself into something more relevant to the modern world was an attractive option:

Queen E should resign and let Charles have a go and he should marry Camilla. They should cut down on houses, palaces and staff and show all their paintings and treasures to the nation; turn that awful Buckingham Palace into an art gallery and generally cost the nation less. There should

A TENTATIVE RECOVERY? THE ROYAL FAMILY IN THE 2000S

be less trooping about with crowns on, black rod etc, and those ridiculous judges with their wigs and robes.

But the Monarchy is still basically a good thing, holding the nation together and unelected. Better than an elected president. Most of those about the place do not inspire one with confidence.[45]

Others went further and questioned the point of the royal family in a modern era. A 43-year-old office worker living in the London suburbs wrote:

In my experience there is very little place in modern society for the royal family. My two teenage children seem rather puzzled at the amount of fuss that surrounds anything that happens in the royal family, and certainly they would have trouble in naming all the major members.

I think future generations will come to regard the royal family as totally unimportant. Certainly I have no plans to celebrate the Queen's jubilee and despite media pressure to do not feel it is going to be a major event. The silver jubilee was celebrated with much more enthusiasm than the golden one appears to be. I am not sure if it [is] general apathy or the fact that the majority of British people feel the royal family have no bearing upon their lives.[46]

This sense of generational detachment was reinforced by a 29-year-old communications consultant living in South East London who stated:

I think the royal family are irrelevant to my life. And I think that this is probably a view shared by lots of my generation. I can't think of any of my friends who are particular fans of the Royal family; maybe they just keep quiet about it.[47]

Many of the Observers noted that although they may not be comfortable with the monarchy, the alternative of a presidency did not appeal either, outweighing the disadvantages of maintaining a royal family. Despite describing himself as a 'lounge republican' the sentiments expressed by a 43-year-old working in HM Customs and Excise in Essex appear supportive when faced with the alternatives, even if this opinion seems more based on respect for the Queen rather than loyalty to the concept of monarchy:

The royal divorces and annus horribilis of 1992 have shown the monarchy to be normal – totally dysfunctional like many of her subjects. As to the position of the Queen constitutionally, these events have not diminished her constitutional position even if her family have done all they can to turn the public against the 'Firm'. In fact the events have actually strengthened her position (excepting the poor way in which the death of Diana was handled), and I have great respect for her dedication and duty to her role. And that is something coming from a 'lounge republican'.

There may be less 'royal' feeling in 2002 – but this term is too vague. I think there is less patience with the antics of the 'family', including the Duke of Edinburgh, rather than a declining respect for the role and work of the Queen. She still maintains a central constitutional role, a unifying institution in an often unsavoury and dishonest political world. As a republican I do find it hard to identify an equally detached, noble and statesman like figure in Parliament, who could equal the Queen's stature to act as Britain's first president.[48]

Other Observers declared themselves republicans and were less tolerant of the institution, including a 47-year-old teacher from Manchester who declared:

I have always been a staunch republican – in 1977 I was in a very small minority. Now in 2002 I am still in a minority but the numbers have grown.[49]

Another staunch republican, a 28-year-old researcher from the Midlands, wrote:

1992 had no effect on how I feel about the royal family; I have always been a republican. I think people are generally less in awe of the monarchy now, but many still seem to see them as a 'good thing' for no particular reason. My view is that the monarchy should 'die' with the Queen; I feel it is irrelevant in today's society. Although it could be argued that royalty do no real harm because they have no power and do make some people happy, I believe the end of the monarchy would help to overcome class division, privilege and inequality.[50]

Spring Directive 2005 – Charles and Camilla

On 10 February 2005, Clarence House[51] announced the engagement of the Prince of Wales to Camilla Parker-Bowles. The engagement came over twenty years after the couple first met. Their on-and-off relationship has been well documented in the press, especially in the wake of publications and interviews given by both the Prince and Princess of Wales in the 1990s. The involvement of Camilla Parker-Bowles in the break up of the Wales's marriage caused many people to take a negative view of her relationship with the Prince, and following the death of Diana in 1997, a concerted effort was made by Prince Charles's staff to 'rehabilitate' Camilla's reputation with the British public.[52] Camilla was gradually introduced to the public stage as the Prince's companion, beginning to appear in public together and eventually being accepted by the Queen as her son's companion. By November 1998, a Daily Mail headline declared that despite a 'warming' by Britain to the relationship, eight out of ten were still fiercely opposed to her ever becoming Queen.[53] By 2001, the same paper had started to suggest that the couple might marry, and Camilla eventually become Queen.[54]

A civil ceremony was held at Windsor Guildhall followed by a religious ceremony to bless the marriage at St George's Chapel in Windsor Castle on Saturday 9 April, moved from its original date on the previous day due to a clash with the funeral of the recently deceased Pope John Paul II. The Saturday ceremony also clashed with the running of the Grand National horse race at Aintree, which subsequently was moved to a slightly later time of day to avoid conflict.

The Directive

Maintaining its tradition of recording responses to royal events, Mass-Observation chose to mark the wedding of the Prince of Wales to Camilla Parker-Bowles with a Directive asking Observers their views on the marriage and a request to keep a diary for the day.

Perhaps in line with the relatively low-key event, activities on the day were markedly less than other royal weddings, with little evidence of social gatherings to watch the wedding or local celebrations. For those whose day did mention the wedding, it was largely intertwined with the rest of their daily activities. This included a sixty-year-old teacher from Devon who wrote about her antipathy towards the monarchy but nonetheless admitted to a 'Hello magazine mentality':

He has shown himself to be out of touch, remote but interfering and in fact irrelevant. The monarchy, with all its hangers-on has become anachronistic, and the only good thing about the royal family is the queen herself, by virtue of her commitment and her knowledge gained through the years ...

Basically they don't interest me. Which is a surprise to me, because I used to be pro the royal family, but now I just think they're interested in feathering their own nests.

Had a shower and washed my hair and then sat down to watch Charles and Camilla arriving at Windsor Guildhall for their wedding. I know I'm not interested, but having a 'Hello magazine' mentality, I like to see what's going on ...

Went round dead-heading the daffodils and then went to watch the royal wedding blessing at St George's Chapel. Everything looked nice and happy, so perhaps they can get on with their lives and we can get on with ours. Back to the garden to do some more, and then to watch the re-run of the Grand National.[55]

This 'low-brow' interest in the wedding was shared by others, including 39-year-old senior prescribing support technician from Wales who admitted to her interest being kindled by the fashions worn by guests:

> When I came back I did the housework – hoovering and dusting and I cleaned the bathroom. Whilst I was doing this I had the royal wedding on the TV. Though I had only a passing interest in it up to this point, I got really into it and kept stopping the housework to watch. I was especially interested in who was there and the outfits.[56]

Other Observers chose to actively include the wedding in their day. For a 75-year-old retired primary schoolteacher from Newcastle it was an opportunity to indulge in some royal watching:

> Then ready to watch the royal wedding, still comfortable on the settee and a large glass of brandy for a treat. I thoroughly enjoyed everything. I enjoyed the atmosphere of the Family as they settled themselves for the Blessing. Ceremony without too much pomp. I think it was as nice a Royal Wedding as any of the earlier weddings. Camilla's two outfits were beautiful and as a couple they showed dignity and happiness. The people outside who'd turned out to cheer put into words a warmth towards them that I felt myself.
>
> The hymns brought tears and I thought of my husband and missing him. The wedding continued on TV, a happy event, 750 guests and a 'Finger Buffet'. I liked the way the Queen kept back a little, acknowledging it was Charles and Camilla's day. She wasn't brimming with happiness but was allowed to feel her age and opinions of age as she had seen it all before. I loved the way the Grand National was postponed till 4.10 pm instead of 3 o clock. I can picture the disappointment and exasperation of the Queen for this treat to be at the same time as the Buffet she was giving. This would give her a chance to 'slip away'. It also confirmed the feeling that the Royal Family is also a 'family' and there is too much stuffed shirt baloney around giving the newspapers half-baked attitudes. A bit of common sense toleration and forgiveness wouldn't come amiss. In the end the newspapers did cover the event well.[57]

Opinions on the marriage itself taking place were divided, with many wishing the couple well, whilst others still felt strongly about their responsibility for the fate of the late Princess of Wales. Others used the Directive to reflect on the future of the royal family, in particular the role of Charles and Camilla. Inevitably there were reflections on Diana, Princess of Wales, eight years on from her death in Paris, and as ever, the longitudinal nature of Mass-Observation enables us to witness how the passage of time affects opinion as well as giving Observers space to explore the broader context of the subject.

For a 54-year-old freelance writer from Norfolk, the Directive enabled her to reflect on tradition and change:

> I wish people would leave Charles and Camilla to get on with their lives. I think it was sad that they were not allowed to marry when they first met and so obviously fell in love, but from what I have read, it appears they were discouraged, along similar lines to Princess Margaret and Group Captain Townsend presumably, they were not considered 'right' for each other. Charles had to think if the future of the monarchy ahead of his own future, and needed 'good breeding stock', as I heard it described somewhere, some young woman from a perfect background who would provide future sons and heirs to the throne.
>
> And so along came Princess Diana, just fitting the bill, and so personal feelings had to be cast aside in the name of duty to one's country. How awful . . . how lucky the rest of us mere mortals that we are not bound by such antiquated ideas.
>
> I am not without sympathy for Princess Diana, for here was a young girl who was so obviously in love with her prince, the stuff of little girls dreams, some big girls dreams maybe too. But his heart obviously wasn't really in it, and so the marriage fell apart, each of them doing their own thing in private whilst the world and its mother speculated about the real state of their marriage.
>
> The fact that anyone wanted to know what was really going on is not something I understand. How many of these voyeurs would have been happy to be on the receiving end of all that attention, all that stress?
>
> Prince Charles seems to me to be at his most happiest and relaxed now. Both of them look happier together the more time passed. At first you felt Camilla was a little nervous, and why wouldn't she be? But she seems to be getting easier with the attention, and it is clear they are a couple in love. And so they should now be allowed to have their wedding, get married, and in true fairy tale story ending, live happily ever after.
>
> On a cynical note, they are not getting any younger either, so deserve to spend the rest of their days together. As for whether or not she should be Queen, I don't think the situation will arise. Personally I don't think Charles has much interest in being King, and that it will be his eldest son who takes that role, leaving Charles and Camilla to live their lives out of the limelight less than were he King.[58]

Relief that they married

For many Observers the marriage on 9 April came as a relief on behalf of the couple. Sympathy with their past seemed to have grown, perhaps as a result of the rehabilitation mentioned earlier that resulted in more positive press coverage as the notion of 'three in a marriage' started to become history. A 41-year-old business analyst put his view across succinctly:

> As a republican; utter contempt and disinterest. As a human; good luck to them, it's absolutely none of my business.[59]

Whilst a 39-year-old from York agreed that the couple should marry, she also recognized the 'grief' that their not having done so in the first place had caused to so many.

> I was curious but bored by all of this. Relieved in a way that they'd just got married so we wouldn't have to keep talking about whether or not they would. It seemed stupid for them not to get married now because they live together and everyone knows that, but I did feel very uncomfortable about it. I wish they'd done it years ago and saved a lot of people a great deal of grief. Generally I really do believe people should marry their soulmate, and Charles and Camilla seem to be each other's soulmates; but I can't forget how their closeness destroyed Princess Diana, who was very young and vulnerable.[60]

Those against the marriage

Other Observers were not so reconciled to the marriage, citing what they perceived as the effect of the couple's relationship on the Wales's marriage. For a 58-year-old personal assistant from Derbyshire, hearing the announcement manifested in physical shock for her:

> I sat at my desk in total bewilderment. Surely he wouldn't be allowed to do that. No-one would want her as queen. I certainly didn't. Surely there would be a massive outpouring of protest? Perhaps people would take to the streets and demand he give up his right to the throne. I really believed it would stir the country to its foundations. No way would it be allowed to go ahead. Then I read how pleased the Queen was – or said she was.

> A few days later I was really taken aback to discover that not only had I now accepted he would marry her but I really didn't care what he did.

> Now for me this was a bit worrying. I'm quite a loyal Royalist – far better a Royal than a President – and probably less likelihood of corruption, but I now realise I had quite gone off Prince Charles, even though I always thought him stiff and pompous and wimpy before. He's never going to change at all.

> I don't expect she will ever become Queen and to be honest I think he would do the country a favour if he did an Edward VIII. He and us would

A TENTATIVE RECOVERY? THE ROYAL FAMILY IN THE 2000S

probably be happier in the long run and Prince William seems to be coming along nicely.[61]

The exercise cited earlier to 'rehabilitate' Camilla Parker-Bowles's public image had clearly not influenced the feelings of a 73-year-old female writer from Kent who along with several other Observers did not want to ever see Camilla as Queen:

I don't see them as star-crossed lovers. More like selfish, arrogant aristocrats who consider themselves above reproach whatever they do.

There is no way I have <u>any</u> respect for Camilla in particular. As I'm never going to meet her it doesn't matter of course, but as far as being <u>Queen</u>! what a travesty.

Whatever Diana's faults and she had quite a few, – when she married Charles, if he had allowed her, she could have been a splendid Queen . . .

I wouldn't even buy a <u>stamp</u> with Camilla's face on it.[62]

Others took a less extreme view of Camilla's role, including a 61-year-old retired auditor who, despite not being a monarchist, reflected on what she perceived as the 'sheer nastiness' within the media towards Camilla, identifying wider cultural influences at work:

Why has she so upset people? People are so hypocritical, pretending that she has done something (never quite defined but somehow understood) to render her unacceptable. It is just 'understood' that you can slag her off in any way you like. But most of these comments are childish, personal and usually rather cruel. As a people-watcher I find that is the reactions to Camilla that are fascinating rather than the event itself . . .

I tend to believe the argument that much of the anti-Charles attitude in the country comes from the steady anti-royal propaganda from the Rupert Murdoch press. This is simply a continuation of it. It is easy to work on basic human prejudice against perceived ugliness, especially coming after the sainted Diana.

More generally about Royalty – it is not so easy these days to distinguish between any genuine feeling for royalty in the population, and what I suspect is no more than a following for yet another group of celebs. That is why we insist that they should be beautiful. Diana did this, she was like a film star. Poor old Camilla cannot live up to the celeb standard of glamour so she is alleged to be letting us down.[63]

The influence of the press was identified by others, including a 66-year-old illustrator from the South East who not only recognized the influence of the media on the response to the wedding but also laid some responsibility with the reading and watching public:

> Is all the fuss generated by the press? Of course it is, but as I have already mentioned, it is what the people want. They want their drip feed of royal gossip. 'Do people really care?' was another question. Depends what is meant by 'care'. They care enough to be absorbed by the royal soap opera. They cared enough to put out all those flowers for Princess Diana and wait overnight to be close to her funeral. The caring might have been a protest against the Queen, Duke of Edinburgh, Prince Charles etc but it still shows that people care about what is going on. The Press and Media generally care to tell us about royalty because they know many of us are interested.[64]

A 32-year-old female student living in the Midlands took a more nuanced analysis of the press attitude towards female 'in-comers' to the royal family:

> Perhaps it's a controversial viewpoint, but I never did understand the whole 'Princess Diana hysteria'. Sarah Ferguson was vilified as fat and ugly yet Diana came in for none of this. People talked endlessly of her glamour, poise, beauty etc – all superficial nonsense. 'Fergie' seemed like much more of a person to me, in her expressions and actions. Perhaps that's why she was unpopular.
>
> It seems that Camilla is similarly vilified – well, she's just not Diana, is she? Well, a big fat so?! to that. I know very little of Charles and Camilla's relationship, but the depictions of Camilla as a horse really angered me. If the sole purpose of female royalty is to smile nicely and be a clothes hanger, then no wonder Charles gets so mad – who do the press think they are?! I am very happy for Charles and Camilla – they obviously get along very naturally and well, and I don't see why the media are so horrible to them. I suppose the Sun would prefer Peter Andre and Jordon on the palace, nothing like a vapid and plastic Ken and Barbie couple to aspire to and represent us. Ugh.[65]

Evolution of the royal family? Into the future . . .

Several Observers took the opportunity to reflect on the changes in the royal family and its place in society through their lifetime, including a 48-year-old male town planner from Gloucester, who concluded that the royal family had not evolved in the previous half-century:

> The late 'Queen Mother' appears to have succeeded in keeping the royal family in a more or less suspended state of how it was when her husband

A TENTATIVE RECOVERY? THE ROYAL FAMILY IN THE 2000S

King George VI died in 1952. This might have helped with her grief for all I know but it certainly makes for a strange spectacle in the early C21st, her surviving daughter seems bent on continuing this time capsule approach to life for the family. (I was unsurprised to see on a recent television programme that the Royal palaces still regularly transfer mail between their various establishments by horse drawn carriage).

Charles wouldn't look out of place in a newsreel of c.1950 in his old fashioned coats and suits. This unfortunate man has been struggling with the anachronistic nature of his family ever since he reached adulthood, one recalls scenes like the rather gauche photo opportunities with 'The Three degrees' all those years ago. He seems to have found some kind of role in championing a reactionary (and amateur) view of architecture in the National Gallery row in the 1980s which I admired in a way because he was being controversial.[66]

The perceived lack of adaptation to the modern world was held as being responsible for the royal family's lack of relevance in modern life, according to a forty-year-old male from Staffordshire:

In many ways the whole 'affair' illustrates the irrelevance of and inconsistency of the Monarchy to daily life. The Queen has been responsible for much divisive legislation in recent times, positively discriminating in the worst possible way; what 'safe guards' did having a Monarch have when accepted human rights principles were being flouted by a Post-War British government? Not much in truth!

She has said that she valued the support and advice of her mother (for most of her reign since 1953) but will not extend the same benefit to her son as she will not stand down; only being succeeded in the traditional way! What progress in the c20th? Very little.

The Royals are out of touch with most people's ordinary lives and seem to be kept there by a conservative hierarchy to justify their existence.

I hope they are happy after many years of waiting.[67]

But not everyone agreed that some traditional values held by the royal family should adapt, with a 70-year-old former radio programme monitor perceiving similarities between the situation of Edward VIII and Prince Charles. She felt that the Prince should follow the precedent of his great-uncle and forego his right to the throne:

Generally I feel people don't really care what the 'Royals' do, especially the younger generation born after the war, but for the rest of us, I think we do care. I feel very strongly on Charles and Camilla's relationship as people did on Edward 8th. Over the years, the Royal Family have felt they can do whatever they like, but with their status responsibility comes with pleasure. Edward 8th soon learnt they can't just do what they like, he had to choose whether to marry the woman he loved (who wasn't in a position to be Queen of England) or become King. I feel Prince Charles is in the same position – 2000+ or not, that he can happily marry Camilla now, but forfeits the right to be King, as did Edward 8th. Camilla no way should become Queen. I hope our Queen reigns for many more years, then William becomes King. Look at the misery caused by Charles and Camilla over the years. The way Charles treated Diana once she had had his children was disgraceful, irrespective of whom had what affair.[68]

Other Observers took the opportunity to state where they believed the future of the royal family lay. A twenty-year-old undergraduate student living in North London argued:

I think that the most important factor about the coming wedding is that nobody really cares. Just as people have become apathetic about politics, so about the Royal Family. The only reason that people turned on for the Silver Jubilee or Charles and Diana's wedding was that it was a huge ceremony with helicopters, men in funny outfits etc. Since Charles and Camilla are getting married in the Royal equivalent of the all-night Elvis chapel in Vegas, without even the presence of the mother-in-law, things are different.

Those who do express an opinion seem to be divided by age – the older generations (60+) tend to be traditionalists, harking back to the old days when the Monarchy 'did things properly' and so on to 'Diana, Queen of our Hearts, the People's princes etc etc'. So these are the people who tend to be against the marriage. Younger people tend to take the view 'Well, they're in love, why can't we all butt out and let them get on with it' and yet everyone still buys the tabloids to find out what they are doing (recently there was a huge w-day news festival when Charles insulted some journalists under his breath). The Royal Family have become no different from 'The Osbournes' (fly-on-the-wall documentary about a delinquent family if an aging rock star).

For my part, I firmly believe that Britain should become a Republic and that the monarchy serves no useful purpose. The only main arguments that people seem to bring up to deny this are that (1) They are traditional, and therefore good; (2) They make the money back that we give them through encouraging tourism. The taxpayer subsidises these people to live, and so they owe us something in return. If the only reason that they have anything to offer is that they are traditional, then they should live by their own traditions – Prince Harry should not go off getting drunk, doing drugs and embarrassing himself and Prince Charles should not marry a Catholic divorcee. If they want to keep their jobs, they should start playing by the rules – they are paid to be performing monkeys, so they jolly well should perform.[69]

A male 41-year-old university lecturer from Essex went even further, suggesting that the family should be sacked from their positions:

Whilst I don't feel any ill will towards the Royals per se I feel that they are a self-serving institution that should have no place in modern democracy. Over the years I have shifted from being quite a little monarchist to being an out and out republican. It seems crazy that in this age that someone should be a head of state, by virtue of their parentage. What nonsense and what a clutch of hangers on and flunkies.

Sack the lot; give the Queen, Charles and the Princess Royal a sizable pension. Let the Queen keep Sandringham and Balmoral (the latter for her lifetime only). The kids can keep theirs – Anne gets Gatcome Park; Charles gets Highgrove; Andrew Southfork[70] and Edward his pile. The rest (Kents, Gloucesters and any others) get twelve months grace and favour to vacate state buildings and palaces – or pay the full London rents.[71]

Summary

The years following the Golden Jubilee seemed to mark a more settled period for the royals, to the extent that Prince Charles was able to marry Camilla Parker-Bowles. It was perhaps inevitable that the remarriage of Prince Charles would attract reflection on his marriage to the late Diana, Princess of Wales, and as ever, the Mass-Observers provided an insight into the range of opinion on the marriage that provides an insight into the evolving relationship between royals and people. The deaths of the Queen's mother and sister in such close succession garnered sympathy for the monarch, highlighting a facet that was apparent in the response to the death of Diana, Princess of Wales – the universal experiences around death, loss and mourning creating a way of connecting personal experiences with that being experienced by the royal family.

9

A decade of recovery? The 2010s

The decade of 2010s provided a renaissance in the relationship between royal family and the press with the marriage of Prince William to Kate Middleton and in the following year the celebration of the Queen's Diamond Jubilee. The Queen's sixtieth year on the throne coincided with the nation hosting the London Olympics resulting in a summer of positive stories.

2011 – marriage of Prince William to Kate Middleton

On 16 November 2010, the engagement of Prince William to Kate Middleton was announced. The wedding of the couple, who had met ten years earlier whilst students at the University of St Andrews, took place at Westminster Abbey on 29 April 2011. An estimated 24.5 million UK residents watched the wedding ceremony, whilst 5,500 applications to hold street parties were made to local councils.[1]

On the day of the wedding the Queen conferred the Dukedom of Cambridge on Prince William, meaning that the couple became known as the Duke and Duchess of Cambridge following their marriage. The new Duchess reverted to the more formal name of Catherine, having been known as Kate whilst at University, a moniker that continued to be used in news reports after the wedding. Catherine Middleton came from an upper-middle-class family and had received a private education before attending the University of St Andrews. Despite coming from a background of wealth and privilege, much has been made of the Duchess's 'commoner' background due to not having an aristocratic pedigree. Thirty years following the wedding of his parents, it was perhaps inevitable that comparisons would be made between the two couples, demonstrating how the royal family had changed within those decades.

The Directive

Thirty years after sending out one of its first Directives asking Observers to record their activities on the day of the Prince and Princess of Wales's wedding, Mass-Observation had the opportunity to repeat the exercise for the wedding of the couple's eldest son. Observers were asked to

> document your activities, thoughts, and feeling on this day, paying particular attention to the royal wedding. If the wedding does not affect your day in any way then we would still like to hear about whatever you are doing.[2]

The request was the third theme in that Directive, which included questions about donor conception and gambling in the other two parts.

Unlike the previous royal wedding of Charles and Camilla, the marriage of Prince William to Kate Middleton was a much higher-profile affair and as such is reflected in the activities of many of the Observers over the weekend of 29 April. Accounts include those who went to London to witness parts of the celebration in person and others who gathered together in social groups to watch the events on television.

As ever, the Observers took the opportunity to comment on their current opinions of the royal family and the impact of the wedding on their opinion. The accounts selected later in the text are highlights of the variety of opinions and experiences narrated by the panel and reflect some of the discourses active in the press and social media at the time of the wedding.

Watching the wedding

A 74-year-old retired civil servant decided to make the trip from her home in Brighton to London to enjoy the wedding, much to the surprise of the ticket clerk at the station who suggested that she would see more by staying at home and watching on the TV. However, having 'been at Buckingham palace to see the royal family on VE Day, VJ Day, the wedding of Princess Elizabeth to Phillip Mountbatten, watched the funeral of King George Sixth, slept on the pavement all night for a front row seat for the Coronation' as well as attending the lying-in-state of the Queen Mother and the wedding of Charles and Diana, she could not miss the opportunity to add this event to her list. She provided a detailed account of her day, reminiscent of the early Mass-Observation investigators on the streets on 12 May 1937. The following extract describes the atmosphere she encountered in central London on 29 April:

> I made my way out of the crowd and onto the grass behind me and found a fence around yet another camera installation. I sat down on the

grass leant against the fence and ate my sandwiches while waiting for the appearance of the Royal family on the balcony. The small area of grass was packed with picnickers many of them young, other families with small children and lots of visitors of all hues from overseas some of whom have probably made their homes in the UK. I heard a lot of American accents. Most of the people old and young had Union Jack flags, red white and blue hats, tee shirts with the Union Jack printed on them. Many people carried cardboard periscopes to help them to see more. I did not see any alcohol, no cans of beer and no bottles of wine. The age groups of the hundreds of people in the immediate vicinity surprised me but gave me hope for the survival of our system of Constitutional Monarchy which with all its' faults; unelected, gives credence to the class system and privilege, out of date in a meritocracy and so on. It does seem to work still for the majority of the population and long may it continue to do so.[3]

Another Observer who decided to experience the atmosphere in person was a 36-year-old telecommunications engineer, an ardent royalist who having watched 'all the buildup on TV with excitement' travelled up to London from Northamptonshire with his Canadian wife and eight-year-old daughter to watch parts of the wedding celebration from The Mall and the Victoria Memorial outside Buckingham Palace. Conscious of the many non-British onlookers that he was standing with throughout the day he commented that

There were plenty of foreign tourists around and it made me feel very proud to be British. I love the whole ceremonial side of things – the history and the tradition and I loved the fact that the world was looking at Britain – for all the right reasons. There were plenty of flags being waved and massive Union Jacks hanging along The Mall. The coverage from the foreign press had been amazing in the days leading up to the Wedding and here was our opportunity to show the world what we do best. Let's face it – our history and culture and traditions are why tourists come here.[4]

Not everyone who was keen to celebrate the wedding could afford to travel to London, so for an unemployed single mother from Leicestershire her celebrations were planned on a smaller scale at home with her young daughter. For them, the event was on a par with the most special celebratory days, signalled by the purchase of croissants for breakfast normally reserved for Christmas Day only:

The Royal Wedding completely took over the day of myself and my daughter and we wanted it this way. We had both been excited about it, both looked at merchandise in supermarkets. My daughter had been working on a Royal Wedding Challenge badge at Rainbows since January

A DECADE OF RECOVERY? THE 2010S

and had taken part in a sponsored Royal Quiz at school (to raise money for the school). Her school held a Royal Wedding street party just before they broke up for Easter in which they all had to wear red, white and blue. Every child took food and together we made fairy cakes which we iced with the British flag and on some we wrote 'Kate heart Wills'. The school put all the dinner tables out in the playground and they had a proper street party. My daughter wore special Royal Wedding deeley boppers from Tesco and was tremendously excited. The day of the Royal Wedding was meant to be the last day of our Easter holiday in Great Yarmouth, but we came back a day early so we could make sure we were at home to watch it all.

On the day of the wedding we woke at 6.30 am (naturally). By 7 am we were waiting outside a small Tesco to get the newspapers and croissants as a treat for breakfast. We only ever have croissants for breakfast on Christmas Day so this is how special the day was to us. We flicked around channels until 8 am then stuck with BBC coverage for the rest of the day. It seemed a long wait until the guests started arriving at the Abbey and I was desperate to see someone I knew. Finally I saw Victoria Beckham in the queue (I loved that they had to queue) but was disappointed in her boring navy blue dress which looked more suited to a funeral. David Beckham looked an idiot wearing his OBE. There were many people there that have medals but he was the only one stupid enough to wear it. I read afterwards he even wore it on the wrong side and it was against protocol to wear it. Doh! . . .

On the whole it was a happy experience for me and made me feel that some people really do find true love and it's not all fairy stories, although this is rather a great fairy story in a way. I think they will make a great King and Queen but hope they have some time together before all that starts.[5]

The reference to the Beckhams' appearance illustrates an element common to many of the accounts of sitting to watch the wedding ceremony. This focus on famous, non-royal guests was not so evident in accounts of earlier royal occasions, perhaps signalling the progression of celebrity culture fuelled by social media and the 'Hello magazine mentality' mentioned earlier. The presence of so many famous faces seemed to be an attraction to watch the ceremony for some Observers, perhaps indicating that royal occasions concerning the younger generation of the royal family are starting to be regarded as celebrity events. A 66-year-old retired nurse from Derby had woken up with a sense of excitement for the day:

Back home for 10 am and switch TV on, I sit watching everyone arriving at the Abbey. By now I am feeling very excited, here are the Beckhams, my goodness she looks in a furious mood. Oh. Dear Princess Beatrice who on

REFLECTIONS ON BRITISH ROYALTY

earth advised you that the hat looks great, IT IS AMAZING and I think we shall be hearing a lot more about it. Eugenie looks very awkward in her outfit too, I bet Fergie has had hand in this! I think it's sad that Sarah Ferguson has been left out, I know she is what some would call a walking disaster but a lot of the public like her for that very reason, and she will not conform. Here come Camilla and Charles, Camilla does her best but she still looks wooden.[6]

A 73-year-old retired trademark attorney watched the wedding with his wife hoping to spot familiar faces amongst the guests.

Of course the TV lingered over the more famous faces, such as Elton John (looking very chubby) with his partner; Chelsy Davy who was Prince Harry's erstwhile girlfriend; Tara Palmer-Tomkinson; and David Beckham with is pregnant wife who was wearing a hat that defied gravity. He was wearing a medal (I guessed it was an OBE) but on the wrong side! You never wear it on the right. I shouted this out to him, and I am told by someone that he changed it over later. Then the more important guests began to arrive.

I pointed out to my wife that all the guests had different coloured tickets according to their degree of importance. Earl Spencer – the bridegroom's uncle – for example had the very prestigious yellow ticket, but poor Elton John had to content himself with a green one. Others, who were even further 'below the salt', had blue or white ones. Most of the men not in uniform were in morning suits – including the Prime Minister, David Cameron (despite the suggestions in the press a few days earlier that he might eschew a morning suit as being too 'posh' in favour of a lounge suit), the Deputy Prime Minister, Nick Clegg, and the Leader of the Labour Party, Ed Miliband (his was clearly hired) who was accompanied by his frumpish partner whom he has not yet bothered to marry despite having fathered 2 children with her.[7]

The outfits of the princesses Beatrice and Eugenie, daughters of the Duke and Duchess of York, probably provoked the most comment, and hilarity, among the guest's outfits on the day, which were revealed upon their exit from minibuses that were hired to bring minor members of the royal family to Westminster Abbey:

Like most people I was amazed at how the minor royals all turned up in minibuses and would've loved to have been a fly on the wall in that cab office when that booking was taken. I was aghast at the outfits of Princesses Beatrice and Eugenie who resembled pantomime ugly sisters. The beige alien toilet seat antenna hat had me in stitches. Poor girl – did no one think to tell her she looked like one of the Teletubbies? I thought she had something wrong with her back-the way she was sitting in the car but when she emerged I realised it's because her hat was so big it had been touching the ceiling! And of course the two main outfits people were looking for were what the queen wore (someone on Twitter compared her to Jim Carrey in the Mask) and of course the bride's dress.

Pageantry – not so many people saying it made them proud and we do it better than everyone else – in fact some people disputing that altogether.[8]

Other Observers were even less inclined to watch the wedding, with some actively ignoring the event, including a 66-year-old retired film editor from Scotland who chose to spend the day meeting friends and attending a beer festival in Glasgow:

A day of Ruritanian flummery, surrounded by weeks of hysteria. I am a republican – but not an aggressive one. So, to me, the hysteria and cost of this affair is absurd. Buckingham Palace insists that this is a private family wedding, NOT a state occasion. If only this was the truth. I have absolutely no interest in either of those being married. I wish them (as I would anyone) the best of luck, but why is it necessary to ram the entire, expensive farrago in our faces? Why could the 'private family wedding' not have taken place at one of their many palaces, attended by as many of their friends as they wished, without bothering the rest of us? The press and media are of course much to blame – the loud, in-your-face froth, humbug and sycophancy (with the BBC at the forefront) is intellectually crass and frivolous. It comes over as nothing more than another celebrity event. The guest list gives much away; it clearly IS a state occasion, with far too many of the world's vicious dictators invited – men who would chop of your hands as soon as look at you. And even at that, the business was not well-managed, with the Syrian ambassador invited and then dis-invited at less than 24 hours' notice. Meanwhile former PMs Blair and Brown have apparently been snubbed, while Thatcher and Major are 'in'. Very British. Scotland will observe with, at best, benevolent detachment.[9]

Social media and community

One aspect of some people's day exemplified a technological change in the way that people were able to interact with the events of the day. Several Observers commented on sharing information or opinion on the events by text and social media, including a 33-year-old living in Cardiff who had the day off from his role as a radio broadcast assistant:

A friend and I talked about watching it together and then going out but when we discovered it was on so early we decided to watch it at our homes and meet up for lunch later on. I watched the ceremony in my pyjamas in front of the TV – with half of my attention dedicated to following all the Facebook statuses and Tweets commenting on the events as they unfolded. That was as much fun as watching the event – seeing what other people thought. It seemed to me that everyone in some way had something to say on the matter and it united people – even the curmudgeons who threatened to close their Facebook and twitter accounts because they were fed up hearing about Wills and Kate. I'm a big softy where romance is concerned and was fluctuating between a sucker for the soppiness of the whole occasion and flippancy.[10]

Social media also provided an outlet for less respectful responses to the royal family. Writing from Grimsby, a 39-year-old teacher's account of her day included coverage of tweets from the @Queen_UK, a spoof Twitter account, which provided an 'alternative' view of the day's events:

I settle down to watch the wedding coverage with a blueberry muffin and a cup of coffee. The kids are a bit unsettled as they've watched a lot of coverage already and it has mainly consisted of people they've never heard of arriving at Westminster Abbey. While we are watching, my husband has Twitter on his I-phone and is following a spoof of the Queen, he reads various tweets out to me including:

@Queen_UK: Packed one's handbag for tomorrow's wedding (miniature gin, remote weapons button, reading glasses, I-phone, bag of peanuts)

@Queen_UK: No Philip, you cannot go attend the wedding in a Tony Blair mask.

@Queen_UK: Having an early gin and tonic to help with the wedding preparations. Being Queen of the world is all go. #ginoclock

@Queen_UK: One can confirm that there will be a fruitcake at the wedding. In fact there will be two as Mr. Cameron is bringing Mr. Clegg

@Queen_UK: Middletons are round for a BBQ. They've brought an ASDA value box of meet and a case of Fosters. Awkward.[11]

A modern royal family

The marriage of Prince William and Kate Middleton drew comparisons with the wedding of William's parents thirty years earlier, giving cause to reflect on the possible modernizing effect as the new generation of royals started to take centre stage. Comparisons were made between the relationships perceived between the two couples, in particular given the hindsight afforded by the breakdown of the Wales's marriage. Observers commented on the

A DECADE OF RECOVERY? THE 2010S

balance of the younger couple, their apparent ease with each other and their publicity. A female 54-year-old writer from Watford observed:

1.30 pm: I am still watching the television and have just seen the couple kissing on the balcony of Buckingham Palace. Something that strikes me as very appropriate is that William and Catherine look very balanced and equal to each other in their clothing, neither of them overshadowing the other, and I think this is important. It shows that they are good friends and are happy to support and complement one another. Again I have to contrast this with the upstaging antics of Diana, the late Princess of Wales, who started off in a vulgar, trashy dress that was bigger than herself and Prince Charles put together, and then she went from bad to worse to disastrous. I very much hope that, by contrast, Catherine's sensible elegance and grace presage a future of sensible, gracious and dignified behaviour.[12]

A 52-year-old male civil servant from Tyne and Wear thought the way the couple met, in a 'very middle-class' way, was part of the reason they seem so well suited and easier for the public to identify with:

Thinking back thirty years, to the wedding of Prince Charles and Lady Diana, I can see that that time around both the groom and the bride seemed to be very much 'other': very much not ordinary people, I mean. And that social distance between the couple getting married and the millions watching the event helped to build up the glamour and enchantment of the occasion. But even then there were people saying, he'd never have got her if he wasn't Prince of Wales.

I've always had a soft spot for Prince Charles, poor devil that he is: a man who'd have been happy as a country architect, married complaisant to a discreetly flighty wife, forced into the role of heir to the throne and surrounded from his earliest days by hearty bullies like his old man. His sheer awkwardness in the role was what leant him such charm as he possessed. And people tend to remember the more mature Diana and forget what a nullity she was at the time of her marriage.

I felt none of this during the run-up to today's wedding, however. Prince William looks to me like a young man who's happy in his own skin, doing a job he loves and more than capable of making his own way in the world; I get the feeling that if the monarchy were to be abolished tomorrow he'd shrug his shoulders and carry on being an RAF helicopter pilot, and probably feel quietly relieved at being spared all the ceremonial nonsense that goes with the Royal job description. Above all, he looks like a young man who could have won his bride on his own merits, and in fact I'm sure he did just that, for all the spiteful remarks one hears about Kate Middleton being a gold-digger. There's something

226 REFLECTIONS ON BRITISH ROYALTY

very 'middle class' about the way the couple met, started and carried on their relationship, including that interlude in which they worked out that they really did want to be together. Not a fairy tale wedding, then, but all the better for it. All the Royal marriages there have been in my lifetime have failed, I think, but this one looks as though it'll endure and be happy, and that fact alone is worth celebrating. If only even one commentator had thought to say so, before switching off his microphone and shutting up for good.[13]

The concept of the Prince marrying a 'commoner' was referred to by several Observers, most of whom questioned the notion of what a commoner actually was in today's society, considering Kate Middleton had a comparatively privileged upbringing. A twenty-year-old student, from North Wales but studying in London at the time of the wedding, commented that she was irritated by the press coverage of this:

I find it annoying when the press speak of Kate Middleton as a 'commoner' because she is clearly so wealthy, and went to Marlborough school, which costs thousands of pounds to attend. However, I have become more interested in the couple, partly because they're both so attractive and seem – through media portrayal anyway – to be quite genuine, and in love. Compared to Diana and Charles' wedding, which was very stiff by the looks of things on archive TV broadcasts I've seen (I wasn't born when they married), Kate and William's looked more fun.[14]

Observers noted other differences from the wedding of thirty years earlier, perhaps more demonstrative of the changes in society and the concept of 'modernizing' the royal family that were exemplified in the wedding of William and Kate. A 44-year-old Union administrator was critical of attempts at informality that he identified on the day:

The attempts by the Royals to strike an informal, modern and maybe even cost-cutting note. It seemed to me that the media must have been briefed on this because all the commentators were parroting the same line: how successfully the day combined both tradition and modernity; how it illustrated the ability of the Windsors to adapt to changing conditions, etc. Yet to me these attempts at informality fell flat and often seemed rather silly: the minor royals trooping on and off minibuses on their way to the Abbey as though on a work outing; the reports of the catering at Buckingham Palace being canapés and finger food; the sight of William and Kate pootling down the Mall in a sports car after the reception. The point of a Royal Wedding is surely the pageantry, and that's what we want to see; I hardly think the cost of a few extra limousines in place of the minibuses would have added appreciably to the enormous cost of the day.[15]

A DECADE OF RECOVERY? THE 2010S

Others, including a 42-year-old female researcher from Cheltenham, were more appreciative of the changes.

> The crowds are very heartening: for years the royal family has taken a bashing for the way the royals behave, and lots of people lost respect for the royal family. But people have real affection for William and Kate, and that was evident. Such a contrast between the stuffy, dull ceremony and the sense of real celebration amongst the ordinary people on the streets of London. And at the end of the day, it's the ordinary people who will choose whether or not a monarchy is still relevant in Britain today. In contrast to the people in the Abbey (mostly white and from privileged backgrounds), the crowds were made up of people from all ethnic backgrounds and all parts of the country.[16]

One aspect of the event that appeared markedly different in accounts was the low level of local community engagement with organized street parties and events. Several Observers did mention gatherings but not on the scale of the royal wedding of 1981. A 73-year-old retired civil servant from Bath considered this:

> There was a lot of rather silly discussion in the press about the low number of street parties being planned, suggesting that it was due to lack of interest. Several correspondents pointed out that a lot of people no longer live in settled communities, or even know their neighbours. If you have lived in the same street for years and have had parties before, everyone knows what to do and they almost arrange themselves, but this is often no longer the case. Arranging a party among semi-strangers takes a lot of time and determination to organise and so many people these day work long hours and no longer have the energy to do it.[17]

Inevitably, the subject of a royal wedding gave Observers an opportunity to reflect on the place of the monarchy in 2011. As with previous royal-related Directives, opinions ranged across republicans, monarchists and those who just saw the event as an opportunity for celebration in a way similar to other national events. A 30-year-old living in Watford wrote of wanting to create a 'republican refuge' at her house and hoping to avoid any activity or coverage of the wedding:

> So, we managed to avoid the wedding. How do I feel about it? It just makes me angry to think that so many people in this country continue to be duped into deferring to a ridiculous system where one family of people have an almighty privilege over the rest of us, purely as a result of their birth. I do see how in history it's been relevant, but I think nowadays the royal family is so anachronistic. I just don't understand why we need it. Some people say they are good for tourism, but in countries like France

where they did the sensible thing and got rid of their monarchy, tourists still visit royal palaces like Versailles. It makes me so mad to see people on the TV going on about how wonderful it is to catch a glimpse of these people – like they think they themselves are worthless, when in actual fact they probably lead much more meaningful lives.

I just think it's a huge symbol of the inequity that continues to exist in this country. A display of wealth like that is vulgar at the best of times, but in the middle of the worst public spending cuts since the war, it just goes to show how out of touch they are with everyday people's lives. It's disgusting. The fact that they invited all sorts of awful people from countries where human rights abuses are going on right this minute (Saudi Arabia etc) is also incredibly insensitive and just goes to show where their interests lie.

I do and I don't feel sorry for Kate Middleton. I think she's probably aware of what she's getting herself in for and if she's that hungry for wealth etc then I think she deserves what she gets. But just to have your life controlled like that – not even being able to keep your first name as you want it for goodness sake. Plus, she's already started losing weight and it's not like she was fat to start with. She will be hounded and criticised from left right and centre and completely defined by the man she's married to or what she's wearing and looks like. Then expected to churn out babies till she has a boy. Awful.[18]

In contrast, a 25-year-old government worker watched the wedding ceremony in her local pub in Birmingham and enjoyed it so much that she and her partner, 'both into our tattoos . . . jokily discussed the idea of getting matching royal wedding commemorative tattoos done by P. We said we would get "Kate & Will 4eva. IDET" (= if destroyed ever true. This was a standard format for declarations of love throughout both of our school days!).' She went onto reflect on the symbolism of the event for her:

My favourite part of the wedding was the journey from Westminster Abbey to Buckingham Palace. I love to see the carriages and soldiers, everything red and gold and baroque and so so over-the-top! To me that is a real symbol of England, and speaks volumes of a heritage that we should be proud of. It is hard sometimes to be patriotic because of associations with the BNP and football hooliganism, but the royal wedding seemed to be a wonderful opportunity for the country to pull together in celebration. It is odd, I suppose, to care about a wedding between two people I have never met, but it was a great symbol of pride and of a glorious, grand shared history.[19]

A 57-year-old writer from Harrogate agreed that the event showcased a ceremonial side of Britain that reminded him of support of the monarchy despite initial disinterest in the event:

My conclusions? Nobody does pomp and ceremony so well as we British. What's more, we manage to make it look as if it belongs to the people and isn't just for the VIPs involved. William and Kate's wedding was in weather that started off indifferently – as I did – warmed and became brighter as the day wore on. As I did. I started off without any strong opinions either way and ended the day as a re-confirmed royalist . . .

The above feeling was similar but a little more intense than how I was before other big royal events in my lifetime. These were principally the Queen's Silver Jubilee, followed by the wedding of Charles and Diana and then the latter's funeral. The other weddings of which I was aware – Princess Ann, Prince Andrew, Prince Edward and a plethora of lesser royals – were either not televised and in any event of much less interest. These three events, involving the monarch, her heir to the throne and a woman who had posthumously become almost a goddess in the eyes of the Nation's media were, without doubt, big occasions.

I was not interested up to the day of each televised event but ended up watching all the live footage I could. Each occasion reminded me that I am a Monarchist and confirmed my opinion that there is no other Head-of-State model suitable for our country. Also that we are lucky to have them. At least the 'main players' in the family – the Queen, Duke of Edinburgh, Prince of Wales and Princess Royal. I have much less time and tolerance for those who appear to do nothing for their income and lifestyles, in particular, Andrew and his daughters, Edward and the lesser princes, princesses, dukes and duchesses.[20]

A 35-year-old counsellor from Exeter used her account of the day to reflect on the meaning of royalty, referencing the fairy-tale quality that always seemed to accompany royal weddings:

I'm kind of sad tonight because she was so beautiful and he was so handsome and it made me want that fairy tale. I know that everyone has shied away from saying that they have a fairy tale because of Diana and Charles but actually the magic came back today. There is so much hope in the monarchy for me. I know that there are so many objections to all that they stand for but I really loved every minute of it and felt proud to be a part of Britain today. I love that this matters. I love that we enjoy having street parties and things like that. I wanted to be Kate today and I wanted to marry a handsome prince and to have that life. I know that it's going to be really hard for her and for them both really. It's going to be pressure and difficulty. I know that really it's not going to be all that glamorous but oh – they looked so in love and I wanted so much to be in a royal palace and to be dressed in really beautiful clothes and look the part and to be able to act the part. I know that it's not my life and that is not a road

I'll ever go down. I am married to my own Prince Charming! He's a bit ill tonight though and wasn't very impressed with all the wedding stuff.[21]

Summer 2012 – the Diamond Jubilee

The royal family were kept firmly in the public eye as a year following the wedding of the Duke and Duchess of Cambridge, the Queen celebrated her Diamond Jubilee. The Diamond Jubilee year was markedly different to the Queen's fortieth anniversary (celebrated in her 'annus horribilis' of 1992) and her fiftieth, which had been predicted by the media to 'flop' but which surprised many in its success, perhaps due to an updated format of royal celebration that included a rock concert at Buckingham Palace featuring Brian May, Paul McCartney and Phil Collins. Each jubilee thereafter was celebrated with a 'party at the palace', with a memorable takeover of the palace staged by Madness playing 'Our House' in 2012.[22]

The year 2012 felt different for the Windsors, who at that point were experiencing what the Telegraph *described as 'a surge of interest after the Duke and Duchess of Cambridge's wedding'.[23] The impending Olympic Games which were to be held in the UK the month following the jubilee also added to a sense of well-being in the country. The* British Medical Journal *reported on the significantly higher rates of satisfaction with life in the UK found in the Office for National Statistics annual household survey for that year, which showed 'that 2012 was a good year for happiness, possibly boosted by the Queen's diamond jubilee, with its extra bank holidays, and the success of the Olympic and Paralympic Games in London'.[24]*

The jubilee was held over the weekend of 2–5 June, with two additional bank holidays being declared for the event to make a long weekend break for many. The events included a 'Big Jubilee Lunch' to encourage 'neighbours to get together', a jubilee pageant along the Thames in London which comprised a seven-mile-long flotilla of over 1,000 vessels and a flypast by the Royal Air Force, watched by the royal family from the balcony at Buckingham Palace.[25] A concert was televised from Buckingham Palace on the Monday evening, to include the lighting of a network of 2012 beacons around the UK. The celebrations were completed by a Service of Thanksgiving at St Paul's Cathedral and carriage procession by the Queen through the streets of London.[26]

The Directives

Mass-Observation kept with its tradition of recording royal events and asked the Observers to note their activities and opinions of the jubilee in the form of a diary for jubilee weekend, 2–5 June 2012. As with previous events, there was a mix of Observers who actively participated in celebrating the jubilee, either by visiting London for the official events or organizing their own activities. Unlike festivities in 1977, street parties seemed to feature far less in people's activities, with events being limited to local celebrations or at home, alone or with a small group of friends and family, interacting with events via televised broadcasts. The following accounts exemplify some of these different engagements with the jubilee celebrations.

Living in Central London, a 48-year-old psychology PhD student decided to take advantage of his proximity to the celebrations and head to the Thames to watch the river pageant on 3 June:

> On the Sunday we got up, breakfasted as usual and got ready to go out. Sundays are normally very slow days for us, so even though we planned to go to the Thames, we still took our time. We left the house around midday and began our walk to the Thames. Even though the event was publicised, I never really expected that much, I don't know why, since William and Kate's wedding 2011 was highly supported. However, as we walked down Park Lane in the general direction of the river, it became evident there were a number of people who to me were on a mission the same as us. We had planned to go to Lambeth Bridge, we felt that given it was a lesser known bridge, maybe there would not be many people there. By the time we got to the other side of Victoria the groundswell of people swarming to the river was huge, hundreds of people heading in the same direction. It was actually quite an exhilarating feeling knowing we were heading toward the same place with the same thought. Actually we were very unprepared for the experience and for the scale of interest that people would have in the event, so when we actually got to the Thames and saw the crowds of people lining the river, and several layers deep it was a surprise. It was impossible to see the river. People were milling around, seeing if they could get a view, others were standing on top of bollards and benches. Others were more prepared, they had brought periscopes, we even saw people carrying stepladders! We could not find anywhere comfortable stand, so we ended up about 15 feet away from the river, but with our backs to it and watching one of the many screens placed along the route of the pageant, showing TV coverage of it.
>
> After a few minutes we realised the irony! We were by a major event with our back to it! We decided to return home, set the TV to record the pageant and have a meal instead, which is what we did.[27]

The majority of Observers celebrated closer to home, in their local area, and were usually dependent on television broadcasts to keep them updated on events in London. Coverage of the events was mentioned by many, although unlike previous events, complaints were not so much about the amount of coverage leading up to the event but more on the quality of coverage. A

69-year-old former bookkeeper watched the celebrations with her husband from their home in Milton Keynes:

> All in all I thought it a wonderful celebration and I thoroughly enjoyed it. I have heard criticism of the BBC's coverage and I do agree with much of it. They annoyed me by constantly going back to the studio when things were still happening. I didn't want to see Huw Edwards any more than I wanted to see the two presenters on the day of the pageant. I did want to know what I was looking at some of the time when they didn't tell us. Interviewing people in the studio, asking inane questions like 'How do you think the Queen's feeling right now?' is not what I expect from the BBC. But as we know standards have slipped.[28]

A retired 74-year-old civil servant from Bath also complained about the quality of the BBC coverage:

> Afterwards, we watched the BBC broadcast of the Jubilee river pageant. A lot was said later about the weather and it was used as an excuse by the BBC Director for technical failings in the broadcast, but in fact the rain we had here from midday did not reach London until after the first part – the 'oared boats' preceding the Royal Barge had reached the end. The wind too, which would have made the barge difficult to control, remained fairly light. I thought the whole pageant a wonderful piece of planning. The idea of a full peel of bells on the first boat being answered by all the church bells along the riverside was a brilliant idea, very traditional, very jubilant. Sadly, we could hardly hear them, or the music from the other boats. Many other aspects of the broadcast disappointed. Far too little information about the boats and people in them – all of them with a story to tell. Nothing more than a distant view of the 'Avenue of Sail' – the boats which had to stay down river from Tower Bridge, which I had been looking forward to. If only we had known, we could have watched a much better broadcast from ITV or Sky TV if we had had it, or even German television which were better and more informative.[29]

One aspect of jubilee coverage that garnered a positive note from a 23-year-old medical student from Cornwall was the way that insights through television programmes could make the royal family feel more accessible, thereby reinforcing their relevance to contemporary society:

> 3 June: After Lunch I did some work and then ironed while watching the documentary about Gary Barlow making the Jubilee song 'Sing'. It was a really engaging and vibrant documentary and I think the song is spectacular. Again we saw a bit of the royal family in the show. It strikes me how lucky we are to have such insight into their world. There are lengthy and detailed interviews with Prince Charles

A DECADE OF RECOVERY? THE 2010S   233

which is such a privilege when you think he is heir to the throne. I can't think of similar interviews with the Queen but it reflects the changing and progressing role the royal family plays. Media such as television makes them much more accessible and I think the future of the royal family lies in them engaging more with the media and taking a more public role as to justify their relevance in a modern world.[30]

Some Observers were uninterested in the celebrations but found it hard to escape them, including a 38-year-old police officer with a young child in Wales who admitted:

I'm sorry but I just can't get myself excited about it. Everything's covered in union jacks and if I see another piece of bunting, I will hang myself from it. I'm not patriotic at all. Ok fair play, the old birds done well. What's she going to try? 70 years next so she'll be the longest ever? I would, may as well get your name in the Guinness book of records for good measure. May as well be remembered for something. I certainly won't be having a street party. I'll be using the day off from work to hopefully if weathers permitting take my little boy out for the day but apart from that, I won't be doing much at all.[31]

The notion of collective celebration, supported by the build-up to the events within the media and commercial spheres, was accepted or rejected by most Observers, but for a 31-year-old fledgling writer from Scotland, the jubilee weekend was not the joyful event she had planned. The resulting account of her weekend underscores how important social gathering might be for some, especially in relation to large-scale celebrations and festivals (such as the jubilee or Christmas):

Yesterday (Friday 1st June 2012) I spent the day cleaning the house and tidying, in preparation for the Jubilee. I had invited my Mother to stay, and was looking forward to it, with bunting and Jubilee-themed cake and had got her a box of commemorative biscuits in a special tin from Marks & Spencer's and made a cushion for her in red cotton with white crowns printed on it, edged in black pom-pom trim. It didn't take long to do the main cover, but I sat and hand sewed the trim in place to get a better finish.

I was excited about spending the weekend watching the celebrations on TV, eating cake, sitting in the garden if it was nice, and talking and laughing and maybe doing a jigsaw.

In the morning (2nd June) her text saying she was going to get her hair done for a night out she had on the Tuesday, and that my husband and I could stop by if we wanted. It felt like a mute response to the efforts I had put in. I was hurt, with everything ready for a party, but no-one to share it with.

My husband isn't very interested, and had an exam to prepare for, so was planning on getting on with that while my Mum and I celebrated. I wanted to nip round the shops and pick up the last round of knick-knacks and bargains and branded Jubilee things, but felt there was no point. He accused me of being materialistic, buying things we don't need, bringing more crap/junk into our house.

I couldn't help tears, feeling somewhat useless and at a loose end. As my husband rightly said: we don't know anyone else who is interested in the Jubilee – just me and my Mum.

The house was ready, and I had even created a space in the living room with a union jack box and a tin in the shape of a London bus with 'Marble Arch' as its destination. On top of the box I put the commemorative plate of William and Kate that was made for their wedding, and called it 'Royal Corner' and thought Mum would have appreciated it. I stared at it feeling really stupid.

I said to my husband, how I'd always wanted to be part of a big family, to have brothers and sisters and cousins living nearby, but my family is spread out and even though we are married, he isn't close to his family/siblings, which means I am not either. I realised that if I wanted to have a party with someone, I would have to have my own family. The thought was at once sobering, sad and a little distasteful. Why didn't my Mum want to come and celebrate all together, rather than sit alone?[32]

Opinions on monarchy

The jubilee became an opportunity for some Observers to reflect back on earlier times and the role of royalty within their own lives. A 55-year-old writer from Watford demonstrated this nostalgia when reflecting on how the jubilee provided a cohesion, albeit temporarily, to the fractures she saw in modern society:

I have been quite depressed lately by the dreadful state of the world, with all the troubles in the middle-east, and the economic problems in Europe, and especially the austerity policy in Britain which will deprive chronically sick and disabled people like me of the state benefits upon which we rely. The future looks very bleak, and my husband and I had been staying indoors, feeling miserable and unsociable, scared of the uncaring, brutal society in which we are living. Strangely, the Jubilee changed that, bringing an atmosphere which was surprisingly uplifting and encouraging. Seeing on television all the people who had gone to

A DECADE OF RECOVERY? THE 2010S

London to join in the events, and seeing such large crowds which were totally peaceful, with ordinary people waving flags and smiling, despite the rain, I was reminded of a Britain of former times, perhaps in my childhood, when people were decent and respectable, and when it was safe to walk out in the street.

When I was a child, the Queen represented the respectable standard by which we lived. My mother would say, 'Sit nicely at the table, like the Queen does', or, 'Say please and thank you, like the Queen'. She would even say, 'Go to the lavatory when you need to. Don't be too embarrassed to ask. The Queen goes to the lavatory.' My mother would also take notice of what the Queen wore, as a guide to what it was acceptable for her to wear herself. To respect the Queen and to try to live up to her standards was comforting and reassuring, and it was a sign that everything was all right. When people speak disrespectfully of the Queen, it distresses me and makes me feel very angry and almost personally threatened. It was wonderful during the Jubilee celebrations to witness the love and respect shown to the Queen, and I found this enormously comforting and reassuring. It was a sign to me that there are still an enormous number of people out there who hold the same fundamentally decent values that I hold myself, and that perhaps all this loose living, materialism and drunkenness we so often see is just some superficial dross perpetrated by a minority of people who have been given undue attention in the media.[33]

For others, the jubilee celebrations allowed them to reflect on the place of patriotism within the different regions and home nations of the UK. A PhD student in Newcastle outlined the discussion she had with fellow students:

We mainly discussed it in terms of national identity because a couple of students are studying the topic of 'Englishness' for their theses. Two Scottish students had opposing views which we discussed. They are on opposite sides of the Scottish independence debate and felt the same towards the Jubilee with the pro-independence student against what he considers the 'English' monarchy, and the anti-independence student enjoying it and looking forward to the street party in her area. A German student I work with took the opportunity to find out what 'Englishness' was from the coverage. He summed it up as 'still managing to have a good time despite the weather' which is probably fairly apt.[34]

A retired civil servant from Bath repeated a theme common throughout this volume about the role of the monarchy and republican alternatives to the institution:

It was great to see all the crowds, such a wonderful mix of generations and diversity of British people of all backgrounds and visitors from abroad, especially from the Commonwealth, and all looking so happy to be there.

The dwindling minority of republicans really want their heads examined. They are either so blinkered and hidebound in their prejudice, or just plain thick. Some of them witter on about democracy, quite missing the point of a Constitutional Monarchy. The Queen has no political power, and some foreigners just don't get it, but that is the whole point. She has no political power and does not rule. She only reigns. Why would we want some sleazy politician as our head of State? The Queen is a leader and she represents our country to the rest of the world who respect her, to our enormous benefit. She holds together the Commonwealth, which seems an increasingly valuable relationship when you look at the EU in comparison.

No elected leader could unite a population as diverse as ours. Regular elections, besides being disruptive and enormously costly, could never provide anyone chosen by more than a minority and however popular at first, they would soon disappoint. Those who had not voted for the winner would start to go over their background and look to 'dig the dirt'. One has only to look at the opposition to someone with such popular support as President Obama. Would the crowds turn out like this for Angela Merkel or the new French leader? The Irish president seems to live in obscurity. People who complain about the cost of the monarchy do not realise that some European leaders cost their countries more and for the price of one, we get the whole royal family to cheer us up, provide recognition to those who truly serve the country and their communities. This Jubilee has made so many people happy, whether they went to London or celebrated with family or neighbours. My sister-in-law planned to combine the party with her mother's 90th birthday.

There are more important things in life than national politics, and it is vital that we have a monarch who is above it all. We maybe do not know how fortunate we are.[35]

Writing on Sunday, 3 June, a 33-year-old administrator from Cardiff reflected on the place of monarchy in today's society:

On the way home we talked about the jubilee a little. My husband doesn't get what we were celebrating. Why we were celebrating. A lot of people see it as a reinforcement of class hierarchies, and the pomp and ceremony do little to dispel that belief. I see it a bit differently. I'm not a royalist, so I don't exactly care or have any nationalistic feeling towards the jubilee, but I see it as a marker of a generation. To me, the queen represents a dying breed of old lady. The fact she is so active well in her 80s is an inspiration to a generation. I feel she really believes she has sacrificed a lot for the country. And in many ways, she probably has. But I'm not sure I can feel much sympathy or gratitude for someone sacrificing stuff for me from their castle, travelling around in their private jet, etc. I guess as a person, I do admire the queen, but as an institution or a symbol, I don't really have much feeling either way.

She went on to reveal a generational divide between her siblings and her parents:

I spoke to my sister, who lives in London. My parents had been down to visit for the pageant, along with my brother-in-law's sister and nephew. My mum had turned up with loads of union jacks and flags sticking out of her bad. Apparently she tried to get everyone involved until a pissed skin head started going on about 'rule Britannia' at her. I don't think my mum gets what the union jack can mean to people outside of their little country village, especially to British Indians in their 40s (my brother-in-law and family). They then didn't get to see much of the pageant because of the crowds and people weren't allowed on the bridges because of the security risks. My sister wasn't too impressed with the whole affair, but my mum gets very enthusiastic about these things. Like my husband, my sister found the whole thing strange, celebrating social hierarchies. I mean, it is a strange thing to have two days off for, but I really enjoyed having the extra time out of work. I think, to me, it was just a really nice long weekend.[36]

A female 44-year-old financial risk manager from the Midlands suggested that the dominant public discourse around the jubilee weekend was less about the unfairness of social hierarchies and more about the Queen herself:

Overall the view of people I have overheard has been less about inherited privilege and more that the Queen has a remarkable sense of duty and works really hard. There has been some limited chatter about whether people would prefer to see the Duke of Cambridge accede to the throne after the Queen but less than I expected. It was a pleasure to be spared too much political focus – there were no politicians on the Royal barge and few interviews with any of them – it is hard to imagine that Tony Blair would not have been keen to participate and provide some historical soundbites if this had still been his premiership.[37]

2018 – Prince Harry marries Meghan Markle

On 27 November 2017, Prince Charles released a statement announcing the engagement of his youngest son Prince Harry to Meghan Markle, with a wedding planned for the following spring.[38] The couple met eighteen months earlier but made their first public appearance as a couple at the Invictus Games in Toronto in September 2017. Prince Harry's previous relationships had all been subject to headlines; Harry and Meghan's courtship was no different, though Markle did appear, as headlines stated, 'Not your average royal'.[39] Famous in her own right as an actress on popular US television shows, Markle was marked out as different from other royal brides for several reasons. A US citizen, Markle was divorced and of mixed race, had an established career and was known for speaking up on various social issues, including feminist causes. Press coverage focused on the differences in this royal union, with the couple being described as 'thoroughly modern'.[40]

The wedding ceremony was held on Saturday, 19 May 2018, at St George's Chapel in Windsor with approximately 600 guests in attendance, including members of the royal family and celebrity friends of the couple. On the morning of the wedding, the Queen conferred the titles of Duke of Sussex, Earl of Dumbarton and Baron Kilkeel on Prince Harry, and following their marriage the couple became known as the Duke and Duchess of Sussex.

The wedding contrasted in many ways with that of Prince William's, largely due to the latter's position as a future monarch – smaller in size and with less of the pomp and ceremony than had accompanied the wedding of the Duke and Duchess of Cambridge. Following extensive media speculation around Meghan Markle's relationship with her family, only her mother attended the ceremony, whilst Prince Charles walked her down the aisle in place of the traditional role of father of the bride. The ceremony itself also introduced less traditional inclusions – a gospel choir and a sermon by Michael Curry, the first African American leader of the American Episcopalian church who preached on the power of love, 'in complete contrast', the Guardian argued, 'to the solemn and stationary ecclesiastical address that preceded his'.[41]

Directives

Unlike Prince William's marriage to Kate Middleton in 2011, there were 'no plans' for a bank holiday to mark the marriage of Prince Harry to Meghan Markle. The BBC reported that a spokesman for the prime minister, Theresa May, stated that there had been 'no bank holiday to mark the weddings of Charles's younger brothers Prince Andrew in 1986 or Prince Edward in 1999',[42] as none of the men were directly in line to the throne at the time of their marriages. Perhaps because of this, the wedding of Harry and Meghan did not seem to attract the same level of community celebration as that of William and Kate, as testified by Observers' accounts.

Part 3 of the Spring Directive for 2018 asked Observers to share their thoughts and feelings on the upcoming royal nuptials, including any conversations they may have had and any reactions to media coverage of the event. In addition, they were asked to keep a Day Diary for the Saturday of the wedding, regardless of their personal engagement with the royal wedding.

Quite a few Observers sat down to watch the ceremony on television or caught glimpses of the ceremony in passing, whilst quite a few actively avoided coverage. The selections reproduced here are selected from those *who participated in a wedding-related activity on the day, including one Observer from Jersey, who decided to celebrate the day with friends at a wedding-themed hotel event.*[43]

It is interesting to note the role that social media and mobile communication played on the day, replicating the chatter around guests, outfits and the ceremony itself that took place around the television set in earlier events, such as the wedding of Prince Harry's parents in 1981. A 26-year-old archivist from the Midlands watched the wedding on television alone at home but shared the experience with her friends and family through social media platforms.

Despite looking forward to the wedding, I hadn't planned to watch the wedding live. Due to unforeseen circumstances, my plans were canceled at the last minute. I tuned into the BBC coverage (the @Queen_UK parody account on twitter made it clear watching on ITV was illegal!!) just in time to see George and Amal Clooney arrive, shortly followed by David and Victoria Beckham. I remember thinking how stunning Amal looked, top to tail in sunshine yellow, and how Victoria Beckham was still sucking lemons. I think this was about 10:15 am. They were followed by a whole host of celebrities – from Sir John Major to Sir Elton John. Princess Anne's daughter, Zara Tindall looked decidedly uncomfortable and very pregnant, while you wouldn't have known that the Duchess of Cambridge had a 3-week-old baby at home.

I used WhatsApp to message my family in our group chat, as I expected them to be watching. I wasn't disappointed, we were all tuned in. We started to place bets on what colour the Queen would be wearing. I opted for yellow, my sister for purple. I maintain that 'lemon-lime' = yellow, even though it was embellished with purple. I joked about how disappointed I was that Princesses Beatrice and Eugenie were wearing actually lovely and sophisticated hats this time – their attire to William and Catherine's wedding in 2011 was one of the most-discussed of the whole event . . .

All in all, it was the epitome of British pomp and circumstance – nobody does it better. Thousands lining the streets, everyone celebrating, whether at the wedding or camped outside. The sun shone but it wasn't uncomfortably hot either. As Katy Brand reminded us all on Twitter, considering the horrendous loss of his mother when he was just 12 years old, and having to do that awful walk behind her at her funeral, Harry absolutely deserved to have a fantastic and memorable day, and to feel part of an institution that is loved worldwide. I hope they are both very happy together and do plenty of good in the years to come. The phrase 'with great power comes great responsibility' remains apt.[44]

Others watched the television coverage of the ceremony around their daily activities, again sharing comment with friends and family through technological means. The proliferation of mobile technology and social media platforms on which people were able to communicate with others during the event is in marked contrast to earlier royal events covered in this book. It is interesting to note the sense of community sought by many of those watching the events and how this effects feelings of participation and methods of celebration – the virtual version of a street party perhaps. For a 55-year-old homemaker, despite feeling unwell on the day, she was still able to share the event with family by chatting on the phone with family:

> As a Black British/Caribbean woman I and my extended family were intrigued and excited by the idea of these forthcoming nuptials. We joined in the speculation about what she and her mother might wear and, of course, if her father might attend.
>
> I did not feel well on the day and was mostly asleep for the morning build up but I watched the guests arriving and the ceremony while chatting on the phone to my younger sister. We broke off and redialled when the hour was coming up on our phones. We watched until they left the chapel and drove off. We mainly commented on and applauded the outfits worn by the black women and thought that Meghan's mother was so dignified and gorgeous and loved the way Prince Charles took her hand and escorted her to the private registrar's part of the ceremony.
>
> We agreed that the Kingdom choir was sensational and took a comfort break during the lengthy sermon.[45]

Critique of media commentary appears in responses to all Mass-Observation Directives relating to royal events as we have seen, and the wedding of Prince Harry to Meghan Markle was no exception.

A 51-year-old administrator living in Bristol who professed to not being a fan of royalty found himself watching highlights of the wedding that evening and being 'moved by Harry and Meghan's obvious love for one another'; he was nonetheless critical of the media coverage that acted as 'cheerleaders' for the monarchy:

> The run up to the wedding I said to somebody at work on the Friday before, 'It wouldn't be so bad if it could just happen, and we didn't have to hear about it.' There are quite a number of things which irritate me about this Royal Wedding, and the inanity of the advance coverage comes pretty high on the list. Politicians complain about the supposed political bias of the BBC, but who is there to complain about the monarchist bias of all the major broadcasters? Why do the BBC and ITV appoint themselves as cheerleaders for the monarchy? On the day itself, their combined TV coverage lasts for twelve hours. BBC Radio 2 will be live from Windsor from eight a.m. with wedding-themed programmes scheduled to run until six p.m. Who can possibly want so much of this stuff? A recent opinion

A DECADE OF RECOVERY? THE 2010S

poll reported that 66% of those interviewed were uninterested in the wedding; you'd never guess from the adulatory tone adopted by our broadcasters.[46]

Moving away from tradition

Many Observers commented on the contrast in Meghan Markle's background to previous royal brides. Markle's nationality, previous career and marriage all came under significant media scrutiny, and whilst her 'difference' was celebrated in many quarters, it was also viewed with suspicion in others. A 59-year-old male civil servant from Tyne and Wear noted the negative images of the new Duchess:

I get an impression that many people disapprove of Meghan Markle, though not to the point where they'd become involved in a row or even a heated discussion about her character or her suitability as a bride for Prince Harry.

Actually, when I say 'many people' what I really mean is, just about all women and some men I've spoken to, but I think they're reasonably representative of the wider populace.

I understand that prior to taking up with Prince Harry Ms Markle had a career as a television actress and starred in a drama series of the kind watched almost exclusively by women, so possibly the women I've been listening to have based their dislike of her on a mistaken impression that she must be just like the character she plays on screen. I wouldn't know as I wouldn't watch the show in question. The explicit criticisms I've heard are (a) that Meghan Markle is a Wallis Simpson type who has played Prince Harry like a fish on a line, for her own personal advancement, (b) that 'someone like her', who has achieved success in one field, should have refrained from crossing over into another, completely different field, and (c) again, that 'someone like her' will surely prove to be temperamentally unsuited to the duties she'll have to undertake.[47]

A 35-year-old property inventory clerk from London made similar observations about the sense of difference attributed to Meghan Markle by what he describes as 'voices'. Whether these are opinions picked up from the media, social media (although he does mention this as a source) or from those around him is unclear:

As soon as the engagement has been announced, voices were raised that she might not be the right choice. She is not an aristocrat, she is American; she is a divorcee, someone even whispered or shouted (after carefully hiding behind anonymity) that her mother is black. I must admit, these were correct observations, however I find it difficult to accept them as a reason why she was not a good candidate for marrying Prince Harry.

1. The Duchess of Cambridge, formerly known as Catherine Middleton, now the wife of Harry's older brother and second in line for the throne (after his father) has come from an upper-middle class, hardworking and entrepreneurial family, received good education, but hardly represents better or worse odds than Meghan, who comes from a less prominent, less wealthy family, but proved that she can make a career of her own and has done it rather successfully. (I don't watch TV or follow the latest series, but she has already been a celebrated young actress at the time of her introduction to Harry.)

2. The fact that she is not British: for centuries the royal family choose spouses from various countries, some from royal families, some from among celebrities, and it hardly made any difference, if it made any at all. I am not convinced that this should be a problem even is Harry was the first in line for the throne, but his situation is even less prominent, so it is just a fact, that he fell in love and decided to marry someone from another country.

3. Is she a divorcee? It has been often quoted, that a second marriage is a triumph of hope over experience. I am Presbyterian so I am less familiar with the Church of England's views on marriage and divorce, but I think it is human to make a mistake and it takes courage to face up with it and take action instead of suffering in a bitter and poisonous relationship for life. It is best for both parties to admit a mistake and move on instead of sucking the life out of each other. Should I care more about it, I might consider why she divorced her first husband, but I am not interested and it is not my business either.

4. Racism is out of fashion in Britain, at least by law. However, people are still conditioned to recognise differences and associate them with virtue or vice. As far as I am concerned, I haven't even thought of her African American origins until someone points the fact out: I have seen darker skin on chevs and chevettes living in the direct vicinities of tanning shops than Meghan's. An interesting note on this: while secretly and openly racist people were bewildered that fact that a black mother-in-law now stands a better chance to be invited to smart royal parties than they are, a friend of mine with Indian origins posted on social media the following: *'His marriage to Megan brings another major change to the Royal family and the world watched on Saturday when Megan became a member of the British royal family. There were a lot of people of colour who went to London to see the procession and said that normally they would never have come to see a royal wedding but now that a woman of colour was joining the family they themselves felt that they were now being repre-sented.'* There is a flip side of this coin, after all.[48]

Another Observer admitted suspicions regarding Meghan Markle, in part aroused by stories and coverage within the media:

> I'm pleased if it makes them both happy, though I'm a bit cynical about Meghan Markle. I just get the feeling that she's always been determined to marry extremely well, and that she was very focused on getting him. I think I've been influenced by the fact that her 'friends' say that she's always been obsessed by the Royal Family, and a comment that someone made to me that she also seemed to have made a point in mixing in the right circles to get to know him. On the other hand, I don't always believe what I read in the papers, and I bet there are millions of women who would have gone for it if they'd thought they stood a chance (and hopefully also thought they loved Harry). If I'd been an appropriate age, and mixed in similar circles, maybe I'd have given it a shot, as he does seem a very nice man (though I wouldn't have got very far, and am probably not at all suited to the life of a royal).[49]

Other Observers were much more positive about the effect that Meghan Markle could have on the royal family and the country more broadly. A 75-year-old housewife from Milton Keynes was one:

> Meghan was a wildcard, ticking a number of uncharted boxes for the Royal Family (those who wanted to retain their place in the line of succession, anyway) – mixed race, American and divorced. The comparisons to Wallis Simpson flooded in, but what a difference 80+ years makes. We shouldn't be surprised by Harry's choice of bride – he's always been more rebellious than many royals of recent years. But I genuinely believe that she can do a lot of good for the Royal Family. Yes, she is an actress, and American, but she is also passionate about human rights, and an excellent speaker – using her voice for good, which is what the Royal Family is for. When people talk about the relevance of the Royal Family today, we don't need to look too hard to find the relevance. They represent the biggest platform Britain, arguably, the world, has to offer – probably the most famous family in the world too. And while I don't want to dwell on the impending Brexit, but we will need strong ties with our allies, including America, and this certainly lays the ground work.[50]

Another facet of the difference that Observers related to this marriage was the nature of the ceremony itself. For some it illustrated how the royal family was moving into a new era, but for others it was more reflective of the couple's roles and personalities. A 59-year-old from Tyne and Wear attributed these changes to the fact Prince Harry had the 'freedom to deviate from tradition' in a way impossible for his brother:

Taking the wider view of whether, and if so how and to what extent Prince Harry's marrying Meghan Markle might have changed the Royal Family and the public's perception and expectations of it: this might sound like a copout but I think it's far too early to say. I'm fairly sure the public was looking for a large measure of traditional process and pageantry when Prince William married Kate Middleton, and would have been some what alarmed by some of the elements of Saturday's service: certainly the Reverend Michael Curry's sermon would have jarred, and I don't think the gospel choir would have met with universal approval either. Prince Harry had much more freedom to deviate from tradition because when all's said and done he doesn't count for much anymore, in the line of succession, and as a consequence can indulge a different and more frivolous strain of Royal behaviour, last seen perhaps when the future King Edward VII was Prince of Wales.[51]

The deviation from tradition towards an effort to appear 'normal' was picked up by a 50-year-old retired teacher who wrote that although the event was lovely, it did not feel 'royal' to them:

I am a royalist. I like, admire and respect our royal family enormously. I always have. I remember watching the wedding of Prince Charles and Diana avidly; also watching at least some of Prince William and Kate Middleton. So why not this one? Possibly some of it has to do with the way in which this younger generation of the royal family have been at such pains to appear more 'normal' and less specially removed from the rest of the world. And yet that's not really it either – I like the way they have embraced causes, been more emotional, public and open. I've read some of the after-reports of the wedding – I think it sounded lovely, enjoyable – and yet somehow not royal, in spite of all the wonderful pomp and ceremony which the British do so well.[52]

A 66-year-old retired teaching assistant from Brighton felt that the changes signalled by the marriage were refreshing. She drew on the troubled marriage of the Prince and Princess of Wales as an example of what happened when the expectations of royal protocol were put ahead of human feeling:

I'm not a royalist and I avoided most of the pre-wedding media coverage. One couldn't deny the fact though that this was a major event. It was refreshing of course to have a mixed-race, divorcee welcomed into the royal family. No longer have sacrifices had to be made such as Princess Margaret having to give up the divorcee she loved to keep her HRH title or Edward VIII having to give up the throne to marry his divorcee. There was also Prince Charles of course who was not allowed to marry the woman he loved – Camilla, because she was a divorcee and instead married a 'suitable young virgin' – Diana, with disastrous consequences.

After Diana's tragic death he was allowed to finally marry Camilla and they are happy so all's well that ends well perhaps. Anyway putting all the ridiculous pomp aside it was very nice to see a couple so obviously in love. Meghan Markle is giving up her career to become a duchess but clearly she thinks it is worth it and all that acting experience will no doubt come in very handy.[53]

Anti-royal sentiments

As ever, the occurrence of a royal event, with its associated coverage, expense and commentary, caused many Observers to reflect on what having a royal family meant to them and to the country. One viewed this in the context of how the young generation of royals affected the image and future of the family:

I have never seen the point in retaining the Royal Family, but I think the current generation (Princes William and Harry) have worked hard for many good causes which has endeared them towards me. I also can't quite put my finger on it, but both William and Harry actually appear to be genuine people keen to do good. They don't seem to be acting when they interact with people or the media, which is a massive plus for them.

As for the future of the Royal Family, only time will tell. I think they could be in for a rocky time when Charles becomes king as I don't feel people universally warm to him or particularly like his wife. I do also fear for Megan Markle as I believe she married with good intent, but I imagine life in the Royal Family to be quite restrictive. Hopefully the change in approach of William and Harry will mean Megan can pursue her interests such as charity work and she won't be stifled by life in the palace.

All in all I think everyone wished Megan and Harry well, although I don't think their wedding was compulsory viewing in many of my social circle's homes.[54]

For plenty of Observers with republican tendencies, the Directive provided an opportunity to express their disdain for the monarchy. A seventy-year-old retired university worker in Brighton, undertaking voluntary work with migrants, contrasted the media focus on the wedding received to the level of coverage of other events that she believed more worthy of attention:

Well, as you can see from the above I am hardly likely to be a royalist. Indeed I find the displays of wealth and privilege quite appalling . . . and yet I confess to a certain degree of fascination and curiosity. It makes me angry that the wedding receives such a huge amount of media coverage, and such an enormous amount of public resources are devoted to the event in all sorts of ways, when there are such inequalities within the UK, never mind within the world. Does it help that Meghan Markle is a woman of colour? Maybe. She is so beautiful and her hair is so straight (how can that be?) that she seems to me to transcend racial categories. All the same, I can't really claim her for the alternative or oppositional world. How do the Windrush generation feel? Does it help them get over the traumas they have been put through by the Home Office? And what about the survivors of the Grenfell Tower fire? And all the other people who are destitute, homeless, hopeless, alienated, angry, excluded? Does this wedding have a meaning for them? Or does it just underline their otherness and deprivation? The debates about sweeping the homeless people off the streets of Windsor in preparation for the wedding brought these issues into stark relief. As for the ranks of the world's media, especially from the US, they make me want to vomit. The hypocrisy, the selectivity in what they cover, the enormous resources they are able to draw on for this coverage. It's both a money absorbing event and a wealth creation event – for some people.

Anyway, so what's new? There's no point in my being apoplectic about it all. People will go on being homeless, people will die in tragedies (the Cuban air crash this morning, the volcanic eruptions in Hawaii), people will go on being oppressed and killed (on the Gaza border, or in Syria, or Eritrea, or almost everywhere else in the world including the USA – another school shooting yesterday). There is an argument to say, let's focus on something more positive – two young people in love getting married. A time for the nation to unite and celebrate. Hmmm. Bread and circuses.[55]

A 41-year-old male carer from Sunderland described the wedding as a 'slap in the face' given the level of social and economic problems he perceived in British society:

I'll admit that the Royal Family are in a catch 22 situation – if they are aloof aristocrats that don't involve the commoners in their lives then they are an irrelevant anachronism, yet if they are down-to-earth and approachable individuals that act like ordinary people then you wonder what the justification is for their special treatment. Yes, they make a lot of money for the country in terms of tourism, but the French have no royal family anymore and yet tourists still flock to Versailles. I don't really have anything against the royal family as people. I actually like some of them, especially Kate whom I think will become a very popular and competent queen, but if the monarchy has any real influence then it should be exerted – speaking up for its most needy subjects perhaps, or would that just draw attention to their own excessive wealth?[56]

Summary

Those who watched the celebrations reported their enthusiasm, indicating that interest in pomp and ceremony and the role of continuity still had a place in public interaction with the royal family and national identity. The popularity of the new Duke and Duchess of Cambridge also appeared to usher in a new era of royal protocol, an increase in emphasis on ordinariness and identification with the wider public. The description of William and Kate as a modern couple, along with continued discussion by some that Prince William should be next in line to the throne instead of his father, might exemplify the kind of royal family Observers imagined.

The marriage of Prince Harry to Meghan Markle also gave rise to optimism for some Observers in terms of the modernization of the royal family by embracing causes relevant to their generation and creating personas that enabled the public to identify with them in ways unthinkable for previous generations of royals. Even for some of those declared as republicans, there appeared to be some softening towards the younger royals.

However, with the benefit of hindsight it is interesting to note comments on the extent of change that Meghan Markle symbolized. Mass-Observation's next Directive on royalty addressed these questions and underscored the dichotomy of opinion regarding the new Duchess of Sussex, as well as royal scandal, celebration and ceremony over the intervening four-year period.

10

The British Royal Family in 2022

The year 2022 marked the Platinum Jubilee of Queen Elizabeth II, an unprecedented anniversary for the British monarchy. Although the seventieth anniversary of the Queen's accession to the throne occurred in February, the celebrations were delayed until the summer with four days in June set aside, including two additional bank holidays. Whilst such an occasion would be enough to merit a request to Observers to respond to a Directive on royalty, the previous two years had also seen great change and disruption within the royal family.

Following months of speculation of rifts between the Duke and Duchess of Sussex and the rest of the royal family, the Sussexes announced their intention to step back from royal duties in March 2020, splitting their time between the United Kingdom and the United States. Rumours of a split in the royal family were further compounded by revelations made by the couple during an interview with Oprah Winfrey in March 2021, which alleged mistreatment by the British press and by members of the royal family itself.[1]

Further deepening royal crisis, an interview in November 2019 with British journalist Emily Maitlis on the BBC's Newsnight programme was almost universally agreed to have deeply tarnished Prince Andrew's image, with the Washington Post *describing it as 'nuclear explosion level bad'.[2] Following long-running criticism of his association with convicted sex offender, Jeffrey Epstein, the Duke of York was forced to resign from public roles in May 2021. His involvement in a US civil action over sexual assault allegations was settled out of court in early 2022 but not before the Prince found himself stripped of his military titles and the right to use the title, His Royal Highness.[3]*

On 9 April 2021, Prince Philip, Duke of Edinburgh, died at Windsor Castle at the age of 99. His funeral took place at St George's Chapel, Windsor, on 17 April 2021. Due to the Covid-19 regulations in place at the time of the funeral, arrangements were modified but 'the day was still very much in line with His Royal Highness's wishes'.[4]

The Queen's Platinum Jubilee took place in June 2022. Official celebrations included Trooping the Colour, the lighting of jubilee beacons across the country and the Commonwealth, a 'Party at the Palace' comprising musical tributes from acts through the years and a Platinum Jubilee Pageant along the Mall that reflected the music, innovation and cultural changes in the UK during the seventy years of Queen Elizabeth's reign.

Directives

In the context of the above-mentioned royal events, Mass-Observation issued its Directive in June 2022. In a break with tradition, M-O did not ask Observers to keep a diary for the Platinum Jubilee but instead encouraged Observers to share their thoughts and opinions on the British monarchy and its future. Additionally, the Directive sought opinions on individual members of the royal family, particularly in light of some of the events listed earlier, and asked about Observers' level of involvement in jubilee events.

Opinion on the royal family

As with other reflections on the royalty, some Observers had difficulty imagining a republican future, such as this retired 72-year-old from Leicester, who linked disappointments regarding Prince Andrew's behaviour and Prince Harry's departure from the royal family to the experiences of ordinary British families:

Once the present monarch has departed, I do not see a great future ahead under the reign of King Charles III. William, however, poses a different scenario. He is already a popular figure in this country and I am sure he will make a fine monarch. I doubt that Britain will ever become a full republic and depose the monarchy as part of the state, in my lifetime.

In my view, the commonwealth has a future and will continue to bring together a wide range of nations in what, for them, is and will continue to be a commonwealth and political alliance. The Duke of Edinburgh played a key role in the survival of the British monarchy. He will, I am sure, be given a critical assessment by the historians of the future. But his influence over the Queen and other members of the royal household will be seen as being crucial to its popularity and survival. I cannot see how it could be otherwise, based on what we know of his life and works. He might be seen as a controversial figure but it is hard to imagine historians awarding him anything other than a considerable role during his lifetime.

Prince Harry (as he was once known) poses a range of problems both for me and will do so for those who record history. Before he stood down from royal duties and moved to America, Harry showed a lot of promise. His involvement in work with charities and social issues was all to the good. He was a popular celebrity during his time in this country. What he did after his marriage to Megan Marple [*sic*] was as surprising as it was disappointing. Many of us, myself included, viewed the whole sorry episode with disdain as being just another machination of the traditional royal household who have clearly failed to move with the times. I watched the broadcast of his interview with Oprah Winfrey and found it most interesting even if it was not all that surprising.

Many, like me, will have doubts about Andrew. The scandal that surrounds him is murky and full of contradictory evidence. The Windsor/ Mountbatten family shares much in common with many families in this country. Just as other families have their 'black sheep' and share of marital problems, so too does the royal family. In this regard, they are just like the rest of us. They might enjoy high social status, but as a group of people they are not unlike many other families. The present royal family has all the kinds of problems seen in most other British families. That would include marriage breakdowns, sexual rule-breaking, mental health issues and lack of moral integrity. Why should the Windsor family be any different? If I weigh up the pros and cons of having royalty, I think, on balance, they do more good than otherwise.[5]

A retired 72-year-old psychotherapist living in the Midlands used the Directive to reflect on some of the more problematic aspects the family faced:

We have had the splitting from Royal duties Prince Harry and Megan. That has caused divided feelings across the country. Personally, I was full of hope when that wedding took place. But as the months went on it seemed that things were not at all ok between the Sussex's and the rest of the Royal family. Who knows the truth of the gossip and speculation? I can only judge on the evidence, and I found and continue to find that damming. The interview with Oprah Winfrey was such an attention seeking exhibition of entitlement. I actually couldn't bear to watch all of it, the bits I did see felt so stage managed and spiteful. Whoever you are and whatever your grievances, true or just perceived are private family affairs. How humiliating for the Queen and other senior royals to have such dirty linen washed in public. Prince Harry I am afraid comes across as whiney and wanting his status still without any responsibilities. The couple live a hugely privileged lifestyle and can have no understanding of hardship. Easy to sit back and moan and backbite secure in the knowledge of a healthy bank balance and a sycophantic following. I may be writing more harshly than I otherwise would but I can't bear the thought of the Queen passing away without being reconciled with Harry.

The passing of Prince Philip was also terribly sad, what a wonderful husband and loyal statesman he had been for so many years. He had made sacrifices but still carried out his duties with intelligence and mainly good humour. Yes, he made many a gaffe sometimes extremely inappropriately, but we sort of just thought 'oh that's just Philip' sometimes they were wickedly funny and as the world quite rightly has become more PC they were sometimes cringe moments but I believe that in the main he was forgiven. His funeral in the midst of lockdown was a lonely occasion for the Queen and the sight of her sitting alone in the chapel was heart breaking. He was by her side for so many years, it must have felt like losing a limb . . .

Prince Andrew, well what can you say? Ill-advised in so many ways. It has always been said that he was the Queen's favourite, but who knows. His car crash interview where he was trying to distance himself from Epstein was such an embarrassment not just for himself but his family as a whole. I don't know the ins and outs or the truth of what occurred between Prince Andrew and young girls. Some evidence would point to him having some knowledge of their age but as I say I don't know. I do know that rich and powerful human beings can and do get what they want perhaps more easily than others.[6]

A 75-year-old retired teaching assistant from Edinburgh considered what made a good value member of the royal family, deciding on behaviour and hard work as critical:

I suppose I am still a Royalist, though not strongly so. I am more interested in the Royal family than my Scots husband; I don't know if we are representative of the UK as a whole in this. One family member I rate highly is Princess Anne. She does a great job wherever she shows up, and is completely matter-of-fact about it all. I have grown up alongside Charles, a near-contemporary of mine, and feel for him, living so long in the shadow of his mother and never becoming King. If and when he does reach that dizzy height, he may well not have very long in the role unless he has inherited the longevity gene from his grandmother and parents. The Diana saga was utterly tragic and I'm glad he ended up with Camilla, who is another good-value member. A third member who is playing her part splendidly is Kate, Duchess of Cambridge. I heard today that the Cambridges are to move from Kensington Palace to a quite modest house near Windsor, to give the children, who are all due to start at the same school near Ascot shortly, as normal as possible an upbringing. How sensible! As to Harry and Meghan, I feel some at least of the criticism heaped upon her in particular is unfair, but on the other hand I suspect she is quite manipulative and has Harry, and her life, just where she wants them. The less said about Prince Andrew and his doings, the better!

Through seventy years of her family's fortunes, good and bad, the constant bright star has of course been the Queen herself. What a sterling job she has done all this time, and how deeply we will miss her! She will leave a gaping hole in the fabric of our national life. Can we expect Charles to even begin to fill that hole? The Platinum Jubilee in June was quite a jamboree, of which we watched a fair amount and concurred with most of the populace's opinion that the best moment was the Queen's little teatime sketch with Paddington Bear. She is an actress manque! God save the Queen![7]

Press and media

As ever, commentary on the Windsors also included discussion of the role of the press and media in shaping their image. The following two extracts provide insights into aspects of this relationship. A retired 67-year-old psychotherapist from West Sussex focused on the funeral of Prince Phillip in April 2021. Like many other Observers, the images of the Queen in St George's Chapel at Windsor Castle, having to sit apart from her family in respect of Covid-19-related social distancing restrictions, were particularly poignant:[8]

News, stories and images of the royal family are deeply embedded in the fabric of our lives. For me their comings and goings have created a backdrop against the drama of my own life. I have never expected individual members of the royal family to be anything other than human. Why should they be? Rather, I have both marvelled and sympathised with the pressures of living life under scrutiny. These public figures can become so powerful in the collective imagination. When Prince Philip died it was as if I too had lost a member of my extended family. And who can forget that image of the Queen, solitary in lockdown, attending the funeral service of her beloved husband and companion. We watch these scenes unfold and wonder 'how would I cope in that situation?' We watch newsreels of a more carefree Princess Elizabeth on her honeymoon and project our own desires and wishes for a happy ending, untroubled fortunes and an archetypal fairy-tale life. The media has brought these images into our lives in an increasingly powerful way over the years. One could argue that those solitary images at Prince Philips funeral were intrusive. How many of us face the prospect of being recorded as we mourn the death of a partner. That the Queen was able to contain and manage her feelings under such scrutiny also fuels our desire to know this woman more, her innermost thoughts, her inner resources, dreams, fears, motivation.

The self-contained aspect of the Queen's demeanour stands out the more in this age of reactionary tweets, self-indulgence, self-exposure, entitlement overload. The Prince Harry and Meghan Markle Oprah interview is of its time where to tell all despite the consequences has become the norm. Should tight-lipped self-composure have been more appropriate?[9]

A 38-year-old librarian from Leeds found sympathy with some members of the royal family following their treatment by the press:

The press attitude to the Monarchy annoys me most I think. Literally responsible for the deaths of George V and Princess Diana, they act like they own the Royals and if they go off-piste and/or happen to be non-white (like Harry and Meghan) then you have to feel their wrath. I honestly don't blame Harry and Meghan for leaving for America. If my wife had to endure day after day of negative press for no other reason than her being black then I'd give the country up too. Of all of the Royals I'm closest in age to Harry who has always seemed like a decent person, so maybe that affects my view of him. I've grown up alongside him in a way. My parents are the same age as Diana too (which is strange to think of now because Diana died when she was my age). And why shouldn't Harry and Meghan have done the Oprah interview? They certainly weren't given any chance by the British press to voice their opinions fairly. I think a lot of people describe themselves as Royalists but what they actually mean is that they like the Queen. I honestly can't see people having such a strong attachment to Charles or William. But I guess that the Monarchy has always had to change to survive.

I do have to say that I found the commentary around this jubilee very different to the last one. Last time around it felt like universal praise was heaped on the Queen. I remember approval rates in 2012 being 90% across age groups. This time around, with the country being in much more of state, I definitely saw much more criticism centred around the cost of these events in the shadow of a cost of living crisis. People seem to struggle with nuanced opinions about the Royal Family. When Prince Philip died I saw a lot of cries of 'he was racist!' and yes, while technically true he also helped to modernise the Royal family. Sometimes it's possible for members of the Royal family to have good qualities alongside their bad but people seem to struggle to hold both ideas in their head. After saying that I'm fairly ambivalent about the monarchy I ended up watching nearly all of the pageant on the Sunday of the Jubilee. I do moan about this country a lot but it's mostly in relation to the UK being harangued by a right wing media that constantly undermines our ability to be something great. Also, our politicians submit to the press in the most servile of ways. It's frustrating.[10]

The role of the royal family in 2022

Observers considered the role of the British royal family in Britain. A 61-year-old solicitor was critical of the Queen's continued reign, suggesting that she should follow the example of other European monarchs and abdicate. She also took the opportunity to analyse other senior members of the royal family:

> I am unimpressed by the Queen's Platinum Jubilee. The fact that she continues to think she should rule and thereby deny her son his turn on the throne, is just selfish and ridiculous. It smacks of the divine right of kings. A few years ago there was a photo in The Times of Queen Beatrice of the Netherlands, signing abdication papers and appointing her son as King. She looked so proud and happy. They both did. That's what the Queen should have done years ago.[11]

A 78-year-old community youth and community officer from Sheffield who described himself as having been brought up to respect the monarchy in his youth, following commonplace rituals such as singing the national anthem, was far more critical of the family, believing them to have no place in modern society:

> For most of my life, and increasingly so as time passes, I have come to regard the Royal Family as utterly irrelevant. Indeed, I regard them as a dysfunctional family. Perhaps that is not surprising when they have had to live their lives under a national, and international, microscope. Failed marriages for three of the Queen's four children – with the media speculating and reporting on every real, or invented, detail of the break-ups. And I, and every taxpayer, has to fund this dysfunctional family. Why? I'm not quite at the 'off with their heads' stage, I don't wish them any personal harm. But we really don't need them. They were simply born into a particular (and disputable) lineage. They have done nothing at all to deserve the privileges and deference they enjoy. This country can never attain equality for all whilst it keeps one particular family that is excluded, by accident of birth, from being treated like the rest of us. I did not join in any celebrations of the Queen's Platinum Jubilee. I try to avoid all news about the Royals as they have no bearing whatsoever on my life. Unlike when I was seven and unavoidably witnessed the Coronation of Queen Elizabeth II – I shall ignore the Coronation of Charles if and when that happens. 'The King is dead – long live the Republic'.[12]

A 37-year-old charity worker from Newcastle also shared an aversion to the concept of privilege as birthright, stating that the Queen and her family played absolutely no role in his life:

> I think the Royal Family are undeniably an anachronism, and that causes them all sorts of problems. The idea that political power should be a function of ancestry is obviously nonsense, but it's not one which is easy to abandon because most people's position in society is entirely due to

THE BRITISH ROYAL FAMILY IN 2022   255

the circumstances of their birth. You don't get rich by working – all the oligarchs and great men who run the world got their starts from the money their parents loaned them or their family connections which got them their first over-paid job; our politicians all come from the same private schools paid for by their rich parents; the people buying politicians and political parties all want to retain their wealth so they can hand it on like it was handed on to them. Heredity is written into our economic and political system, so the Royal Family aren't exactly an outlier, and you can't really attack the principle in one place without laying bare the injustice of it everywhere else. Which, I think, is why people like politicians and the press are so keen on glorifying them.[13]

Other Observers also expressed their belief that the royal family was an anachronism, including a 58-year-old woman living in Wales and on employment and support allowance who imagined the end of royal privilege:

I find it really hard to understand how anyone can think that the Royal Family should still exist in the 21st century. When inequality is increasing in the UK and we have the hereditary class system being reinforced by a Royal Family who are there by luck and not for any other reason I don't understand it.

I think it's time to completely downsize them, the land and properties should be income generating for the population for social care and for health care. No one family should have so much. I don't dislike them as people but obviously I don't know them, but I do resent them and their wealth at our expense. When the Queen dies or abdicates it needs to end. She has worked 'hard' in a Royal sense and done her duty as prescribed by the system of the time but things have changed. The world has moved on.

I also feel that the Queen should have intervened politically to protect the public but she never has. She has allowed the Tory government to destroy this country. There is no point in a Royalty who do not support their population. A ceremonial Royalty is pointless. The homelessness, poverty, decline of the wealth fare state all of this on her watch. To say that she is not political is not true, she is not allowed to state her views but she does so behind closed doors. I had no time for Prince Philip, he sounded incredibly racist and out of touch. The Harry and Megan situation could have been avoided if they had managed the situation better. It appears that they are more interested in how things look or rather than dealing with problems. Harry has had to cope with the trauma of losing his mother in a very public way and then his father getting together with the woman he was having an affair with. Diana's life was destroyed by the Royals. Charles should have had the backbone to not marry her if he didn't love her and he clearly didn't. I don't know Harry or Megan but

I do feel she is a mistake for him. He needs less limelight not more. He needs to be nurtured and needs time away from the press and pressures of Royal life. It feels like the Royals are emotionally stifled.

The arrogance of Prince Andrew comes from his privileged upbringing and sense of entitlement. If he was not Royal he would be in prison, the system has protected him. He is not bright, has never worked. He is lazy, obnoxious and self-important.

The Duke and Duchess of Cambridge visit to the Caribbean was a total disaster. It was outdated, the Royals are finished. The visit looked like an imperial throw back. I was so embarrassed. It is not about them as people but about the system. It really needs to end now. Prince Charles should never be King and Camilla should have nothing to do with the Crown. I have not forgiven nor forgotten Charles's behaviour around his marriage to Diana. Although I appreciate it's not anything to do with me, but I have not time or respect for him or the Royals. Their behaviour is dreadful. It is also sad that Charles is so inadequate but part of a family that are lacking those normal qualities. We just need to reassess our whole system. We need the Royal family to step down. We need to change the class system starting with the closure of private/public schools.[14]

An 82-year-old artist from East Yorkshire considered the current state of the monarchy, before going on to suggest the future direction of the royal family:

THE MAGIC HAS GONE Here lies the problem. As monarch Elizabeth II has been exemplary. As head of her own family she has been subjected to realities experienced by the rest of us. The various personalities that make up the royal family have produced an ongoing soap-opera watched avidly by the public both here and abroad. Wonderful entertainment perhaps, but it has shattered the myth of royalty as a 'magical' institution; Its members a kind of earthly deity to whom we must kneel, nod or curtsey. And yet there are those who strenuously maintain this belief as well as those in thrall; willing and wanting to believe in the 'magic'; they 'love' the queen. How can that be if they have never known her? – respect her, yes; admire her, certainly; but love her? One only loves someone close and intimate whom you know well.

In some ways I can appreciate this mass hysteria. Most of our population has known no other British Head of State. Only once has the queen incurred any serious criticism, at the death of Diana, but in 70 years she has won universal respect. In the near future I see problems for the royal family after Elizabeth II. The queen is the keystone of an ancient and damaged structure; previous efforts at modernisation have proved ineffective or disastrous. But this is Britain and no matter the arguments as to the costs of royalty, its undemocratic privileges and the frailties of its members, it is still 'The Royal Family' so the greater population suspends reason and reality – the show must go on; on with the bow, the curtseys and the fawning. Republicanism is but sideshow for cranks in spite of asking unanswered questions as to the cost, meaning and sheer hypocrisy of an unelected family of moderate intellectual abilities being somehow 'above' the rest of us . . .

THE ROYAL FUTURE: I expect to be long dead before we reach the next episode in this royal saga. Shakespeare would have thrilled at the dynamics of the brotherly face-off between William and Harry. The bard would have had them vying for the throne of their father. Harry self-exiled with his 'foreign' bride, raising a media army to claim his rights (is the old king really his father? – only the ghost of Diana might tell). And William as today's 'Prince Hal' with divine wife and angelic children prepares to defend the throne with the aid of the barons – press barons in this case; and all to be resolved in Act V.

That is make believe but of what I see and read I think the royal family's best chance of long term survival would be for William to become king at the death of the present queen. Royalty, to preserve the myth, must look ahead well into the new century. Charles will probably be dead in 20 years which is not long compared to the reign of his mother. A new start is urgent with much of the wastage and flummery expelled from the royal household, a working royal family of maximum six members – the rest to find work in the real world. Away with the ceremonial throwbacks to Victorian Britain, the fancy dress, the courtiers, the mistress and masters of this and that. Fewer castles and estate holdings (open them up to all of us) – proper taxes paid and less secrecy (what is there worth hiding?). We fund the enterprise as 'subjects' so open the books. And let's have King William V soon – but don't expect me to bow or nod to any of them.[15]

EPILOGUE

The announcement of the Queen's death on the eighth of September occasioned a pause – a momentary pause for many, an officially ordained ten-day pause for the nation. The ten-day mourning meant the pre-empting of television programs, the cancelation of sports events and the donning of black armbands by MPs, newsreaders and many others, including university leadership; transport workers postponed scheduled strikes and Morrisons lowered the volume of the beeps on its registers. Official 'National Mourning Guidance' stated that there was 'no expectation on the public or organisations to observe specific behaviours during the mourning period'.[1] Perhaps because of the discretionary nature of the national mourning, questions abounded: will work be cancelled? How should one act? What should one wear? (Is it appropriate, for instance, to wear bright colours during the official mourning?) In Devizes, one 47-year-old woman recalled that on the day after the announcement:

> Work was a bit weird . . . there were questions about what we should be doing. But as I don't work doing anything directly related to the Queen or Op London Bridge, I found that strange. Surely we just had to get on and do our work? If the Queen was all about doing her duty, wasn't doing my duty as a civil servant the best way to honour her?[2]

Another Observer, a 38 year-old female social worker from Leeds, wrote:

> As a civil servant I've been a bit taken aback by the scale and seriousness of the response from my employer. We've been issued with official mourning guidance, attended special meetings about the Queen's death, received emails from senior leaders and staff working in London have been asked to dress in black or dark clothes when attending the office.[3]

For many – in Britain, Commonwealth countries and countries and peoples touched by empire or the celebrity of the royal family – the death of the Queen was a moment to remember, to reflect, to cry, to celebrate, to question, to criticize; and for some, it was a moment of disbelief: disbelief that a 96-year-old woman who seemed like she might reign forever (or at least stay on a bit longer) was now gone – alternatively, disbelief at the wave of grief and emotion swept over a nation in political and economic turmoil.

For some, that grief was appropriate: 'Two things struck me', wrote a 69-year-old married woman from Morpeth:

The first was that Morpeth was so quiet. There were very few people about and hardly anyone was in the restaurants. In the place where we were there was only one other couple and when the news was confirmed the girl, (only around her early twenties), burst into tears. I was quite surprised at this, as I had made the perhaps mistaken assumption that younger folk would not find it too upsetting, maybe to the point of indifference. I was clearly wrong about this as subsequent events would show. I was pleased about this and found it to be reassuring.

This Observer reported feeling a 'strong urge' to go to London and travelled down with her husband to watch the procession from Buckingham Palace to the lying-in-state at Westminster Hall.

From our point of view, this was a unique and historical event, something that we might never be able to experience again, and we wanted to be a part of it. It is an experience which I shall always remember. Whilst it was obviously very sad it was also memorable for the spirit of camaraderie and kindness which we experienced. The organisation was absolutely magnificent. Given the level of the crowds and the area which had to be covered it was truly superb and a real credit to the country.[4]

Others found the collective grief embarrassing or overwrought, some connecting it to the response to Diana's death 25 years earlier, as did one 71-year-old woman who wondered, 'When did the English get to be so sentimental?'[5] Another – a 39-year-old woman – called it 'misery porn'.[6]

Others responded with angry disbelief at what they believed was an undeserved, overly emotional reaction, as one forty-year-old female from Bristol wrote:

this has been the most horrifyingly ludicrously disgusting week of mawkish, sentimental, pompous bathos that I have ever experienced. I have honestly felt quite scared at what has been going on around me – I suddenly don't recognise this country, my colleagues, the media – anything . . . Why are people so upset, why are people reacting like this, what is the big deal? . . . I just don't get it . . . My university offered me counseling as if I was sad about the Queen's death – WTAF? Will they offer me counselling when an actual member of my family dies?[7]

Another Observer from Oldbury was also incensed by the public grief and the pressure to take part in it:

So this old woman, who had led a life of incredible privilege at public expense, never having to go cold in winter, always having enough to eat

EPILOGUE 261

for her (and her dogs and race-horses) and having, no doubt, the very best of medical care right to the end even though the NHS is almost destroyed, is now dead, and I'm no doubt expected to be full of grief and sympathy. Well, I'm not.[8]

The following 37-year-old male charity worker from Newcastle upon Tyne felt the Queen's passing was sad but had little relevance to him personally. Indeed, he reported that he and his friends engaged in a lot of 'mutual shoulder shrugging' in response to the Queen's passing:

Yeah, so this is one of those odd ones where you realise that other people are completely alien and see the world completely differently to you.

The Queen, and the Royal Family more generally, play absolutely no role in my life. I've never met them . . . They appear on currency, but I don't really use cash any more, and they appear on stamps, but stamps with heads on them were something which was being phased out anyway. And that's more-or-less it. They're just people on TV.

So it's sad she's dead, in the sense that it's sad when people die. I can empathise with the family, because members of my family have died and it's not a nice thing to have to deal with. But it's not something which has had any emotional impact on me.

This Observer described learning of the Queen's death through social media, pondering the jarring ways in which one consumed the knowledge:

Because my friends are pretty indifferent, we've had a certain amount of mutual shoulder-shrugging and reflection on what this says about us as outsiders to all this. In fact, I think I found out when someone in a WhatsApp group started sharing pictures of BBC online sub-sites (like BBC Food and their Boxing page) where the normal content had been replaced by an announcement of the death. Which, in the case of the Boxing page, made it appear that the Queen had died in the ring. There is something very odd about replacing non-news content with an obit – someone will have discovered the Queen was dead because they were trying to find out how to cook a flan. There feels something absurd about it.[9]

As part of the Queen's seventieth jubilee, Mass-Observation put out a Summer Directive asking Observers to write down their thoughts and opinions about the royal family. When the Queen died, many posted updates to their Directive responses and still others, who had not yet responded by September 8, answered the Directive through the lens of her passing. A month later, over seventy people had written to M-O regarding the Queen's death.

262 EPILOGUE

Responses to the Queen's death, and to the official mourning period, varied from positive royalist vantage points to scathingly critical republican invectives. Many commented positively about the Queen's sense of duty, moral and spiritual strength and longevity. It was a moment for some to remember Coronation activities in 1953 or the mourning of George VI in 1952 or ponder the intertwining of a royal life with one's own. One 75-year-old divorced teacher from York marked the Queen's passing by flipping through the pages of a book she received upon the Coronation of Elizabeth II and reminiscing over her childhood.[10]

Some registered unease or disgust at the way that the long national mourning felt more akin to the enforced veneration seen with the passing of dictators. One female 68-year-old retired civil servant from Weymouth felt the mourning ceremonies and processions were emblematic of British white supremacy and jingoism and thought: 'If such scenes of regimented "adoration & respect" were taking place in North Korea, Russia or China, then the U.K. media would have been "horrified".'[11] *Another Observer, a 48-year-old poet and library assistant, also linked the official mourning to dictatorial regimes like Russia and North Korea.*[12]

The 2022 responses to the Queen's death were often set within the context of political and economic chaos and numerous anxieties about global concerns (such as Ukraine). The chaotic premiership of Liz Truss featured in the responses, as did austerity and the economy. The passing of an era, which was expressed repeatedly in the media and in conversations, at a moment of political and economic uncertainty, exacerbated a feeling that the world was 'out of control', as this 38-year-old woman from London wrote:

I felt a little sad and shocked when I found out . . . Now though I feel increasingly republican. The TV coverage and expense . . . People are literally going to die and end up in hospital this winter because of the cost of living crisis and they waste millions, and Charles isn't going to pay any inheritance tax. One rule for them, one for the rest. I hope his reign is as short as possible and the monarchy is abolished.

The Queen's death has been repeatedly called the end of an era, setting off a feeling which seems to amplify anxiety and deepen feelings of a nation – and a world – out of control.

A 36-year-old archaeology student and avowed republican put it this way:

[the queen] represented the wartime generation. Now that she's gone, we're left in the hands of public-school boys with abandonment issues, constantly and desperately seeking approval from parents who sent them away to be institutionalised in prep school at age 8. It feels like all the adults have left the room and the nation is being babysat by a bunch of drunk teenagers vulnerable to peer pressure.[13]

EPILOGUE

One Observer wondered whether

> people are grieving about the state of the country rather than the Queen, whether this is public outcry of hopelessness and a failing UK and whether they saw her as the last thing to go before the collapse of our country as we get further into crisis. We had financial collapse, Brexit, Covid, Cost of living crisis and the one familiar thing in most of our lives dies. It is national grief of all the above and the Queen dying has made people more upset as everything they thought they knew is going.[14]

Others thought it offered the government an excellent distraction: one non-binary 57-year-old Observer from Aberystwyth thought that

> it is clear that there is a highly politicised process underway, which is masquerading as a traditional ritual above politics . . . There is something of a cotton wool effect as politics has been dampened. What have we heard of the cost of living crisis, the Ukraine war or anything else?[15]

Observers offered insight into another phenomenon expressed by some in the British press, that the Queen's passing was intimately bound up in the personal; New Statesman *writer Andrew Marr illuminated this point when he confessed his surprise at the emotion he felt upon announcing the Queen's death, until he realized that her passing reminded him of his own father's death two years prior.[16] The archaeology student mentioned earlier explains her reaction:*

> She reminded me of my Nan. Not just because they shared a birth year, but because of all the small visual cues – the 40s perm, the woollen shin-length skirts, *those* shoes that only Nan's seem to have, the enormous plastic-framed glasses. Now that the queen has gone from public life, these small visual cues that defined that generation of women will fade, and it's another facet of my Nan that I lose touch with.[17]

This 71-year-old divorced female expressed anxieties about social and cultural change, worrying over younger generations who seemed to threaten the monarchy and the stability of British society:

> So sad to hear of this event. I was two years old when she was crowned. She has set such a good example for everyone on how to behave and be diplomatic with all. She has worked so hard. To get up from what must have been her death bed, to see Boris Johnson and Liz Truss her final prime minister, just demonstrates her total dedication to duty. We will never see the like again . . .
>
> What with this and the new government, plus the energy crisis, the war in Ukraine, the cost of living crisis, the future is not looking very rosy for

any of us, except the energy companies!!

A coronation in a few months will be a very special thing for people to look forward to. I have seen Queen Elizabeth's coronation on TV but of course, now it will be all over the internet, on our phones and everywhere. This will be a very special event.

The difference of course is that the Queen was on the throne for over 70 years, Charles will probably manage it for 20 years and this amount of time will probably be the same for all future monarchs, unless something dire happens.

I think eventually, the monarchy may go. I hope it does not as it adds pomp and ceremony to our country and brings in lots of tourists. Sadly, the latest generation are so different in that they only think about themselves, feel they should get everything given to them, feel they can do what they like regardless of others (I am generalising here). The fact they pulled down statues demonstrates their lack of true historical knowledge or care for public objects. They are not even sure what gender they are. What hope is there for them, us and the future?[18]

The following retired widow's response demonstrates the complexities of grieving a woman one does not know yet has been a constant in one's life. Her response also articulates the uncertainties facing the future of the monarchy:

I am writing this just over a week after the death of The Queen. There is always sadness when people one knows die; but did I ever know The Queen in the same way as I knew my parents and grandparents, uncles, aunts and cousins whose death I have witnessed? Or indeed in the way I knew friends and colleagues who are no longer alive?

Well yes as this women's life was deeply embedded within the fabric of the society I live in. I can remember being told at my primary school when coming inside after morning playtime that her father had died and there would now be a Queen. We have the same name as was pointed out to me then and on other occasions. I watched her coronation on a friend of my family's TV. . . . It was a very tiny box in the corner of the living room and other neighbours had also been asked in throughout the day. I recall going to see the film of the coronation at the local cinema when it was released with my parents.

Following the coronation there was a national tour undertaken by The Queen and the Duke of Edinburgh and as a brownie I remember marching to our allotted spot in Newcastle upon Tyne to watch as she drove past . . . it was a wet and cold day. I have a fonder memory of seeing the Royal Family as they drove from Aberdeen to Balmoral one summer when we were staying with my grandparents nearby . . .

The next 'encounter' would have been at the opening of The University of Sussex library. Students were given lunch in various lecture theatres . . . I think it was another wet day!

So I've seen the Queen, but I do not know her. It has been written that the Royal Family are like a soap opera, key events punctuate their lives when they interface with the public. They live private lives but in a goldfish bowl. They are at the centre of gaze . . . this has certainly been the case this week. I gazed sadly as I saw the Queen with Liz Truss on Tuesday . . . much diminished in stature but determined to carry out her constitutional duty. This sense of duty and service has been much spoken and written of and I think it is in this role that I will remember Queen Elizabeth II . . . Opinions had to be shared with great care, a bit like walking on egg shells. But this was a human being with feelings too.

I am not sure what will now follow. We have a King who has expressed opinions in a far more open and controversial way than his mother, a duke who has all but admitted to child abuse and trafficking and a younger duke who has opted out of the family firm. The goldfish bowl will not go away as both are watched for clues of remorse or seeking ways back into the firm. Is it the advisers who need to change, or the members of the Royal Family? I suspect both. . . . How long will the House of Windsor reign? Watch this space.

Mass-Observation writing can provide more nuanced insights than traditional opinion polling into the subtle shifts in the relationship between royalty and public since 1937. The continuities seen across this volume also are suggestive of the ways in which public opinion has remained relatively stable over this period and demonstrate the acceptance of much of the Windsor Brand. That brand has evolved over that time in response to modern – often contradictory – expectations of the public: the paradoxes of tradition and modernity, respect and celebrity, public figure and private individual. The public persona of an infallible monarch who leads the country's moral and religious tone has been tested over the past eighty-five years, revealing the only too human foibles of a family with their share of marital woes and personal tragedies. The survival of the Windsor Brand has always depended on the royal family navigating this terrain, and the extent of the royalty's success in doing so can be charted across time within the Observer responses.

Perhaps the greatest recent achievement of the monarchy has been the seamless transition of the Crown to King Charles III in September 2022. Writing only weeks before the death of Queen Elizabeth, some Observers were still of a mind that the Crown would never pass to Charles but straight on to his son William, a theme recurring in responses since 1992. Others wrote of their hopes that the death of the Queen would spell the end of the institution altogether. The fact these notions were still being aired in 2022 with the current monarch already in her late nineties implied a precarity of the institution built on tradition. Yet, whilst the public were still digesting the news of the passing of the UK's longest reigning monarch, the institution (or rather, the various royal advisors and behind-the-scenes individuals who ensure its continuation) and the media hummed into action, leveraging tradition and ceremony to deliver a new monarch with little meaningful protest.

The death of Queen Elizabeth II, whose reign witnessed significant social, cultural and technological change, marks the end of an era but her passing also demonstrated the robustness of the Windsor institution as it continues to adapt itself to the contemporary world. As we enter the reign of King Charles III and his Queen Consort, Mass-Observation will continue to record the public response to British royalty into the twenty-first century.

NOTES

Introduction

1 John Harris, 'Life after the Queen's Death: "I Care, but I Don't Care"', *Anywhere but Westminster* (Guardian News & Media, 15 September 2022), https://youtu.be/8M_yH-e9cq8 (accessed 1 December 2022).

2 For more about the manipulation of opinion regarding the abdication by the establishment, see Kingsley Martin, *The Magic of Monarchy* (New York: Alfred Knopf, 1937), especially pp. 76–111.

3 For an excellent history of early Mass-Observation, see James Hinton, *The Mass Observers: A History, 1937-1949* (Oxford: Oxford University Press, 2013).

4 On this phenomenon in entertainment, see Jennifer Purcell, *Mother of the BBC: Mabel Constanduros and the Rise of Popular Entertainment on the BBC, 1925-1957* (New York: Bloomsbury Academic, 2020).

5 Roger Mortimore, 'Measuring British Public Opinion on the Monarchy and the Royal Family', in *The Windsor Dynasty: 1910 to the Present, 'Long to Reign over us?'*, ed. Matthew Glencross, Judith Rowbotham, and Michael D. Kandiah (London: Palgrave MacMillan, 2016), 136.

6 P3209, M82M. 2022 Jubilee Directive, ad hoc response to the Queen's death on 8 September 2022.

7 Mortimore, 'Measuring Public Opinion', 139.

8 Andrzej Olechnowicz, '"A Jealous Hatred": Royal Popularity and Social Inequality', in *The Monarchy and the British Nation 1780 to the Present*, ed. Andrzej Olechnowicz (Cambridge: Cambridge University Press, 2007), 301.

9 British Social Attitudes polling asked a question about monarchy versus republic in 1983 but did not ask it again until 1994. Ipsos Mori polling began asking this question regularly in 1993. One-off polling in the media has taken place since the 1960s. Mortimore, 'Measuring Public Opinion', 139–49.

10 Olechnowicz, '"A Jealous Hatred"', 292.

11 Frank Prochaska, 'George V and Republicanism, 1917-1919', *Twentieth Century British History* 10, no. 1 (1999): 27–51. Matthew Glencross, 'George V and the New Royal House', in *The Windsor Dynasty: 1910 to the Present, 'Long to Reign over us?'*, ed. Matthew Glencross, Judith Rowbotham, and Michael D. Kandiah (London: Palgrave MacMillan, 2016), 34.

12 John Plunkett, *Queen Victoria: First Media Monarch* (Oxford: Oxford University Press, 2003), 14.

13 Ibid., 14 and 166–71.

14 Ibid., 170.

15 David Cannadine, 'The Context, Performance and Meaning of Ritual: The British Monarchy and the "Invention of Tradition" c. 1820-1977', in *The Invention of Tradition*, ed. Eric Hobsbawm and Terence Ranger (Cambridge: Cambridge University Press, 1983), 102.

16 Matthew Glencross, Judith Rowbotham, and Michael D. Kandiah, *Introduction*, ed. Matthew Glencross, Judith Rowbotham, and Michael D. Kandiah (London: Palgrave Macmillan, 2016), 13.

17 Ibid., 5.

18 Ibid., 13.

19 Ibid., 20. The entire volume discusses many aspects of this 'branding'.

20 For more on this in the early twentieth century, see Philip Williamson, 'The Monarchy and Public Values, 1910–1953', in Olechnowicz, *The Monarchy and the British Nation 1780 to the Present*, 223–57.

21 Olechnowicz, '"A Jealous Hatred"', 280–314.

22 Michael Billig, *Talking of the Royal Family* (London: Routledge, 1992), 114–15.

23 Ibid., xii.

24 Cannadine, 'The Context, Performance and Meaning of Ritual', 102.

25 Ibid., 137.

26 Glencross, et al., 'Introduction', 13.

27 Edward Shils and Michael Young, 'The Meaning of the Coronation', *Sociological Review* 1, no. 2 (December 1953), 74.

28 Ibid., 68.

29 Emily Mayne, 'Shows of Joy and Malice: Performance, the Star Chamber, and the Celebration of James I's Coronation in Norwich in 1603', *Early Theatre* 1, no. 2 (December 2020), 169–82.

30 Samuel Pepys, 'The Diary of Samuel Pepys: Diary Entries from the 17th Century Diary', 22 April 1661, https://www.pepysdiary.com/diary/1661/04 /22/ (accessed 22 June 2021). For the power of royal ceremonial in the reign of Charles II, see Anna Keay, *The Magnificent Monarch: Charles II and the Ceremonies of Power* (London: Continuum, 2008).

31 Glencross, et al., 'Introduction', 17.

32 Cannadine, 'The Context, Performance, and Meaning of Ritual', 102.

33 Cameras were at every subsequent royal event, such as Victoria's funeral in 1901, Edward VII's coronation (1902) and funeral (1911), George V's coronation (1911) and the Delhi Durbars of Edward VII (1903) and George V (1913). Jeffrey Richards, 'The Monarchy and Film, 1900-2006', in Olechnowicz, *The Monarchy and the British Nation 1780 to the Present*, 260.

34 Richards, 'The Monarchy and Film', 258.

NOTES

35 See chapter (REF).

36 For instance, Chris Stone, 'Andrew Marr: Why I Broke Down when Announcing the Queen's Death', *New Statesman*, 9 September 2022, https://www.newstatesman.com/politics/uk-politics/2022/09/andrew-marr-why-i-broke-down-when-announcing-the-death-of-the-queen (accessed 17 October 2022).

37 Bruce Lenthall, *Radio's America: The Great Depression and the Rise of Modern Mass Culture* (Chicago: University of Chicago, 2007), 55. Experiments in the 1920s by psychologist T. H. Pear demonstrated how people believed they could discern personality and trustworthiness through the medium. Purcell, *Mother of the BBC*, 36.

38 See Laura Mayhall, 'The Prince of Wales versus Clark Gable: Anglophone Celebrity and Citizenship between the Wars', *Cultural and Social History* 4, no. 4 (2007): 529–43.

39 Tom Nairn, *The Enchanted Glass: Britain and its Monarchy*, 2nd edn (London: Verso, 2011), 27.

40 Billig, *Talking of the Royal Family*, 221.

41 November 1955 directive, 3627 M37M.

42 James Hinton, 'Bloomsbury Academic's Mass Observation Critical Series Launch Event', Mass Observation 85th Anniversary Online Series, 7 June 2022, https://youtu.be/gziDGWbGSgo.

Chapter 1

1 Piers Brendon, *Edward VIII* (London: Penguin, 2018), 50.

2 Edward VIII, 'Abdication Speech', (1936), https://youtu.be/wBn06A-sdok (accessed 29 December 2022).

3 As evidence of the 'shock of the crisis', Kingsley Martin reported that, during the week of uncertainty about the King's fate, trade dropped off precipitously. *The Magic of Monarchy* (New York: Alfred Knopf, 1937), 8 fn.

4 Martin, *The Magic of Monarchy*, 8–11.

5 Philip Gibbs, *Ordeal in England* (New York: Doubleday, 1937), 65.

6 'Effect in Potteries', *Times*, 4 December 1936, 18.

7 'House of Commons', *Times*, 12 December 1936, 7.

8 Keith Middlemas, *The Life and Times of George VI* (London: George Weidenfeld and Nicolson, 1974), 92.

9 James Hinton, *The Mass Observers: A History, 1937-1949* (Oxford: Oxford University Press, 2013), 7.

10 Quoted in Ben Highmore, '"The Observation by Everyone of Everyone": The Project of Mass-Observation in 1937', in *Mass-Observation: Text, Context and Analysis of the Pioneering Pamphlet and Movement*, ed. Jennifer J. Purcell (London: Bloomsbury Academic, 2022)9.

11 On Edward's visit to south Wales, see Brendon, *Edward VIII*, 60–1.

12 Hinton, *The Mass Observers*, 66.

13 Humphrey Jennings and Charles Madge, *May the Twelfth: Mass-Observation Day Surveys 1937 by over Two Hundred Observers* (London: Faber and Faber, Ltd., 1937), 89.

14 Ibid., 89–90.

15 Ibid., 89.

16 Hinton, *The Mass Observers*, 66–7; Nick Hubble, *Mass Observation and Everyday Life: Culture, History, Theory* (Houndsmills, Basingstoke: Palgrave MacMillan, 2010), 120; for instance, Day Survey Respondent 135 listened in from Switzerland and DS 277 reported from Bulawayo.

17 Jennings and Madge, *May the Twelfth*, 345–414.

18 Hinton, *The Mass Observers*, 67; Hubble, *Mass Observation and Everyday Life*, 123. For more on the subversive intentions of the organization, see Jennifer Purcell, ed., *Mass-Observation: Text, Context, and Analysis of the Pioneering Pamphlet* (London: Bloomsbury, 2023).

19 Hinton, *The Mass Observers*, 68.

20 Hubble, *Mass Observation and Everyday Life*, 127.

21 For instance, DS 213, who went to Northern Ireland to hike.

22 DS 428.

23 Oswald Moseley's Union of British fascists fervently supported Edward VIII during the Abdication Crisis.

24 DS 346. Listed in *May the Twelfth* as CM2. See pages 108–9, 111–12, 121–2, 126–7, and 131–5 for the extracts chosen for the 1937 publication.

25 DS 538.

26 DS 044.

27 DS 170.

28 DS 482.

29 DS 461.

30 DS 396.

31 DS 264.

32 DS 220.

33 DS 431.

34 DS 076.

35 DS 510. The first paragraph can be found in *May the Twelfth*, 119.

36 DS 164.

37 DS 135.

38 DS 461.

39 DS 080. While much of this individual's account is reproduced in the *May the Twelfth* volume, the extract included here is not found in the volume.

40 DS 431.

NOTES

41 DS 118.

42 DS 197.

43 DS 081.

44 DS 57.

45 DS 258.

46 DS 149.

47 DS 163.

48 Tim Crook, *Radio Drama: Theory and Practice* (London: Routledge, 1999), 54..

49 DS 241.

50 DS 277.

51 DS 277 (Bulawayo).

52 DS 482.

53 CL10.

54 DS 538.

55 DS 118.

56 DS 090 31-year-old female social worker.

Chapter 2

1 Fiona Courage, 'The National Panel Responds: Mass Observation Directives 1939-1945', *Mass Observation Online*, 2011, http://www.massobservation .amdigital.co.uk.library.smcvt.edu/FurtherResources/Essays/TheNational PanelRespondsMassObservationDirectives1939-1945 (accessed 20 July 2022).

2 Ibid.

3 FR 22. Newsreel report. The Cinema in the first three years of war, 31.

4 FR 57. Film Report, March 1940, 20; FR 141. Newsreels (2). May 1940, 6.

5 FR 215. Newsreels in Early June, 19 June 1940, 5. The French had not yet capitulated at the time of this report.

6 FR 314. Newsreels, August 1940, 2.

7 FR 444. Newsreels, October 1940, 7.

8 Seventy-five per cent of the time. Jeffrey Richards and Dorothy Sheridan, eds, *Mass-Observation at the Movies* (London: Routledge and Kegan Paul, 1987), 413.

9 See entries for 11 November 1943 and 4 October 1944.

10 FR 181. Capitulation Talk in Worktown. 19 June 1940, 8.

11 FR 247. The Royal Family, July 1940, 1–2.

12 Ibid., 3–4.

13 An October 1945 file report noted indirects regarding the Duke of Windsor's trip to Britain in that month. Comments are generally ambivalent or negative, pointing to his money and privilege.

14 Bob Malcomson, 'Diaries for Mass Observation 1939-1940', *Mass Observation Online*, 2009 (accessed 21 July 2022).

15 FR 574. War in December Diaries, February 1941, 25.

16 D5353.

17 D5231.

18 D5141.

19 D5269.

20 D5353.

21 D5419.

22 D5445.

23 D5333.

24 D5319.

25 Piers Brendon, *Edward VIII* (London: Penguin, 2016), 78–9.

26 D5396.

27 D5083.

28 D5294.

29 D5419.

30 D5342.

31 D5269.

32 D5419.

33 John W. Bennett-Wheeler, *King George VI: His Life and Reign* (New York: St. Martin's Press, 1958), 466.

34 Ibid., 468.

35 TC23 Air Raids. 23-5-C. 'Buckingham Palace'.

36 D5170.

37 D5103.

38 D5296.

39 D5117.

40 D5419.

41 D5419.

42 D5296.

43 D5296.

44 D5296.

45 D5419.

46 D5333.

47 D5240.

NOTES

48 D5390.

49 D5443.

50 D5447.

51 D5443.

52 D5296.

53 D5047.

54 D5447.

55 D5412.

56 D5447.

57 D5423.

58 D5443.

59 D5052.

60 Reference to a poem by William Schwenck Gilbert, from 1889 comic opera, *The Gondoliers*. The Duke is always at the head of a retreat.

61 At sixteen Princess Elizabeth became colonel of the Grenadier Guards.

62 D5423.

63 D5301.

64 D5301.

65 D5443.

66 D5301.

67 D5443.

68 D5277. Ellipses are in original.

69 FR 1392. Death of the Duke of Kent, August 1942.

70 D5447.

71 D5205.

72 D5390.

73 D5177.

74 D5447.

75 D5277.

76 D5342.

77 D5443.

78 D5337.

79 D5372.

80 D5390.

81 D5445.

82 D5447.

83 D5447.

84 D5337.

NOTES

85 D5443.

86 D5349.

87 D5337.

88 D5447.

89 D5445.

90 D5443; diarist is on holiday near Dunoon, Scotland.

91 D5296. Reference to Leopold III of Belgium.

92 D5447.

93 D5447.

94 D5443.

95 FR 2190D. Indirects about King's speech, December 1944.

96 D5447.

97 D5447.

98 D5296.

99 FR 2263. Victory in Europe, June 1945, 28–30.

100 D5337.

101 D5447.

Chapter 3

1 Peter Hennessy, *Never Again: 1945–1951* (London: Jonathan Cape, 1992).

2 David Kynaston, *Austerity Britain, 1945–1951* (London: Bloomsbury, 2008), 243.

3 Robert Lacey, *Majesty: Elizabeth II and the House of Windsor* (New York: Harcourt Brace Jovanovich, 1977), 129.

4 Like the Windsors, the Battenbergs anglicized their name to Mountbatten during the First World War, though Philip's mother chose to keep Battenberg. See Lacey, *Majesty*, 129–30.

5 'A Royal Betrothal', *Times*, 10 July 1947, 5. As it turned out, these machinations were not entirely necessary, since it was learned that Philip was already a British national and a member of the British royal family due to the stipulation in the 1701 Act of Settlement that bestowed all descendants of Sophia, Electress of Hanover, British nationality and royal status. Lacey, *Majesty*, 129n. The title of Duke of Edinburgh was bestowed the day before the wedding, on 19 November 1947, 'Duke of Edinburgh', *Times*, 20 November 1947, 4.

6 Kynaston, *Austerity Britain*, 244.

7 Emily Brand, *Royal Weddings* (Oxford: Shire Publications, 2018), 39.

8 Lacey, *Majesty*, 131.

9 'Royal Gifts on Show', *Times*, 18 November 1947, 4 and 10.

NOTES

10 Ibid., and Lacey, *Majesty*, 134n.

11 Princess Elizabeth kept five of the dresses. There is no record in the Royal Archives that other wedding gifts were redistributed. Many thanks to Julie Crocker of the Royal Archives for this information. Personal Communication, email, 27 September 2022.

12 'Clothing Coupons', *HC Deb*, 22 October 1947, vol 443 cc1-2W, https://hansard.millbanksystems.com/written_answers/1947/oct/22/clothing-coupons-royal-wedding (accessed 11 August 2022); 'Princess in Ivory Satin', *Times*, 20 November 1947, 4.

13 'Gratitude of Royal Pair', *Times*, 22 November 1947, 4.

14 'Royal Wedding Cake', *Times*, 15 November 1947, 4.

15 See map on 'To-Day's Processions', *Times*, 20 November 1947, 6.

16 'Wedding Day in the North', *Times*, 21 November 1947, 7; 'Broadcasting', *Times*, 20 November 1947, 9.

17 Kynaston, *Austerity Britain*, 243.

18 DR1054.

19 DR2142.

20 DR2903.

21 Walter Bagehot, *The English Constitution*, ed. Paul Smith (Cambridge: Cambridge University Press, 2001), 71.

22 DR1014.

23 DR3960M.

24 DR1147.

25 Michael Billig, *Talking of the Royal Family* (London: Routledge, 1992), 114–15.

26 DR2776.

27 DR3319.

28 DR2795.

29 DR3397.

30 DR2675.

31 DR3635.

32 DR3371.

33 DR1679.

34 DR3005.

35 DR2511.

36 DR4315.

37 DR2984.

38 DR3015.

39 DR3572.

40 DR4004.

41 Lacey, *Majesty*, 131; *Times*, 10 July 1947.
42 DR3484.
43 DR1061.
44 DR2584.
45 DR1079.
46 DR2686.
47 DR2903.
48 DR1048.
49 DR3799.
50 DR3795.
51 DR3820.
52 DR3613.
53 DR1016.
54 DR3642.
55 DR3899.
56 DR1095.
57 DR2923.
58 DR3789.
59 DR1669.
60 DR2783.
61 DR3811.
62 DR3644.
63 DR3678.
64 DR3785.
65 DR3035.
66 DR3793.
67 DR1642.
68 DR1980.
69 DR1264.
70 DR3602.
71 DR3053.
72 DR3434.
73 Billig, *Talking of the Royal Family*, xi.
74 DR1362.
75 DR1644.
76 DR2254.

Chapter 4

1 Val Gielgud, *Years of the Locust* (London: Nicholson and Watson, 1947), 188.

2 Wesley Carr, 'The Intimate Ritual: The Coronation Service', *Political Theology* 4, no. 1 (2002): 11.

3 Joe Moran, *Armchair Nation*: *An Intimate History of Britain in front of the TV* (London: Profile, 2014), 52.

4 Pre-Coronation activities, 69/5/E, Naomi Mitchison.

5 A court which adjudicates petitions to serve the monarch at the Coronation ceremonies.

6 Statues of the giants of London were destroyed when the Guildhall was bombed in the blitz. In early 1953, newspapers carried pictures about 9-foot replicas to be installed in the Guildhall in June. See, for instance, Our Special Correspondent, 'Plans for a Double Assault on Peak of Everest: Colonel Hunt Picks his Final Teams', *Times*, 19 May 1953, 14.

7 Pre-Coronation Activities, 69/5/E, 'March 1953 The Coronation', no name.

8 Pre-Coronation Activities, 69/5/E, 'Report', Bradford, Yorkshire.

9 Pre-Coronation Diary, 69/5/M, MT.

10 Pre-Coronation Diary, 69/5/M, DLD.

11 Pre-Coronation Diary, 69/5/M, DLD.

12 Pre-Coronation Diary, 69/5/M, Ivy Williamson.

13 Pre-Coronation Diary, 69/5/M, DLD.

14 Pre-Coronation Activities, 69/5/E, Norman Pollard.

15 Pre-Coronation Activities, 69/5/E, 4072.

16 Pre-Coronation Activities, 69/5/E, student from Edinburgh.

17 Pre-Coronation Activities, 69/5/E, 'Part C', no name.

18 Pre-Coronation Diary, 69/5/M, DLD.

19 Pre-Coronation Diary, 69/5/M, DLD.

20 DR676, M M Hearing Aid Technician.

21 Corley Coronation Activities circular, with DR1971.

22 Mount Pleasant, Pontypridd. M92.

23 Coronation Surveys and Questionnaires, 69/1/B, 'Coronation directive, part C'.

24 Coronation Day Accounts 69/6/D, 'Combe Hay Ox Roasting'.

25 Our Special Correspondent, 'Plans for a Double Assault on Peak of Everest', 6.

26 'The Challenge of Everest: A Brave Chapter in the Story of Human Endeavour', *Times*, 2 June 1953, 7.

27 N60 (RD).

28 Comedian – Potter's routine that day was to 'recount events' in fictional Hogsnorton.

29 Band leader – the programme was 'The Kingdom Dances'. For Potter and Shand, see *Radio Times*, programming on BBC Home Service 2 June, https://genome.ch.bbc.co.uk/schedules/service_home_service/1953-06-02.

30 DR676.

31 Of Scone.

32 Naomi Mitchison.

33 DR0240.

34 DR0214.

35 DR0161.

36 MM 37.

37 F45S.

38 MM29.

39 W. r/01.

40 M37.

41 DR0708.

42 D. FS.

43 Widowed Social Worker.

44 DR4256.

45 DR4696.

46 DR254.

47 DR1061.

48 DR767.

49 MS61.

50 DR1971.

Chapter 5

1 For a discussion on the establishment of Mass-Observation as a limited company, see James Hinton, *The Mass Observers: A History, 1937-1949* (Oxford: Oxford University Press, 2013), 298–9 and 359–60.

2 November 1955 directive.

3 Robert Lacey, *Majesty: Elizabeth II and the House of Windsor* (New York: Harcourt Brace Jovanovich, 1977).

4 Quoted in John Pearson, *The Ultimate Family: The Making of the Royal House of Windsor* (London: Bloomsbury, 2013), 146.

5 *The People*, 'They Must Deny It Now', 14 June 1953, 1.

6 Mentioned in *Leicester Mercury*, 'Cabinet Said No to Princess's Wedding', 9 June 1953, 1.

7 Quoted in *Manchester Guardian*, 'Poll on Princess', 22 July 1953, 3.

NOTES

8   Reported in the *Birmingham Mail*, 'Townsend Denies "Exile" Story', 14 March 1955, 1.

9   Quoted in *The Daily Telegraph*, 'Princess Margaret: No Marriage', 1 November 1953, 1.

10   Ibid.

11   'Sacrifice to Duty', 1 November 1955, 6.

12   Responses to this question are not included in this chapter, but the overwhelming response to this question was negative – many respondents had little to no interest in television or were strongly against commercialization. The few who were in favour took an interest in breaking the monopoly of the BBC.

13   The overheard can be found on a telephone report to Mass-Observation, (O 167) F55B 69/11/B.

14   Claire Langhamer, *The English in Love* (Oxford: Oxford University Press, 2013), 1.

15   DR3627, cannot remember when last attended church.

16   DR3351, not a regular churchgoer.

17   DR2818, had not attended church in years.

18   DR1048.

19   DR2903.

20   DR2173, not a regular churchgoer.

21   DR2975, C of E, not regular churchgoer.

22   DR4701, 'I last went to church in 1952. That was the christening of a child. I do not attend Church to worship, I am not a welcome visitor at Church through my opinions and outspoken condemnation of their policies.'

23   DR3052.

24   DR2795, Quaker.

25   DR2675, C of E.

26   DR3388, C of E every fortnight.

27   DR3811, not a regular churchgoer.

28   DR3678, has not attended church in years.

29   DR1061.

30   DR1046.

31   DR1079, Catholic.

32   DR2316, Regular C of E.

33   DR1403.

34   Anthony Eden divorced in 1950, remarried 1952.

35   DR1066.

36   DR2512, C of E, 'High Anglican' but not regular churchgoer.

37   DR1015.

38   DR3810, had not attended church in forty years.

NOTES

39 Malcolm Muggeridge's article was cited by several Observers and was considered shocking to the establishment when it was published. See reprint, with and introduction by Paul Johnson, on the occasion of the 2012 Jubilee: https://www.newstatesman.com/politics/2012/05/royal-soap-opera (accessed 26 November 2022).

40 DR1534.

41 DR3121, has not attended church in years.

42 DR3844, Methodist, regular churchgoer.

43 DR1362.

44 G. K. Chesterton. See footnote 39 regarding Malcolm Muggeridge, who quoted Chesterton as such: 'when people cease to believe in God, they do not then believe in nothing, but in anything.'

45 DR2686.

46 Langhamer, *The English in Love*, 169.

47 DR1325.

48 DR3806, had not attended in years.

49 DR3875, not a regular churchgoer.

50 DR4689, attended 'a long, long time ago'.

51 DR4964, C of E, last attended in April 1955.

52 DR4687, Catholic.

53 DR2984, C of E.

Part II

1 *Plummer 2001: 7*

Chapter 6

1 P. Ziegler, *Crown and the People* (London: Collins, 1978).

2 Ibid.

3 0001.

4 017.

5 050.

6 018.

7 018.

8 087.

9 The Queen's Silver Jubilee Appeal was set up in 1977, to focus on raising funds to support young people and on encouraging and helping young people to serve others in the community.

NOTES

10 087.

11 069.

12 010.

13 Willie Hamilton was a British politician who served as a Labour Member of Parliament for Fife between 1950 and 1987 and renowned for his anti-royalist views.

14 019.

15 012.

16 W. Shawcross, *Rupert Murdoch: Ringmaster of the Information Circus* (London: Chatto & Windus, 1992), 412.

17 C143.

18 G234.

19 W624.

20 G229.

21 W630.

22 C140.

23 A18.

24 F208.

25 F210.

26 H256.

27 C126.

28 Autumn Directive 1986.

29 M1757.

30 R1478.

31 W625.

32 *Daily Mail*, 15 February 1981, https://link-gale-com.ezproxy.sussex.ac.uk/apps/doc/EE1862279986/DMHA?u=sussex&sid=bookmark-DMHA&xid=ba09d4de.

33 The *Telegraph* dedicated two pages of its 20 March 1986 broadsheet to the engagement, including establishing the Ferguson family tree's 'royal roots', implying that much as her status of a 'commoner' was celebrated, a pedigree of some sort was still required to ensure the public's acceptance of Sarah Ferguson into the royal family.

34 A1516.

35 B1486.

36 W625.

37 J1797.

38 H1635.

39 B1898.

40 B1654.

NOTES

41 B58.

42 A1412.

43 B1215.

44 H1703.

45 L1919.

46 H1651.

47 A1126.

48 A2.

49 B1722G.

50 M1812.

51 H1651.

52 A1412.

53 B1492.

54 Q1834.

55 B71.

Chapter 7

1 A. Hamilton, I Sad Queen dubs 1992 her 'annus horribilis' in *The Times*, 25 November 1992 (accessed 25 October 2022).

2 Newspaper coverage of the separation culminated in an infamous photograph headlining the *Daily Mirror* in 20 August 1992 of Texan millionaire John Bryon sucking the Duchess's toes whilst her young daughter looked on.

3 *Diana: Her True Story* was written by Andrew Morton who, following the death of Princess Diana in 1997, admitted that the Princess was herself a significant source of information for the book.

4 A. Hamilton, *The Times*, 21 November 1992, 1. Seven-hour fire wrecks state apartments, https://link-gale-com.ezproxy.sussex.ac.uk/apps/doc/IF0503347262/TTDA?u=sussex&sid=bookmark-TTDA&xid=2876a547.

5 http://news.bbc.co.uk/onthisday/hi/dates/stories/november/26/newsid_2529000/2529209.stm.

6 B34.

7 C1878.

8 B736.

9 B58.

10 C108.

11 B60.

12 F1614.

13 L1002.

14 R2143.

NOTES

283

15 L318.

16 M1593.

17 B2154.

18 H1705.

19 J1549.

20 M381.

21 C1624.

22 M1450.

23 H1451.

24 C2142.

25 L318.

26 A2635.

27 L1789.

28 B89.

29 H2269.

30 http://news.bbc.co.uk/onthisday/hi/witness/november/20/newsid_4407000/4407752.stm.

31 F1634.

32 C2579.

33 A2464.

34 G2701.

35 P1730.

36 C1786.

37 B1120.

38 G2089.

39 F1560.

40 S2305.

41 O2349.

42 H1709.

43 G1241.

44 L1477.

45 D2239.

46 Quoted in C. Harris, 'Secular Religion and the Public Response to Diana's Death', in *The Mourning for Diana*, ed. T. Walter (Oxford: Berg, 1999).

47 W1893.

48 M2665.

49 S1383.

50 https://ukpressonline.co.uk/ukpressonline/database/search/preview.jsp?fileName=DMir_1997_09_04_001.

51 A2801.

52 C110.

53 A2212.

54 N2148.

55 R1025.

56 P416.

57 K2241.

58 S2191.

59 S2305.

Chapter 8

1   https://www.theguardian.com/uk/2000/aug/05/queenmother.monarchy.

2   http://news.bbc.co.uk/1/hi/uk/841740.stm.

3   http://news.bbc.co.uk/1/hi/uk/746429.stm.

4   https://www.theguardian.com/uk/2000/may/18/monarchy.mattwells.

5   J2893.

6   B2240.

7   C2834.

8   G2883.

9   H260.

10 H260.

11 C2654.

12 A. Barnett, 'Prince Harry Taken to Drink and Drugs Rehabilitation Clinic', *The Guardian*, 13 January 2002, https://www.theguardian.com/uk/2002/jan/13/monarchy.antonybarnett.

13 Stephen Bates, 'Palace Plays Down Fears of Jubilee Flop: Website List of Local Events has Forlorn Look but Officials Remain Unconcerned', *The Guardian (1959–2003)*, 24 January 2002, https://ezproxy.sussex.ac.uk/login?url=https://www.proquest.com/historical-newspapers/palace-plays-down-fears-jubilee-flop/docview/188857663/se-2 (accessed 29 October 2022).

14 John O'Farrell, 'God Save the Jubilee', *The Guardian (1959–2003)*, 2 February 2002, https://ezproxy.sussex.ac.uk/login?url=https://www.proquest.com/historical-newspapers/god-save-jubilee/docview/188886807/se-2 (accessed 29 October 2022).

15 P. Thompson, 'Save the Jubilee', *The Sun*, 23 January 2002.

16 http://www.massobs.org.uk/images/Directives/Spring_2002_Directive.pdf.

17 S2574.

18 S1534.

19 P1796.

NOTES

285

20 O2349.

21 W2950.

22 R2065.

23 J1890.

24 B1426.

25 B1426.

26 C2722.

27 C2091.

28 J2893.

29 P1796.

30 A2801.

31 C110.

32 C2901.

33 B1771.

34 B1771.

35 The UK experienced a serious outbreak of foot-and-mouth disease in 2001 causing a crisis in British agriculture. The disease resulted in the slaughtering of over 6 million cows and sheep, along with the closure of many open spaces and a ban on moving livestock, the latter of which lasted into 2002.

36 H1709.

37 A2801.

38 P2819.

39 C108.

40 C41.

41 G2486.

42 W2322.

43 G2941.

44 B2240.

45 M2290.

46 M2892.

47 G2776.

48 W2924.

49 G2818.

50 M2933.

51 Clarence House became the official residence of Prince Charles following his inheritance of the property on the death of his grandmother, the Queen Mother, in 2002.

52 Andrew Pierce, 'How the Mistress Became a Partner', *Times*, 9 June 2000, 26. *The Times Digital Archive*, link-gale-com.ezproxy.sussex.ac.uk/apps/doc

/IF0501359588/TTDA?u=sussex&sid=bookmark-TTDA&xid=14301a8e (accessed 31 October 2022).

53 Richard Kay, '8 out of Ten Say No to Queen Camilla', *Daily Mail*, 9 November 1998, [1]+. *Daily Mail Historical Archive*, link-gale-com.ezprox y.sussex.ac.uk/apps/doc/EE1860489379/DMHA?u=sussex&sid=bookmark-D MHA&xid=cacbc81f (accessed 31 October 2022).

54 Geoffrey Levy and Richard Kay, 'So could it be Queen Camilla?', *Daily Mail*, 17 March 2001, 16–17. Daily Mail Historical Archive, link-gale-com.ezproxy .sussex.ac.uk/apps/doc/EE1861077492/DMHA?u=sussex&sid=bookmark-D MHA&xid=6cd0b4db (Accessed 31 October 2022).

55 R1227.

56 M3203.

57 S2574.

58 K798.

59 G3025.

60 A2801.

61 H1703.

62 B1898.

63 B1475.

64 L2604.

65 L3175.

66 C3006.

67 K3125.

68 C1939.

69 N3060.

70 The former home of the Duke and Duchess of York, Sunninghill Park in Berkshire, was nicknamed 'SouthYork' due to its apparent resemblance to Southfork, the fictional residence of the Ewing family in the popular 1980s US soap opera *Dallas*.

71 H3204.

Chapter 9

1 https://www.bbc.co.uk/news/entertainment-arts-13248199.

2 http://www.massobs.org.uk/ima ges/Directives/Spring_2011_directive.pdf.

3 L1991.

4 W4092.

5 R4503.

6 H1836.

7 T3686.

NOTES

8 G4296.

9 H1541.

10 G4296.

11 M4130.

12 A2212.

13 M3190.

14 V4661.

15 B3227.

16 F3137.

17 P1326.

18 C3210.

19 W4421.

20 Z4682.

21 B4750.

22 See, for instance, Alexis Petridis, 'Queen's Diamond Jubilee Concert a Tough Gig for Rock and Royalty', *Guardian*, 5 June 2012.

23 How the Queen's Silver, Gold and Diamond Jubilees compare in *The Telegraph*, 6 June 2022.

24 N. Hawkes, '2012 was a Good Year for Happiness in the UK, Finds Survey', *BMJ* 347 (2013): f4842, https://doi.org/10.1136/bmj.f4842 (Published 31 July 2013).

25 https://www.gov.uk/government/news/the-diamond-jubilee-weekend#:~:text =The%20Diamond%20Jubilee%20marks%2060,large%20contingent%20of %20military%20involvement.

26 https://www.royal.uk/announcement-plans-central-diamond-jubilee-weekend -2012.

27 E5040.

28 R1025.

29 P1326.

30 C4958.

31 P3373.

32 J4793.

33 A2212.

34 C4271.

35 P1396.

36 S4002.

37 S4872.

38 https://www.royal.uk/prince-harry-and-ms-meghan-markle-are-engaged-be -married.

39 *The Guardian*, 1 December 2017, https://www.theguardian.com/uk-news/2017 /dec/01/not-your-average-royal-what-we-know-so-far-about-meghan-markle.

288 NOTES

40 *Express Online*, 28 November 2017 – How Prince Harry and Meghan Markle engagement shows couple will be thoroughly modern, https://advance.lexis.com/document/?pdmfid=1519360&crid=1b945b98-4509-4f0c-8b2f-eabb2f3f17d4&pddocfullpath=%2Fshared%2Fdocument%2Fnews%2Furn%3AcontentItem%3A5R2C-N111-JCJY-G247-00000-00&pdcontentcomponentid=408506&pdteaserkey=sr185&pditab=allpods&ecomp=zbzyk&earg=sr185&prid=86326d18-86be-4ab3-bc5f-dd8561351b3c.

41 D. Evans, 'Michael' Curry's Royal Wedding Sermon will Go Down in History', 20 May 2018, https://www.theguardian.com/commentisfree/2018/may/20/bishop-michael-curry-sermon-history-harry-meghan-wedding.

42 https://www.bbc.co.uk/news/uk-42138938.

43 B3010.

44 B5125.

45 G6209.

46 B3227.

47 M3190.

48 O6203.

49 V3773.

50 B5125.

51 M3190.

52 M3412.

53 S2207.

54 E4014.

55 S4743.

56 N5744.

Chapter 10

1 https://www.bbc.co.uk/news/uk-51040751; https://www.nytimes.com/2021/03/08/world/europe/recap-of-harry-meghan-oprah-interview.html.

2 A summary of the interview is available on the BBC's website: https://www.bbc.co.uk/news/live/uk-50447028/page/4.

3 https://www.bbc.co.uk/news/uk-59987935.

4 https://www.royal.uk/funeral-duke-edinburgh-0.

5 L6048.

6 H1776.

7 G7202.

8 At the time of Prince Phillip's funeral the Covid-19-related legal restrictions on social contact in England included two-metre social distancing from anyone not in a person's household.

NOTES 289

9 S6892.

10 O4128.

11 A7000.

12 C3603.

13 J5734.

14 J2891.

15 P3209.

Epilogue

1 'The Demise of Her Majesty Queen Elizabeth II: National Mourning Guidance', 9 September2022, https://www.gov.uk/government/publications /the-demise-of-her-majesty-queen-elizabeth-ii-national-mourning-guidance /the-demise-of-her-majesty-queen-elizabeth-ii-national-mourning-guidance (accessed 19 October 2022).

2 M7490 F47M, 2022.

3 T7345.

4 K7522, 2022 Jubilee Directive.

5 O7647, F71M.

6 D7175, F39M.

7 H7408, F40M.

8 P6638.

9 J5734.

10 T7449.

11 03436.

12 M5645.

13 M6759, F36M, 2022 Jubilee Directive.

14 MOJ2891 58-year-old married woman.

15 H6949.

16 Chris Stone, 'Andrew Marr: Why I Broke Down When Announcing the Queen's Death', *New Statesman*, 9 September 2022, https://www .newstatesman.com/politics/uk-politics/2022/09/andrew-marr-why-i-broke -down-when-announcing-the-death-of-the-queen.

17 M6759, F36M.

18 L7499, F71D.

BIBLIOGRAPHY

Bagehot, Walter. *The English Constitution*, edited by Paul Smith. Cambridge: Cambridge University Press, 2001.

Bennett-Wheeler, John W. *King George VI: His Life and Reign*. New York: St. Martin's Press, 1958.

Billig, Michael. *Talking of the Royal Family*. London: Routledge, 1992.

Brendon, Piers. *Edward VIII*. London: Penguin, 2018.

Cannadine, David. 'The Context, Performance and Meaning of Ritual: The British Monarchy and the "Invention of Tradition", c. 1820–1977'. In *The Invention of Tradition*, edited by Eric Hobsbawm and Terence Ranger, 101–64. Cambridge: Cambridge University Press, 1983.

Carr, Wesley. 'The Intimate Ritual: The Coronation Service'. *Political Theology* 4 (2002): 1.

Courage, Fiona. 'The National Panel Responds: Mass Observation Directives 1939–1945'. *Mass Observation Online*, 2011.

Gibbs, Philip. *Ordeal in England*. New York: Doubleday, 1937.

Gielgud, Val. *Years of the Locust*. London: Nicholson and Watson, 1947.

Glencross, Matthew. 'George V and the New Royal House'. In *The Windsor Dynasty: 1910 to the Present, 'Long to Reign Over Us?'*, edited by Matthew Glencross, Judith Rowbotham, and Michael D. Kandiah, 33–56. London: Palgrave MacMillan, 2016.

Harris, C. 'Secular Religion and the Public Response to Diana's Death'. In *The Mourning for Diana*, edited by T. Walter, 97–108. Oxford: Berg, 1999.

Hennessy, Peter. *Never Again: 1945–1951*. London: Jonathan Cape, 1992.

Highmore, Ben. '"The Observation by Everyone of Everyone": The Project of Mass-Observation in 1937'. In *Mass-Observation: Text, Context and Analysis of the Pioneering Pamphlet and Movement*, edited by Jennifer J. Purcell, 7–28. London: Bloomsbury Academic, 2022.

Hinton, James. *The Mass Observers: A History, 1937–1949*. Oxford: Oxford University Press, 2013.

Hubble, Nick. *Mass Observation and Everyday Life: Culture, History, Theory*. Houndsmills, Basingstoke: Palgrave MacMillan, 2010.

Jennings, Humphrey and Charles Madge. *May the Twelfth: Mass-Observation Day Surveys 1937 by Over Two Hundred Observers*. London: Faber and Faber, Ltd., 1937.

Keay, Anna. *The Magnificent Monarch: Charles II and the Ceremonies of Power*. London: Continuum, 2008.

Kynaston, David. *Austerity Britain, 1945–1951*. London: Bloomsbury, 2008.

Lacey, Robert. *Majesty: Elizabeth II and the House of Windsor*. New York: Harcourt Brace Jovanovich, 1977.

BIBLIOGRAPHY

Langhamer, Claire. *The English in Love*. Oxford: Oxford University Press, 2013.

Lenthall, Bruce. *Radio's America: The Great Depression and the Rise of Modern Mass Culture*. Chicago: University of Chicago, 2007.

Malcomson, Bob. 'Diaries for Mass Observation 1939–1940'. *Mass Observation Online*, 2009.

Martin, Kingsley. *The Magic of Monarchy*. New York: Alfred Knopf, 1937.

Mayhall, Laura. 'The Prince of Wales Versus Clark Gable: Anglophone Celebrity and Citizenship between the Wars'. *Cultural and Social History* 4, no. 4 (2007): 529–43.

Mayne, Emily. 'Shows of Joy and Malice: Performance, the Star Chamber, and the Celebration of James I's Coronation in Norwich in 1603'. *Early Theatre* 1, no. 2 (December 2020): 169–82.

Middlemas, Keith. *The Life and Times of George VI*. London: George Weidenfeld and Nicolson, 1974.

Moran, Joe. *Armchair Nation: An Intimate History of Britain in Front of the TV*. London: Profile, 2014.

Mortimore, Roger. 'Measuring British Public Opinion on the Monarchy and the Royal Family'. In *The Windsor Dynasty: 1910 to the Present, 'Long to Reign Over Us?'*, edited by Matthew Glencross, Judith Rowbotham, and Michael D. Kandiah, 135–56. London: Palgrave MacMillan, 2016.

Nairn, Tom. *The Enchanted Glass: Britain and its Monarchy*, 2nd edn. London: Verso, 2011.

Olechnowicz, Andrzej. '"A Jealous Hatred": Royal Popularity and Social Inequality'. In *The Monarchy and the British Nation 1780 to the Present*, edited by Andrzej Olechnowicz, 280–314. Cambridge: Cambridge University Press, 2007.

Pearson, John. *The Ultimate Family: The Making of the Royal House of Windsor*. London: Bloomsbury, 2013.

Plunkett, John. *Queen Victoria: First Media Monarch*. Oxford: Oxford University Press, 2003.

Purcell, Jennifer. *Mother of the BBC: Mabel Constanduros and the Rise of Popular Entertainment on the BBC, 1925–1957*. New York: Bloomsbury Academic, 2020.

Richards, Jeffrey. 'The Monarchy and Film, 1900–2006'. In *The Monarchy and the British Nation 1780 to the Present*, edited by Andrzej Olechnowicz, 258–79. Cambridge: Cambridge University Press, 2007.

Richards, Jeffrey and Dorothy Sheridan, eds. *Mass-Observation at the Movies*. London: Routledge and Kegan Paul, 1987.

Shew, Betty. *Queen Elizabeth, the Queen Mother*. London: Hodder and Staunton, 1955.

Shils, Edward and Michael Young. 'The Meaning of the Coronation'. *Sociological Review* 1, no. 2 (December 1953): 63–81.

Stone, Chris. 'Andrew Marr: Why I Broke Down When Announcing the Queen's Death'. *New Statesman*, 9 September 2022.

Williamson, Philip. 'The Monarchy and Public Values, 1910–1953'. In *The Monarchy and the British Nation 1780 to the Present*, edited by Andrzej Olechnowicz, 223–57. Cambridge: Cambridge University Press, 2007.

Ziegler, Philip. *Crown and the People*. London: Collins, 1978.

INDEX

Abdication crisis 5, 15–16, 30, 39,
            56, 114, 270 n.23
    and coronation of George VI 28,
            100–1
    and creation of Mass-
            Observation 2, 13,
            15–16
    and Townsend Affair 118–19,
            130, 133, 199
Abyssinia 31
Africa 55–6, 59, 81, 86, 188
AIDS (autoimmune deficiency
            syndrome) 160
Air-raids 40–1, 44–8
Albania 44
Alfonso XIII, King of Spain 67
Alfred, King 7
Americanization 74, 120–1
Americans 15, 29, 45, 48, 53, 55–8,
            63, 74, 77, 90, 154, 196,
            220, 238, 241
Andrew, Duke of York 217, 229,
            256
    Jeffery Epstein scandal 248–51
    marriage to Sarah Ferguson 159–
            66, 229, 238
    media coverage of separation and
            divorce 166–7, 170–3,
            175
Anne, Princess Royal 115, 153, 167,
            217, 229, 239
annus horribilis 5, 166–8, 173–4,
            204–5, 207, 230
anti-monarchism 1, 4, 8, 18, 79, 81,
            143, 152, 154, 158, 183,
            201, 213, 245–6
anti-Semitism 36, 38
Armstrong-Jones, Antony, Earl of
            Snowdon 170, 199

Armstrong-Jones, Sarah (Lady
            Chatto) 153
Attlee, Clement 16, 62
austerity 10, 64, 69–71, 75, 79, 82,
            234, 262
Australia 54, 86, 141, 151
Auxiliary Territorial Service
            (ATS) 61, 70

Baldwin, Stanley 28, 53, 119
Balmoral 91, 157, 185–6, 194, 217,
            264
Bashir, Martin 176
Battle of Britain 39, 43, 114
Beatrice, Princess of York 221–2,
            229, 239
Beatrix, Queen of the
            Netherlands 254
Blair, Tony 189, 223–4, 237
Blitz, the 39, 44–5, 48, 277 n.6
Borga, Mohammed Ali (Prime Minister
            of Pakistan) 100
Brexit 243, 263
Briggs, Asa 139
Britain Revisited (1961) 14
British Broadcasting Corporation
            (BBC)
    and Andrew sex scandal 248
    beacons, lighting of 26, 230, 249
    and Charles and Diana's
            wedding 152
    and Diana's death 176, 183
    and Elizabeth and Philip's
            wedding 65–6, 71–2,
            85
    and Elizabeth II coronation 87,
            93, 97–8, 102, 104,
            106–10
    and Elizabeth II death 261

INDEX

and Elizabeth II Diamond Jubilee (2012) 232
and George VI coronation 18–19, 30–5
and Harry and Meghan's wedding 238–40
and Queen Mother's 100th birthday 192–3, 196–7
support for monarchy 240
in wartime 38, 42, 50–1, 55, 60, 62
and William and Kate's wedding 221, 223
British Empire 8, 16, 19, 23, 33–5, 41, 46–9, 51, 59–60, 64, 80–1, 100, 119, 155, 259
British Expeditionary Force (BEF) 43–4
British Legion 26, 93
British Medical Journal 230
British monarchy
 alternatives to 4, 16, 79, 176, 206–8, 235
 and Americans 29, 53, 55–6, 74, 76–7, 90, 154, 196, 200
 attitudes to 1, 4, 36, 39–40, 57, 69, 72, 79, 81–4, 112, 141–7, 157, 216
 and celebrity 9, 34, 84–5, 116, 126, 221, 223, 238–9, 242, 250, 259, 265
 and ceremony 2, 6–8, 24, 28, 31–6, 39, 67–80, 82–3, 87, 102, 110, 112, 118, 154, 158, 164, 191, 196, 210, 220, 223, 225–6, 228–9, 236, 238, 244, 247, 255, 257, 262, 266
 and class 18, 24–5, 30, 36, 78, 80, 91, 220, 225–6, 236, 255–6
 compared to Continental monarchy 5, 131–2, 176, 254
 compared to republics 70, 98, 176, 194, 206–8, 216, 227–8, 235–6
 cost of 19, 35, 49, 74–80, 84–5, 125, 145, 156–7, 164, 223, 226, 236, 253, 256–7

 criticism of 1–2, 4–6, 8, 35, 50, 61, 74–6, 79, 81, 110, 129, 144, 156–7, 165, 173–4, 177, 186, 188, 191, 194–5, 206, 217, 253–4, 256, 259
 duty 6, 9, 15, 59, 66, 116, 121–3, 130, 135, 195, 200, 207, 211, 237, 255, 259, 262–3, 265
 events
  as holidays 19, 23, 65, 69, 73, 102, 108, 111, 143, 146, 161, 163–5, 230, 238, 248
  as national celebrations 203
 future of 174–5, 204, 208, 220, 249, 257, 262–5
 as Head of Church 6, 97, 114, 118, 126, 170
 as Head of State 4–5, 83, 176, 181, 206, 217, 236, 256
 humanity of 9, 15, 55, 62, 67–70, 122, 131, 165, 169, 181, 185, 195, 202, 204, 252, 265
 identification with 6, 9, 67–9, 125, 165, 181, 185, 199, 201–2, 225, 229, 247
 ideological reversal 68
 and imperialism 8, 19, 35, 41, 46–7, 51, 80–1, 256
 and the media 8–9, 151–2, 175–6, 201, 205, 240, 253, 266
 in military uniform 30, 43, 51–2, 59, 61
 and modernity 5–7, 15, 28–9, 61, 86, 116, 122, 131–2, 158–9, 166, 189–91, 196, 206–7, 215, 217, 224, 226, 233, 238, 247, 253–4, 256, 265
 and national identity 7–8, 83, 196, 220, 235, 247
 popularity of 35, 38, 101, 122, 124, 131, 162, 178, 197, 200–1, 246, 249–50
 privacy 34, 66, 72, 75–6, 116, 118, 125, 129, 160–1, 165, 175–6, 223, 240, 265

294   INDEX

and privilege 7, 36, 68, 120, 170,
  176, 181, 184, 193–5,
  199, 205, 208, 220, 227,
  237, 245, 250, 254–6, 260
relationship to the people 1, 5–6,
  8–10, 140, 165–6, 168,
  176, 192, 217, 265
relevance of 2, 10, 130–1, 172,
  177, 205–6, 208, 215,
  227, 246, 254, 256–7
role of 6, 190, 235–6
scandal 14–16, 114–16, 169–73,
  187, 247, 250
soap opera 214, 256, 265
and stability 61, 190, 263
support of 4–5, 18, 67, 78, 80–3,
  98, 118, 126, 159, 173,
  189, 201–4, 228–9, 235
as symbol 6–7, 9, 15, 39, 46–7,
  61, 83, 112, 118, 153,
  169, 190, 228, 237
sympathy for 9, 33, 54, 68, 101,
  116–17, 121–3, 168–9,
  172, 174, 176, 179, 184,
  186, 188–9, 191, 198–202,
  211, 217, 253–4
tourism 87, 89, 144, 146, 154,
  175, 196, 216, 220,
  227–8, 246, 264
and tradition 2, 7, 22, 26, 76, 82,
  84, 95, 98, 116, 122–3, 132,
  137, 143, 146, 159, 163,
  165–6, 189, 191–2, 195–7,
  211, 215–16, 220, 226,
  232, 241–4, 263, 265–6
and unity 17, 40, 45, 71, 102,
  112, 146, 151, 180–1,
  184–5, 191, 224, 228,
  235–6, 240, 246
upholding values 6, 8, 16, 70, 75,
  165, 195
British National Party (BNP) 228
Brown, Gordon 223
Brussels 115
Buckingham Palace 29, 40, 44–7, 52,
  54, 65, 74, 81, 103, 108,
  145, 177, 192, 196, 203,
  206, 219–20, 223, 225–6,
  228, 230, 249, 260

Buddhism 109
bunting 23–4, 26, 35, 91, 145, 233
Burma 50–1, 64
Bush, George W. 175

Caballero, Francisco Largo (Spanish
  Prime Minister) 37
Cameron, David 222, 224
Camilla, Queen
  Camilla-Gate 167, 170–3
  Duchess of Cornwall 222
  marriage to Charles 10, 191–2,
    206, 208–13, 216–17, 219,
    244–5, 251
  possibility of becoming
    Queen 209, 213,
    215–16, 256
  rehabilitation of image 208,
    213–14
Campbell, Margaret, Duchess of
  Argyll 98
Canada 43, 53, 58, 65, 75, 86
Cannadine, David 7
Carey, George, Archbishop of
  Canterbury 184
Caribbean 240, 256
Carol II, King of Romania 67
Catherine, Princess of Wales
  background 218, 226, 242
  as commoner 218, 226
  marriage to William 140, 218–31,
    234, 238, 244, 247
  popularity of 227, 246–7
  royal duties 251, 256
Catholicism 97, 131, 136, 159, 216
Cavendish, Mary, Duchess of
  Devonshire 98
Celebrity. See British Monarchy, and
  celebrity
Ceylon 86
Challenger disaster (1986) 160
Chamberlain, Neville 41–2
Charles II, King 8
Charles III, King
  becoming King 5, 146, 160, 170,
    172, 206, 209, 211–13,
    215–16, 245, 249, 251–4,
    256–7, 264–6
  Camilla-Gate 167, 170–3

INDEX

comparison to Edward VIII   212,
215–16
and Cornwall   143
death of Diana   5, 178–9, 184–90,
208
divorce from Diana   169–72, 174,
176
media coverage of separation
and divorce   17, 173–5
engagement to Diana   151
investiture as Prince of Wales   157
marriage to Camilla   10, 191–2,
206, 208–14, 216–17, 219,
244–5, 251
marriage to Diana   3, 140, 151–9,
162–3, 166, 213, 216–17,
219, 225–6, 229, 244
Prince Charles   103, 115, 132, 148,
161, 193, 196, 201–2,
204–5, 217, 222, 225,
232, 237–8, 240, 244,
255, 262
relationship with Diana   171–2,
179, 185, 211–12, 216,
255–6
Welsh opinions of   157–8
Chernobyl disaster (1986)   160
Chesterton, GK   133, 280 n.39
and   44
China   160, 262
Christmas   23, 43, 50, 66, 97,
111–12, 220–1, 233
Churchill, Sir Winston   3, 42, 45, 47,
49–50, 52, 54, 56–7, 61–2,
86, 99–100, 104–5, 107,
109, 111, 128–9
Church of England   6, 124, 129, 170
views on divorce   114, 125, 131,
134, 242
cinema   8, 27, 44, 57, 77, 87, 91, 182
Civil List   72–5, 82, 143
Clarence House   65, 208, 285 n.51
class   18–19, 23–5, 30, 36, 39, 60, 78,
80–1, 91, 95, 132, 143–6,
175, 180, 208, 218, 220,
225–6, 236, 242, 255–6
Clegg, Nick   222, 224
colonialism   1, 18, 23, 31, 45, 48, 65,
77, 80–1, 130, 142, 256

Commonwealth   1, 8, 61, 83, 89–90,
96–8, 116, 119, 130, 132,
235–6, 249, 259
communism   29, 37, 53, 64, 82–3,
144
Conservative Party   3, 37, 61, 98
coronations   2–3, 7–11, 102, 110, 114
anointing   8, 26, 86, 108–9
Coronation Committee   16, 86
Court of Claims   89
decorations   23–5, 28–9, 36,
89–92, 101–3
music   7–8, 19, 29, 31, 98–100,
111
processions   8, 15–21, 24, 27,
31–2, 86–7, 90–1, 93,
97–100, 102–9
programmes   15, 24, 87, 89, 91–3
souvenirs   15–16, 22, 87, 89–90,
92, 95, 101, 118
street parties   18, 23, 91–3, 95,
104
Cost of Living Crisis   253, 262–3
COVID-19   248, 252, 263, 288 n.8
Coward, Noel   44
Cronin, A. J.   52
Crystal Palace   13, 16
Curry, Michael   238, 244
Czechoslovakia   41, 47

Daily Express   46, 60
Daily Mail   208
Daily Mirror   2, 89, 115, 185
Daily News (New York)   115
Daily Worker   82
Dallas (TV programme)   286 n.70
dancing   22–3, 28, 38, 95, 149
D-Day   58
de Casalis, Jeanne   30
de Gaulle Charles   60
Derby, the   52
Diana, Princess of Wales   161, 169,
190, 205, 210, 216, 225,
257
compared to Camilla Parker-
Bowles   213–14, 244–5,
251
compared to Sarah Ferguson   166,
214

296 INDEX

death of 5, 166, 176, 189, 192,
   202, 208, 245, 253
 emotional response to 178,
   180–3, 260
 floral tributes 177, 180–1,
   185–6, 214
 funeral 178, 182, 187, 229
   Earl Spencer's speech 178,
   188
 media coverage 177, 181, 183
 public mourning 177, 179–80,
   184, 195, 217
 response of royal family 177,
   185–7, 194, 204, 207,
   256
divorce from Charles 169–72,
   174, 176
 Andrew Morton
   biography 171–3, 282
   n.3
 Martin Bashir BBC
   interview 176
 media coverage of 17, 173–5
and James Gilby ('squidgey-
   gate') 167
marriage to Charles 3, 140,
   151–9, 162–3, 166, 171,
   213, 216–17, 219, 225–6,
   229, 244
popularity of 162
relationship with Charles 171–2,
   179, 185, 211–12, 216,
   255–6
divorce 5, 10, 15, 57, 82, 114–16,
   118, 120, 123–9, 131–7,
   140, 167–9, 172, 175,
   183, 188, 195, 200,
   204–5, 207, 216, 238,
   241–4
dogs
 dressing up 29–30
Douglas-Hamilton, Douglas 14th
   Duke of Hamilton 60
Drake, Francis 96
dreams 17, 27–8, 105
drinking 21–2, 27, 31, 95, 134, 150,
   197–8, 200
Dunkirk 38, 43, 59
Dylan, Bob 205

Eden, Anthony 37, 115, 128, 135,
   279 n.34
Edinburgh 110, 200, 251
Edward VII, King 5–8, 81, 244
Edward VIII, King (later Duke of
   Windsor) 18, 20, 56,
   122, 191
 abdication 15–16, 30, 39, 85, 101,
   118–19, 130, 244
 compared to George VI 26–9, 43,
   51, 101, 118–19
 compared to Prince Charles 212,
   215–16
 Duke of Windsor 31–2, 39, 42,
   44, 50, 53, 58–61, 78, 91,
   120, 126, 272 n.13
 as governor of the Bahamas 40,
   43–4, 47, 53
 Prince of Wales 41, 81
Edward, Duke of Edinburgh 229,
   238
Edward, Duke of Kent 97
Edward, Duke of Windsor. *See* Edward
   VIII, King (later Duke of
   Windsor)
Edwards, Huw 232
Elgar, Edward 7
Elizabeth, Queen Mother 9, 153–4,
   179, 214, 285 n.51
 100th birthday 192–7
 Death and funeral 191, 197–8,
   200–2, 204–5, 219
 and George VI coronation 20, 22,
   24, 26–30, 34–5
 and Princess Elizabeth's
   wedding 67, 72, 80, 85
 and Second World War 38–40,
   43–9, 51–3, 56–60, 62
 speeches 49, 51, 55
 and Townsend Affair 114–15,
   130
Elizabeth I, Queen 29
Elizabeth II, Queen
 abdicate in favor of Charles 206,
   254–5
 annus horribilis 5, 166–8, 173–4,
   204–5, 207, 230
 Big Jubilee Lunch 230
 birthday 160

INDEX

coronation of 7–8
  Americans 90
  comparison with 1937 100–2
  Coronation committee 86
  Coronation Week 93–5
  crowd experience 92–3, 106–8
  decorations 90–2, 101, 103
  Elizabethan celebrations 91, 93
  Mount Everest summited 96–7
  MPs attendance of 87–9,
    98–100
  ox-roasting 95–6
  preparations for 86–93
  processions 97, 106–7
  souvenirs 87, 89–90, 92, 95,
    101
  speech 102, 105, 111–12
  street parties 92–3, 104, 156
  television broadcast of 86–7,
    93, 101–8, 112
  TV parties 86–7, 91, 99, 102–5
  wireless broadcast of 108–10,
    112
death of 1–5, 9–10, 259–66
  "the queue" 1
  official mourning 1, 259, 262
  Operation London Bridge 259
Diamond Jubilee 218, 230–7
  decorations 233
  memorabilia 233–4
  pageant 231–2
  street parties 231, 233, 235
  television coverage of 231–5
Golden Jubilee 192, 198, 202–5,
  217
  street parties 197
income tax 168, 172–5, 180, 186
marriage to Prince Philip 9, 65–7
  broadcast of wedding 65
  choice of Philip 62, 81–2, 84
  cost of 65, 68, 73–84
  described as 'fairy tale' 66
  engagement to Philip 63–4
  gendered response to 77–9
  honeymoon publicity 71–2, 85
  as national celebration 68–72
  procession 65, 71
  wedding dress 65
  wedding gifts 65, 81

Platinum Jubilee 1, 140, 248–9,
  252–4, 261
Princess Royal 19, 21–2, 27, 30–1,
  43, 51, 53, 57, 59–61, 63,
  65
respect for 69, 142, 146, 174, 204,
  207–8, 235–6, 256
response to Diana's death 177,
  185–6, 194–5, 202, 207–8,
  217, 256
Silver Jubilee 139–52, 155, 157–8,
  165–6, 197–8, 203–4, 207,
  216, 229
tours 86, 264
Townsend Affair 114–15, 119–20,
  126–31, 136–7
Elvis 216
Empire 8, 16, 19, 23, 25, 33–5, 41,
  46–9, 51, 59–60, 64, 80–1,
  100, 119, 155, 259
Epstein, Jeffrey 248, 251
Essex 195, 207, 217
Eton 58
Eugenie, Princess 222, 239
Europe 5, 42, 58–9, 61–2, 64, 75, 79,
  155, 234, 236, 254
European Economic Community
  (EEC) 140
European Union (EU) 236
everyday, the 1, 3, 10, 17, 40, 91, 96,
  112, 128, 139–41, 158,
  228
Evita 179

Facebook. *See* social media
fascism 17, 20, 33, 42, 64, 83
Fifth Column 44, 49
fireworks 89, 101, 104–5, 154
First World War 5, 65
Fisher, Geoffrey Archbishop of
  Canterbury 86, 106, 109,
  129
Fitzalan-Howard Bernard, Duke
  of Norfolk, Earl
  Marshal 86, 97–8
Foot, Michael 158
foot and mouth disease 203, 285
  n.35
football 160, 198, 228

INDEX

Fortnum and Mason   145
Fosters (beer)   224
France   17, 37–9, 43–4, 47, 55, 98,
    227, 236, 246
Franco, Francisco   36

Gallup polling   3
Gascoyne, David   16
gas masks   41
Gatcome Park   217
George, Duke of Kent   19, 40, 53–5,
    65
George IV King   6
    Prince Regent   133
George V, King   5–7, 26, 30, 155, 253
George VI, King   9, 16–17, 33, 56–7,
    59, 65, 67, 72, 77, 80, 82,
    85, 101, 118, 133
    compared to Edward VIII   27–8
    coronation   2, 8, 19, 22–4, 26–9,
        35, 155
        acclamation   21
        ceremony   33–4
        decorations   23–4, 30
        fears   28
        procession   20–1, 26, 33, 36,
            206
        programmes   36
        speech   30
    death of   86, 114, 199, 215, 262
        funeral   219
    Second World War   40, 56
        bombed   45–8
        newsreels   38–9, 44, 57
        rumours   39, 43, 47, 49, 58
        speeches   41–3, 50–1, 60, 62
        tours   48, 51–3, 56, 58–9
    wedding of   51
Germany   26, 34, 36, 41–2, 44, 46,
    50, 55, 60, 83, 97, 232,
    235
Gert and Daisy   30
Gibbs, Philip   16
Gilby, James   167
Glasgow   16, 25, 49, 223
"God save the King." *See* National
    Anthem
Gog and Magog   89
Golancz, Victor   57

Gordon, John   46
Grand National, the   209–10
Greece   54, 64–5, 81–2
Grenfell Tower fire   246
Guardian, the (formerly *Manchester
    Guardian*)   2, 36, 87, 89,
    100, 151, 192, 197, 238
Guinness Book of World Records   233
Gurkhas   90

Hamilton, Willie   150, fn   281
Harris, John   2
Harris, Leonard   14
Harrisson, Tom   2, 139, 141
Haw-Haw, Lord (William Joyce)   52
Hello! magazine   209, 221
Henry VIII   6, 97
Henry, Duke of Gloucester   19, 21,
    48, 97
Henry, Duke of Sussex (Prince
    Harry)   9, 197, 216, 245,
    255, 257
    death of Diana   187–8
    interview with Oprah
        Winfrey   248, 252–3
    marriage to Meghan Markle   237–
        44, 247
        Kingdom Choir   238, 240, 244
    move to America   248–50, 253
    resigns royal duties   249–51
Hillary, Edmund   96–7
Hinton, James   10, 17
Hitler, Adolf   19–20, 41–2, 44–5, 48,
    57, 175
Hollywood   84–5, 120, 132, 135
Home Guard   60
homelessness   246
Hong Kong   48
horse racing   52, 209, 261
housing   38, 64–5
Hussein, Saddam   175
Huyton, Chris   156
Hyde Park   16, 154, 187–8

ideological reversal   68
imperialism. *See* colonialism
India   50, 64, 81, 98, 107
inequality   208, 220, 246, 255
Invictus Games   237

INDEX

IRA (Irish Republican Army)   151
Ireland   97, 236
Italy   34, 44, 55, 59, 61, 98
ITV   192, 232, 239–40

James I, King   8
Japan   48
Jazz   38
jingoism   18, 83, 262
Joad, C. E. M.   60
John, Elton   222, 239
John Paul II, Pope   209
Johnson, Boris   263
jokes   20, 66, 92, 96, 136, 228

Kensington Palace   177, 180, 187,
   251
Korea   100, 171

Labour Party   3, 16, 61, 67, 70, 72–4,
   87–8, 91, 98, 189, 222
Lang, Cosmo Gordon, Archbishop of
   Canterbury   28, 50, 57
Langhamer, Claire   117
Lansbury, George   57
Lascelles, George   7th Earl of
   Harewood   58
Last, Nella   41, 109, 125–6
Las Vegas   216
Lenin, Vladimir   24
Leopold III, King of Belgium   60, 274
   n.91
Libya   52, 160
London   52, 60, 62, 74, 85–6, 116,
   142, 185–6, 217, 259
   Blitz   40, 44–8
   and coronations   8, 16, 18–21, 29,
     32, 89–91, 99, 106–8, 110
   East End   45–6
   Londoners   77, 150
   and Mass Observation   2, 17
   Olympics   218, 230
   Paralympics   230
   and royal events   167, 177–9,
     186–7, 192, 196, 203,
     206, 230–2, 235–7, 260
   and royal proclamations   16, 86
   and royal weddings   151, 153–4,
     219–20, 227, 242

love   15, 66, 68–9, 73, 76, 78, 85,
   115–16, 119–21, 126–7,
   129–30, 158, 170, 178–9,
   181, 199–200, 211, 213,
   216, 221, 226, 228–9,
   235, 238, 240, 242,
   244–6, 255–6

Madge, Charles   2, 16–17
Maitlis, Emily   248
Major, John   223, 239
Margaret, Princess   19, 21–2, 27,
   30–1, 43, 53, 65, 153, 170
   death of   192, 197–200
   media coverage   115, 119–20, 200
   Townsend Affair   114–16, 125–7,
     130, 132, 199–200
     Church role in   114, 118–19,
       121–6, 129–35, 137
     compared to Charles and
       Camilla   211, 244
     compared to Edward VIII   119,
       126, 130, 191, 244
     decision not to marry   117–18,
       120, 122–6, 128–9, 136–7
     Elizabeth II handling of   114–
       15, 126–31
Mariana, Princess, Duchess of
   Kent   20, 54–5, 65, 81
Marks & Spencers   233
Marr, Andrew   263
Marshall, Howard   33, 60
Mary, Queen   19–21, 30, 32, 54, 67,
   153
Mass-Observation   2–5, 10–11,
   13–14, 38–9, 61
   day surveys   13–14, 17, 38, 87
   diaries   10–11, 13–14, 40–2
   directives   3, 5, 10–11, 13, 14, 38,
     66, 114, 116–17
   file reports   38–40, 53–4, 272 n.13
   May the twelfth (1937)   2, 14,
     17–18, 38
   overheards   39–40, 87, 92
   preparations for Elizabeth II
     coronation   87–8, 95,
     100
   preparations for George VI
     coronation   16–17

300 INDEX

Mass Observation Project   114,
  265–6
  day surveys   140, 152, 238
  diaries   149, 177
  directives   139–41, 151–2, 159,
    166–8, 177–8, 192–3, 195,
    197–9, 201, 206, 208–9,
    219, 230, 238, 240,
    247–9, 261
  methods   139–41, 210
  overheards   162, 237
Maxton, James   16
May Day   19–20
media   1–2, 5–10, 15, 39, 45, 66,
    68–9, 115, 117, 121,
    135, 151–2, 154, 159–62,
    165–6, 168, 170–1, 177–9,
    181–4, 187, 189, 191,
    195, 198, 200–3, 205,
    207, 213–14, 223, 226,
    229–30, 233, 235, 238,
    240–1, 243–6, 252–4, 257,
    260, 262, 266
Meghan, Duchess of Sussex
  background   241–3
  compared to Wallis Simpson   241,
    243
  criticism of   241, 243, 251
  interview with Oprah
    Winfrey   248, 252–3
  marriage to Prince Harry   237–45,
    247
    Kingdom Choir   238, 240,
    244
  media coverage   238
  move to America   248–50, 253
  race   241–2, 246, 253
Merkel, Angela   236
Miller, Paul   156
Milliband, Ed   222
Mitchison, Naomi   87–8, 98–100,
    131
Montgomery, Bernard, Field General
    ('Monty')   59, 99
morale   38, 50, 70, 173, 193
Morton, Andrew   171–3, 282 n.3
Moscow   182
Moss Bros   88
Mountbatten, Lord Louis   57, 64, 82

Mount Everest   96–7, 109
Muggeridge, Malcolm   131, 280 n.39,
    280 n.44
Murdoch, Richard   151–2, 175, 183,
    197, 213
Murrow, Edward   52
Mussolini, Benito   20, 57, 61

Nairn, Tom   9
National Anthem (British)   20, 25, 27,
    29, 41–3, 60, 92, 98, 144,
    154, 196, 205, 254
National Gallery   215
National Health Service (NHS)   157,
    170, 261
national identity   7–8, 70, 235, 247
National Savings   89
Nazis   41, 43, 48, 55, 58
Nazism   17
Nehru, Jawaharlal, Prime Minister of
    India   100, 107
Newcastle   264
New Labour   189
Newmarket   52
News Chronicle   27
News of the World   151
Newspapers   2, 5, 6, 8, 9, 23, 28, 30,
    42, 44, 67, 74, 77, 87, 89,
    95–7, 106, 107, 110, 115,
    118, 119, 121, 123, 125,
    133, 159, 160, 164, 169,
    175, 183, 192, 210, 221
newsreels   38, 42, 76, 87, 252
New Statesman   2, 17, 131, 263
New York Institute of Dress
    Designers   65
New Zealand   86, 141
Norgay, Tenzing   96–7
Normandy   58
North Korea   262
nostalgia   160, 198, 234
nuclear fears   100
Nuffield, Lord (William Morris)   59

Obama, Barack   236
old age pensioners   92, 95
Olympics (2012)   218, 230
opinion polling   3
ox-roasting   95–6

INDEX

pacifism   43
Paddington Bear   252
Paddington Station   92
pageantry   2, 35, 36, 68–70, 72, 79,
        80, 82, 83, 110, 154, 158,
        164, 196, 223, 226, 244
Pakistan   86, 98, 100, 107
Paralympic Games (2012)   230
parasocial relationship   9, 69
Paris, France   43, 176, 199, 210
Parliament   16, 41, 47, 65, 87, 121,
        175, 194, 208
Patricia, Princess of Connaught   65
patriotism   18, 19, 23, 32, 34, 36, 39,
        103, 161, 162, 200, 205,
        228, 233, 235
Pearl Harbor   48
People, The   115
Pepys, Samuel   8
Peter Townsend, Group Captain   9–
        10, 14, 114–34, 136–7,
        175, 199, 200, 211
Philip, Duke of Edinburgh   14, 86,
        99, 105, 132, 141, 144,
        145, 224, 229, 255, 264,
        274 n.5
    death   248, 252–3
    funeral   248, 251
    funeral of Diana, Princess of
        Wales   187, 214
    Greek ancestry   64, 81–2
    role in family   125, 208, 249
Pocock, David   17, 139
Poland   41–2
Potter, Gillie   98
Press   2, 6, 10, 17, 34, 57, 65, 71–3,
        84, 114–16, 118–19, 124,
        126, 128, 133, 152, 157,
        159, 165–6, 197, 208,
        212–14, 218–20, 222,
        223, 226, 227, 238, 248,
        252–3, 255–7, 263
    coverage of royal divorces   10, 175
    coverage of the death of Diana,
        Princess of Wales   176,
        180, 181, 185, 188, 191,
        202, 203
    intrusion   169, 187
Press Council   115

Private Eye   181
Privy Purse   194
processions   8, 16–21, 24, 27, 31, 52,
        60, 65, 66, 68, 76, 79, 86,
        87, 90, 91, 93, 97–100,
        102–9, 141, 148, 152,
        187, 192, 206, 230, 242,
        260, 262
    royal coaches   19–21, 29, 32, 85,
        89, 107, 141, 148, 164
propaganda   34, 47, 73, 213
psychology   3
pubs   21, 27, 35, 83, 95, 228
Punch and Judy   80
punk rock   156

race   238, 240–4, 253
radio   8–10, 18–19, 21–2, 25, 27,
        29–33, 35, 42, 51, 57, 60,
        68, 87, 93, 102, 104, 106,
        108–12, 158, 182, 183, 240
Radio Times, the   109
Rathbone, Eleanor   36
rationing   50, 52, 64–5, 96
Red Cross   59
religion   10, 38, 116, 133, 134, 137,
        184
Representation of the People Act   3
republicanism   4, 5, 16, 28, 41, 59,
        74, 78–80, 86, 135, 172,
        175, 194, 201, 206–8,
        212, 216, 217, 223, 227,
        235, 245, 249, 254, 257,
        262
Reynolds, Quentin   49
riots   151, 155
Romsey Abbey   71–2, 85
Roosevelt, Franklin Delano   57
Royal Air Force (RAF)   51, 69, 106,
        225, 230
Royal tours   86, 141, 171, 264
rumour   43–4, 58–9, 136, 248
Runcie, Robert, Archbishop of
        Canterbury   153
Russia. *See* USSR

St. Andrews, University   218
St. George's Chapel   209, 238, 248,
        252

302 INDEX

St. James's Palace 65
St. Johns Ambulance 20, 106–7
St. Paul's Cathedral 47, 141, 148,
 151, 155, 159, 192, 230
Salote Tupou III, Queen of Tonga 97,
 100, 105
Sandringham 217
Sands, Bobby 151
Sarah, Duchess of York 159, 166,
 172, 214, 222, 281 n.33
 life before marriage 162
 nicknamed Fergie 165
 personality 161–4
Sargent, Malcolm 60
Saudi Arabia 228
Scotland 53, 60, 87, 115, 195, 223
 devolution 145, 235
scouts 23, 24
Second World War. *See also* Blitz, the
 declaration of war 41
 invasion fears 45, 47–8, 56
 rationing 50, 52, 64–5, 96
Selaisse, Haile 44
sensationalism 121
sexuality 38
Shakespeare 80, 257
Shand, Jimmy 7–8, 98
Shils, Edward 7
Simpson, Wallis (later Duchess of
 Windsor) 15, 29–30,
 43, 53, 60, 118, 163, 170,
 241, 243
SkyTV 232
Sloan, Pat 35
socialism 73–4, 76, 79, 81, 85, 131,
 146
social media 8–10, 166, 219, 221,
 223–4, 239–42, 261
sociology 3
South Africa 74, 86, 188
souvenirs 15–16, 22, 87, 89–90, 92,
 95, 101, 142–3, 149–50,
 154, 228, 233–4
Spain 17, 18, 31, 35, 36, 43
Spencer, Charles, Earl Spencer 178,
 187–8, 222
Spencer, James, Earl 153
'squidgey-gate' 167
Stack, Prunella 60

Stalin, Joseph 57, 182
Stone of Scone 98
street parties 18, 91–3, 141, 148–9,
 155, 157–8, 196–7, 218,
 227, 229, 231
Sun, The 151, 197, 214
Sunday Express 91
Sunday Mirror 170
Sunday People 170
Sunday Pictorial 64, 66, 115
Sunday Times, The 151
Sunninghill Park 65, 289 n.70
Swedish Royalty 132
Syria 223, 246

tabloid press 116, 126, 152, 159,
 165, 171, 187, 216
tattoos 228
Telegraph, the 183, 230
Teletubbies 222
television 8–10, 86–7, 90, 92–3, 99,
 101–8, 112, 117, 142,
 152–3, 155, 158–9, 161,
 163–4, 175, 183, 187,
 192, 200, 201, 203, 205,
 210, 215, 219–22, 224–6,
 228, 231–4, 238–42, 259,
 261–2, 264
Temple, William, Archbishop of
 Canterbury 28
Thatcher, Margaret, Baroness 151,
 223
Times, The 15, 34, 64, 105, 131–2,
 151, 158, 167, 254
Tindall, Zara 239
Tobruk, Libya 53
Toronto 237
Tottenham Hotspurs, (Spurs) 156
Townsend, Peter, Group Captain 9–
 10, 14, 114–37, 175,
 199–200, 211
tradition 2, 7, 16, 22, 26, 29, 34, 65,
 74, 76, 82, 84, 95, 98, 116,
 121–2, 127, 132, 143,
 146, 159, 163, 165–6,
 189, 191–2, 195, 211,
 215–16, 220, 226, 232,
 241–4, 250, 265–6
Trafalgar Square 108, 206

INDEX

traffic 51, 76, 92, 111, 153
Travolta, John 156
Tribune 115
Trooping the Colour 249
Truss, Liz 262–3, 265
TV. *See* television
Twitter, (now X) 223–4, 239

Ukraine 160, 262, 263
unemployment 16, 18, 36, 77, 101, 151, 152, 155, 157
United States of America (USA) 3, 4, 9, 23, 45, 47, 64, 74, 154, 243, 248, 250, 253
University of Sussex 14, 139, 141, 265
USSR 37, 42, 74, 83, 160, 262
Uxbridge 21

VE Day 62, 219
Victor Emmanuel III, King of Italy 44
Victoria, Queen 5, 6, 75
   Diamond Jubilee 8
VJ Day 206, 219
Voltaire 35

Wales 17, 157–8
Washington Post 248
Waterloo Bridge 76
Waters, Elsie. *See* Gert and Daisy
Wedgewood 90

Welsh 157
Westminster Abbey 8, 16, 23, 29, 65, 86–7, 97–8, 106, 110, 161, 187, 201, 218, 222, 224, 228
Westminster Hall 1, 260
William, Prince of Wales 140, 213, 238–9, 244–5, 247, 249, 253, 257, 265
   death of Diana, Princess of Wales 187–8
   marriage to Kate Middleton 216, 219, 224–7, 229, 231, 234
Windrush Generation 246
Windsor Brand 5–9, 116, 265
Windsor Castle 209, 246, 248, 251–2
   fire 167, 173–5
Winfrey, Oprah 248, 250
Winnington-Ingram, Arthur, Bishop of London 33
Women's Institute 149
Woolton, Lord (Frederick Marquis 1st Earl of Woolton) 50
working classes 18, 24–5, 30, 78, 144, 146, 180
World Cup 160, 198

Y.M.C.A. 58

'Zadok the Priest' 99
Ziegler, Philip 141

INDEX OF MASS OBSERVER LOCATIONS

Aberdeen   171
Aberystwyth   263
Ashford (Kent)   22
Ayr   143

Barrow-in-Furness   41, 109, 125
Bath   91, 227, 232, 235
Bedfordshire   188
Beer, Devonshire   23, 29
Berkshire   200
Birmingham   197, 228
Bolton   39, 182, 199
Bridlington   188
Brighton   143, 219, 244, 245
Bristol   184, 240, 260
Bromley   151

Cambridgeshire   150
Cardiff   157, 223, 236
Chelsea   28
Cheltenham   227
Cleveland   148
Combe Hay   95–6
Corley   93
Cornwall   142, 159, 232

Dartmoor   168
Derbyshire   170, 212
Devizes   259
Devon   209

East of England   152
East Sussex   149, 201
East Yorkshire   256
Edinburgh   110, 200, 251
Ely   178
Essex   195, 207, 217
Exeter   179, 229

Fulham   155

Glasgow   223
Gloucestershire   171, 206, 214
Grimsby   224

Hampshire   170, 205
Harrogate   228
Hereford   25

Jersey   239

Kent   22, 23, 34, 168, 213

Lancashire   101
Lancaster   205
Leeds   132, 253, 259
Leicester   249
Leicestershire   220
Lewes   149
London   18–21, 28, 32, 106, 151, 153, 155–7, 169, 173, 179–81, 184, 187, 204, 207, 216, 226, 231, 241, 262

Manchester   176, 193, 199, 208
Midlands   208, 214, 237, 239, 250. *See also* West Midlands
Milton Keynes   232, 243
Moreton   93, 94
Morpeth   260

Newcastle   198, 210, 235, 254, 261
Norfolk   26, 147, 148, 182, 190, 211
Northamptonshire   220
Northumberland   144, 146
North West   160, 170, 184
Nottingham   175, 189
Nottinghamshire   171

INDEX OF MASS OBSERVER LOCATIONS

Oldbury, West Midlands   260
Orford, Suffolk   22
Oxfordshire   194

Pontypridd, Wales   93
Prestwick, Scotland   24, 25

Ryhope, Sunderland   148

Scarborough   175
Scotland   223, 233, 244
Scottish Islands   147
Sheffield   254
Shetland   204
Shropshire   189
Somerset   183
South East   157, 160, 185, 186, 206, 207, 213

Southend-on-Sea, Essex   35
South West   175, 183
Staffordshire   215
Stockton-on-Tees   179
Stoke-on-Trent   150
Suffolk   22, 178
Sunderland   148, 246
Surrey   200, 202, 203

Wales   93, 157–8, 174, 181, 182, 203, 210, 223, 226, 233, 255
Watford   186, 225, 227, 234
West Midland   74, 175, 205, 260
West Sussex   195, 252
Weymouth   262

York   201, 203, 212, 262
Yorkshire   160, 169, 172, 185